TIMELINES
OF EVERYONE

DK SMITHSONIAN ✺

TIMELINES OF EVERYONE

**From Cleopatra and Confucius
to Mozart and Malala**

DK LONDON
Senior Editor Steven Carton
Senior Art Editor Smiljka Surla
Project Editors Edward Aves, Thomas Booth
Project Designers Sunita Gahir, Joe Lawrence, Jessica Tapolcai
Editors Ben Ffrancon Davies, Tayabah Khan
US Editor Megan Douglass
Design Assistants Naomi Murray, Lauren Quinn
Illustrators Peter Bull Art Studio, Gary Bullock Illustration,
Barry Croucher/The Art Agency, Rob Davis/The Art Agency, Sunita Gahir,
Peter Johnston/The Art Agency, Naomi Murray, Lauren Quinn,
Claudia Saraceni/The Art Agency, Gus Scott, Peter David Scott/The Art Agency
DK Media Archive Romaine Werblow
Senior Picture Researcher Myriam Megharbi
Managing Editor Lisa Gillespie
Managing Art Editor Owen Peyton Jones
Production Editor Gillian Reid
Senior Producer Meskerem Berhane
Jacket Designer Surabhi Wadhwa-Gandhi
Jackets Design Development Manager Sophia MTT
Publisher Andrew Macintyre
Art Director Karen Self
Associate Publishing Director Liz Wheeler
Publishing Director Jonathan Metcalf
Consultant Philip Parker
Contributors A. M. Dassu, Mireille Harper, Lisa Sade Kennedy,
Susan Kennedy, Francesca Kletz, Sally Regan

DK DELHI
Jacket Designer Tanya Mehrotra
Senior Picture Researcher Taiyaba Khatoon
Senior Picture Researcher Surya Sankash Sarangi
Assistant Picture Researcher Vagisha Pushp

First American Edition, 2020
Published in the United States by DK Publishing
1450 Broadway, Suite 801, New York, NY 10018

Copyright © 2020 Dorling Kindersley Limited
DK, a Division of Penguin Random House LLC
20 21 22 23 24 10 9 8 7 6 5 4 3 2 1
001–316701–October/2020

A catalog record for this book is available from the Library of Congress.
ISBN 978-1-4654-9996-7

DK books are available at special discounts when purchased
in bulk for sales promotions, premiums, fund-raising, or educational use.
For details, contact: DK Publishing Special Markets,
1450 Broadway, Suite 801, New York, NY 10018
SpecialSales@dk.com

Printed and bound in China

For the curious

www.dk.com

Smithsonian

THE SMITHSONIAN
Established in 1846, the Smithsonian—the world's largest museum and research complex—includes
19 museums and galleries and the National Zoological Park. The total number of artifacts, works of art, and
specimens in the Smithsonian's collection is estimated at 154 million. The Smithsonian is a renowned research
center, dedicated to public education, national service, and scholarship in the arts, sciences, and history.

Including everyone

This book was created, designed, written, and edited by a multicultural team of women and men from many different nations, heritages, and communities. Some of them hold different and varied religious beliefs, and others have no religious beliefs. We believe that the diversity of this team has helped make this book inclusive of lots of different people and their lives, stories, and cultures. Readers should see themselves reflected in the books they read.

Traditionally, history has been recorded and written by men from privileged backgrounds, who often have a European focus when they assess the past. This has meant that most history books have hidden, overshadowed, and excluded the exciting lives and amazing accomplishments of women, and of people from different ethnic and cultural backgrounds. In making this book, we have intentionally sought out those people and their stories. Here you will find wonderful timelines that profile people regardless of their gender, nationality, beliefs, heritage, religion, or sexuality.

Traveling through time

The earliest events in this book took place a very long time ago. Some dates may be followed by MYA, short for "million years ago," or YA, short for "years ago." Other dates have BCE and CE after them. These are short for "before the Common Era" and "Common Era." The Common Era dates from when people think Jesus Christ was born.

Where the exact date of an event is not known, "c." is used. This is short for the Latin word *circa*, meaning "around," and indicates that the date is approximate.

RAMSES THE GREAT TO IBN SINA

CONTENTS

ARTEMISIA GENTILESCHI TO ADA LOVELACE

WINSTON CHURCHILL TO GRETA THUNBERG

WILLIAM RANDOLPH HEARST TO OODGEROO NOONUCCAL

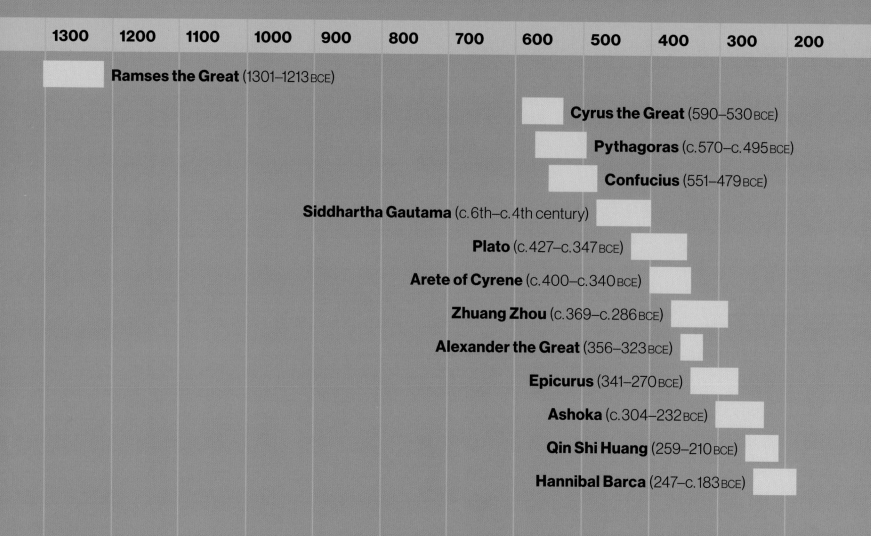

Ramses the Great (1301–1213 BCE)

Cyrus the Great (590–530 BCE)

Pythagoras (c.570–c.495 BCE)

Confucius (551–479 BCE)

Siddhartha Gautama (c.6th–c.4th century)

Plato (c.427–c.347 BCE)

Arete of Cyrene (c.400–c.340 BCE)

Zhuang Zhou (c.369–c.286 BCE)

Alexander the Great (356–323 BCE)

Epicurus (341–270 BCE)

Ashoka (c.304–232 BCE)

Qin Shi Huang (259–210 BCE)

Hannibal Barca (247–c.183 BCE)

Ramses the Great
to Ibn Sina

The ideas of ancient scholars and thinkers in the time between Ramses the Great and Ibn Sina still influence the way we think today. Our belief that mathematics and physics can explain the Universe can be traced back to the theories of Pythagoras and his followers. The teachings of Confucius have shaped Chinese culture for more than 2,000 years. And Fatima al-Fihri is believed to have established the oldest university anywhere in the world.

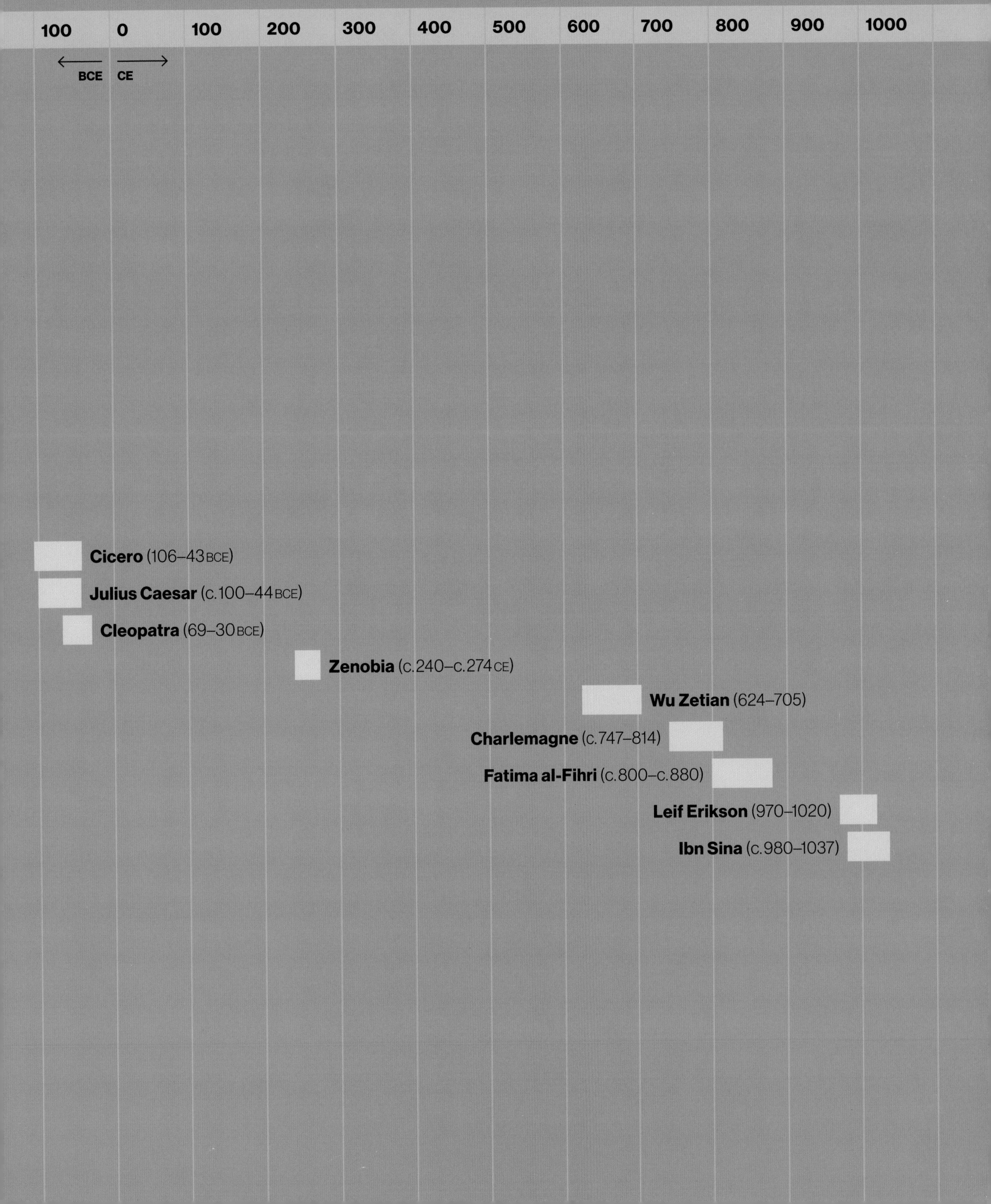

100
0
100
200
300
400
500
600
700
800
900
1000
BCE
CE
Cicero (106–43 BCE)
Julius Caesar (c. 100–44 BCE)
Cleopatra (69–30 BCE)
Zenobia (c. 240–c. 274 CE)
Wu Zetian (624–705)
Charlemagne (c. 747–814)
Fatima al-Fihri (c. 800–c. 880)
Leif Erikson (970–1020)
Ibn Sina (c. 980–1037)

First tools

The earliest hominins live in West Africa. They learn to make simple tools by striking stones against each other. They use these tools to crack nuts, chop wood, and scrape meat from the carcasses of animals.

c.2.5 MYA

Fire

Hominins use fire to cook meat. Cooking makes it easier for people to digest their food. The extra calories and nutrients allow the brain size to increase. Groups spend time around the hearth, preparing and eating food, and caring for their young.

c.800,000 YA

Humans through time

About 7 million years ago, a species of ape appeared in East Africa that could walk upright on two legs. It was the first of the hominins—a group that includes modern humans and our ancestors. Over millions of years, humans evolved into the species that has today populated almost every part of planet Earth.

Farming

Humans domesticate pigs, sheep, and goats for their meat and skins. They harvest wild plants, such as wheat and barley, storing some seed for sowing next spring. In time, they become farmers, and settle in one place. Humans no longer have to rely on hunting and gathering to survive.

Using metal

People use copper, a soft metal that can be found easily, to make tools for harvesting crops. About 5,500 YA, humans also learn to make bronze (which is harder and stronger) by melting copper and tin together. They start using iron, a very hard metal found in rocks, about 2,000 years later.

c.9000

c.12,000 YA

A house in Çatalhöyük
Houses were often decorated with wall paintings and the skulls of bulls.

Urban living

In the Middle East, people begin living in towns and cities. One of the largest is Çatalhöyük, in modern-day Turkey, which has a population of about 6,000 people. They live in small mud-brick houses crowded close together. Each house is entered through a hole in its roof.

c.8000

Hunting with spears

Hominins begin to hunt in groups using spears. This means they have to cooperate with each other while hunting. They communicate by gestures and shouts. Hominins also begin to build shelters out of rocks and branches.

c.400,000 YA

Around the world

By this time, *Homo sapiens* (modern humans) are present in Africa, Asia, Europe, and Australia. By about 15,000 YA (years ago), they will also reach the Americas. They make a variety of stone tools, and use needles made from bone to make animal skins into clothes. They even make flutes from bones.

40,000 YA

Cave art

Humans around the world decorate rock faces and caves with carved or painted designs. Many of these artworks are of animals, such as horses, rhinos, and deer. The art may be connected to rituals asking for successful hunts.

44,000 YA

Dogs and humans

Some wolves begin to hang around human campsites looking for food. Over time, they lose their fear of people and become friendlier. Later, people use their descendants (the first dogs) for hunting and protection.

c.14,000 YA

Shelter from the cold

Europe is much colder than today. Hunters there use the bones of mammoths to build shelters. By about 10,000 YA, mammoths will have disappeared from Europe. Hunting and climate change leads to their total extinction by 1700 BCE.

c.15,000 YA

Pottery

By this time, people are making pottery in China. Over the following 10,000 years, humans in all parts of the world discover independently how to mold clay and bake it in a fire. This new technology allows them to make pots for cooking and storing food and drink.

20,000 YA

Writing

The first writing systems are invented in Sumer (modern-day Iraq) and Egypt. Other early writing systems using simple pictures as signs develop separately in India, China, and Mexico. Writing allows humans to record their history.

c.3400 BCE

Crossing oceans

New shipbuilding technology means European sailors can cross oceans to reach the Americas and the eastern parts of Asia. People from different parts of the world meet for the first time, sharing cultures and goods. Sailors carry diseases, which kill many people who have no natural resistance to them.

c.1500 CE

New technology

The development of steam-powered machines brings about the Industrial Revolution. The way humans live, work, and travel speeds up. People leave the countryside to find work in factories and mills in cities.

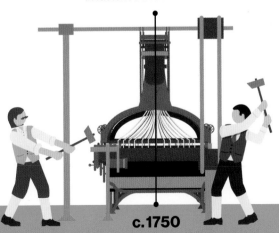

c.1750

Computer age

The rapid development of computer technology in the late 20th century brings enormous changes to the workplace. The internet and smartphones transform the way people communicate and spend their leisure time.

c.1990

Ramses the Great

Pharaoh Ramses II (c. 1301–1213 BCE) used diplomacy, a huge building program, and endless self-promotion to become the greatest pharaoh of ancient Egypt. His long rule brought unprecedented stability and prosperity to the nation, and led nine further pharaohs to take his name in a bid to mirror his success.

Notable pharaohs

Over the course of about 3,000 years, 170 pharaohs ruled Egypt. Each pharaoh left a unique legacy that shaped the culture, religion, and traditions of the country.

Khufu (reigned 2589–2566 BCE)
This pharaoh's best-known contribution was the construction of the Great Pyramid of Giza, the largest of the Egyptian pyramids.

Amenhotep III (1411–1351 BCE)
Egypt reached its pinnacle of power during the 38-year reign of Amenhotep III. He inherited a vast empire, and kept peace with his neighbors though diplomacy and marriage. He was the first pharaoh to send out royal news bulletins inscribed on stone seals, documenting significant events during his reign, such as his marriages and building projects. Amenhotep III was later revered as a fertility god by Egyptians as a result of the abundant crops harvested during his reign.

Tutankhamen (c. 1344–1327 BCE)
The grandson of Amenhotep III, Tutankhamen became pharaoh around the age of nine, and reigned until his death at the age of about 17 years old. He is most famous today for his lavish tomb, which was so well hidden that grave robbers never found it.

Battle of Kadesh
The young pharaoh leads his forces to recapture Kadesh, but is tricked by spies into thinking the Hittites are far from the Egyptian camp. They are actually lying in wait nearby, and attack. The Egyptians are on the brink of defeat, but reinforcements arrive just in time.

1274 BCE

Invasion
When Ramses becomes pharaoh, the Hittites see an opportunity to test the young king and his empire's northern border. They invade and take over the important trading town of Kadesh (in modern-day Syria).

1274 BCE

Ramesseum
Ramses begins work on a temple that will record important events in his reign, the Ramesseum. Located on the west bank of the Nile, the huge site features a courtyard, a hall, painted scenes from the pharaoh's life, and a giant statue of Ramses himself.

c. 1279 BCE

Pharaoh
After the death of Seti I, Ramses ascends the throne. Along with his new title, he inherits the kingdom's many problems and conflicts. It is a lot to take on for a 25 year old, especially as Egypt is surrounded by enemies.

1279 BCE

Prince regent
From an early age, Ramses accompanies his father on his military campaigns. At the age of 14, he is appointed prince regent—making him Seti's stand-in when the pharaoh is not around. By the time he is 22, he is the commander of the Egyptian army, leading it into battle.

1289 BCE

Birth of a king
Ramses is born to Pharaoh Seti I and Queen Tuya during a time of war. Egypt has lost several provinces in the north to the Hittites of Anatolia (in modern-day Turkey). Seti battles against the Hittites to get these provinces back.

c. 1301 BCE

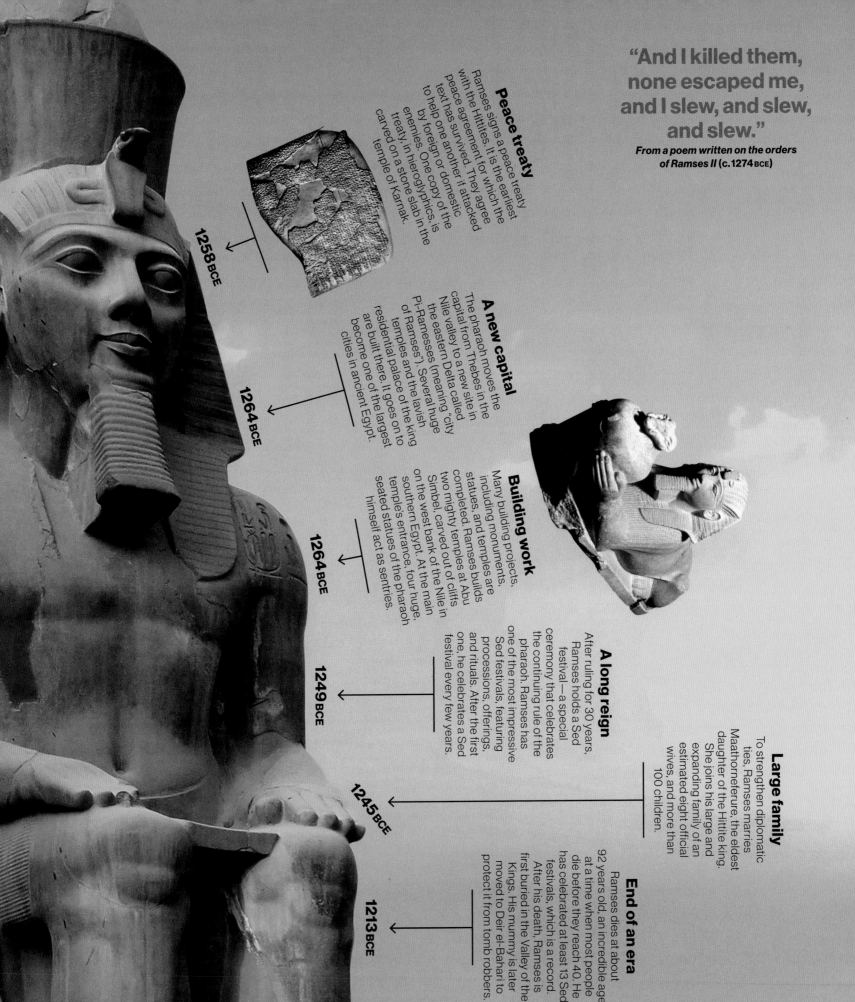

"And I killed them, none escaped me, and I slew, and slew, and slew."

From a poem written on the orders of Ramses II (c. 1274 BCE)

Peace treaty

Ramses signs a peace treaty with the Hittites. It is the earliest peace agreement. They agree to help one another if attacked by foreign or domestic enemies. One copy of the treaty, in hieroglyphics, is carved on a stone slab in the temple of Karnak.

1258 BCE

A new capital

The pharaoh moves the capital from Thebes in the Nile valley to a new site in the eastern Delta called Pi-Ramesses (meaning "city of Ramses"). Several huge temples and the lavish residential palace of the king are built there. It goes on to become one of the largest cities in ancient Egypt.

1264 BCE

Building work

Many building projects, including monuments, statues, and temples are completed. Ramses builds two mighty temples at Abu Simbel, carved out of cliffs on the west bank of the Nile in southern Egypt. At the main temple's entrance, four huge, seated statues of the pharaoh himself act as sentries.

1264 BCE

A long reign

After ruling for 30 years, Ramses holds a Sed festival—a special ceremony that celebrates the continuing rule of the pharaoh. Ramses has one of the most impressive Sed festivals, featuring processions, offerings, and rituals. After the first one, he celebrates a Sed festival every few years.

1249 BCE

Large family

To strengthen diplomatic ties, Ramses marries Maathorneferure, the eldest daughter of the Hittite king. She joins his large and expanding family of an estimated eight official wives, and more than 100 children.

1245 BCE

End of an era

Ramses dies at about 92 years old, an incredible age at a time when most people die before they reach 40. He has celebrated at least 13 Sed festivals, which is a record. After his death, Ramses is first buried in the Valley of the Kings. His mummy is later moved to Deir el-Bahari to protect it from tomb robbers.

1213 BCE

Cyrus the Great

One of the greatest leaders in the ancient world, Cyrus the Great (c. 590–530 BCE) was a talented military commander who conquered three other empires to establish the first Persian Empire. Cyrus is recorded as being a wise ruler, respecting the religions and customs of all the lands he ruled. He remains a hero to many in modern-day Iran.

"**I am Cyrus, who won the Persians their empire. Do not begrudge me this bit of earth that covers my bones.**"

Inscription on Cyrus' tomb

Croesus (c. 595–545 BCE)
King of Lydia (the western part of modern-day Turkey), Croesus was worried about the rise of the Persian Empire. According to legend, he asked an oracle for advice, and was told that if he attacked the Persians, he would destroy a great empire. Croesus attacked Cyrus in 547 BCE, but the following year Croesus was himself defeated. It turned out that the oracle had foretold the end of his own empire.

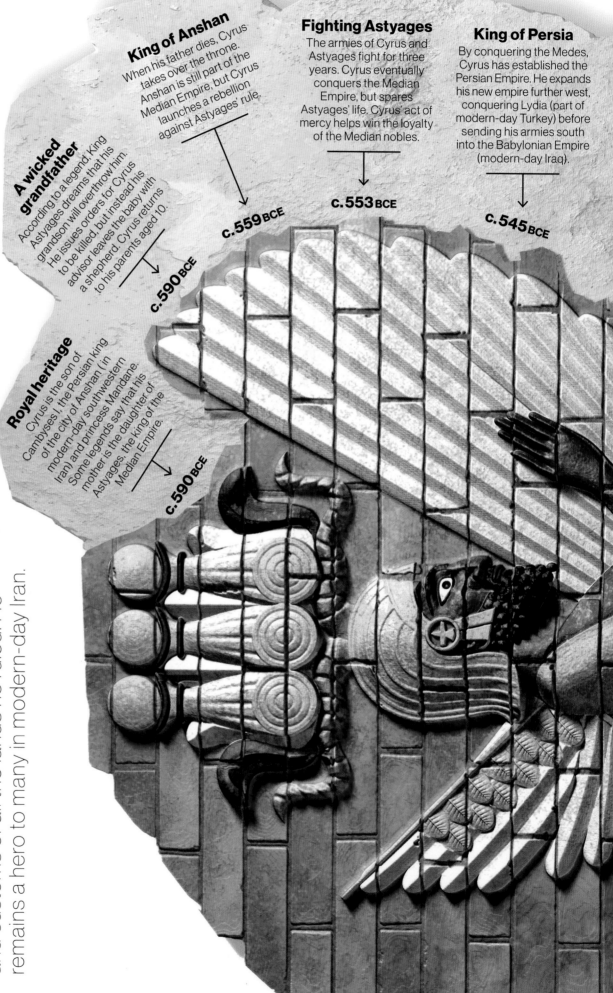

A wicked grandfather
According to a legend, King Astyages dreams that his grandson will overthrow him. He issues orders for Cyrus to be killed, but instead his advisor leaves the baby with a shepherd. Cyrus returns to his parents aged 10.

c. 590 BCE

King of Anshan
When his father dies, Cyrus takes over the throne. Anshan is still part of the Median Empire, but Cyrus launches a rebellion against Astyages' rule.

c. 559 BCE

Fighting Astyages
The armies of Cyrus and Astyages fight for three years. Cyrus eventually conquers the Median Empire, but spares Astyages' life. Cyrus' act of mercy helps win the loyalty of the Median nobles.

c. 553 BCE

King of Persia
By conquering the Medes, Cyrus has established the Persian Empire. He expands his new empire further west, conquering Lydia (part of modern-day Turkey) before sending his armies south into the Babylonian Empire (modern-day Iraq).

c. 545 BCE

Royal heritage
Cyrus is the son of Cambyses I, the Persian king of the city of Anshan (in modern-day southwestern Iran) and princess Mandane. Some legends say that his mother is the daughter of Astyages, the king of the Median Empire.

c. 590 BCE

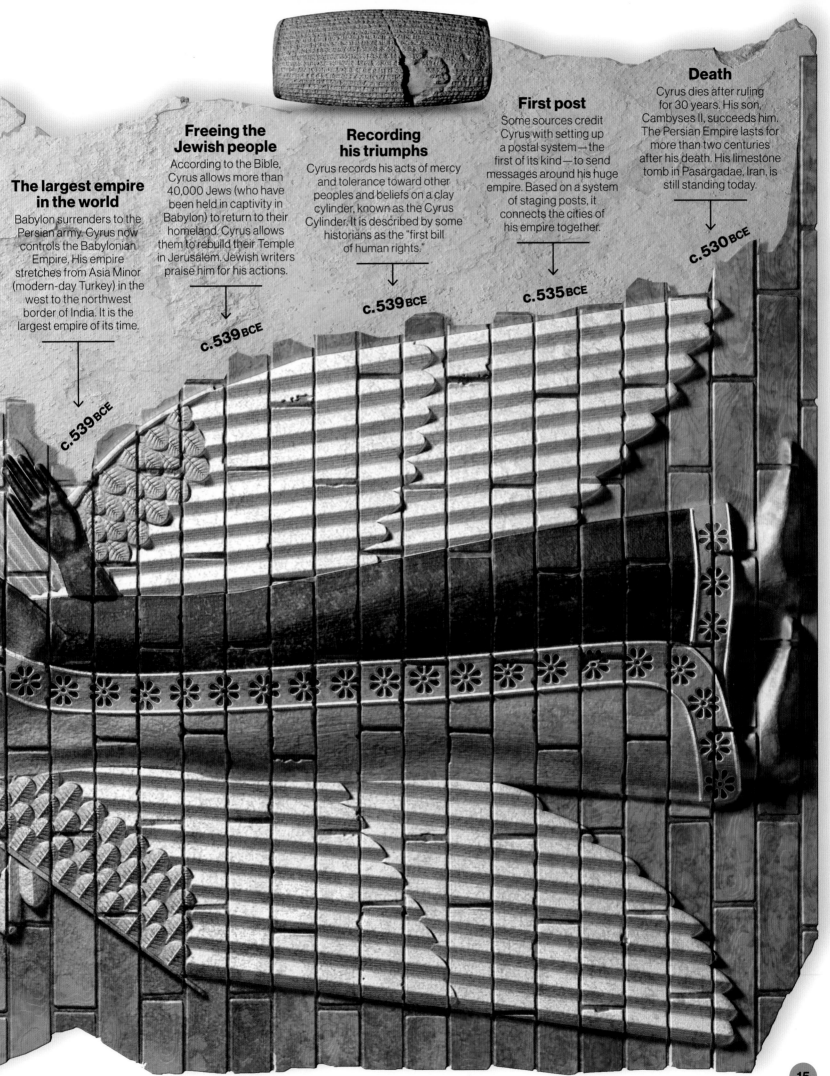

The largest empire in the world

Babylon surrenders to the Persian army. Cyrus now controls the Babylonian Empire. His empire stretches from Asia Minor (modern-day Turkey) in the west to the northwest border of India. It is the largest empire of its time.

c.539 BCE

Freeing the Jewish people

According to the Bible, Cyrus allows more than 40,000 Jews (who have been held in captivity in Babylon) to return to their homeland. Cyrus allows them to rebuild their Temple in Jerusalem. Jewish writers praise him for his actions.

c.539 BCE

Recording his triumphs

Cyrus records his acts of mercy and tolerance toward other peoples and beliefs on a clay cylinder, known as the Cyrus Cylinder. It is described by some historians as the "first bill of human rights."

c.539 BCE

First post

Some sources credit Cyrus with setting up a postal system—the first of its kind—to send messages around his huge empire. Based on a system of staging posts, it connects the cities of his empire together.

c.535 BCE

Death

Cyrus dies after ruling for 30 years. His son, Cambyses II, succeeds him. The Persian Empire lasts for more than two centuries after his death. His limestone tomb in Pasargadae, Iran, is still standing today.

c.530 BCE

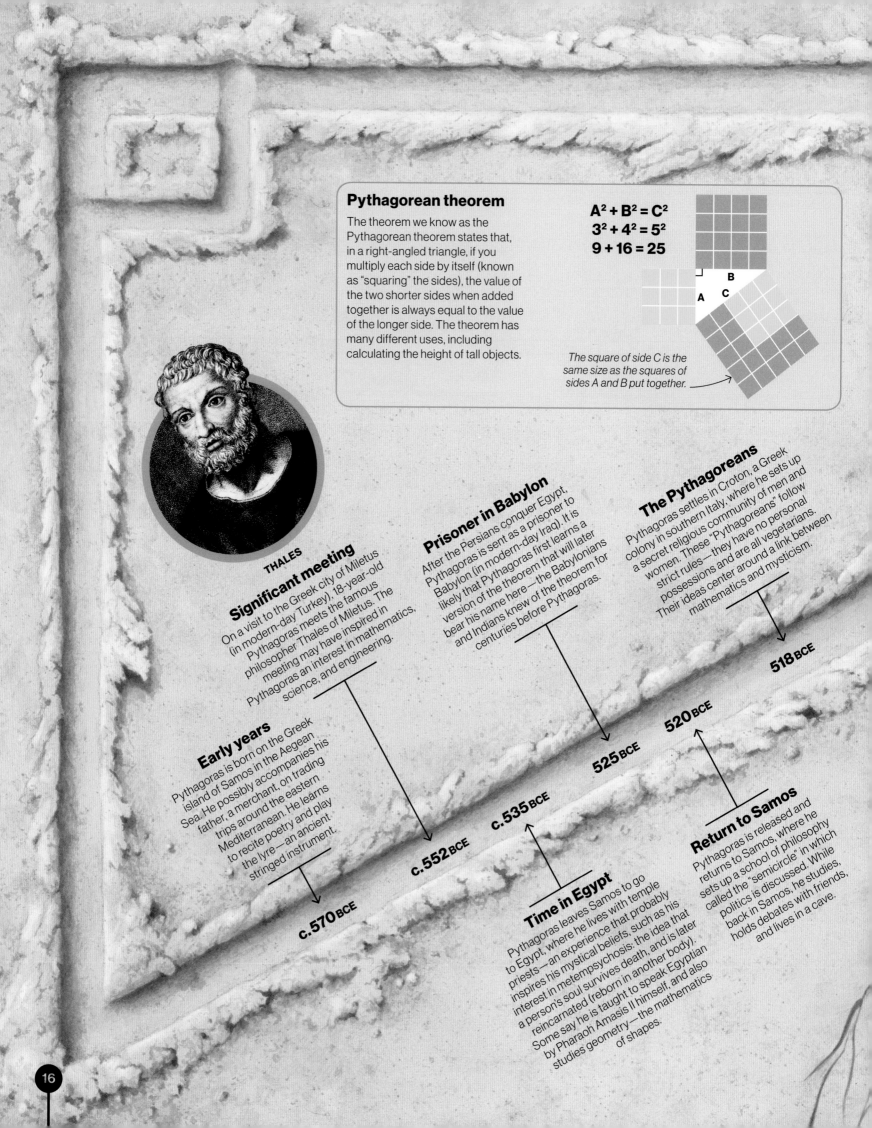

Pythagorean theorem

The theorem we know as the Pythagorean theorem states that, in a right-angled triangle, if you multiply each side by itself (known as "squaring" the sides), the value of the two shorter sides when added together is always equal to the value of the longer side. The theorem has many different uses, including calculating the height of tall objects.

$$A^2 + B^2 = C^2$$
$$3^2 + 4^2 = 5^2$$
$$9 + 16 = 25$$

The square of side C is the same size as the squares of sides A and B put together.

THALES

Significant meeting

On a visit to the Greek city of Miletus (in modern-day Turkey), 18-year-old Pythagoras meets the famous philosopher Thales of Miletus. The meeting may have inspired in Pythagoras an interest in mathematics, science, and engineering.

Prisoner in Babylon

After the Persians conquer Egypt, Pythagoras is sent as a prisoner to Babylon (in modern-day Iraq). It is likely that Pythagoras first learns a version of the theorem that will later bear his name here—the Babylonians and Indians knew of the theorem for centuries before Pythagoras.

The Pythagoreans

Pythagoras settles in Croton, a Greek colony in southern Italy, where he sets up a secret religious community of men and women. These "Pythagoreans" follow strict rules—they have no personal possessions and are all vegetarians. Their ideas center around a link between mathematics and mysticism.

518 BCE

Early years

Pythagoras is born on the Greek island of Samos in the Aegean Sea. He possibly accompanies his father, a merchant, on trading trips around the eastern Mediterranean. He learns to recite poetry and play the lyre—an ancient stringed instrument.

520 BCE

525 BCE

c. 535 BCE

c. 552 BCE

Return to Samos

Pythagoras is released and returns to Samos, where he sets up a school of philosophy called the "semicircle" in which politics is discussed. While back in Samos, he studies, holds debates with friends, and lives in a cave.

c. 570 BCE

Time in Egypt

Pythagoras leaves Samos to go to Egypt, where he lives with temple priests—an experience that probably inspires his mystical beliefs, such as his interest in metempsychosis: the idea that a person's soul survives death, and is later reincarnated (reborn in another body). Some say he is taught to speak Egyptian by Pharaoh Amasis II himself, and also studies geometry—the mathematics of shapes.

Family life

Pythagoras marries Theano, one of his pupils and a philosopher in her own right. They have several children, and one of their sons later becomes a teacher in the community Pythagoras set up in Croton.

c. 515 BCE

Pythagorean theorem

Although Pythagoras did not discover the rule that bears his name, it is possible that he is the first to introduce the rule to the Greeks. It is also possible that he or his students were among the first to prove why it works.

c. 500 BCE

c. 495 BCE

Unclear death

We don't know how or when Pythagoras died, but we know that he was famous for his outspokenness and often upset people. According to one story, his enemies set fire to his school at Croton. He escapes and flees to the town of Metapontum, where he starves himself to death.

Ancient Greek scientists

The ancient Greeks made many advances in science. The word *scientist* did not exist then—they called themselves philosophers ("lovers of wisdom").

Hippocrates (c. 460–c. 377 BCE)
Greek physician Hippocrates changed medicine forever by arguing that diseases had natural causes and were not sent by the gods to punish people, as was previously believed.

Democritus (c. 460–c. 370 BCE)
Greek philosopher Democritus believed that everything in the universe is made up of tiny particles called atoms that cannot be divided or changed.

Archimedes (c. 287–c. 212 BCE)
The story goes that Sicilian-born Archimedes had the original "Eureka!" ("I have it!") moment in the bath, when he realized that the volume of an object can be found by measuring the water it displaces.

Pythagoras

Although his ideas have been passed to us through other people, we know that Pythagoras of Samos (c. 570–c. 495 BCE) was one of the most influential thinkers of the ancient Greek world. He believed that mathematics held the key to the universe, and was interested in the mystical powers of numbers. While he did not discover the Pythagorean theorem, his ideas were important for his time, and some are even still around today.

497 BCE

"If you see what is right and fail to act on it, you lack courage."

Analects, Book II

Now disillusioned with politics, Confucius is disappointed when the Duke of Lu spends more time with the performers at court than performing his duties. He decides to leave his position and go into exile.

497–484 BCE

"Let the state of ... harmony exist, and a happy order will prevail."

Doctrine of the Mean

Confucius sets off traveling across China's kingdoms, trying to find a ruler who will put his teachings into practice. Many people are interested in what he has to say, and his ideas spread.

484 BCE

"If I hear the Way [of truth] in the morning, I am content even to die in that evening."

Analects, Book IV

After 13 years, Confucius returns to Lu and devotes the final years of his life to teaching. He dies in 479 BCE. His followers later collect his ideas in a text called the *Analects*. For 2,000 years, all Chinese officials have to pass an exam based on Confucius' philosophy, later called Confucianism, and it remains a guiding force in the Chinese way of living today.

500 BCE

"When a country is ill governed, riches ... are things to be ashamed of."

Analects, Book VIII

Lu state is governed by three corrupt aristocratic families under a ruling duke. Confucius wants to introduce further reforms, with the duke taking sole power. He leads a plot against the families, but it fails, and he makes some powerful enemies at the duke's court.

501 BCE

"Guide [the people] by example; they will ... come to be good."

Analects, Book XVII

He is made governor of a town in Lu state, and eventually rises to become minister of justice. He argues that rulers should not order their people around, but set a good example. The reforms he introduces are so successful that crime is almost eliminated.

519 BCE

"What you do not wish for yourself, do not do to others."

Analects, Book VI

Confucius' reputation grows as he gathers a dedicated group of followers. Among his teachings is the Golden Rule: the idea that you should treat people the way you would like to be treated.

Confucius

Confucius (551–479 BCE) was China's first great philosopher. He believed in respecting tradition, and being loyal and kind to other people. He also developed new ideas for how society should work, arguing that people could only be happy if their rulers treated them well. Confucius' simple but powerful ideas gradually spread and became a huge part of Chinese life.

551 BCE

"A young man should serve his parents ... and be respectful to elders."

Analects, Book I

Confucius is born in the state of Lu in China, to a once-rich aristocratic family that has fallen on hard times. When he is just three years old, his father dies and he is brought up in poverty by his mother.

536 BCE

"At fifteen my heart was set on learning."

Analects, Book II

Confucius has an appetite for books and decides to devote his life to philosophy. When he leaves school, he works in various government jobs to make ends meet, including as a bookkeeper and as a stable manager.

519 BCE

"Reviewing what you have learned and learning anew, you are fit to be a teacher."

Analects, Book II

After his mother's death, he opens a school in the family home. He believes that everyone has a right to education, and even allows some poorer students to live with him for free.

PLATO

Socrates (469–399 BCE)
One of the first philosophers to be interested in human behavior, Socrates taught by asking questions and then discussing possible answers. When his political enemies accused him of having dangerous ideas, he refused to defend himself, and was sentenced to death.

Hypatia (c.370–415 CE)
Some think this likeness is of Raphael, but others feel it is Hypatia, one of the last great thinkers of the ancient world. She was a teacher of astronomy, mathematics, and philosophy in Alexandria, Egypt. She was murdered by a Christian mob as she returned from a lecture because she did not believe in their God.

Athenian youth
Plato is from an aristocratic Athenian family, and is educated by the best teachers. He is a good wrestler, and some sources say that he competes in the Isthmian Games, an important local sporting festival.

Turning point
When Plato hears the philosopher Socrates teaching, he is struck by his ideas. He decides to devote himself to philosophy, spending the next eight years as a follower of Socrates.

Plato's dialogues
It is possible that Plato begins writing his dialogues around this time. In these, he sets out Socrates' ideas in the form of conversations with other thinkers. They discuss topics such as how to live a good life, the nature of love, and the ideal state.

Leaving Athens
Deeply upset by Socrates' death, Plato leaves Athens. He spends several years traveling widely around the Mediterranean world, visiting Italy, Sicily, and Egypt.

The Republic
In his influential dialogue *The Republic*, written around the middle part of his career, Plato imagines what a perfect society would be like. He believes it would be ruled by a "philosopher king" with the help of wise people known as "guardians."

| c.427 BCE | c.409 BCE | c.407 BCE | c.399 BCE | 398 BCE | 390s | c.387 BCE | c.375 BCE |

Military service
Plato serves in the Athenian army at the end of a long war with the city of Sparta. The war results in defeat for Athens, and the collapse of democracy. Plato decides to become a poet.

Death of Socrates
Socrates is found guilty of corrupting the youth of Athens with his ideas. He is put to death by poison. Plato later writes a detailed account of Socrates' trial and death.

The Academy
Plato sets up a school called the Academy, which is based in a garden of olive trees just outside Athens. Students come here to discuss philosophical questions with their teachers. They do not have to pay fees.

Aristotle (384–322 BCE)
Aristotle was interested in understanding the natural world around us. He believed that all theories should be proved by observation. Aristotle became tutor to Alexander the Great, and later set up his own school in Athens called the Lyceum.

The School of Athens
Philosophers made Athens the center of learning in the ancient world. In this fresco from 1511, the Renaissance artist Raphael shows Plato, Aristotle, and Socrates mingling with other Greek philosophers and thinkers from other ages.

Plato

Born in the Greek city-state of Athens, Plato (c. 427–c. 347 BCE) was one of the greatest philosophers of all time. He set up the Academy, a school where he and his students discussed subjects such as politics, religion, and morals. His ideas still influence thinkers today.

C. 367 BCE

Great student
Aristotle arrives to study at the Academy. He stays for 20 years, composing many of his most famous works. He becomes Plato's most famous student.

C. 367 BCE

In Sicily
Plato is invited to Syracuse, in Sicily, to advise the ruler and hopefully make him a "philosopher king." The experiment ends in failure because of court politics, and Plato is forced to leave.

C. 347 BCE

Death in old age
Plato is in his early 80s when he dies in Athens. The Academy he established continues as a center of philosophical learning for several centuries after his death.

Ancient philosophers

Siddhartha Gautama (c. 6th–c. 4th century BCE)

Though historians disagree about exactly when the events of his life happened, we know that Siddhartha Gautama taught his followers that suffering was a part of life, and that they must accept this to be at peace. His ideas became the basis of Buddhism, one of the world's major religions.

c. 563 BCE
Siddhartha Gautama is born in Lumbini (in modern-day Nepal). His father is a wealthy ruler. Siddhartha is brought up in his father's luxurious palace, where he has the best of everything.

c. 534 BCE
Siddhartha leaves his palace for the first time and sees an old person, a sick person, a dead person. For the first time in his life he comes face to face with suffering, and the fact that everyone must die. These encounters lead him to abandon his life of luxury.

c. 525 BCE
Siddhartha spends six years under the guidance of many spiritual teachers. While he is meditating beneath a bodhi tree, he receives enlightenment, or awakening. After his awakening, he understands that we must accept suffering in order to reach nirvana (liberation from suffering).

c. 525 BCE
Now known as the Buddha (meaning "Enlightened One"), he spends the next 45 years traveling throughout northern India to spread his teachings. After his death, his ideas become a religion, Buddhism, which has about 500 million followers worldwide today.

Arete of Cyrene (c. 400–c. 340 BCE)

Arete of Cyrene played an important role in developing the ancient Greek school of thought called "hedonism." She believed that the supreme goal of life is pleasure, because it is pleasure that makes people happy.

c. 400 BCE
Arete is born in the Greek colony of Cyrene (in modern-day Libya). She learns philosophy from her father, Aristippus, who had set up a school of philosophy in Cyrene. At the time it is very unusual for women to study philosophy, as most women of the time are prevented from pursuing study or taking part in public forums.

c. 380 BCE
Arete begins teaching people about hedonism. She believes that in order to be happy, we must pursue the things that bring us pleasure, and avoid things that increase our suffering. But we also must not become obsessed with seeking pleasure, because pleasure will then lose its power.

c. 356 BCE
When her father dies, Arete takes over leadership of the hedonist school in Cyrene. She teaches there for more than 30 years, developing and building on her father's ideas.

c. 340 BCE
Arete dies. Her importance to her students and fellow philosophers is etched in an inscription on her tomb, which says that she has the "soul of Socrates, and the tongue of Homer"—two of the greatest thinkers and writers of ancient Greece.

Epicurus (341–270 BCE)

Epicurus believed that seeking pleasure is the goal of life. Epicurus believed that knowledge, friendships, and eating simply are ways of achieving peace.

341 BCE
Epicurus is born on the Greek island of Samos to Athenian parents.

323 BCE
He moves to Athens to serve in the Athenian army. Later, he studies with various philosophers, including Plato and Socrates.

c. 311 BCE
Epicurus sets up a school of philosophy in Mytilene on the island of Lesbos. He begins to develop his ideas on how best to live. He teaches and attracts followers in the cities of Mytilene and Lampsacus.

c. 306 BCE
He returns to Athens and sets up a philosophical school called "The Garden." While there, Epicurus and his followers live in line with his teaching that pleasure comes from knowledge, enjoying good friendships, and avoiding rich food. He is unusual in allowing women and enslaved people to attend his school.

270 BCE
Epicurus suffers from a painful disease, but, thanks to his philosophical ideas, he manages to remain cheerful. He dies at the age of 71.

Since the beginning of time, people have wondered, debated, and formed opinions on how best to live. Philosophers have emerged at different times and places with thought-provoking suggestions. Some of their ideas became ways of organizing governments, sciences, and even religions.

Zhuang Zhou (c.369–c.286 BCE)

An ancient Chinese sage, or philosopher, Zhuang Zhou wrote the *Zhuangzi*. It became one of the most important books of Daoism—an ancient Chinese system of beliefs which teaches that we should live simply, avoid conflict, and find ways around problems.

c.369 BCE
Almost nothing is known about Zhuang Zhou's life. Meng, in China, is often given as his place of birth.

c.340 BCE
According to one story, he is offered the post of chief minister by the king of Chu. He refuses the job as he prefers to live an independent life, and does not want to be constricted by the stresses of the royal court.

c.350 BCE
He writes the *Zhuangzi*, a collection of stories and fables. The book teaches that there is no difference between good and bad, life and death, and humans and nature. Everything is connected: a central idea of Daoism.

c.286 BCE
When Zhuang Zhou is about to die, his friends say they are planning a grand burial for him. Instead, he puts an end to the idea, pointing out his body will soon be food for crows and worms.

Cicero (106–43 BCE)

The Roman lawyer and politician Cicero wrote many influential books on philosophy. His ideas emphasized that a person's well-being is based on living in a good society.

106 BCE
Marcus Tullius Cicero is born in the town of Arpinum, not far from Rome. His father, a wealthy landowner, pays for his education in law, writing, and philosophy.

81 BCE
Cicero begins to work as a lawyer. He has a reputation for being intelligent and ambitious.

58 BCE
Cicero makes an enemy of Julius Caesar, one of the most powerful men in Rome. As a result, he is forced into exile in Macedonia for a year.

57 BCE
After returning home, Cicero dedicates himself to writing about philosophy. He studies Greek philosophers, including Epicurus. He writes that the ideal government is a blend of royalty, aristocracy, and democracy, and the formation of laws that must be in harmony with nature.

44 BCE
Caesar is declared dictator (sole ruler) of Rome for life. Cicero criticizes him for seizing power, but is not involved when Caesar is murdered by his political enemies.

43 BCE
Cicero criticizes Marcus Antonius, a powerful political ally of Caesar's. Cicero is murdered on the orders of Marcus Antonius.

Alexander the Great

One of the most successful military generals who ever lived, Alexander the Great (356–323 BCE) never lost a battle. He became king of Macedonia, a kingdom in northern Greece, at the age of 20. In just eight years, he created the largest empire ever assembled to that point, which included parts of Europe, Africa, and Asia, and stretched from Greece to northern India.

356 BCE

Hero's training

Alexander is the son of King Philip II of Macedonia. Philip arranges for the Greek philosopher Aristotle to be Alexander's tutor when the boy turns 13.

338 BCE

First taste of battle

At the age of 18, Alexander leads a cavalry charge at the Battle of Chaeronea against the Greek city-states of Athens and Thebes. His victory gives Philip II control over most of Greece, and helps develop Alexander's grasp of battle tactics.

Philip II of Macedon (382–336 BCE)

Although now overshadowed by his more famous son, Philip II was a great military leader. He brought in improvements in how his armies fought, and their success in battle resulted in Philip uniting Greece under his rule.

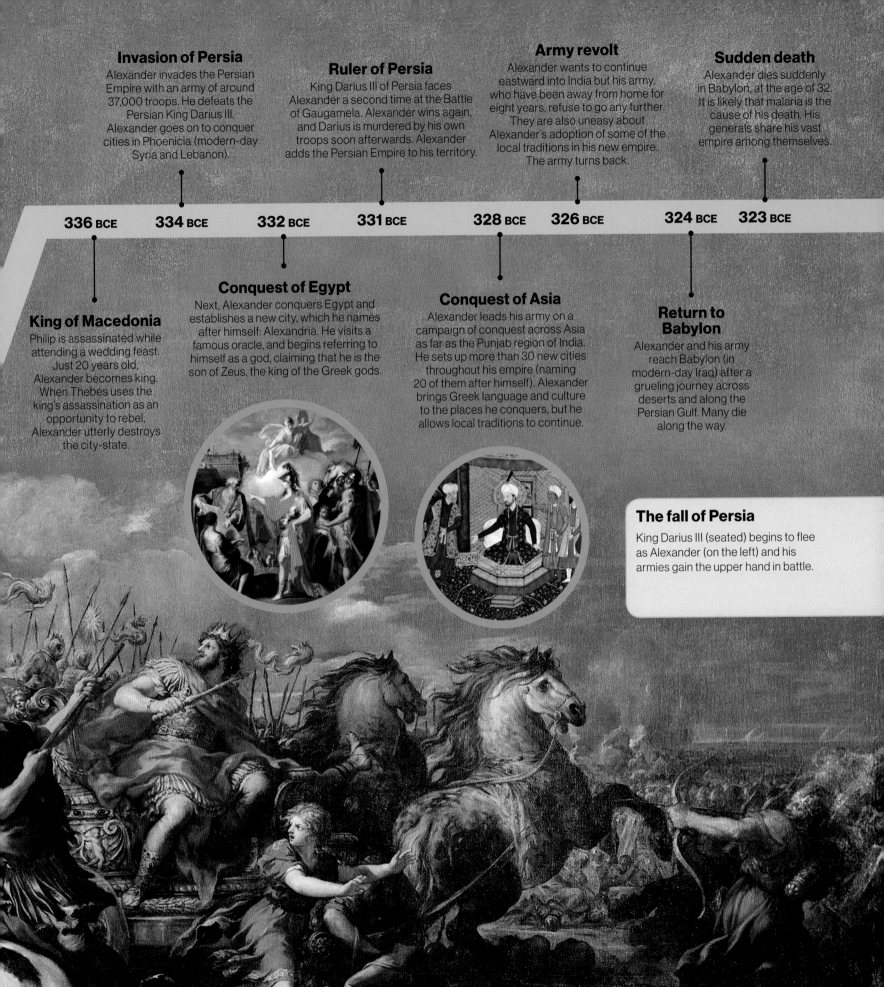

Invasion of Persia
Alexander invades the Persian Empire with an army of around 37,000 troops. He defeats the Persian King Darius III. Alexander goes on to conquer cities in Phoenicia (modern-day Syria and Lebanon).

Ruler of Persia
King Darius III of Persia faces Alexander a second time at the Battle of Gaugamela. Alexander wins again, and Darius is murdered by his own troops soon afterwards. Alexander adds the Persian Empire to his territory.

Army revolt
Alexander wants to continue eastward into India but his army, who have been away from home for eight years, refuse to go any further. They are also uneasy about Alexander's adoption of some of the local traditions in his new empire. The army turns back.

Sudden death
Alexander dies suddenly in Babylon, at the age of 32. It is likely that malaria is the cause of his death. His generals share his vast empire among themselves.

336 BCE **334** BCE **332** BCE **331** BCE **328** BCE **326** BCE **324** BCE **323** BCE

King of Macedonia
Philip is assassinated while attending a wedding feast. Just 20 years old, Alexander becomes king. When Thebes uses the king's assassination as an opportunity to rebel, Alexander utterly destroys the city-state.

Conquest of Egypt
Next, Alexander conquers Egypt and establishes a new city, which he names after himself: Alexandria. He visits a famous oracle, and begins referring to himself as a god, claiming that he is the son of Zeus, the king of the Greek gods.

Conquest of Asia
Alexander leads his army on a campaign of conquest across Asia as far as the Punjab region of India. He sets up more than 30 new cities throughout his empire (naming 20 of them after himself). Alexander brings Greek language and culture to the places he conquers, but he allows local traditions to continue.

Return to Babylon
Alexander and his army reach Babylon (in modern-day Iraq) after a grueling journey across deserts and along the Persian Gulf. Many die along the way.

The fall of Persia
King Darius III (seated) begins to flee as Alexander (on the left) and his armies gain the upper hand in battle.

Ashoka

One of the greatest rulers of ancient India, Emperor Ashoka (c. 304–232 BCE) ruled the Mauryan Empire, which covered most of South Asia. Originally a warrior king, he converted to Buddhism and erected pillars throughout his empire inscribed with its teachings, which helped its ideas spread.

Uprising in Ujjain

Some accounts of Ashoka's life state that Bindusara asks Ashoka to put down an uprising in the province of Ujjain in central India. According to one version, he is injured, and Buddhist monks and nuns nurse him back to health. He is said to marry Devi, the daughter of a merchant.

c. 275 BCE

Out of favor

Ashoka's jealous elder half-brothers persuade Bindusara to send Ashoka away to govern Taxila, on the northwest frontier of the Mauryan Empire. Some stories say that Ashoka later goes into hiding in Kalinga (modern-day Odisha).

280s BCE

Birth of a prince

Ashoka is born in modern-day Patna, India), in father Ashoka (near Pataliputra. His father is Emperor Bindusara. His Mauryan Empire. grandfather is Chandragupta Maurya, and his founder of the empire.

c. 304 BCE

Ashoka Chakra

The Ashoka Chakra, a symbol consisting of a wheel with 24 spokes, is found on several of the stone pillars carved with Ashoka's edicts. Each spoke stands for a particular teaching within Buddhism. The symbol of the Ashoka Chakra appears on the flag of modern-day India.

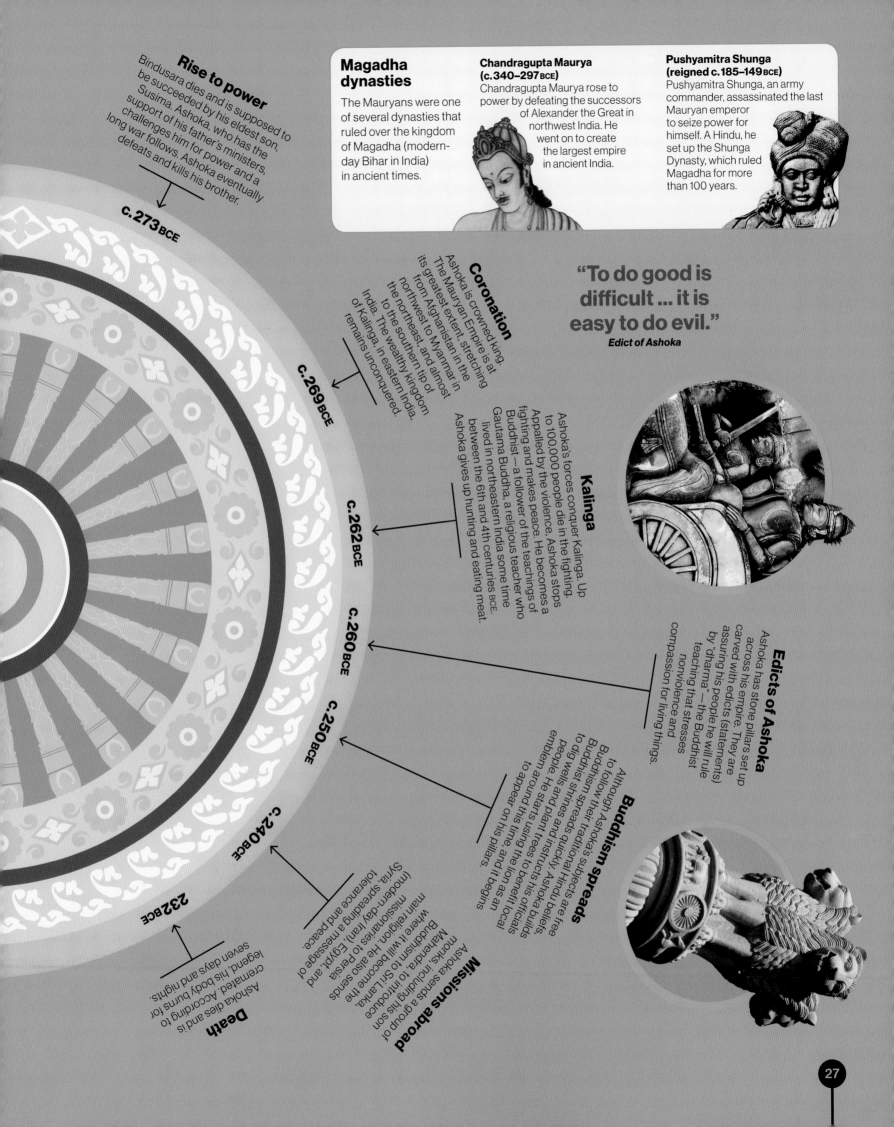

Rise to power

Bindusara dies and is supposed to be succeeded by his eldest son, Susima. Ashoka, who has the support of his father's ministers, challenges him for power and a long war follows. Ashoka eventually defeats and kills his brother.

C.273 BCE

Magadha dynasties

The Mauryans were one of several dynasties that ruled over the kingdom of Magadha (modern-day Bihar in India) in ancient times.

Chandragupta Maurya (c.340–297 BCE)

Chandragupta Maurya rose to power by defeating the successors of Alexander the Great in northwest India. He went on to create the largest empire in ancient India.

Pushyamitra Shunga (reigned c.185–149 BCE)

Pushyamitra Shunga, an army commander, assassinated the last Mauryan emperor to seize power for himself. A Hindu, he set up the Shunga Dynasty, which ruled Magadha for more than 100 years.

Coronation

Ashoka is crowned king. The Mauryan Empire is at its greatest extent, stretching from Afghanistan in the northwest to Myanmar in the northeast, and almost to the southern tip of India. The wealthy kingdom of Kalinga, in eastern India, remains unconquered.

C.269 BCE

> "To do good is difficult ... it is easy to do evil."
> *Edict of Ashoka*

Kalinga

Ashoka's forces conquer Kalinga. Up to 100,000 people die in the fighting. Appalled by the violence, Ashoka stops fighting and makes peace. He becomes a Buddhist—a follower of the teachings of Gautama Buddha, a religious teacher who lived in northeastern India some time between the 6th and 4th centuries BCE. Ashoka gives up hunting and eating meat.

C.262 BCE

C.260 BCE

Edicts of Ashoka

Ashoka has stone pillars set up across his empire, carved with edicts (statements). They are assuring his people he will rule by "dharma"—the Buddhist teaching that stresses nonviolence and compassion for living things.

C.250 BCE

Buddhism spreads

Although Ashoka follow their traditional Hindu beliefs, Buddhism spreads quickly. Ashoka builds Buddhist shrines and temples. He starts using the lion as an emblem. He also instructs his officials to dig wells and plant trees to benefit local people, and to appear on his pillars. Buddhism, their subjects are free to appear around this time to benefit local people, and it begins

C.240 BCE

Missions abroad

Ashoka sends a group of monks, including his son Mahendra, to Sri Lanka, where it will become the main religion. He also sends missionaries to Persia (modern-day Iran), Egypt and Syria, spreading a message of tolerance and peace.

232 BCE

Death

Ashoka dies and is cremated. According to legend, his body burns for seven days and nights.

27

Great emperors of China

China's many leaders have helped to shape its unique history.

Gaozu (256–195 BCE)
Liu Bang led a revolt that overthrew the Qin Dynasty. He established the Han Dynasty, and took on the name Gaozu. He reduced taxes for the common people and made the teachings of the philosopher Confucius an important part of the Chinese government.

Emperor Taizong (598–649 CE)
Taizong brought in many changes to the economy and government that helped bring peace and prosperity to China. The 22 years of his reign became an inspiration to future emperors.

The Great Wall
To protect China from attack from the north, Shi Huang orders the joining up of defensive walls along the Yellow River. The project, during which countless workers die, is the beginning of the Great Wall of China.

221 BCE

Emperor of China
Zheng takes the name Qin Shi Huang, meaning "first emperor of China." In order to suppress any future rebellions, he reforms the government, so that people are promoted based on merit, rather than their social class.

221 BCE

225 BCE

End of war
Zheng eventually conquers the remaining four states. The defeat of Wei is followed by the conquests of Chu and Yan. Zheng finally unites them all under his rule when he triumphs over the state of Qi in 221 BCE.

230 BCE

Unification
Zheng sets about uniting the other six states through conquering them. The first kingdom he successfully invades is Han. Next, in 229 BCE, Zheng uses the chaos caused by an earthquake in Zhao to conquer that state. He makes many enemies, leading to three failed assassination attempts.

237 BCE

Betrayal
Lu Buwei manages the state successfully for several years. Eventually, though, he is implicated in a coup to usurp (seize) the throne and is banished. Zhao Ji is also accused of being involved and is imprisoned. After the coup, Zheng takes full control of Qin.

246 BCE

Early reign
When his father dies, Zheng becomes king. As he is too young to rule, Lu Buwei is chosen as regent. He rules Qin through the Warring States period, as the seven kingdoms fight for land. Even though he is just 13 years old, construction begins on Zheng's burial tomb.

259 BCE

Birth
Ying Zheng is born at a time when seven states struggle for power in China. His father is king of Qin, a state in the northwest. Rumors circulate that Zheng's mother, Zhao Ji, had an affair with an ambitious merchant, Lu Buwei, and Zheng is actually their child.

Qin Shi Huang

One of the greatest leaders in Chinese history, Emperor Qin Shi Huang (259–210 BCE) unified China for the first time in its history. Large sections of the Great Wall of China were built during his reign, and he ordered the crafting of a magnificent army of terra-cotta warriors to protect him in the afterlife.

Eternal life

Shi Huang wants to live forever, and tries out many pills and potions to prolong his life. He even sends out thousands of servants to look for magic herbs which are thought to grow in a mythical land called Penglai.

219 BCE

Language

Prior to his empire, there were several regional languages. Shi Huang orders all writing to be made uniform, so that people from all regions of China can communicate with each other. The new script leads to the establishment of an imperial academy to oversee all books.

213 BCE

Uniformity in China

Shi Huang creates a universal currency, and a national legal system. Books on local histories and traditions are burned. Zheng wants to create a unified China, with one official history.

213 BCE

Silent army

Construction of Shi Huang's opulent tomb is almost complete. A vast underground city, it contains a huge terra-cotta army made up of 8,000 soldiers, 150 cavalry horses, and 130 chariots. This army is meant to guard Shi Huang in the afterlife.

210 BCE

End of a dynasty

Shi Huang dies, possibly from poisoned by mercury, an ingredient in many of the potions he has been taking. His empire falls apart as different areas of the country fight for power.

210 BCE

HANNIBAL BARCA

The military genius who took the long way around to fight Rome

Hannibal Barca (247–c. 183 BCE) commanded the forces of Carthage (in modern-day Tunisia) during the Second Punic War against the Roman Republic. Knowing that the Romans expected him to attack Rome from the south, Hannibal led his huge army—including war elephants—up through what is now Spain and across the snow-capped Alps to attack the city from the north. This bold military gamble paved the way for some of the heaviest defeats the Romans ever suffered.

> "I shall either find a way or make one."
> **Latin proverb attributed to Hannibal**

The threat from Rome

Hannibal was only a child when Carthage was defeated by Rome in the First Punic War in **241 BCE**. To restore Carthaginian wealth and power, his father—Hamilcar—invaded Hispania (modern-day Spain), threatening Roman dominance there. By **221 BCE**, Hannibal was commander of the Carthaginian army, and in early **218 BCE**, he decided to strike at the heart of Rome in central Italy. But trying to defeat the Romans at sea, or to march through Sicily and southern Italy, would end in certain failure. He decided on a move that no one expected: he will strike north from Hispania, cut across Gaul (France), and approach from the Alps mountain range.

Gathering an army

Hannibal gathers a huge army in southern Hispania, drawn from Carthage's allies in Africa and Hispania, including a force of African war elephants. He sets off in **late spring**, defeating hostile tribes en route, and pushes north across Hispania. He enters Gaul with 50,000 infantry, 9,000 cavalry, and 37 elephants. The journey across southern Gaul passes largely without incident, but as the Carthaginians approach the Alpine foothills, mountain tribes attack them repeatedly, inflicting heavy losses.

A tough journey

By the time Hannibal reaches the Alps, winter is coming. To make matters worse, the tribespeople ambushing his troops from their mountain lookouts are difficult to shake off. When Hannibal realizes that they abandon their posts at night, he has his troops sneak past them. In the days that follow Hannibal and his army make good progress, despite dangerous conditions. When the army enters a narrow gorge, ambushers from Gaul send rocks tumbling down on them, but Hannibal's troops escape, mostly unharmed. It starts to snow. When the army reaches the highest pass through the Alps, Hannibal decides to rest his exhausted troops. He gives a stirring speech to urge his tired army on.

The descent

After two days of rest, the army begins the most difficult part of the journey—the descent. The way down the mountains is narrow, steep, and covered in light snow, hiding the dangerous ice beneath. Some foot soldiers slip to their deaths and horses' hooves become stuck. The track becomes too narrow for the elephants to pass, so Hannibal orders his troops to widen the path. It takes three days of back-breaking work. Finally, Hannibal and his army reach the flat plain in northern Italy. Only half of his army have survived, but miraculously all 37 elephants, despite being half-starved, have made it through.

From victory to defeat

Hannibal carries on and fights his way down to Rome through northern Italy. He crushes Roman forces at the Trebia River and at Lake Trasimene. His biggest victory comes in **August 216 BCE**, when his army destroys Rome's largest-ever army in one day in Cannae, southeastern Italy. But by **210 BCE**, the Romans have recovered. Instead of fighting Hannibal, they attack his allies, with success. They then launch an attack on North Africa, causing Hannibal to abandon Italy to defend his lands in **203 BCE**. He suffers a devastating and final defeat at Zama (in modern-day Tunisia) in **202 BCE**. Hannibal later poisons himself, probably around **183 BCE**, in order to avoid being seized by Roman troops.

Julius Caesar

Julius Caesar (c. 100–44 BCE) was a brilliant soldier and ambitious politician during the final years of the Roman Republic. Following a civil war, he became Rome's sole ruler, but, after barely one year in power, he was brutally murdered by senators wishing to defend the republic and its values.

End of the Republic

Following the assassination of Julius Caesar, his former allies fought each other in a bitter civil war. His great-nephew (and adopted son) Octavian emerged as winner, and became the first Roman emperor.

Marcus Antonius (83–30 BCE)

After hunting down Caesar's killers, Marcus Antonius, one of Caesar's closest supporters, ruled in Rome's eastern provinces. He began a love affair with Cleopatra in Egypt. In 31 BCE, his enemy Octavian defeated him at the Battle of Actium. Marcus Antonius fled with Cleopatra to Egypt, where they killed themselves.

Octavian (63 BCE–14 CE)

Aged only 18 when Julius Caesar died, Octavian went on to become sole ruler of the Roman world in 31 BCE, when he became emperor. Four years later, he was given the title of "Augustus," or "honorable one," by which he is best known today. Octavian's 41-year reign was a period of stability.

Livia Drusilla (58 BCE–29 CE)

The third wife of Octavian, Livia Drusilla had great influence over her husband, at a time when Roman women did not play a role in public life. She was fiercely ambitious for her two sons from her previous marriage. The eldest, Tiberius, was adopted by Octavian as his own son and became his successor.

Governor of Spain

Julius is appointed to his first military command as governor of the Roman province of Further Spain. He leads a military campaign during which he takes a lot of plunder. Julius uses it to pay off his debts.

61 BCE

Religious leader

Julius is elected pontifex maximus (the most important position in the Roman religion). This position gives him great power over religious and political affairs. Julius holds it for the rest of his life.

63 BCE

Held ransom

While sailing to the Greek island of Rhodes to study oratory (the art of public speaking), Julius is seized by pirates. They hold him prisoner until a ransom is paid for his release. Julius assembles a small navy, hunts down the pirates, and has them executed.

75 BCE

In the army

Julius is lucky to escape with his life when Sulla, Julius's life's rival, seizes power in Rome. He joins the army to get away from Italy. Sulla's death in 78 BCE. He then returns and becomes a lawyer.

82 BCE

Noble childhood

Gaius Julius Caesar is born into a well-connected noble Roman family. His uncle is Gaius Marius, a successful general. His father dies when he is 15, and Julius becomes head of the family.

c. 100 BCE

Caesar coin

Julius Caesar was the first Roman leader to arrange for coins with his portrait to be issued during his lifetime. Many Roman politicians believed this to be a sign that Caesar saw himself as a godlike figure, not bound by Roman law.

Power-sharing trio

Julius forms an unofficial alliance with two of the most important Roman politicians, Pompey and Crassus. Together, the trio dominate Roman politics, though there are tensions between them.

59 BCE

Gaul

Julius launches the conquest of Gaul (modern-day France and Belgium). The Romans control only a small area to the south, but over the next six years, Julius conquers the whole region, as far as the English Channel and the Rhine River.

58 BCE

Author

Taking time off from his campaigns, Julius begins writing his history of the war in Gaul. He creates it as a work of self-promotion, hoping to boost his reputation in Rome. It also serves as an important historical record.

58 BCE

Attempt to invade Britain

After leading a fleet across the English Channel to invade Britain, Julius is driven back by bad weather. He tries again the next year, but this also results in failure. The Romans will not conquer Britain until 43 CE.

55 BCE

Struggle

Crassus dies, leaving Pompey and Caesar locked in a power struggle. In 49 BCE, politicians, including Pompey, order Julius to disband his army. Instead, he leads his troops across the Rubicon, the river between Gaul and Italy, to seize control of Rome. Civil war follows.

49 BCE

48 BCE

Pompey defeated

Julius chases Pompey to Greece and defeats him in battle. Pompey flees to Egypt but has been murdered by the time Julius reaches him. While in Egypt, Julius has a relationship with Cleopatra, the Egyptian queen.

46 BCE

Triumphant return

Four triumphs (victory parades) are held in Rome to celebrate Julius' victorious campaigns. Wagons of loot plundered during his conquests are rolled into the city. Julius lays on lavish games to entertain the people of Rome.

44 BCE

Assassination

Julius declares himself dictator (sole ruler) for life. This is a step too far, a group of assassins, many of whom are his former friends.

"I came, I saw, I conquered."

Julius Caesar, as quoted by Suetonius (121 CE)

Cleopatra

The life of Cleopatra (69–30 BCE) was intertwined with major political upheaval within Rome. Although Egypt was going through turbulent times, Cleopatra managed to rule the kingdom as pharaoh for almost 30 years. She strengthened her power by forming military alliances with generals and politicians in Rome, including Julius Caesar and Marcus Antonius (also called Mark Antony).

Female pharaohs

Although most pharaohs were men, hundreds of years before Cleopatra women achieved positions of great power in ancient Egypt.

Sobekneferu (reigned 1806–c. 1802 BCE)

The first woman known to have become pharaoh was Sobekneferu, though some scholars believe as many as five women assumed the role before her. She succeeded her father, Amenemhat III, who ruled over a golden age for Egypt's Middle Kingdom, and continued his peaceful reign.

Hatshepsut (c. 1507–1458 BCE)

Egyptian architecture flourished during Hatshepsut's reign. She was regent for her stepson, Thutmose III, but ended up ruling for more than 20 years. She established important trade links, boosted the economy, and built major monuments. Many likenesses of her from the time show her in male regalia, even wearing a fake beard, to fit in.

Nefertiti (c. 1370–c. 1330 BCE)

Queen Nefertiti ruled Egypt alongside her husband, Akhenaten. Their reign was a period of great wealth, but also major upheaval: they banned traditional Egyptian gods and set up a cult around the sun-god, Aten. Some scholars believe Nefertiti ruled alone for a while after her husband's death.

Caesar assassinated

Caesar appoints himself dictator for life, but his enemies in Rome conspire against him. While Cleopatra is in Rome, a group of rival Roman politicians stabs Caesar to death. Cleopatra's main ally is gone, and she flees back to Egypt, her rule in doubt.

44 BCE

Back on top

Using her political skills, Cleopatra manages to persuade Caesar to her side. She is eventually reinstated as leader, and Ptolemy XIII soon dies. Cleopatra rules alone again.

48 BCE

Ousted from power

Ptolemy XIII manages to oust Cleopatra from the throne. In Rome, a power struggle is looming as two powerful generals compete to become leader of the Roman Republic. Julius Caesar and Pompey. Caesar eventually wins, and becomes dictator of Rome.

49 BCE

Egyptian queen

Cleopatra's father passes away. In his will, he requests that Cleopatra and her younger brother, Ptolemy XIII, co-rule Egypt. Cleopatra is 18 years old, and as her brother is still a child, she, in effect, rules alone as pharaoh.

51 BCE

Birth

Cleopatra is born in the Egyptian city of Alexandria, the daughter of Pharaoh Ptolemy XII Auletes. Around this time, Rome had begun to play an important role in Egyptian politics.

69 BCE

Marcus Antonius

Caesar's nephew Octavian, and Caesar's friend Marcus Antonius, join forces to defeat Caesar's rivals at the Battle of Philippi in Greece. Cleopatra and Antonius fall in love and go on to have three children.

Broken alliance

The alliance between Marcus Antonius and Octavian soon falls apart over who should rule Rome. Octavian accuses Antonius of being under Cleopatra's spell and claims that she wants to rule Rome herself. War is looming.

Defeat at Actium

When Octavian declares war, Cleopatra uses her considerable wealth to support Marcus Antonius, but the war quickly slips away from them. They are totally beaten at the Battle of Actium in Greece on September 2, and forced to return to Egypt.

Death of Marcus Antonius

Octavian pursues Marcus Antonius and Cleopatra to Egypt. Severely outnumbered, Marcus Antonius' soldiers abandon him. His cause now hopeless, he stabs himself and dies.

Death of Cleopatra

Rather than be taken prisoner, Cleopatra chooses to allow herself to die by suicide. Some claim she did this by allowing a poisonous asp, or snake, to bite her. Her eldest son Caesarion is murdered, and Egypt becomes a full Roman province—the rule of the pharaohs is over.

42 BCE

33 BCE

31 BCE

August 1, 30 BCE

August 10, 30 BCE

ASP
(EGYPTIAN
COBRA)

35

Noble family
c. 240

Zenobia is born into a noble family. She may be the daughter of Julius Aurelius Zenobius, who is general of the city of Palmyra in modern-day Syria. She becomes fluent in several languages, and is a brilliant horse rider.

Trading routes
c. 250s

Though a Roman territory, Palmyra is largely self-governing. It is a major trading center, and is very prosperous. Zenobia marries Odaenathus. He forms an alliance with Rome, and becomes ruler of Palmyra.

Aiding Rome
260

When the Sassanids invade (an Iranian territory), Palmyra swoops in to help Rome, Roman soldiers is proclaimed and drive the invaders back. Odaenathus is proclaimed "commander of the east" by Rome, and the "king of kings" by his own people.

Assassination
262

It is possible that Zenobia joins her husband on military campaigns, gaining valuable tactical and political skills. Her life changes dramatically when Odaenathus is brutally murdered in mysterious circumstances in 267.

Palmyra

Though never finished, the ancient city of Palmyra's 302-ft- (92-m-) wide Roman Theater dates from the 2nd century CE, just before the time of Zenobia. Palmyra grew rich thanks to its position on the Silk Road— a network of trading routes between Europe, Asia, and the Middle East.

Queen regent
267

Zenobia proclaims her son, Vaballathus, as Odaenathus' heir, but he is too young to rule. Zenobia becomes queen regent (rules in his place until he is old enough) and immediately secures the support of her husband's army. She seizes control of the eastern provinces recently claimed from the Sassanids.

Seizing territory
269

Gallienus, emperor of Rome, is killed. This throws Rome into turmoil, but Zenobia sees an opportunity to expand her territory. She begins to seize what are today Syria, Iraq, Egypt, and Turkey from the Romans.

Zenobia

In 270 CE, Palmyra (in modern-day Syria) came under the rule of a remarkable woman. Zenobia (c. 240–c. 274 CE) declared herself empress, and set about conquering half of the Roman Empire by seizing territories in what are today Syria, Iraq, Egypt, and Turkey.

> **"You demand my surrender as though you were not aware that Cleopatra preferred to die a queen rather than remain alive."**
>
> Zenobia, quoted in
> *Historia Augusta* (c.375–400)

Female rulers of antiquity

Though ancient times were dominated by male rulers, women did lead from time to time.

Boudicca of Britain (died c.61 CE)
Boudicca was a courageous warrior queen who united several British tribes in revolt against the Roman Empire in 60–61 CE. She famously succeeded in defeating the Romans in three great battles, though Rome eventually put down her rebellion.

Theodora (c.495–548)
Theodora, Empress of the Byzantine Empire and wife of Justinian I, was empress from 527 until her death in 548. Theodora was the most powerful woman in the Byzantine era, and the first ruler to recognize the rights of women.

273
End of rule
Zenobia is taken to Rome as Aurelian's prisoner. She is paraded through the streets, bound in gold chains. It is not clear how her life ends, but it is possible that she marries and settles in Rome before her death in around 274.

272
Defeat by Rome
Rome lays siege to Palmyra. Zenobia is sure that she can resist them. Aurelian increases his efforts, and things turn his way. According to one historian, Zenobia escapes the city on a camel, but is captured when she reaches the Euphrates River (in western Asia). Palmyra soon surrenders.

272
Rome strikes back
Zenobia's rebellion spurs Aurelian to action. Leading his army, he takes some of the lost territory. Although Zenobia's weaker army tries to hold the Romans off near Antioch (in modern-day Turkey), they are pushed back toward Palmyra.

271
Empress of the east
Zenobia breaks all ties with Rome by declaring Palmyra an independent empire and herself its Augusta (empress). As this title is the birthright of the royal family of Rome, Zenobia's use of it angers the new Roman Emperor, Aurelian.

Wu Zetian

Though many parts of her life are shrouded in mystery, we know that Empress Wu Zetian (624–705 CE) was the only woman who ruled China in her own name. She was a skillful leader, and introduced many reforms that improved Chinese society.

Early life
Wu Zetian is born. Her mother belongs to the powerful Yang family, and her father is a high-ranking government minister. He encourages his daughter to study Chinese history and literature.

624

Imperial court
Zetian is sent to the imperial court to be a concubine (a lesser wife) of Emperor Taizong. She makes a good impression on the emperor.

638

A new emperor
Emperor Taizong dies, and his son Gaozong becomes emperor. Zetian is said to have been sent away from court to become a Buddhist nun. The new emperor pays her a visit, and, dazzled by her intelligence and beauty, he brings Zetian back to court to be one of his concubines.

649

Murder
Zetian gives birth to a daughter, who dies in mysterious circumstances. She accuses Empress Wang of murdering the baby. The emperor eventually agrees with Zetian. He demotes Empress Wang and Consort Xiao, and promotes Zetian. The following year, she accuses Wang and Xiao of witchcraft, and they are executed.

Position of power
Zetian becomes Emperor Gaozong's first concubine, an important position at court. She gives birth to two sons, Li Hong and Li Xian. Gaozong's wife, Empress Wang, and his former first concubine, Consort Xiao, become jealous of Zetian's growing influence.

652

654

Zhou Dynasty
Empress Wu introduced new Chinese characters (symbols). This one is for the Zhou Dynasty.

Ruling alone
When Emperor Zhongzong rebels against his mother, Zetian removes him, replacing him with her youngest son, Li Dan (who becomes Emperor Ruizong). Six years later, she forces him to abdicate, and she decides to rule alone.

Reforms
As sole ruler, Zetian introduces many reforms. She improves the education system, lowers taxes for farmers, and introduces exams for people who want to become public officials.

Death
Aged 80, Zetian is finally overthrown by her son, Emperor Zhongzong. He seizes control of the throne. Zetian dies later that year.

684

685

705

Change of emperor
When Emperor Gaozong dies, Zetian's third son, Li Xian, takes the throne as Emperor Zhongzong. Zhongzong is emperor in name only, as Zetian continues to hold on to power.

In power
Emperor Gaozong is in poor health. He recommends that Zetian rules in his place. Zetian proves herself to be a great ruler—displaying excellent management skills, a strong will, and courage when needed.

683

674

Empress Wu
Zetian is now empress and her son Li Hong is heir to the imperial throne. She persuades the emperor to demote, exile (force to leave), or execute people who oppose her rise to empress.

Mount Tai
Zetian asks for blessings from heaven and Earth as she carries out ancient rituals on Mount Tai. This event is important as these rituals have only ever been carried out by men.

655

666

Empresses of China
The wives of emperors played an important role in shaping Chinese history. Empresses often ruled China in place of their sons or husbands, when those men or boys were too ill or young to take on their own roles.

Empress Lü Zhi
(c. 241–180 BCE)
Lü Zhi was the wife of Emperor Gaozu, the founder of the Han Dynasty. Following her husband's death, she became ruler, as their son was still a boy. She is remembered for ruthlessly attempting to keep her family in power.

Empress Wei
(c. 664–710 CE)
The wife of Emperor Zhongzong (Wu Zetian's son), Empress Wei handled government matters during her husband's rule. After his death, she planned to rule alone, but was removed from power and killed shortly after.

Empress Dowager Guo
(c. 778–848 CE)
Empress Guo lived through the reigns of seven emperors, during an unstable period in Chinese history. She advised her son and grandson when they each became emperor.

European rulers

Charles I and the Frankish kings dominated western Europe in the early medieval period.

Clovis I (c.466–c.511)
Clovis united the Frankish tribes, who lived in parts of modern-day Germany and Belgium. He became the first king of the Franks. He conquered most of modern-day France. He converted to Christianity on Christmas Day, 496.

Otto I (912–973)
After Charles I's death, the Carolingian Empire gradually broke up. One of the sections became Germany, where Otto I became king in 936. Otto modeled himself after Charles, and was crowned Holy Roman Emperor by the pope in 962, just like his hero.

Frederick I (1122–1190)
Known as Barbarossa (meaning "red beard" in Italian), Frederick was one of Germany's greatest rulers. During his long reign, he displayed excellent abilities in fighting, organization, and negotiation. He died from drowning while leading armies during the Third Crusade.

Crowned as Emperor
Pope Leo III (standing, on the left) crowns Charles I as Holy Roman Emperor in 800.

Joint rule
When Pepin dies, Charles and his younger brother Carloman become joint rulers of the Frankish kingdom. When Carloman dies suddenly aged 20 in 771, Charles is left to rule alone.

Lombardy
Charles conquers the kingdom of Lombardy (in modern-day Italy). He defends the lands of Pope Adrian I (the leader of the Christian church) from invasion.

Saxon massacre
As the Saxon wars rage on, Charles orders the executions of 4,500 Saxon prisoners in a single day. It is possible that this is a punishment for the deaths of some of Charles' nobles.

Palace at Aachen
Charles builds a magnificent palace for himself at Aachen (in modern-day Germany). He makes the city the capital and center of his kingdom.

c.747   768   772   774   778   782   782   790s   795

Birth
Charles is born. When he is young, his father, Pepin, becomes ruler of the Frankish lands.

Saxon Wars
Charles launches the first of a series of wars against the pagan Saxon tribes to the northeast of his kingdom. Charles hopes to conquer their lands, and convert them to Christianity.

Defeat in Spain
At this time, Muslim rulers control the majority of Spain's regions. The Frankish armies fight tough battles, often in difficult conditions. They are ultimately defeated, and return home.

Learning and books
Charles invites scholars from across Europe to his kingdom to study and teach. He opens schools throughout his lands to copy and preserve religious books.

Conquering the marches
Charles conquers many of the marches—areas of land that nobody really owns, and where few people live—to the east. He further extends his lands eastward by conquering the Avars, former nomads who have settled by the Danube River.

800

804

814

Emperor

Pope Leo III crowns Charles Holy Roman Emperor in Rome. This title is a reference to the Roman Empire. The crowning shows the alliance between Charles and the Christian Church.

Death of Charlemagne

Charles dies in his palace at Aachen. Over time, he becomes better known as "Charlemagne" in English.

End of the Saxon Wars

Charlemagne crushes the last resistance to his rule in Saxony, bringing the 32-year-long war to an end. The territory he now rules becomes known as the Carolingian Empire—in honor of his name. Some begin to refer to him as "Charles the Great."

Charlemagne

Charles I (c. 747–814) was the most powerful European ruler of his time. He inherited the Frankish kingdom (made up from parts of modern-day France and Germany), and added to it by conquering lands on its borders. His reign was so successful that he is more commonly known by the name "Charlemagne," which means "Charles the Great."

FATIMA AL-FIHRI

Founder of the world's oldest university

Fatima al-Fihri (c.800–c.880) is said to have established the University of al-Qarawiyyin in Fez, Morocco. The university became one of the leading educational centers of the Muslim world, and is believed to be the oldest existing college of higher education that awards its students degrees.

The founding of Fez

In the early **9th century**, the territory that will later become Morocco was ruled by King Idris II, whose father established the Idrisid Dynasty. The Idrisids are considered the founders of the Moroccan state. They initially established their capital at Walili (near modern-day Meknes) but about **809**, Idris moved the center of government to the market town of Madinat Fas, now part of the city of Fez. The town grew to become a center of politics, culture, and religion. It drew people from elsewhere in North Africa and Islamic Spain.

The al-Fihri family

In **824**, a rebellion in the town of Qairawan (Kairouan, in modern-day Tunisia) sparked a wave of emigration to Fez. One of the families that migrated, scholars believe, was the al-Fihri family. Little is known about them, but it is believed that Muhammad bin Abdullah al-Fihri arrived in the city with little money. According to most stories, he brought his wife, their daughters Fatima and Maryam, and their son with him. Muhammad valued learning, and ensured that all his children received a good education. Through hard work, he became a successful businessperson and merchant. However, tragedy struck when he, his son, and then Fatima's husband died within a short period of time.

A place for the community

After these deaths, Fatima and her sister Maryam inherit a lot of money. This makes both women financially secure and independent. It leads them to question what they should do with the money. They decide to invest in something that will benefit their community. The sisters were raised in a religious home so they choose to establish two places of worship. As more people, this time from Islamic Spain, are attracted to Fez, Maryam decides to create a magnificent

mosque for them to worship in. Work starts in **857** on what is now known as the Andalusian Mosque. Meanwhile, Fatima purchases an existing mosque, which had been constructed about 845, along with the land around it. She sets about rebuilding this mosque on a much larger and more lavish scale.

Al-Qarawiyyin Mosque

Reconstruction of the mosque starts in 857. Fatima oversees every aspect of the work. It is said that every day she prays and fasts until sunset for good luck until it is complete. As well as a prayer hall, library, schoolrooms, and courtyard, the mosque will include a *madrasa*—a place of learning, where religious lessons will be taught. Two years later, in **859**—the same year that the Andalusian Mosque is completed—the al-Qarawiyyin Mosque opens its doors. In the early days of the *madrasa,* only courses in religious teaching and the Quran are taught, but before long it becomes a center of even more studies. It grows into a college (now regarded as a university) where scholars teach students about mathematics, music, medicine, and Arabic grammar. Students are awarded degrees for the successful completion of their studies— another novel idea.

Influence

Fatima dies in about **880**, but during the coming years, the university becomes a center for scholars of the Islamic world, with students from all faiths coming to study from across the globe. The idea of an institution that offers opportunities for advanced study spreads to Egypt, where Al-Azhar University is established in Cairo in **970**, and later to Europe, where the universities of Bologna and Oxford are both set up in the **11th century**. Al-Qarawiyyin produces some of the most renowned medieval thinkers, including the Jewish philosopher Maimonides (c.1135–1204), the Islamic scholar and traveler Leo Africanus (c.1485–c.1554), and (it is believed) the French scholar Gerbert of Aurillac (c.945–1003), who later becomes Pope Sylvester II. By the **14th century**, the university has 8,000 students. In **1965**, the institution is officially named the University of al-Qarawiyyin, more than 1,000 years after welcoming its first students.

Leif Erikson

A renowned 11th-century explorer, Leif Erikson (970–1020) became one of the most important figures in the Viking sagas (stories). The details of his most famous voyage differ from one saga to another, but few now dispute that Erikson was the first European to land in North America, hundreds of years before Christopher Columbus.

c.975

Son of Erik
Leif is born in Iceland. His father, Erik the Red, gets into trouble and is banished to Greenland with his family. He sets up the first Viking colony there. Leif learns sailing and survival skills in the new colony.

999

Blown off course
Leif begins to set sail on his own expeditions. On his way to give gifts to King Olaf of Norway and pick up supplies, Leif's ship is blown off course and he spends the summer in the Hebrides Islands, off the Scottish coast. He eventually arrives in Norway and becomes a member of the king's official entourage.

c.1000

Norway
King Olaf converts Leif from Norse paganism to Christianity. Acting on behalf of the king, Leif returns to Greenland with a priest to convert the Norse settlements. He is welcomed home.

c.1000

Mysterious land
Leif hears the tale of Bjarni Herjólfsson, an explorer who, on attempting to find Greenland for the first time with his crew, was blown off course and sighted hospitable land with mountains, hills, and forests to the west.

c.1000

Leif the explorer
Desperate for timber, or perhaps curious to discover new territory, Leif sets off from Greenland to try and find Bjarni Herjólfsson's land. He first encounters a land of ice and stone, which he names Helluland ("Land of the Flat Stones"). This was perhaps Baffin Island in modern-day Canada. Seeing little of interest, he sails on.

1002

Wild grapes
Leif arrives in a place he calls Vinland ("Land of Wine"), possibly because of the plentiful wild grapes growing there and the fertility of the land. Archaeologists later discover that the location was Newfoundland in eastern Canada.

Viking explorers

Vikings have a notorious reputation for plundering and pillaging, but they were also brilliant explorers. Their state-of-the-art ships allowed them to travel far and wide, and discover new territory.

Erik the Red (c.950–c.1003)
Leif's father, Erik Thorvaldsson (Erik the Red), was a Viking adventurer. He discovered a new territory and called it Greenland because he hoped the name would make people want to live there.

Freydís Eiríksdóttir (c.970–?)
A daughter of Erik the Red, Freydís is said to have chased off indigenous attackers on Vinland when the men around her panicked—all while eight months pregnant!

1003

Founding a settlement

Leif and his crew establish a settlement on Vinland— the first European settlement in the Americas. Some sail back to Greenland in the spring, loaded with timber, wheat, and grapes. The settlement breaks up in around 1010, possibly due to fighting with the local indigenous people, whom the Vikings call "Skraelings."

1010–1020

Leif's last years

Leif returns to Greenland and dedicates his time to spreading Christianity. He never returns to Vinland, and dies in around 1020.

Leif Erikson Day

Leif landed on North American soil nearly five centuries before Christopher Columbus in 1492. In recognition of his achievement, "Leif Erikson Day" is observed on October 9 in the US. Statues such as this one in Iceland commemorate the first European to settle in the Americas.

Viking settlement
This is a reconstruction of a Viking home at L'anse aux Meadows in Newfoundland, Canada—the possible location of Leif's settlement.

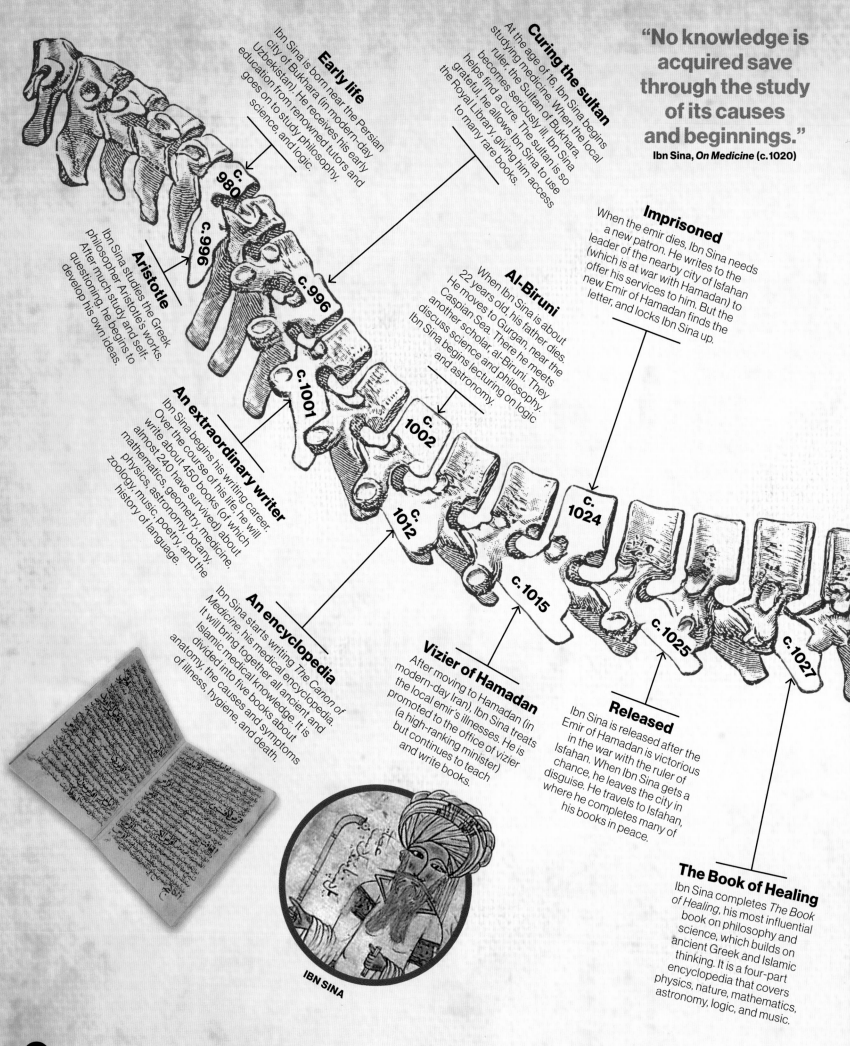

Early life

Ibn Sina is born near the Persian city of Bukhara (in modern-day Uzbekistan). He receives his early education from renowned tutors and goes on to study philosophy, science, and logic.

c. 980

Aristotle

Ibn Sina studies the Greek philosopher Aristotle's works. After much study and self-questioning, he begins to develop his own ideas.

c. 996

Curing the sultan

At the age of 16, Ibn Sina begins studying medicine. When the local ruler, the Sultan of Bukhara, becomes seriously ill, Ibn Sina helps find a cure. The sultan is so grateful, he allows Ibn Sina to use the Royal Library, giving him access to many rare books.

c. 996

An extraordinary writer

Ibn Sina begins his writing career. Over the course of his life, he will write about 450 books (of which almost 240 have survived) about mathematics, geometry, medicine, physics, astronomy, botany, zoology, music, poetry, and the history of language.

c. 1001

Al-Biruni

When Ibn Sina is about 22 years old, his father dies. He moves to Gurgan, near the Caspian Sea. There he meets another scholar, al-Biruni. They discuss science and philosophy. Ibn Sina begins lecturing on logic and astronomy.

c. 1002

"No knowledge is acquired save through the study of its causes and beginnings."

Ibn Sina, *On Medicine* (c. 1020)

Imprisoned

When the emir dies, Ibn Sina needs a new patron. He writes to the leader of the nearby city of Isfahan (which is at war with Hamadan) to offer his services to him. But the new Emir of Hamadan finds the letter, and locks Ibn Sina up.

c. 1024

An encyclopedia

Ibn Sina starts writing The Canon of Medicine, his medical encyclopedia. It will bring together all ancient and Islamic medical knowledge. It is divided into five books about anatomy, the causes and symptoms of illness, hygiene, and death.

c. 1012

Vizier of Hamadan

After moving to Hamadan (in modern-day Iran), Ibn Sina treats the local emir's illnesses. He is promoted to the office of vizier (a high-ranking minister) but continues to teach and write books.

c. 1015

Released

Ibn Sina is released after the Emir of Hamadan is victorious in the war with the ruler of Isfahan. When Ibn Sina gets a chance, he leaves the city in disguise. He travels to Isfahan, where he completes many of his books in peace.

c. 1025

The Book of Healing

Ibn Sina completes The Book of Healing, his most influential book on philosophy and science, which builds on ancient Greek and Islamic thinking. It is a four-part encyclopedia that covers physics, nature, mathematics, astronomy, logic, and music.

c. 1027

IBN SINA

Ibn Sina

One of the founders of modern medicine, Ibn Sina (c.980–1037) was the most influential doctor, astronomer, scientist, and philosopher of the Islamic Golden Age—a great flourishing of science and culture. His most famous book, *The Canon of Medicine*, was used as a textbook for hundreds of years after his death. His influence spread far and wide, including within Islamic countries, across Asia, and even into Europe, where he is more commonly known as "Avicenna."

IBN SINA'S TOMB

Death
Suffering from a serious stomach complaint, Ibn Sina decides to free his enslaved people and spend the rest of his days listening to the Quran being read. He dies about the age of 57. He is buried in Hamadan.

1037

c. 1027

Adviser in Isfahan
He becomes the doctor, and general literary and scientific adviser, to the ruler of Isfahan. Ibn Sina serves him for almost a decade, and even offers his opinion about military issues.

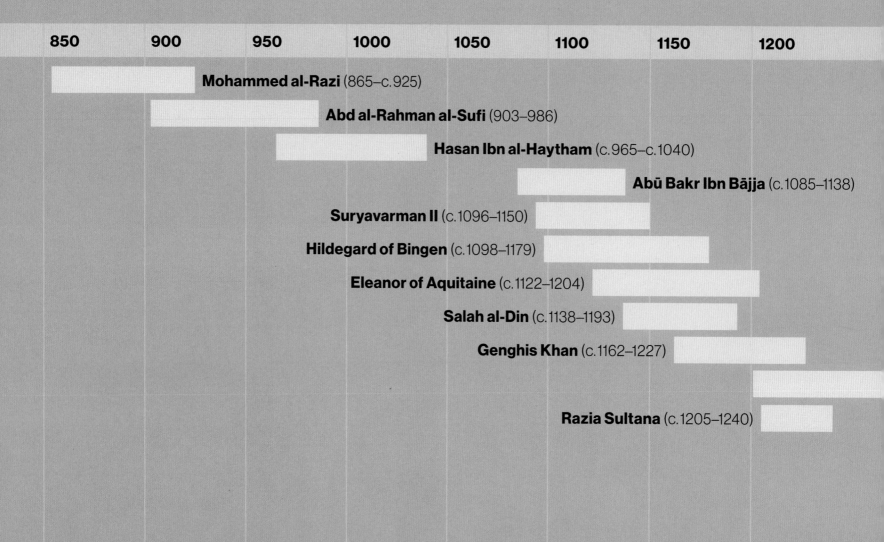

850	900	950	1000	1050	1100	1150	1200

Mohammed al-Razi (865–c.925)

Abd al-Rahman al-Sufi (903–986)

Hasan Ibn al-Haytham (c.965–c.1040)

Abū Bakr Ibn Bājja (c.1085–1138)

Suryavarman II (c.1096–1150)

Hildegard of Bingen (c.1098–1179)

Eleanor of Aquitaine (c.1122–1204)

Salah al-Din (c.1138–1193)

Genghis Khan (c.1162–1227)

Razia Sultana (c.1205–1240)

Mohammed al-Razi
to Mumtaz Mahal

In the time between Mohammed al-Razi and Mumtaz Mahal, great empires flourished, built by powerful leaders. Mongol warrior Genghis Khan created the largest empire ever seen, which stretched from the Pacific Ocean to eastern Europe. In West Africa, Askia the Great transformed the Songhai Empire into a center of Islamic culture. Further south in Africa, Nzinga Mbandi fought to keep her people safe from European armies.

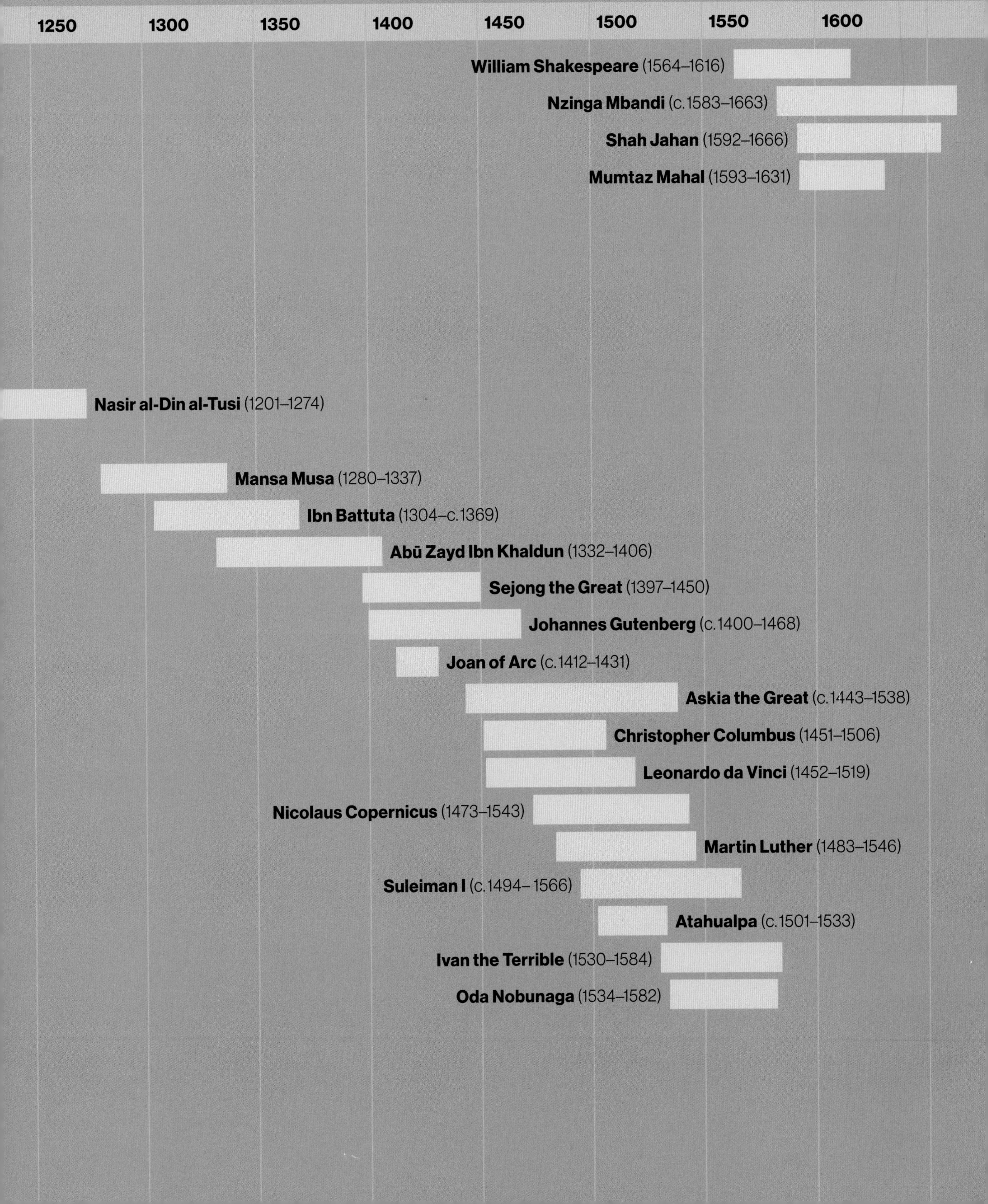

1250	1300	1350	1400	1450	1500	1550	1600

William Shakespeare (1564–1616)

Nzinga Mbandi (c.1583–1663)

Shah Jahan (1592–1666)

Mumtaz Mahal (1593–1631)

Nasir al-Din al-Tusi (1201–1274)

Mansa Musa (1280–1337)

Ibn Battuta (1304–c.1369)

Abū Zayd Ibn Khaldun (1332–1406)

Sejong the Great (1397–1450)

Johannes Gutenberg (c.1400–1468)

Joan of Arc (c.1412–1431)

Askia the Great (c.1443–1538)

Christopher Columbus (1451–1506)

Leonardo da Vinci (1452–1519)

Nicolaus Copernicus (1473–1543)

Martin Luther (1483–1546)

Suleiman I (c.1494–1566)

Atahualpa (c.1501–1533)

Ivan the Terrible (1530–1584)

Oda Nobunaga (1534–1582)

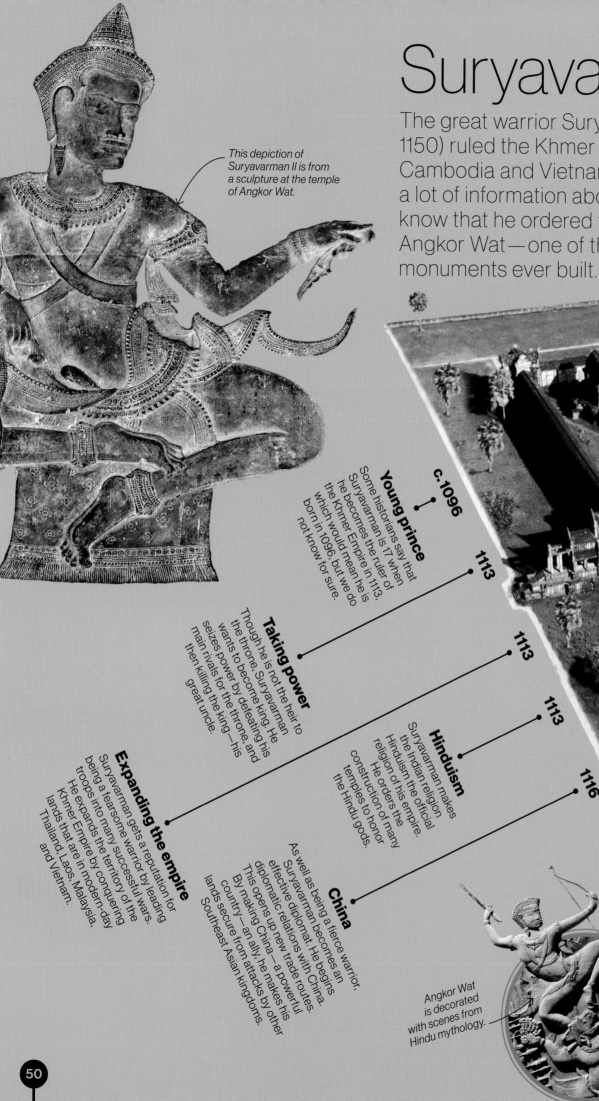

Suryavarman II

The great warrior Suryavarman II (c.1096–1150) ruled the Khmer Empire (in modern-day Cambodia and Vietnam). Though there is not a lot of information about his early life, we do know that he ordered the construction of Angkor Wat—one of the finest religious monuments ever built.

This depiction of Suryavarman II is from a sculpture at the temple of Angkor Wat.

c.1096

Young prince
Some historians say that Suryavarman is 17 when he becomes the ruler of the Khmer Empire in 1113, which would mean he is born in 1096, but we do not know for sure.

1113

Taking power
Though he is not the heir to the throne, Suryavarman wants to become king. He seizes power by defeating his main rivals for the throne, and then killing the king—his great uncle.

1113

Hinduism
Suryavarman makes the Indian religion Hinduism the official religion of his empire. He orders the construction of many temples to honor the Hindu gods.

1113

Expanding the empire
Suryavarman gets a reputation for being a fearsome warrior by leading troops into many successful wars. He expands the territory of the Khmer Empire by conquering lands that are in modern-day Thailand, Laos, Malaysia, and Vietnam.

China
As well as being a fierce warrior, Suryavarman becomes an effective diplomat. He begins diplomatic relations with China. This opens up new trade routes. By making China—a powerful country—an ally, he makes his lands secure from attacks by other Southeast Asian kingdoms.

1116

Angkor Wat is decorated with scenes from Hindu mythology.

c. 1116

Angkor Wat
Suryavarman orders the construction of Angkor Wat ("City Temple") to house his remains after his death. Today, this majestic temple is the largest religious monument in the world.

Mandalas

Power in Southeast Asia radiated out from the center of each kingdom. Historians call these areas of influence *mandalas*.

Queen Soma (1st century CE)

The ruler of the Kingdom of Funan, Queen Soma is today regarded as the first monarch of Cambodia. She unified the country under her rule.

Jayavarman II (c.770–850)

Founder of the Khmer Empire, Jayavarman II united the Khmer kingdoms, which were made up of many cultural groups. He set up numerous cities throughout the Khmer Empire.

Jayavarman VII (c.1122–1218)

Jayavarman VII became king of the Khmer Empire in c.1181. He built the walled city of Angkor Thom ("Great City"), and spread the Buddhist religion. He is regarded as the last of the great rulers of the Khmer Empire.

1123

Dai Viet wars

Suryavarman launches the first in a series of wars against the Dai Viet Kingdom (in modern-day Vietnam).

1131

Defeated in battle

He forces the Kingdom of Champa (also in modern-day Vietnam) to help him in his efforts against Dai Viet. Even with their help, Suryavarman is not successful. In 1136, the Cham king changes sides and supports the Dai Viet Kingdom, which ends the war.

1145

War with the Cham people

Suryavarman removes the Cham king, Jaya Indravarman, and captures the kingdom's capital city. He puts his brother-in-law Harideva on the Cham throne. The Cham people keep fighting and eventually remove Harideva from power in 1149.

1150

Death

During an attempt to recapture the Kingdom of Champa, Suryavarman dies (possibly during a battle). His cousin Dharanindravarman II succeeds to the throne. The Kingdom of Champa eventually wins the war, and conquers Angkor, the Khmer capital.

Hildegard of Bingen

Hildegard of Bingen (c.1098–1179) was one of the great Christian leaders and thinkers of her time. As well as being an abbess (a head nun in a convent), Hildegard was a writer, poet, and composer. She was also an early natural historian, collecting rocks, plants, precious stones, and other natural things to study them.

Benedictine nun

At 14, Hildegard is finally ready to become a nun—meaning she will live, work, and carry out religious duties within the Benedictine community. As a symbol of her pledge, she begins wearing a habit (the clothing and headdress worn by a nun).

Life in the convent

Hildegard's duties in the convent involve working in the garden, tending to the sick, and reciting religious texts. She uses her free time to write, study, and learn to play the psaltery (a stringed instrument).

Jutta of Sponheim

Hildegard is sent to live with a nun, Jutta of Sponheim, so that she can dedicate her life to the Christian Church. Jutta teaches Hildegard the ways of the Benedictine sisterhood—a Christian religious community established by St. Benedict.

Visions

Hildegard is a sickly child. She has regular headaches, and begins to see visions of sparkling light from the age of three. She later believes that these visions are messages of God's love.

Noble birth

The youngest of 10 children, Hildegard is born in Bermersheim, in the County Palatine of the Rhine (in modern-day Germany). Her parents are nobles, and often mix with other members of the aristocracy (high society).

1112

1118

1106

1101

c.1098

Special stones

This piece of agate rock is an example of the kind of stone that Hildegard would have collected. She believed that everything on Earth was created by God, and that the study of nature therefore helped bring her closer to Him.

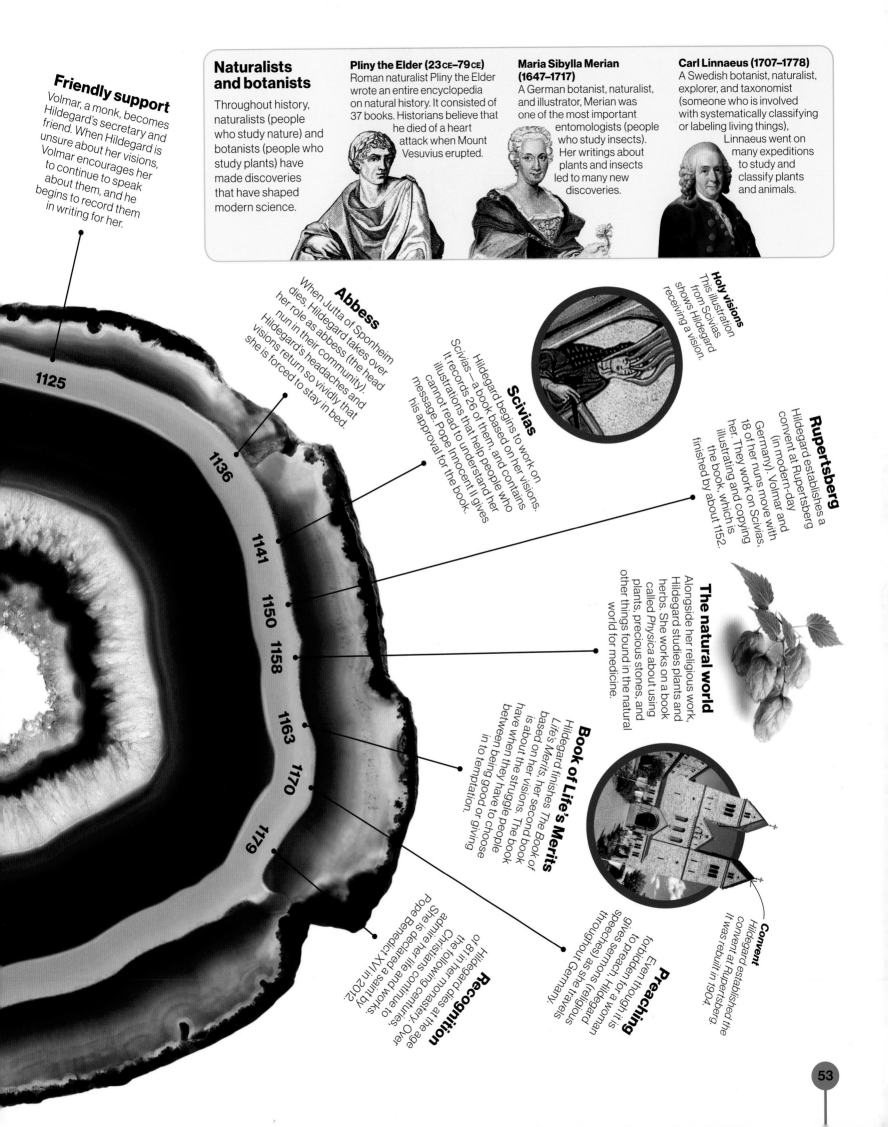

Friendly support

Volmar, a monk, becomes Hildegard's secretary and friend. When Hildegard is unsure about her visions, Volmar encourages her to continue to speak about them, and he begins to record them in writing for her.

Naturalists and botanists

Throughout history, naturalists (people who study nature) and botanists (people who study plants) have made discoveries that have shaped modern science.

Pliny the Elder (23 CE–79 CE)

Roman naturalist Pliny the Elder wrote an entire encyclopedia on natural history. It consisted of 37 books. Historians believe that he died of a heart attack when Mount Vesuvius erupted.

Maria Sibylla Merian (1647–1717)

A German botanist, naturalist, and illustrator, Merian was one of the most important entomologists (people who study insects). Her writings about plants and insects led to many new discoveries.

Carl Linnaeus (1707–1778)

A Swedish botanist, naturalist, explorer, and taxonomist (someone who is involved with systematically classifying or labeling living things), Linnaeus went on many expeditions to study and classify plants and animals.

1125

Abbess

When Jutta of Sponheim dies, Hildegard takes over her role as abbess (the head nun in their community). Hildegard's headaches and visions return so vividly that she is forced to stay in bed.

1136

Scivias

Hildegard begins to work on Scivias—a book based on her visions. It records 26 of them, and contains illustrations that help people who cannot read to understand her message. Pope Innocent II gives his approval for the book.

Holy visions

This illustration from Scivias shows Hildegard receiving a vision.

Rupertsberg

Hildegard establishes a convent at Rupertsberg (in modern-day Germany). Volmar and 18 of her nuns move with her. They work on Scivias, illustrating and copying the book, which is finished by about 1152.

1141

1150

1158

The natural world

Alongside her religious work, Hildegard studies plants and herbs. She works on a book called *Physica* about using plants, precious stones, and other things found in the natural world for medicine.

1163

Book of Life's Merits

Hildegard finishes The Book of Life's Merits, her second book based on her visions. The book is about the struggle people have when they have to choose between being good or giving in to temptation.

1170

Preaching

Even though it is forbidden for a woman to preach, Hildegard gives speeches (religious speeches) as she travels throughout Germany.

Convent

Hildegard established the convent at Rupertsberg. It was rebuilt in 1904.

1179

Recognition

Hildegard dies at the age of 81 in her monastery. Over the following centuries, Christians continue to admire her life and works. She is declared a saint by Pope Benedict XVI in 2012.

Eleanor of Aquitaine

One of the wealthiest and most influential leaders of medieval Europe, Eleanor of Aquitaine (c. 1122–1204) became queen of France in 1137 and then queen of England in 1154. She held significant power in both countries, and became an important patron of the arts.

c. 1122

Wealthy childhood
Eleanor is born in the court (noble household) of Aquitaine, a powerful duchy (land of a duke or duchess) in modern-day France. Her father, the Duke of Aquitaine, is very wealthy and gives her an excellent education.

April 9, 1137

Inheritance
When her father dies, Eleanor becomes Duchess of Aquitaine. Because she is cultured, intelligent, and now very rich, many rulers across Europe want to marry her. The king of France, Louis VI, is appointed as her guardian.

July 25, 1137

First marriage
Planning for Aquitaine to eventually become a part of France, Louis VI arranges for Eleanor to marry his heir, Prince Louis. They marry in Bordeaux. Eleanor's lands will remain independent until she gives birth to a son—as her son will inherit both Aquitaine and France.

Queen of France
Louis VI dies soon after the wedding, and Prince Louis and Eleanor are crowned king and queen of France on Christmas Day. Louis (now Louis VII) spends a fortune making the cold and bare Cité Palace in Paris a suitable home for himself and Eleanor.

December 25, 1137

1141

Religious conflict
Louis lacks experience in ruling, and gets involved in an unnecessary war against the pope and some of his own nobles. His armies set the town of Vitry ablaze, killing more than a thousand people.

1144

Joining the crusade
Edessa, a Christian-held kingdom in the Middle East surrounded by rival Islamic rulers, is captured by the Muslim leader Zengi. The pope calls for a military expedition (the Second Crusade) to win it back. Guilt-ridden over the burning of Vitry, and keen to please the pope, Louis vows to lead the Crusade. Eleanor agrees to join him, and gathers her own army from Aquitaine. The crusaders set off in 1147.

The Court of Love

Eleanor encourages artists to join her court in Poitiers to write romantic poems and songs. Known as the "Court of Love," this patronage shows her interest in arts and culture.

Medieval rulers

During the Middle Ages, rulers in Europe and the Middle East fought battles and made political decisions that have shaped the world ever since.

William the Conqueror (c.1028–1087)
William, Duke of Normandy (in France), became king of England in 1066. His reign brought major changes to England, as he gave land to his leading barons and introduced new laws.

Imad ad-Din Zengi (c.1085–1146)
A Turkish governor of the Zengid Dynasty (in northern Syria and Iraq), Zengi became a hero across the Muslim world when he recaptured Edessa during the Second Crusade.

Henry II (1133–1189)
Ruler of a vast kingdom that stretched from the south of France to Ireland, Henry made important reforms to the English judicial system, but he made enemies of the Church and his own sons.

1168

1167

Return to France

Eleanor and Henry have an argumentative relationship. Fed up with him, she decides to return to Aquitaine, and sets up court in Poitiers. Eleanor and Henry agree to separate.

Queen of England

1154

Eleanor becomes queen of England when her husband ascends to the English throne, becoming Henry II. They go on to have eight children together: five sons and three daughters.

Remarriage

1152

Eventually the pope agrees to the annulment. Eleanor keeps her lands. Now she is single, several nobles ask to marry her. She chooses Henry, Duke of Normandy, and marries him eight weeks later.

Imprisonment

Henry II brings Eleanor back to England. She spends the next 15 years imprisoned in various English castles, seldom seeing her children. Prince Henry's rebellion ends when he dies in 1183.

1173

Rebellion

Looking to seize power, Eleanor and Henry's eldest son, Prince Henry (known as "Henry the Young King"), flees to Paris to start a rebellion against his father. Eleanor supports the plot. Henry II arranges for Eleanor to be captured and imprisoned.

1174

1189

Ruling over England

Henry II dies, and their son, Richard, succeeds him. Richard immediately releases his mother from prison. When Richard is away for several years leading the Third Crusade, Eleanor rules England on his behalf.

1204

Death

Richard I dies in 1199, and Eleanor's youngest (and only surviving) son, John, becomes king. Eleanor dies five years later, and her remains are entombed in Fontevrault Abbey in France.

1149

Failure

The crusade goes badly from the start. After an attempt to besiege Damascus ends in disaster, the royal couple accept defeat and return home. The failure puts a strain on their relationship. Eleanor asks the pope to annul (cancel) the marriage but he refuses.

Citadel of Salah Ed-Din

The crusaders fortified the medieval castle now known as the Citadel of Salah Ed-Din during their occupation of Antioch in Syria. It fell to the forces of Salah al-Din after a three-day siege in 1188, and came to be named after him (though spelled differently) some time later.

Sultan

Nur al-Din dies, and a struggle for his lands begins between powerful nobles. Salah al-Din claims Egypt, and then invades and conquers Syria. He proclaims himself sultan (king) of Egypt and Syria. He gradually builds power by conquering many smaller Muslim states.

Early career

Salah al-Din's uncle Shirkuh is a general to the ruler Nur al-Din. Nur al-Din had unified the divided Muslim states of Syria against the crusaders. Shirkuh brings Salah al-Din on military campaigns, to educate him in battle tactics.

Holy war

Salah al-Din is finally able to turn his attention to the crusaders, who have held the ancient city of Jerusalem since 1099. The city has sites that are holy to Muslims, Christians, and Jews.

Battle of Hattin

After drawing a large crusader army led by King Guy of Jerusalem into a trap, Salah al-Din's forces destroy it during the Battle of Hattin.

End of the Fatimids

Nur al-Din sends Shirkuh and Salah al-Din to help the weak Fatimid rulers of Egypt. Shirkuh becomes the vizier (high official) to the Fatimids. He dies soon after, and Salah al-Din succeeds him in the role. In 1171, Salah al-Din overthrows the Fatimids, and sets up the Ayyubids, a new dynasty.

Righteousness of the Faith

Salah al-Din is born in Tikrit (in modern-day Iraq). His name at birth is Yusuf ibn Ayyub. He is later given the Islamic title "Salah al-Din," meaning "Righteousness of the Faith." Europeans later shorten this to "Saladin."

1174

1180s

1169

c.1138

c.1152

1187

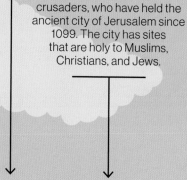

The Crusades

The Crusades were religious wars launched by European Christians from 1095 onward. The crusaders fought to take land they considered holy from Muslim rulers, including the city of Jerusalem.

Melisende of Jerusalem (1105–1160)
The crusaders captured Jerusalem in 1099, during the First Crusade. Melisende was born in the city, and ruled it for more than 30 years—a remarkable achievement given the lower status of women at the time.

Richard I of England (1157–1199)
Though he reigned as King of England for nearly ten years, Richard I spent only about six months of this in the country. For the rest of the time, he was mostly on crusade, held captive by other rulers, or fighting wars to defend his lands in France.

Baldwin IV (1161–1185)
The reign of Baldwin IV of Jerusalem coincided with Salah al-Din's rise to power. Baldwin suffered from leprosy, a skin disease that was feared at the time, and greatly affected his ability to rule.

Salah al-Din

Salah al-Din (c. 1138–1193) was a brilliant military commander who defended Muslim lands against the crusaders—Christian soldiers from Europe who had established their own kingdoms in the Middle East. Salah al-Din was noted for being fair and humane to his enemies.

Jerusalem

Salah al-Din lays siege to Jerusalem, causing it to surrender. Instead of massacring his enemies, as often happens at the end of a siege at this time, Salah al-Din orders his forces to behave with decency to the Christians in the city.

Peace treaty

The crusaders are unable to continue to march on Jerusalem. Richard I and Salah al-Din begin peace talks. A treaty is agreed that leaves Jerusalem in Muslim hands, but allows the crusaders to occupy a strip of land along the coast.

Third Crusade

Crusaders in Europe launch the Third Crusade to defeat Salah al-Din and recapture Jerusalem. Led by King Richard I of England, the crusaders retake the Mediterranean city of Acre and win the Battle of Arsuf.

Death

Soon after Richard departs for Europe, Salah al-Din dies from a fever. He had given away almost all of his wealth to his poor subjects, but dies having achieved his aim of recapturing—and then holding onto—the holy city of Jerusalem.

1187

1189

1191

1193

> **"It is not the custom of kings to kill kings."**
> **Salah al-Din, after the Battle of Hattin (1187)**

The Islamic Golden Age

Mohammed al-Razi (865–c. 925)

Islamic scholar and physician Mohammed al-Razi combined ancient medical knowledge with his own observations. His writings became an important part of teaching in medical schools in both the Islamic world and Europe.

865
Mohammed al-Razi is born in the city of Ray (in modern-day Iran). He later moves to Baghdad, where he studies and practices medicine at the local *bimaristan* (hospital).

902
He is appointed the chief director of a new *bimaristan* in Baghdad. It is one of the largest hospitals in the world at that time.

903
He writes *The Book of Medicine*. It becomes one of the most influential works on medicine. It is translated into many languages, both in the Islamic world and in Europe.

910
He is the first person to describe the symptoms of two deadly diseases in his book *Treatise on Smallpox and Measles*.

c. 925
Mohammed dies. After his death, his students gather together a large collection of his work in *The Comprehensive Book on Medicine*. It is the largest medical encyclopedia at this time.

Abd al-Rahman al-Sufi (903–986)

Abd al-Rahman al-Sufi was instrumental in the development of astronomy during the 10th century.

903
Abd al-Rahman al-Sufi is born in Persia (modern-day Iran). Not much is known about his early life.

964
Abd al-Rahman's influential guide *The Book of Fixed Stars* is published. In it, he provides detailed accounts of the constellations and the sizes and brightnesses of stars. It becomes the standard handbook for astronomers.

969
Emir Adud ad-Daula invites Abd al-Rahman to the city of Shiraz (in modern-day Iran). The king appoints him to the post of chief astronomer, and an observatory is built in the city.

986
Abd al-Rahman dies in Shiraz. His work is an inspiration for generations of Islamic astronomers who come after him.

Hasan Ibn al-Haytham (c. 965–c. 1040)

The Arab mathematician, astronomer, and judge Hasan Ibn al-Haytham is often called the first scientist because he carried out experiments to test his ideas, and recorded his observations. This way of investigating ideas is now known as the "scientific method."

c. 965
Hasan Ibn al-Haytham is born in Basra (in modern-day Iraq). He is educated in the cities of Basra, and later in Baghdad (also in modern-day Iraq).

c. 1011
He writes to the caliph (ruler of Egypt), offering to solve the annual problem of the flooding of the Nile River. Once there, he realizes that he has misjudged the size of the river, and cannot complete the work. He pretends to be mentally unwell to avoid execution.

1021
He is put under house arrest, and he writes his most important study, *The Book of Optics*. In it, he explains how vision works, and includes a detailed diagram of the human eye. The book also includes shadows, eclipses, and the colors of the rainbow.

1027
Hasan leaves his job as a judge to fully devote his time to his scientific research.

c. 1038
He writes his book *The Model of the Motions of Each of the Seven Planets*. In it, he explains the idea that Earth spins on an axis through space.

1040
Hasan dies in Cairo, Egypt, having written more than 200 manuscripts, covering mathematics and medicine, as well as his work on optics and astronomy.

Between the 8th and 14th centuries, Islamic scholars made great advances in science, mathematics, medicine, philosophy, art, and architecture. We call this time the Islamic Golden Age. Here are just a few of the most important people involved.

Abū Bakr Ibn Bājja (c.1085–1138)

Spanish-born scholar Abū Bakr Ibn Bājja wrote about medicine, botany (the study of plants), music, astronomy, physics, and philosophy.

1085
Abū Bakr Ibn Bājja is born in Zaragoza, Spain, which at this time is an independent Muslim state. He is educated in medicine. In his medical writings he investigate diseases and how to cure them.

c.1100s
He writes his detailed and influential book, *The Book of Plants*. It is a highly important contribution to the study of botany.

c.1130s
Abū Bakr begins to focus more on philosophy. In his book *Regimen of the Solitary*, he argues that people must find happiness within themselves and not look for it in society.

1138
Abū Bakr dies. Some suspect that he was poisoned by an enemy, but it is never proved.

Nasir al-Din al-Tusi (1201–1274)

The philosopher, scientist, and mathematician Nasir al-Din al-Tusi was instrumental in the creation of trigonometry—the science of triangles—as a branch of mathematics.

1201
Nasir is born in the city of Tus (in modern-day Iran). He is educated in Tus and later in the town of Nishāpūr (also in modern-day Iran).

c.1250
He writes about trigonometry in his *Treatise on the Quadrilateral*—his most important mathematical work. In it, he establishes trigonometry as its own subject. Before Nasir, it was seen as a branch of astronomy.

1256
Nasir is captured in the city of Alamūt (in modern-day Iran) by the army of the Mongol Empire, who have swept across Asia and the Middle East. He is treated with great respect by the Mongols. They appoint Nasir as their scientific advisor.

1259
Nasir's plan to build an observatory is approved by the Mongol leader. It takes three years to build. When it is completed, Nasir uses the observatory to study and record the movements of the planets. He also produces a catalog of stars. His observational work takes him 12 years to complete.

1274
Nasir dies in Baghdad. During his life, he has written approximately 165 manuscripts.

Abū Zayd Ibn Khaldun (1332–1406)

Abū Zayd Ibn Khaldun was one of the most important Islamic thinkers of his time. He helped advance the recording of history, and paved the way for new sciences, including sociology (the study of human societies).

1332
Abū Zayd Ibn Khaldun is born in Tunis (in modern-day Tunisia), where he receives his education from some of the city's best teachers.

1352
He becomes a politician, holding a number of jobs in both North Africa and Muslim Spain.

1375
Tired of politics, he seeks refuge in a small village in Algeria, where he spends his time writing his masterpiece, the *Muqaddimah*, a detailed history of the world. It also includes sociology, politics, and philosophy.

1378
He returns to Tunis and completes the *Muqaddimah*. The book is influential in Abū Zayd's own time, as well as for centuries to come.

1382
Abū Zayd settles in Cairo, Egypt, where he is appointed chief judge and later becomes a teacher. He also writes an account of his life, and a detailed history of Muslim North Africa.

1406
Abū Zayd dies in Cairo at the age of 73.

Genghis Khan

One of the greatest warriors in history, Genghis Khan (c. 1162–1227) used cunning, military tactics, and mental warfare to unite a collection of tribes and conquer a vast area of land from the Caspian Sea (between Europe and Asia) across to the Pacific Ocean. The Mongol Empire he set up would go on to become the largest empire in history.

Legacy of an empire

Genghis' descendants led the empire to greater prominence, until its end in 1368.

Kublai Khan (1215–1294)

In 1260, Kublai became the fifth Khagan (great khan) of the Mongol Empire. Kublai distinguished himself among the Mongol khans by embracing the customs and cultures of the people he conquered. He became the first non-Chinese Emperor of China in 1271.

Khutulun (c. 1260–c. 1306)

Kublai Khan's niece Khutulun was raised as a warrior. She was very skilled in horseback riding and archery, and was said to have never lost a wrestling match. Her father Kaidu often asked for her opinions on political and military matters, an unconventional situation for a woman of her time and culture.

Jani Beg (reigned 1342–1357)

Khan of a later Mongol state, Jani Beg is notorious for having invented biological warfare. During the siege of Caffa (in the Crimean peninsula) in 1347, he ordered that the bodies of people who had died from bubonic plague be catapulted into the city. The disease spread among the citizens inside, killing many and causing the city to surrender.

c. 1162

Temüjin

Little is known about Genghis Khan's early life, other than the origin of his birth name. To celebrate a victory, Yesukai, leader of the Mongol Borjigin clan, names his son Temüjin Borjigin after an enemy he has defeated.

1171

The Borjigin clan

Temüjin is sent to work with his future bride's family. When his father is killed by the Tatar tribe, Temüjin returns home to take up the role of clan chief, but instead he is expelled from the tribe, along with his family.

1171

Surviving on the steppes

Temüjin leads his family as they scrape a living on the Mongolian steppes — a huge area of flat grassland — dealing with thieves and Yesukai's old enemies.

1178

Tribal alliances

Temüjin begins building alliances with local tribes, starting with the Kereyid tribe. This alliance is cemented by his marriage to Börte, the daughter of the tribe's leader — and the woman he was supposed to marry before his father's death. By 1182, he has developed a reputation as a warrior and begins attracting followers.

c. 1200

Horses and arrows

Temüjin and the Mongols spend their lives on horseback, developing ferocious fighting skills. In battle they maneuver a galloping horse using only their legs, leaving them free to rain arrows down on their enemies, to devastating effect.

1200

Defeat of the Tatars

Using a new alliance with Tughrul of the Kereyid tribe, Temüjin wages war against the Tatar tribe for two years, and is victorious. By destroying the Tatar tribe, Temüjin avenges his father's death, increases his territory, and strengthens his reputation as a warrior.

> "In the space of seven years I have succeeded in ... uniting the whole world in one Empire."
>
> **Genghis Khan, in a letter to Ch'ang Ch'un (1219)**

1227

Ögedei

Genghis dies from injuries he receives from falling off his horse. His son, Ögedei, succeeds him as leader of the Mongol Empire.

1221

Yassa

Drawing on Mongol common law, Genghis creates a legal code known as "Yassa," which forbids feuds, theft, and lying. It also prohibits people from bathing in rivers or lakes and littering, reflecting his respect for the environment.

1221

Pax Mongolica

Genghis uses his newly conquered territories to establish trading routes between Asia and Europe. This time of prosperity is known as "Pax Mongolica" ("Mongol Peace").

1219

Invasion of Khwarizm

The shah (leader) of the Khwarizm Dynasty (which rules parts of Central and southwestern Asia) attacks a Mongol diplomat. Enraged, Genghis takes personal control and leadership of 200,000 fighters for an invasion of the Khwarizm Dynasty. The fighting ends with Genghis victorious, and the death of the Shah of Khwarizm.

1211

Jin Dynasty

Following a successful campaign against China's Jin Dynasty, Genghis takes their capital city of Zhongdu (near modern-day Beijing, China). He then moves deeper into Central Asia.

1207

Expansion into Asia

With the Mongolian tribes now united under him, Genghis turns his attention toward China. He plans to further expand the Mongol Empire and begins by waging war against the kingdom of Xi Xia in northwestern China.

1206

Becoming Genghis

Temüjin destroys the Naiman and Taichi'ut tribes, which gives him control over central and eastern Mongolia. Following this victory, other smaller tribes agree to peace, and grant Temüjin the title of "Genghis Khan," meaning "universal ruler."

c.1205

Beloved daughter

Razia Sultana is born to Shams ud-Din Iltutmish, a former enslaved person from Central Asia who rose to become the Sultan (ruler) of the Delhi Sultanate. Razia is well educated and is trained in archery and martial arts. She also gains experience in governing.

1229

Brother's death

Her brother Nasir ud-Din Mahmud is the heir to the throne, but he dies suddenly. Iltutmish has several other sons, but he does not believe that any of them have the leadership skills that he begins to see in his daughter.

1231

Razia excels

When Iltutmish goes away on a military campaign, he leaves the running of the government to Razia. On his return, he is so impressed with how well she has performed that he decides to appoint her as his heir.

April 1236

Rejection

Iltutmish dies, and the nobility refuse to accept Razia as their ruler because she is a woman. They put her stepbrother, Rukn ud-Din Firuz, on the throne instead. He is an incompetent king, and is often absent seeking fun, leaving his mother in charge.

November 1236

Becoming queen

Razia leads mass protests against Rukn ud-Din's rule. She gains the support of the army and several nobles. While Rukn ud-Din is away from Delhi, they place her on the throne. When Rukn ud-Din returns to the city, Razia has him arrested and imprisoned. He dies soon afterwards.

1237

Defiant queen

Not all the nobles support Razia's accession. She faces multiple rebellions, but she crushes them all. To show her authority, she has coins issued in her name. To appear like previous rulers, she dresses in male clothing in public, which shocks some of her subjects.

> ## "Pillar of Women, Queen of the Eras."
>
> **Inscription on coins commemorating Razia Sultana's rise to the throne (1237)**

Razia Sultana

Raziya al-Din, commonly known as Razia Sultana (c.1205–1240), was the only female ruler of the Delhi Sultanate, an empire that ruled over much of India. Her four-year reign was extraordinary not just because she rose to power in a male-dominated society, but also because her ancestors were enslaved people.

1237

Progressive ruler

Razia gradually restores peace and order, and proves to be an efficient, forward-thinking queen. She orders the construction of roads, schools, and libraries, and the digging of wells to find new supplies of water. She also encourages trade with other lands.

April 1240

Downfall

Her enemies spread rumours that she is in love with a former enslaved person, Jamal ud-Din Yaqut, and has unfairly promoted him in her court. Her childhood love, Ikhtiyar ud-Din Altunia, becomes jealous. He turns against her. Altunia and other nobles kill Yaqut and take Razia captive. Razia's half-brother, Muiz ud-Din Bahram, declares himself sultan.

1240

Marriage

The new sultan ignores the claims of Altunia for power. He returns to Razia's side, and frees her. They marry, form an alliance, and raise an army. They attack the new sultan's forces in Delhi in an attempt to win back her throne, but are badly defeated. The couple flee with their army.

October 1240

Death

Razia and Altunia reach Kaithal, 160 km (100 miles) away from Delhi. There, their army abandons them. According to some sources, they are attacked. They fight bravely, but are killed.

Mansa Musa

One of the greatest African rulers of all time, Mansa Musa (1280–1337) led the Mali Empire at the height of its power, wealth, and creativity. During his reign, the empire stretched for 2,000 miles (3,200 km) across West Africa. His empire's riches caused the value of gold to collapse in the surrounding region.

Egypt
On Musa's journey, he passes through Cairo in Egypt. To show his peaceful intentions and the incredible wealth of his empire, he gives away so much gold that it causes the value of the precious metal to decrease.

Expanding empire
While Musa is extremely generous on his travels, his trip is also political. He acquires Gao, the capital of the neighboring Songhai Empire, which is one of the oldest trading centers in West Africa.

Money matters
Mali is rich in natural resources such as gold, precious stones, minerals, and salt. Musa adds to the empire's wealth by introducing taxes on trade and mining, and by taxing conquered neighboring lands.

Pilgrimage to Mecca
A committed Muslim, Musa makes Islam the official religion of the Mali Empire. In 1324, Musa leaves Mali on the hajj—the pilgrimage to the holy city of Mecca that is seen as a spiritual duty of all Muslims.

Becoming Mansa
Musa is appointed deputy to Mansa Abu Bakr II, who embarks on an Atlantic Ocean expedition but never returns. The throne is passed on to Musa, meaning the title Mansa, becoming the "emperor," becoming the tenth ruler of the Mali Empire.

Born into royalty
Mansa Musa, called the Musa Keita at birth, is the great-nephew of the Mali Musa Keita at Sundiata Keita. Despite Musa's father and grandfather did not rule Mali. Musa's father connection to the royal Empire founder of this royal Empire, and

1280

1312

1320

1324

July 1324

1325

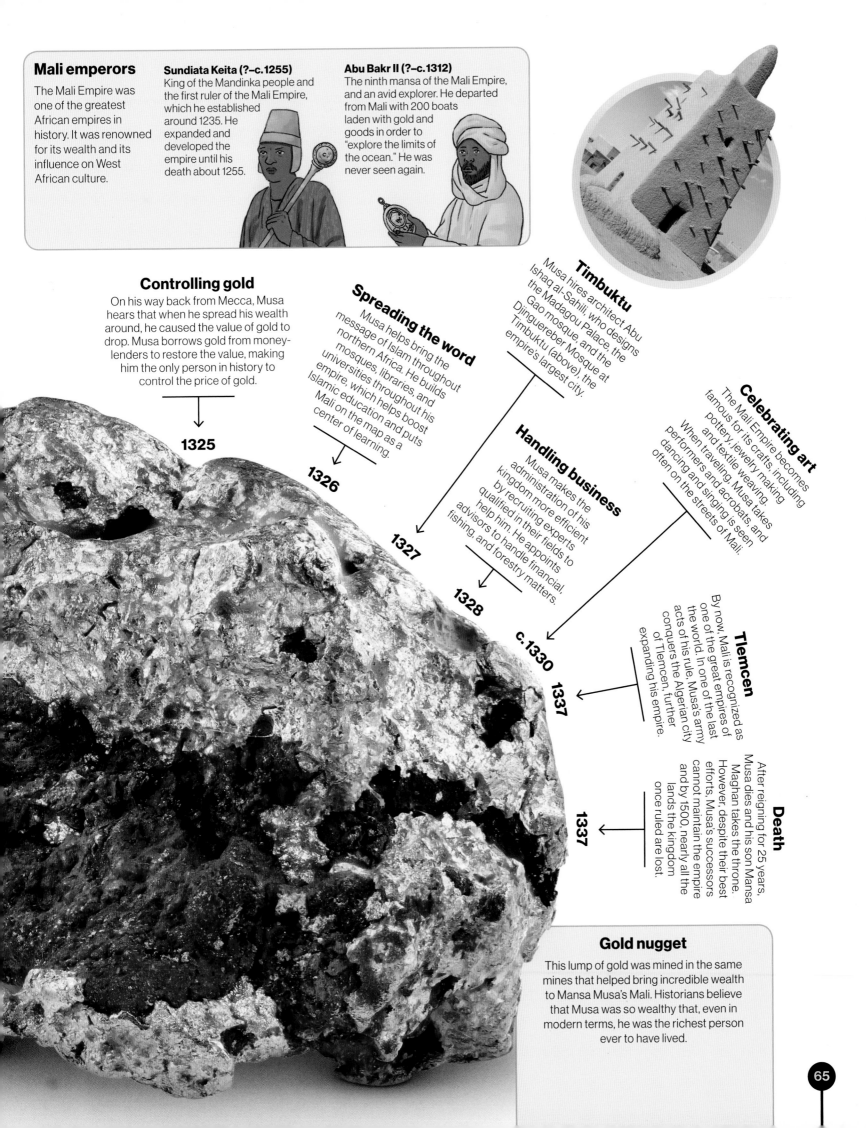

Mali emperors

The Mali Empire was one of the greatest African empires in history. It was renowned for its wealth and its influence on West African culture.

Sundiata Keita (?–c. 1255)
King of the Mandinka people and the first ruler of the Mali Empire, which he established around 1235. He expanded and developed the empire until his death about 1255.

Abu Bakr II (?–c. 1312)
The ninth mansa of the Mali Empire, and an avid explorer. He departed from Mali with 200 boats laden with gold and goods in order to "explore the limits of the ocean." He was never seen again.

Controlling gold

On his way back from Mecca, Musa hears that when he spread his wealth around, he caused the value of gold to drop. Musa borrows gold from money-lenders to restore the value, making him the only person in history to control the price of gold.

1325

Spreading the word

Musa helps bring the message of Islam throughout northern Africa. He builds mosques, libraries, and universities throughout his empire, which helps boost Islamic education and puts Mali on the map as a center of learning.

1326

Timbuktu

Musa hires architect Abu Ishaq al-Sahili, who designs the Madagou Palace, the Gao mosque, and the Djinguereber Mosque at Timbuktu (above), the empire's largest city.

Celebrating art

The Mali Empire becomes famous for its crafts, including pottery, jewelry making, and textile weaving. When traveling, Musa takes performers and acrobats, and dancing and singing is seen often on the streets of Mali.

Handling business

Musa makes the administration of his kingdom more efficient by recruiting experts qualified in their fields to help him. He appoints advisors to handle financial, fishing, and forestry matters.

1327

1328

c. 1330

Tlemcen

By now, Mali is recognized as one of the great empires of the world. In one of the last acts of his rule, Musa's army conquers the Algerian city of Tlemcen, further expanding his empire.

1337

Death

After reigning for 25 years, Musa dies and his son Mansa Maghan takes the throne. However, despite their best efforts, Musa's successors cannot maintain the empire and by 1500, nearly all the lands the kingdom once ruled are lost.

1337

Gold nugget

This lump of gold was mined in the same mines that helped bring incredible wealth to Mansa Musa's Mali. Historians believe that Musa was so wealthy that, even in modern terms, he was the richest person ever to have lived.

Family of judges

Abu Abdullah Muhammad Ibn Battuta is born in Tangier (in modern-day Morocco) to an educated family of *qadis* (Islamic judges).

1304

Pilgrimage

Though sad to say goodbye to his parents, Ibn Battuta leaves home to start the long and arduous *hajj* (Islamic pilgrimage) by traveling to Mecca (in modern-day Saudi Arabia).

1325

Egypt

After traveling more than 1,988 miles (3,200 km) in less than nine months, Ibn Battuta takes a short break on his pilgrimage to take in the sights of Egypt. He sees the pyramids of Giza and spends a month in Cairo, then one of the largest cities in the world.

1326

Ibn Battuta

One of the greatest travelers of all time, Ibn Battuta (1304–c. 1369) spent 29 years venturing further than anyone else of his time. He crossed three continents, visited more than 40 countries, and met at least 60 rulers. He had many adventures and faced countless dangers, but lived to tell the tale!

Judging in Delhi

Ibn Battuta rides into India to become one of the chief judges of Delhi. He joins the sultan (Islamic ruler) on extravagant hunting expeditions on elephants, and his information and stories about other countries and rulers make him very popular.

1333

Robbed and captured

On another adventure, Ibn Battuta and his traveling companions are attacked by bandits as they take treasures from Delhi to the Mongol court of China. The bandits take everything, and kidnap Ibn Battuta. He persuades his captors to release him and he leaves barefoot wearing only his trousers.

1342

Travels in China

He arrives in Quanzhou in China after 40 days at sea. He observes that in the city, even the poor wear silk and have the finest of all pottery. After visiting the Great Wall of China, he begins his journey back home to Tangier.

1345

Black Death

As Ibn Battuta rides through Syria, the bubonic plague (also known as the Black Death) has spread across much of the world. He tries to outrun it, but every city he visits is struggling with an outbreak. He notes that every day, 2,000 people in Damascus and 24,000 people in Cairo die from it!

Buboes
Bubonic plague sufferers break out in painful welts, called buboes.

1348

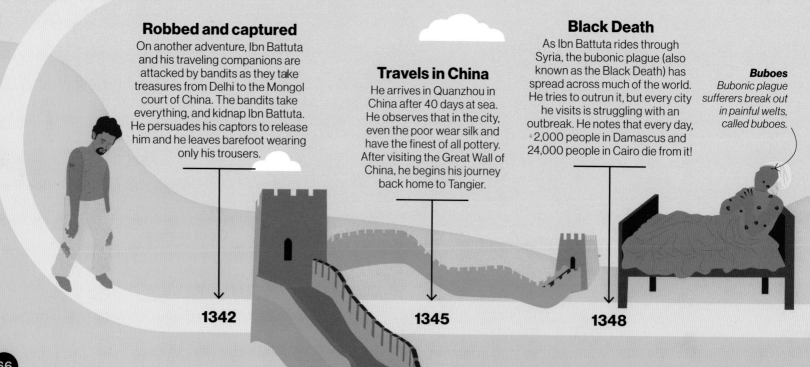
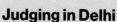

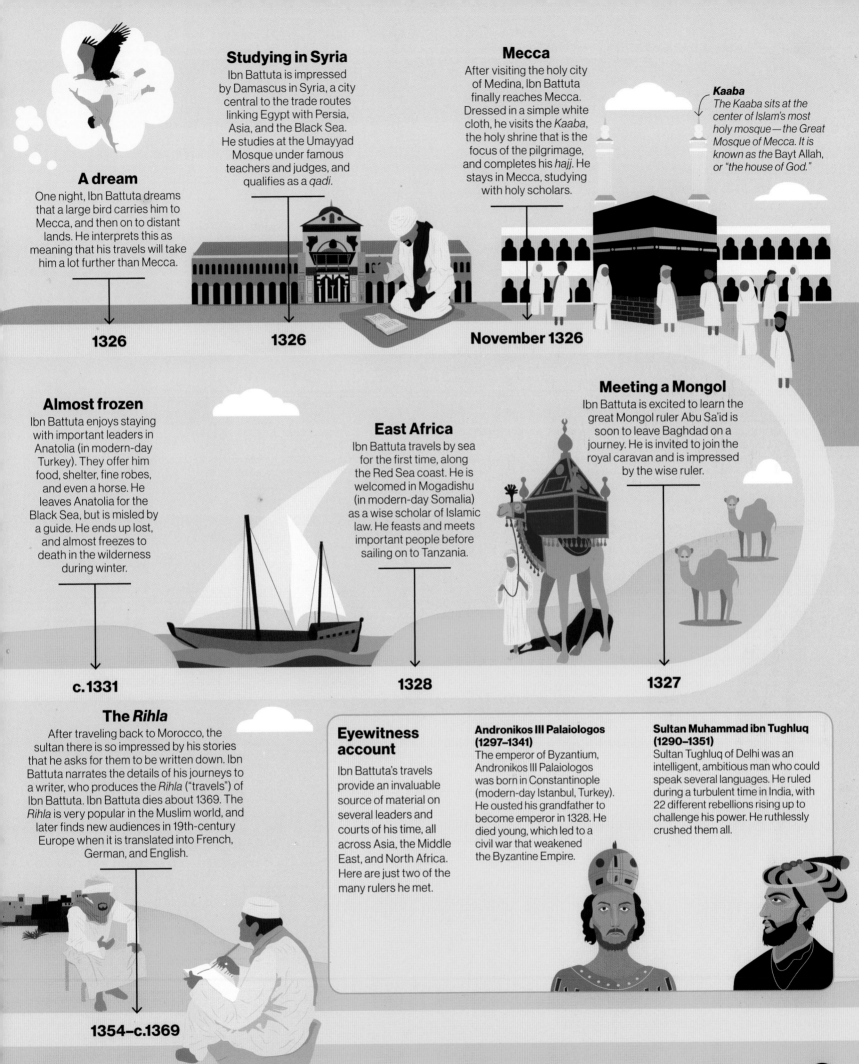

A dream

One night, Ibn Battuta dreams that a large bird carries him to Mecca, and then on to distant lands. He interprets this as meaning that his travels will take him a lot further than Mecca.

1326

Studying in Syria

Ibn Battuta is impressed by Damascus in Syria, a city central to the trade routes linking Egypt with Persia, Asia, and the Black Sea. He studies at the Umayyad Mosque under famous teachers and judges, and qualifies as a *qadi*.

1326

Mecca

After visiting the holy city of Medina, Ibn Battuta finally reaches Mecca. Dressed in a simple white cloth, he visits the *Kaaba*, the holy shrine that is the focus of the pilgrimage, and completes his *hajj*. He stays in Mecca, studying with holy scholars.

November 1326

Kaaba
The Kaaba sits at the center of Islam's most holy mosque—the Great Mosque of Mecca. It is known as the Bayt Allah, or "the house of God."

Almost frozen

Ibn Battuta enjoys staying with important leaders in Anatolia (in modern-day Turkey). They offer him food, shelter, fine robes, and even a horse. He leaves Anatolia for the Black Sea, but is misled by a guide. He ends up lost, and almost freezes to death in the wilderness during winter.

c. 1331

East Africa

Ibn Battuta travels by sea for the first time, along the Red Sea coast. He is welcomed in Mogadishu (in modern-day Somalia) as a wise scholar of Islamic law. He feasts and meets important people before sailing on to Tanzania.

1328

Meeting a Mongol

Ibn Battuta is excited to learn the great Mongol ruler Abu Sa'id is soon to leave Baghdad on a journey. He is invited to join the royal caravan and is impressed by the wise ruler.

1327

The *Rihla*

After traveling back to Morocco, the sultan there is so impressed by his stories that he asks for them to be written down. Ibn Battuta narrates the details of his journeys to a writer, who produces the *Rihla* ("travels") of Ibn Battuta. Ibn Battuta dies about 1369. The *Rihla* is very popular in the Muslim world, and later finds new audiences in 19th-century Europe when it is translated into French, German, and English.

1354–c.1369

Eyewitness account

Ibn Battuta's travels provide an invaluable source of material on several leaders and courts of his time, all across Asia, the Middle East, and North Africa. Here are just two of the many rulers he met.

Andronikos III Palaiologos (1297–1341)
The emperor of Byzantium, Andronikos III Palaiologos was born in Constantinople (modern-day Istanbul, Turkey). He ousted his grandfather to become emperor in 1328. He died young, which led to a civil war that weakened the Byzantine Empire.

Sultan Muhammad ibn Tughluq (1290–1351)
Sultan Tughluq of Delhi was an intelligent, ambitious man who could speak several languages. He ruled during a turbulent time in India, with 22 different rebellions rising up to challenge his power. He ruthlessly crushed them all.

1397

Born into royalty

Sejong is born the third son of King Taejong of Joseon and Queen Wongyeong. His father helped overthrow the Korean kingdom of Goryeo, which established the new Joseon Dynasty.

1409

Royal title

At the age of 12, Sejong is named Grand Prince and marries Soheon, the daughter of a powerful government official. With a keen interest in learning and reading, Sejong excels at his studies.

1412

Fatherhood

Three years after their marriage, Sejong and Soheon welcome their daughter, Princess Jeongso. Sejong goes on to have 29 children, with Soheon giving birth to 10 of them (eight sons and two daughters).

New alphabet

Sejong understands the need to develop literacy as part of Korea's cultural legacy. Inviting scholars to study in his court, he oversees the creation of an alphabet called Hangul, which is still the system used for writing the Korean language.

Peace treaty

In order to prevent Japanese pirate raids on Korean ports, Sejong signs the Treaty of Gyehae with Sō Sadamori, lord of Tsushima Island in Japan. This leads to a peaceful relationship with Japan that lasts throughout Sejong's reign.

Pluviometer

Sejong invites a young inventor from a poor background, Jang Yeong-sil, to his court. Sejong gives him an official position within government and allows him to invent anything he chooses. Jang creates the world's first rain gauge: the pluviometer.

1443

1443

1441

1422

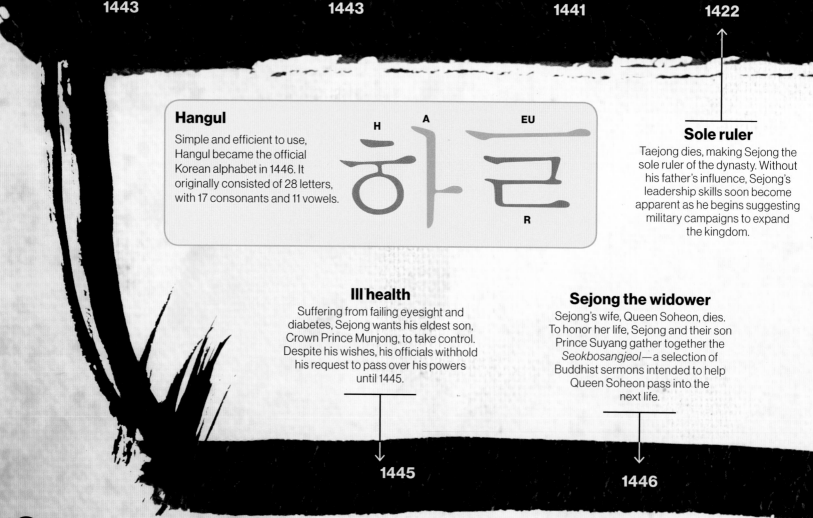

Hangul

Simple and efficient to use, Hangul became the official Korean alphabet in 1446. It originally consisted of 28 letters, with 17 consonants and 11 vowels.

H   A   EU
          R

Sole ruler

Taejong dies, making Sejong the sole ruler of the dynasty. Without his father's influence, Sejong's leadership skills soon become apparent as he begins suggesting military campaigns to expand the kingdom.

Ill health

Suffering from failing eyesight and diabetes, Sejong wants his eldest son, Crown Prince Munjong, to take control. Despite his wishes, his officials withhold his request to pass over his powers until 1445.

Sejong the widower

Sejong's wife, Queen Soheon, dies. To honor her life, Sejong and their son Prince Suyang gather together the *Seokbosangjeol*—a selection of Buddhist sermons intended to help Queen Soheon pass into the next life.

1445

1446

1418

Becoming king

Sejong is favored by his father over his two older brothers. Taejong removes the eldest, Yangnyeong, as heir to the throne, and the next in line, Hyoryeong, becomes a monk. Taejong then steps down, making Sejong king, but he continues to influence government policy.

1420

Royal institute

Gathering scholars from across Korea to advise him on his rule, Sejong establishes an academic institute called the College of Assembled Worthies in the royal palace. The college researches a variety of subjects, creating documents and compiling books on a range of topics.

Death

Sejong dies and his son Munjong takes the throne. However, infighting within the family leads to a period of turbulence. Eventually, Sejong's son Sejo takes the throne in 1455, after executing his nephew and several of Sejong's ministers.

1450

This timeline is designed around the Hangul script for "R."

Long legacy

The Joseon Dynasty (1392–1910) lasted for more than five centuries, and is remembered as the golden age of Korea, with developments in culture, trade, science, and more.

Shin Saim-dang (1504–1551)
A painter, calligrapher, and poet in a male-dominated society, Saim-dang was one of the few women to be known for her art. She became the first woman to appear on a Korean banknote in 2009.

Yi Sun-sin (1545–1598)
A famous naval leader, Sun-sin's victories against the Japanese are still seen by Koreans as some of the most heroic events in their history.

Emperor Gojong (1852–1919)
The last king of the Joseon Dynasty, Gojong changed domestic and foreign policies to protect the empire against Japanese invasion.

Sejong the Great

Best known for creating Hangul, the Korean alphabet, King Sejong the Great (1397–1450) was the fourth ruler of the Joseon Dynasty of Korea. He completely changed the way that government ran by allowing people of all backgrounds to become civil servants. His prosperous reign also led to great advances in literacy and science.

JOHANNES GUTENBERG

Bringing books to everyone

Johannes Gutenberg (c. 1400–1468), a German craftsman from Mainz, changed the world when he invented the movable type printing press. This transformed the way people read and share information through books, newspapers, and other printed materials. His printing press allowed books to be produced in vast numbers for the first time—and it helped spread the ideas that would create the modern world.

JOHANNES
GUTENBERG

Copying by hand

Until the **7th century**, the only way to reproduce a book or a piece of writing was to copy it by hand onto clay, papyrus, wax, or parchment. This was an extremely slow process, done by scribes who carefully copied text from one book to the next. During the **Middle Ages**, only very wealthy people, universities, and religious establishments could afford books, which meant most books were religious in nature.

Printing in China

In Tang Dynasty China (**618–907 CE**), a way of printing that used hand-carved wooden blocks was developed. On one side of the block, words appeared in reverse. After ink was applied to them, these blocks were then pressed onto paper, showing the words the right way around. In the **11th century**, Chinese inventor Bi Sheng (**c.990–1051**) developed a technique known as movable type. This uses individual words made from clay that are then attached to a plate and pressed down onto paper to print text. The words had to be arranged for each page, and with more than 8,000 Chinese characters (symbols for different words or sounds) to choose from, it was a time-consuming process.

Gutenberg's big idea

Johannes Gutenberg, a craftsman working in Strasbourg (in modern-day France), sees the money-making potential of producing books in large numbers. He starts experimenting in about **1436** by taking the screw presses used by farmers to crush olives and grapes, and adapting the screw mechanism so it can be used for printing. He makes individual letters from a mixture of lead and other metals, which is more durable than the wood used up until now. The letters he has made fit together and create lines that are level, making printing much easier than before. He uses an oil-based ink, which sticks better than the water-based inks used for writing. By about **1450**, Johannes' press is ready for use. His new printing system is much more efficient than anything that has come before.

Large-scale printing

Johannes borrows money from Johann Fust, a wealthy moneylender, and builds a workshop. Fust becomes Johannes' business partner, and they begin printing calendars and pamphlets. In **1452**, Johannes begins work on a printed Bible. He prints a set of about 180 illustrated copies in Latin, using 290 molded letter blocks on 50,000 sheets of paper. Although it takes three years to print all of the copies, this is much quicker than producing hand-written manuscripts. Customers are so excited by Johannes' work that he sells every copy before he has even designed the last page for the final Bible. In **1456**, he loses his equipment and workshop to Fust following a court case. Johannes has many money problems after this, but is given a pension by the prince-archbishop of Mainz in **1465**, and he dies there in **1468**.

Printing in Europe

News about Johannes' extraordinary machine spreads across Europe. Printers who helped Johannes in his early experiments teach his techniques to others in the country. In **1464**, the printing press is introduced to Italy, and in **1470**, German printers are asked to set up presses in France at Sorbonne University, and then in Spain in **1471**. William Caxton, an Englishman who lives in Bruges (in modern-day Belgium), brings Gutenberg-style printing to England by establishing a press in Westminster, London, in **1476**. By **1500**, up to nine million books, on subjects ranging from Greek philosophy to the journeys of Christopher Columbus, are available to read.

Changing the world

The invention of the printing press means that ideas are able to spread much more quickly. Works of science and books from the ancient world are now accessible to many more people. In Europe, the Catholic Church no longer has strict control over what is written about the Christian faith, which leads to religious upheaval. The first newspaper, *Relation*, is printed in Strasbourg in **1605**. Soon, newspapers spread across Europe, bringing knowledge about huge issues in the lives of regular people. Although Johannes Gutenberg does not make much money from it in his lifetime, his printing press leads to huge changes in the daily lives of billions of people, right up to today.

Joan of Arc

Seemingly guided by voices from heaven, Joan of Arc (c. 1412–1431) was a military leader who led the French army against the English during the Hundred Years' War. Her unique story meant that she became one of the most famous people of the Middle Ages in Europe.

To battle

At the royal court, Joan promises Charles that he will be crowned king, and demands to lead an army to Orleans. Charles grants her request and Joan sets off dressed in white armor and riding a white horse.

February 1429

Victory

Joan inspires the French troops to win at Orleans. She goes on to defeat the English twice more in stunning victories. It seems a sure sign that Joan, and France, have God on their side.

May 1429

Captive

During a nighttime assault on the town of Compiègne, Joan is thrown from her horse and left stranded outside the town's gates. The Burgundians, allies of England, take her to Beauvoir Castle.

Spring 1430

Imprisoned

The English—seeking to discredit Charles VII—buy Joan and send her to trial before the English clerics who support the English cause. She is imprisoned in Rouen Castle and repeatedly interrogated about her religious visions. She tries to escape many times, but fails.

November 1430

Trial

At Rouen, Joan is accused of witchcraft and dressing like a man—both considered heresies (beliefs or actions against the Church or God). Tired and ill, she agrees that the voices she hears are not God, and that she will not wear men's clothing again. She soon "relapses," however, by admitting it is God talking to her, and by dressing in men's clothes.

January 1431

Burned at the stake

This relapse leads Joan to be sentenced to death for heresy. She is tied to a wooden stake and burned alive. Twenty-five years after her execution, Pope Callixtus III declared her innocent of the charges against her at her trial. After 22 more years of fighting, Charles VII emerges from the Hundred Years' War as the unchallenged king of France.

1431

Other Joans

Joan of Arc became a symbol for people in other countries, often when encountering oppression or war. Many countries around the world have their own people whose stories are similar in some way or another to Joan's. Here are just a few.

Agustina de Aragón (1786–1857)

Agustina de Aragón was a heroine of the Spanish War of Independence and the Peninsular War against France. She is most famous for her bravery at the Siege of Zaragoza (1808). Her actions inspired poetry, paintings, and folklore, both at home and abroad.

Maria Quitéria (1792–1853)

Maria Quitéria dressed as a man in order to serve in the army during Brazil's war of independence against Portugal. By fighting, she defied her father's wishes. He revealed Maria as a woman, but the military respected her skills so much that they allowed her to continue fighting.

Ryu Gwan-sun (1902–1920)

South Korean student Ryu Gwan-sun organized peaceful protests against Japanese colonial rule in Korea. At one protest, Japanese military police shot dead 19 people, including Ryu's parents. She was arrested and eventually died from torture at the age of 17. She has become an important symbol of Korean independence.

Peasant girl
c. 1412

Joan is born to a farming family in Domremy in northeastern France. Her mother, Isabelle, instils in her a devotion to the Christian faith.

Divine mission
1424

Joan hears voices in her head, which she believes are sent by God. These voices give her an important mission: she must save France from English rule in the Hundred Years' War. Joan decides to fight to expel the English, and to install Charles VII as France's rightful king.

Vaucouleurs
1428

Joan goes to Vaucouleurs (a town loyal to Charles VII) to seek permission from soldiers there to visit the royal court at Chinon. She says God has spoken to her, but she is sent away.

Male disguise
1429

In a second meeting with the soldiers at Vaucouleurs, Joan makes a prediction about a battle near Orleans. Her prediction comes true and she is escorted to Chinon. For her own safety, Joan disguises herself as a male soldier by cropping her hair and dressing in men's clothes for the journey.

Askia the Great

Emperor Askia the Great (c. 1443–1538) was a ruler of the Songhai Empire in western Africa. During his reign, he transformed his empire into a strong military power and a center of Islamic culture. He is remembered as a great scholar and leader.

Setting off to Mecca
According to legend, Askia sets off on the hajj—the pilgrimage to Mecca that all Muslims are required to make. To prove he is a strong and wealthy leader, he takes 1,000 soldiers with him, and gives out 300,000 gold pieces to the poor he meets on his travels.

Organizing the empire
Muhammad is now ruler of the Songhai Empire, and takes the name Askia (meaning "usurper"—someone who steals power). He appoints new governors, and develops the city of Timbuktu into a great center of learning and Islamic culture.

The Battle of Anfao
Muhammad plans to take power from Sonni Baru. The two sides go to war at the Battle of Anfao. Even though Muhammad's troops are fewer in number, he defeats Sonni Baru and sends him into exile.

Challenging the king
Muhammad builds a strong relationship with Islamic religious leaders. When Sonni Ali dies, he opposes Sonni Baru, the new king. Muhammad accuses Sonni Baru of being disrespectful to Islam.

Military man
Muhammad joins the Songhai military around this time, and eventually becomes a general in Sonni Ali's army.

Birth
Though we do not know for sure, it is possible that Muhammad Ture is born in western Africa around this time. It is believed that his mother is the sister of Sonni Ali, the king of the Songhai Empire (in modern-day Mali). Muhammad's family has strong connections to the army.

1496

1494

1493

1492

c. 1460

c. 1443

Songhai Empire

The Songhai Empire was one of the most important African empires in the 15th and 16th centuries. It grew rich trading gold and salt along the Niger River and across the Sahara.

Sonni Ali (d. 1492)

One of the first rulers of the Songhai Empire, Sonni Ali reigned from 1464 until his death in 1492. During that time, he built a strong army and navy, and conquered cities, including Timbuktu.

Ahmad Baba (1556–1627)

An Islamic writer, Ahmad Baba was born in modern-day Mali. He is considered to be one of the greatest scholars of the 16th century. Baba wrote about how to live as a good person, and criticized the keeping of enslaved people.

Meeting the caliph

On the way to Mecca, he meets the caliph of Egypt, (the Muslim ruler of the country). Askia is named the caliph's religious representative in West Africa. He completes his pilgrimage to Mecca.

1497

Returning home

Askia makes the journey back to the Songhai Empire. By completing the hajj he has strengthened his authority. His people accept him as their religious leader.

c. 1498

The empire expands

The Songhai Empire expands as Askia conquers neighboring territory. It covers much of modern-day Mali, Niger, and Senegal. This makes it the largest empire in African history.

1500

1505

Facing defeat

Askia has captured a large area of territory from surrounding states, but he faces a setback when he attacks Borgu (the border region between modern-day Niger and Nigeria). The campaign fails, and Askia has to retreat.

Death

Askia dies aged about 95. He is buried in a mud brick pyramid in Gao (in modern-day Mali), which is still standing today.

Fall from power

At the age of 80, Askia is nearly blind and unable to rule. His son, Farimondyo Mousa, revolts against him, and forces him to abdicate. Askia is banished to an island in the Niger River.

1528

1538

Askia and his tomb

We have no confirmed portraits of Askia—this one is based on how rulers of his time and place dressed. His tomb is 56 ft (17 m) high, and is built entirely of mud bricks. The wooden beams give the tomb strength, and allow builders to climb it and carry out repairs.

Spanish exploration

The land Spain claimed as a result of its voyages of exploration transformed it into one of the largest empires in history. But these lands were not empty. People in Spain had varying viewpoints on how to treat these new subjects.

Isabella I of Castile (1451–1504)

Isabella I's marriage to Ferdinand II of Aragon unified Spain. In 1500, she declared that all native peoples not fighting against Spain in the lands that Spain had claimed were considered fully legal citizens, but those fighting were not.

Bartolomé de las Casas (c.1474–1566)

A historian and missionary, Bartolomé de Las Casas wrote about the oppression and exploitation of native people in the Americas living under Spanish colonial rule. Originally a colonist, he got rid of his land and enslaved people in order to campaign against the abuses of power he saw.

Ferdinand Magellan (1480–1521)

A navigator and explorer, Ferdinand Magellan led the first expedition to circumnavigate (sail all the way around) the world. Though the expedition was successful, Magellan himself did not complete it. He died during a battle with native peoples in the Philippines.

Christopher Columbus

An Italian explorer, admiral, and navigator, Christopher Columbus (1451–1506) set sail westwards from Spain in 1492 with the aim of arriving in the Far East. Instead, he landed in the Americas, then unknown to Europeans. He is seen by some as a hero and pioneer, and by others as someone whose arrival brought a lot of suffering to the people living in the Americas.

1451

1465

1479

1485

August 3, 1492

October 12, 1492

Seafaring life
Christopher leaves his home to become a sailor. He sails all around Europe, conducting business and delivering cargo on behalf of wealthy Genoese families.

Marriage
Christopher marries Felipa Perestrello e Moniz, a Portuguese noblewoman, and they settle down in Lisbon, Portugal. Tragedy strikes when Felipa dies a few years into their marriage.

Big idea
Trading with faraway places in the east, such as India and China, is extremely profitable, but difficult and dangerous. Christopher thinks of a new way to get there: by sailing west, a boat will eventually reach the Far East. The royal courts of Portugal, France, and England decline to sponsor his unusual idea.

First voyage
He presents his plan to King Ferdinand II of Aragon and Queen Isabella I of Castile, who are eventually convinced to back him. They provide him with three ships, and 87 sailors. The expedition sets sail from Palos de la Frontera in Spain.

Land sighted
After many weeks at sea, land is sighted just as the expedition is about to turn back. They land on an island in the modern-day Bahamas.

Merchant's son
Christopher Columbus is born in Genoa, Italy, one of five children.

> "When there are such lands there should be profitable things without number."
>
> Christopher Columbus, *Journal of the First Voyage* (1492)

1493

The Americas
Though Christopher believes he has found India, he has actually landed in the Americas. He claims the lands for Spain and for Christianity, but there are already people living there. He brings news of his journey back to Spain.

1493

Second voyage
Ferdinand and Isabella make Christopher governor of the new lands. They sponsor a second voyage, with 17 ships and 1,200 people to set up colonies in the Americas. The king and queen request that he treat the people living there with respect. Christopher claims more islands in the Caribbean for Spain.

1498

Third voyage
A much smaller third voyage sets out, and lands on the northern coast of South America. Reports begin to emerge of Christopher's bad management of the colonies, and terrible treatment of the native people – including torture, enslavement, and murder.

1500

Arrest
After the third voyage, Christopher is arrested for his mismanagement of the Spanish colonies. He is brought back to Spain in chains. His time as governor is over, and he spends six weeks in jail. After his release, he appeals to be allowed to make one more voyage, to which King Ferdinand agrees.

1502

Fourth voyage
Christopher sets off on another expedition, once more looking for a route to China or India. His expedition lands in Central America. After a hurricane, shipwrecks, battles with natives, and a revolt by the sailors, he eventually makes it back to Spain alive.

1506

Death
Christopher spends his final years in Spain, and dies at the age of 54 in Valladolid.

77

Leonardo da Vinci

Leonardo da Vinci (1452–1519) is widely considered to be one of the most remarkable people to have ever lived. He was a painter, sculptor, scientist, engineer, architect, and inventor. Only 15 of his paintings have survived, but their quality is enough for him to be recognized as one of the greatest artists in history.

1452

Early life

Leonardo is born just outside a small town called Vinci in Italy (his surname means "from Vinci" in Italian). There is not much information about his childhood, apart from the fact he grows up in the countryside. His family moves to Florence in the mid-1460s.

c.1468

Apprentice artist

Aged about 17, Leonardo becomes an apprentice to artist Andrea del Verrocchio, in Florence. He finishes parts of Verrocchio's paintings, and his talent is soon recognized.

1478

Independent artist

After leaving Verrocchio's workshop, Leonardo becomes an independent artist. His first job is to produce a painting for the chapel of the Palazzo Vecchio, the town hall of Florence.

1482

Job application

Leonardo writes to Ludovico Sforza, Duke of Milan, asking for work. He talks up his skills as a military engineer rather than as a painter. Sforza hires Leonardo as an artist, and becomes an important patron (financial supporter) to him. Leonardo paints one of his masterpieces, *The Virgin of the Rocks*, soon after arriving in Milan.

c.1490

Vitruvian Man

He draws *Vitruvian Man*, which shows the ideal proportions of the human body, according to ancient Roman architect Vitruvius. It blends Leonardo's interest in art and mathematics.

c.1495

The Last Supper

Sforza employs Leonardo to create a large wall painting for a convent in Milan. It shows the last meal Jesus Christ shared with his followers before his death. The painting takes him three years to complete.

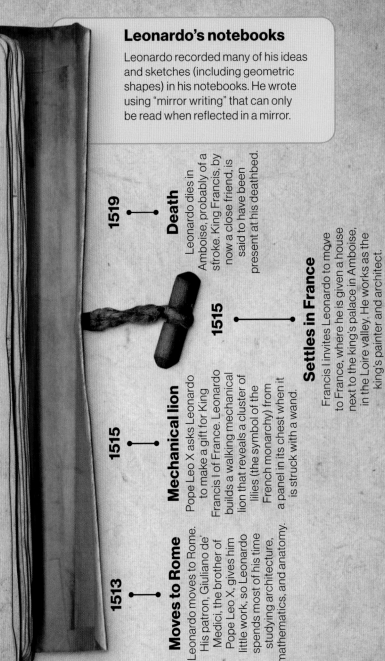

Leonardo's notebooks

Leonardo recorded many of his ideas and sketches (including geometric shapes) in his notebooks. He wrote using "mirror writing" that can only be read when reflected in a mirror.

1519
Death

Leonardo dies in Amboise, probably of a stroke. King Francis, by now a close friend, is said to have been present at his deathbed.

1515
Settles in France

Francis I invites Leonardo to move to France, where he is given a house next to the king's palace in Amboise, in the Loire valley. He works as the king's painter and architect.

1515
Mechanical lion

Pope Leo X asks Leonardo to make a gift for King Francis I of France. Leonardo builds a walking mechanical lion that reveals a cluster of lilies (the symbol of the French monarchy) from a panel in its chest when it is struck with a wand.

1513
Moves to Rome

Leonardo moves to Rome. His patron, Giuliano de' Medici, the brother of Pope Leo X, gives him little work, so Leonardo spends most of his time studying architecture, mathematics, and anatomy.

---

c. 1500
Diving apparatus

At around this time, Leonardo leaves Milan and moves to Venice. He resumes his work there, designing a piece of equipment for breathing underwater. His idea is highly original, but he cannot find a sponsor, so it is never made.

1502
Military engineer

During the wars against the French, Leonardo takes up the post of military engineer to Cesare Borgia—an Italian politician and military leader. He inspects fortifications, builds canals, makes maps, and draws up plans to drain marshes.

c. 1503
Mona Lisa

Leonardo returns to Florence and starts work on the *Mona Lisa*. This small portrait of a woman with a mysterious smile is perhaps the most famous painting in the world today.

c. 1505
Flying machine

Based on his extensive studies of birds, Leonardo sketches designs for a flying machine. He even builds one of these machines and launches it from a hill in Florence, but it does not work as intended.

Italian Renaissance artists

The movement in art, music, and philosophy known as the Italian Renaissance flourished in Italy during the 15th and 16th centuries.

Michelangelo (1475–1564)
Michelangelo was a painter and sculptor from Florence. He is best known for his statue of the biblical figure David, which he carved from a single block of marble.

Sofonisba Anguissola (1532–1625)
A noblewoman from Cremona, Sofonisba Anguissola painted mostly portraits. She was lady-in-waiting to Elisabeth of Valois, the queen consort of Spain, and became her official court painter.

Nicolaus Copernicus

Polish astronomer Nicolaus Copernicus (1473–1543) challenged centuries of belief when he argued that the Earth rotated around the sun, and not the other way around. Fearing punishment by the Christian Church, which taught that God created Earth at the center of the universe, Copernicus delayed making his ideas public until the end of his life. His work was banned for a period by the Church, but became hugely influential. Copernicus' ideas are widely accepted as the starting point of a revolution in scientific thought.

Heliocentric heavens

Published in *On the Revolutions of the Heavenly Spheres*, Copernicus' heliocentric model showed the sun sitting in the middle of the universe, with Earth and the other planets rotating around it. This model explained many things, including why the seasons happen.

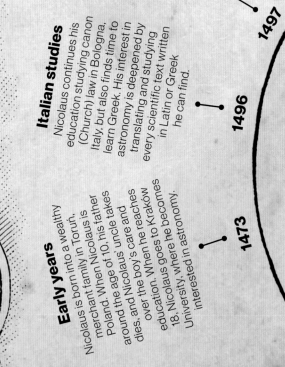

A new theory

Nicolaus moves back to Poland, where he becomes doctor and secretary to his uncle, now a bishop in the Church. He lives in his uncle's castle in the town of Lidzbark, and begins work on his heliocentric model—the theory that the Earth orbits the sun, and not the other way around.

Financial security

Nicolaus is given a Church position in Frombork, Poland. It does not require him to live there but gives him a steady income, and allows him to pursue his passion for astronomy. He stays in Italy, moving to Padua, and begins to study medicine.

Italian studies

Nicolaus continues his education studying canon (Church) law in Bologna, Italy, but also finds time to learn Greek. His interest in astronomy is deepened by translating and studying every scientific text written in Latin or Greek he can find.

Early years

Nicolaus is born into a wealthy merchant family in Torun, Poland. When Nicolaus is 10, his father dies, and Nicolaus' uncle takes around the age of 10 the boy's care and over. When he reaches 18, Nicolaus goes to Krakow University, where he becomes interested in astronomy.

1503

1497

1496

1473

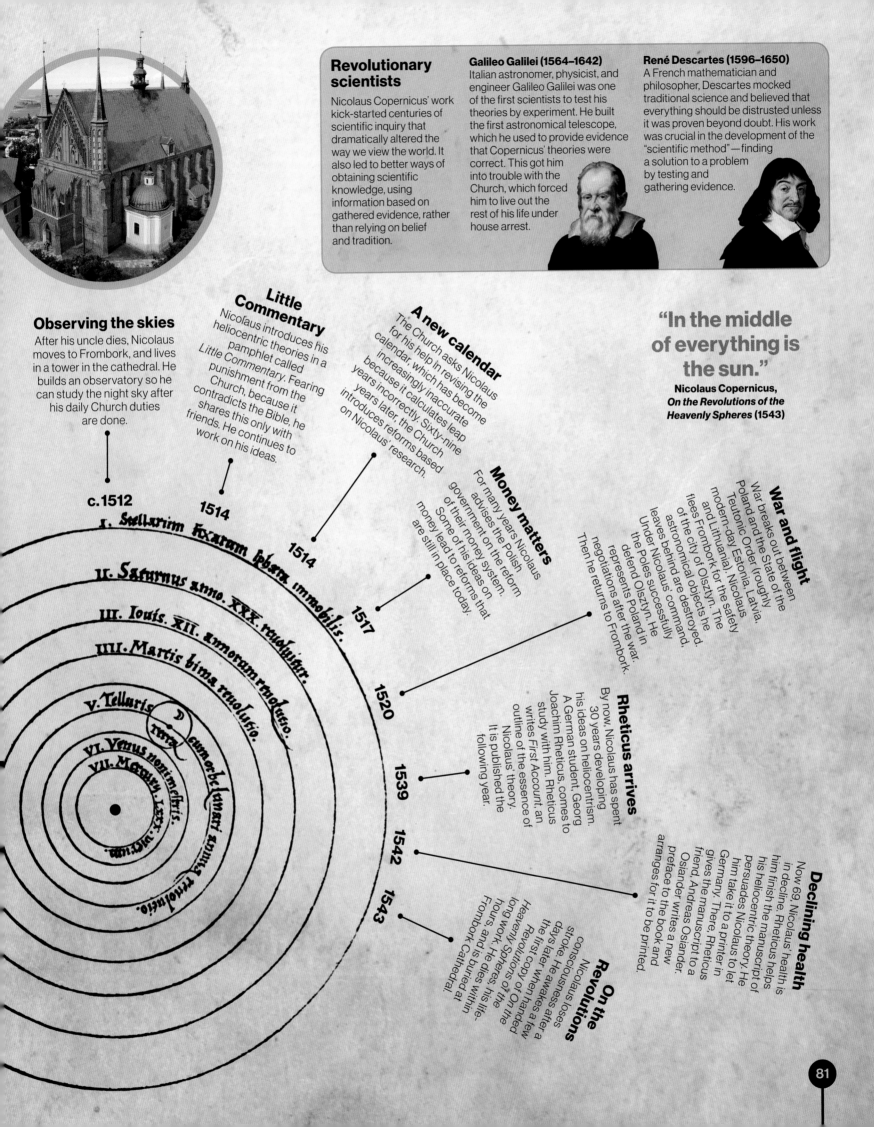

Revolutionary scientists

Nicolaus Copernicus' work kick-started centuries of scientific inquiry that dramatically altered the way we view the world. It also led to better ways of obtaining scientific knowledge, using information based on gathered evidence, rather than relying on belief and tradition.

Galileo Galilei (1564–1642)
Italian astronomer, physicist, and engineer Galileo Galilei was one of the first scientists to test his theories by experiment. He built the first astronomical telescope, which he used to provide evidence that Copernicus' theories were correct. This got him into trouble with the Church, which forced him to live out the rest of his life under house arrest.

René Descartes (1596–1650)
A French mathematician and philosopher, Descartes mocked traditional science and believed that everything should be distrusted unless it was proven beyond doubt. His work was crucial in the development of the "scientific method"—finding a solution to a problem by testing and gathering evidence.

Observing the skies
After his uncle dies, Nicolaus moves to Frombork, and lives in a tower in the cathedral. He builds an observatory so he can study the night sky after his daily Church duties are done.

c.1512

Little Commentary
Nicolaus introduces his heliocentric theories in a pamphlet called Little Commentary. Fearing punishment from the Church, because it contradicts the Bible, he shares this only with friends. He continues to work on his ideas.

1514

A new calendar
The Church asks Nicolaus for his help in revising the calendar, which has become increasingly inaccurate because it calculates leap years incorrectly. Sixty-nine years later, the Church introduces reforms based on Nicolaus' research.

1514

Money matters
For many years Nicolaus advises the Polish government on the reform of their money system. Some of his ideas on money lead to reforms that are still in place today.

1517

War and flight
War breaks out between Poland and the State of the Teutonic Order (roughly modern-day Estonia, Latvia, and Lithuania). Nicolaus flees Frombork for the safety of the city of Olsztyn. The astronomical objects he leaves behind are destroyed. Under Nicolaus' command, the Poles successfully defend Olsztyn. He represents Poland in negotiations after the war. Then he returns to Frombork.

1520

> "In the middle of everything is the sun."
> Nicolaus Copernicus,
> *On the Revolutions of the Heavenly Spheres* (1543)

Rheticus arrives
By now, Nicolaus has spent 30 years developing his ideas on heliocentrism. A German student, Georg Joachim Rheticus, comes to study with him. Rheticus writes First Account, an outline of the essence of Nicolaus' theory. It is published the following year.

1539

Declining health
Now 69, Nicolaus' health is in decline. Rheticus helps him finish the manuscript of his heliocentric theory. He persuades Nicolaus to let him take it to a printer in Germany. There, Rheticus gives the manuscript to a friend, Andreas Osiander. Osiander writes a new preface to the book and arranges for it to be printed.

1542

On the Revolutions
Nicolaus loses consciousness for many days. He awakes a few days later when handed a Revolution of On the Heavenly Spheres of the hours, and is buried at Frombork Cathedral. stroke. He awakes after a long work. He dies his life—first time when handed a copy of his life—

1543

81

(Diagram labels)
I. Stellarum fixarum sphaera immobilis.
II. Saturnus anno. XXX. revoluitur.
III. Iouis. XII. annorum revolutio.
IIII. Martis bima revolutio.
V. Telluris cum orbe lunari annua revolutio.
VI. Venus nonimestris.
VII. Mercurius. LXXX. dierum.

Martin Luther

In 1517, Martin Luther (1483–1546) argued against the huge wealth and practices of the Christian Catholic Church, as well as the right of its leader, the pope, to decide what people should believe. His actions sparked a movement we now call the Reformation, which ultimately led to a split between Catholics and supporters of Luther (who became the first "Protestants"), changing Christianity and the world.

"Why does not the pope ... build the basilica of St. Peter with his own money rather than with the money of poor believers?"
Martin Luther, *Thesis 86 of the "95 Theses"* (1517)

Rome

During his first and only stay in Rome, Italy, Martin becomes disillusioned by what he sees as corrupt practices in the Catholic Church, which is based there. He objects to "indulgences"—the practice of selling forgiveness of sins—and what he sees as ugly displays of wealth by the Church. When he returns home, he writes and distributes pamphlets arguing his views.

Heresy

Pope Leo X charges Martin with heresy (beliefs or actions against the Church or God). Martin defends himself in Augsburg, Germany, with arguments completely based on the teachings of the Bible. Fearing for his life, he soon flees. Martin returns to be under the guard of prince-elector Frederick the Wise, who becomes his protector.

Excommunication

Martin gradually feels that the pope is at the center of all that is rotten with the Church, and publicly calls Pope Leo X the "Antichrist." Leo gives Martin 60 days to appear in Rome and answer charges of heresy. Martin refuses, and the pope excommunicates him—meaning he is no longer considered a Christian.

Thunderstorm

One night, while caught in a thunderstorm so violent that he thinks he might die, Martin prays to God. He vows that if he makes it through the night, he will dedicate his life to Christianity. He survives, and joins the Augustinian order at the monastery in Erfurt.

95 Theses

Martin nails a list of his objections to the Catholic Church's practices to the door of the Castle Church in Wittenberg. The document becomes known as the "95 Theses." Martin hopes and believes his actions will cause the Church to reflect and change course. He does not—at this stage—want to separate from the Church himself.

Early life

Martin Luther is born in Eisleben, Germany. His father, Hans, has a successful copper-mining business, and can pay for his son to receive a great education. Martin studies law at the University of Erfurt but he dislikes it.

1483 **1505** **1510** **1517** **1518** **1520**

Translating the Bible

Thanks to the newly invented printing press, Martin is able to spread his ideas far and wide. He translates the first part of the Bible from Hebrew and Greek into German—something forbidden by the Catholic Church, which felt that only the educated clergy should read the words of God. Martin's translations open the Bible to regular people for the first time.

The Reformation

The Reformation unleashed many ideas about the Christian faith that had been brewing for some time, and it led to a new cultural and religious era in Europe and beyond.

Jan Hus (1369–1415)
Czech philosopher Jan Hus was burned at the stake for advocating reforms very similar to Martin Luther's, and is regarded as a forerunner of Protestant revolt. Unlike Luther, Hus could not rely on the printing press to spread his ideas, nor the support and protection of his local prince.

Henry VIII (1491–1547)
The Reformation came as Henry VIII of England was trying to separate from his wife, as she had not borne him a son. When the pope refused to annul his marriage, Henry declared himself head of the Protestant Anglican Church and divorced her.

Argula von Grumbach (1492–c.1554)
One of Luther's earliest supporters, von Grumbach became the early Reformation's foremost female writer, publishing poems and arguments in defense of Luther and others in the movement.

Fighting for faith

The Church gives Martin one more chance to take back his words, at the Diet (a congregation of officers) in the city of Worms. Martin refuses. His break with the Catholic Church is complete.

Marriage

Martin marries a nun, Katharina von Bora, and they go on to have six children. This is a freedom not allowed under Catholic teaching, which says that clergy are not allowed to marry.

Anti-Semitism

Though initially concerned about the safety of the Jews, Martin turns on them when he realizes that he cannot convert them to his religious ideas. He recommends that Jewish synagogues should be burned, and states that the murder of Jews is justified. His anti-Semitic (anti-Jewish) words are still controversial today.

Death

Martin's protest gradually leads to the emergence of a new branch of Christianity, the Protestant church, and he spends the rest of his life building the "Protestant" movement. He dies of a stroke, aged 62, in Eisleben, the city of his birth.

1521 **1523** **1525** **1543** **1546**

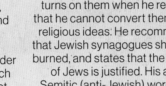

New methods

Irrigation (using channels and reservoirs to supply water to crops) allows farmers to grow crops in drier areas. Farmers grow rice and millet in China. By 3000 BCE, buffalo are used to pull plows (tools used for turning soil before planting seeds).

Fertile Crescent

In the Fertile Crescent (a region in the Middle East), the soil is particularly rich. Sumerian farmers use enslaved people to produce huge amounts of wheat and barley. So much is produced that large numbers of people are able to settle in the first cities.

c.12,000 YA

c.11,000 YA

c.9000 YA

c.3300 BCE

The beginning of farming

Early humans are "hunter gatherers"— they survive by hunting animals and gathering food from wild plants. At the end of the last Ice Age (a long period of cold temperatures), as temperatures grow warmer, some people start growing crops, such as barley and peas. They settle in one place.

Domestication

Sheep and goats are domesticated (tamed) and bred for their wool, meat, and milk. By 10,000 YA, people have domesticated cattle. In the Middle East, donkeys are used to carry things. By 4000 BCE horses are being ridden on the plains of Eurasia.

Farming prospers

In Britain, farming is becoming more efficient. New technology and fertilizers (which improve soil quality) allow farms to produce more food. The growth of towns means there are huge markets for food, and railroads make it easier to transport produce.

Farmers through time

Farmers grow the food that supplies us with the energy and nutrients we need to live. Farming is the world's oldest industry, and farmers began growing crops as long ago as 12,000 YA (years ago), using basic tools. In the modern world, farming uses machinery, fertilizers, and irrigation to meet the needs of the world's growing population.

c.1800

Mechanization

Farmers begin to use machines instead of human labor. Tractors replace horses, and combine harvesters cut crops in the fields. Vast prairie wheat fields in North America provide huge amounts of grain, which is sold all over the world.

New types of crops

Scientists develop new varieties of crops such as wheat and beans, that are designed to meet the demands of a growing population. In Mexico, farmers grow wheat that is disease-resistant and better able to withstand strong winds.

1920

c.1955

Farming on the Nile

In Egypt, the Nile River floods each summer and leaves mineral-rich silt on the land. This silt provides important nutrients that are perfect for growing crops. Farming makes Egypt rich, and pays for the building of beautiful palaces and temples.

c. 3100 BCE

Ancient Greece

Shepherds raise goats and sheep in the mountainous regions of Greece, where the soil is poor. In more fertile areas, farmers grow barley, wheat, olives, and grapes.

c. 800 BCE

The Celts

In what is modern-day France, Britain, and Ireland, the Celts (a group of powerful tribes in central and northern Europe) grow crops in rectangular fields. On small farms, they raise pigs, sheep, and cattle. They store grain in pits sealed with clay, and brew beer from barley.

c. 750 BCE

Making the soil fertile again

Instead of leaving land fallow, farmers in the Netherlands begin to plant turnips, which help restore the soil's fertility. After they are harvested, the turnips can be used as food for farmers' livestock.

1750

Farming revolution

British farmer Jethro Tull, frustrated that planting seeds by hand takes a lot of time, invents a horse-drawn seed drill, which plants seeds efficiently. The seed drill speeds up the farming process, and helps produce more food for Britain's growing population.

1701

The Inca Empire

In the Inca Empire, in South America, farmers grow maize, potatoes, peppers, and tomatoes. In mountainous areas, farmers grow crops on terraces, a system of fields that are cut into hillsides.

c. 1400

Europe in the Middle Ages

Farmers use heavy plows that turn the earth more effectively. They divide their land into three fields. Each year, only two of the fields are sown, while the third field is left fallow (unused) to allow the soil to recover nutrients.

c. 1000 CE

Factory farming

Factory farming, a system where animals are kept indoors in small pens or enclosures, helps farmers produce cheaply large amounts of meat. Though it is financially effective, many people begin to worry about animal welfare.

c. 1960

Moving genes

Scientists develop genetically modified (GM) crops, taking the genes from one plant and inserting them into another plant's DNA in order to make it last longer or taste better. The first product to go on sale is the "Flavr Savr" tomato, engineered to have a longer shelf life.

1994

Veganism

Veganism grows in popularity alongside concerns about animal welfare and the effect of meat production on the environment. Vegans do not eat any meat or dairy products, and do not use any clothing or objects made from animal products. World Vegan Day is launched.

1994

Agricultural engineers

Using computers and Global Positioning Systems (GPS), agricultural engineers plan how best to farm the land. Farming becomes possible in parts of the world that were too arid (dry) or waterlogged.

2001

Going Green

Many farmers produce organic food. This means that they cannot use artificial fertilizers or pesticides (which kill insects). As people worry more about the environment, some farmers use farming methods from the past, which are less harmful to nature.

2020

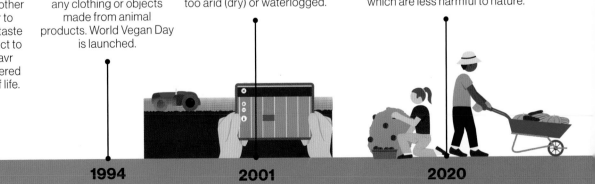

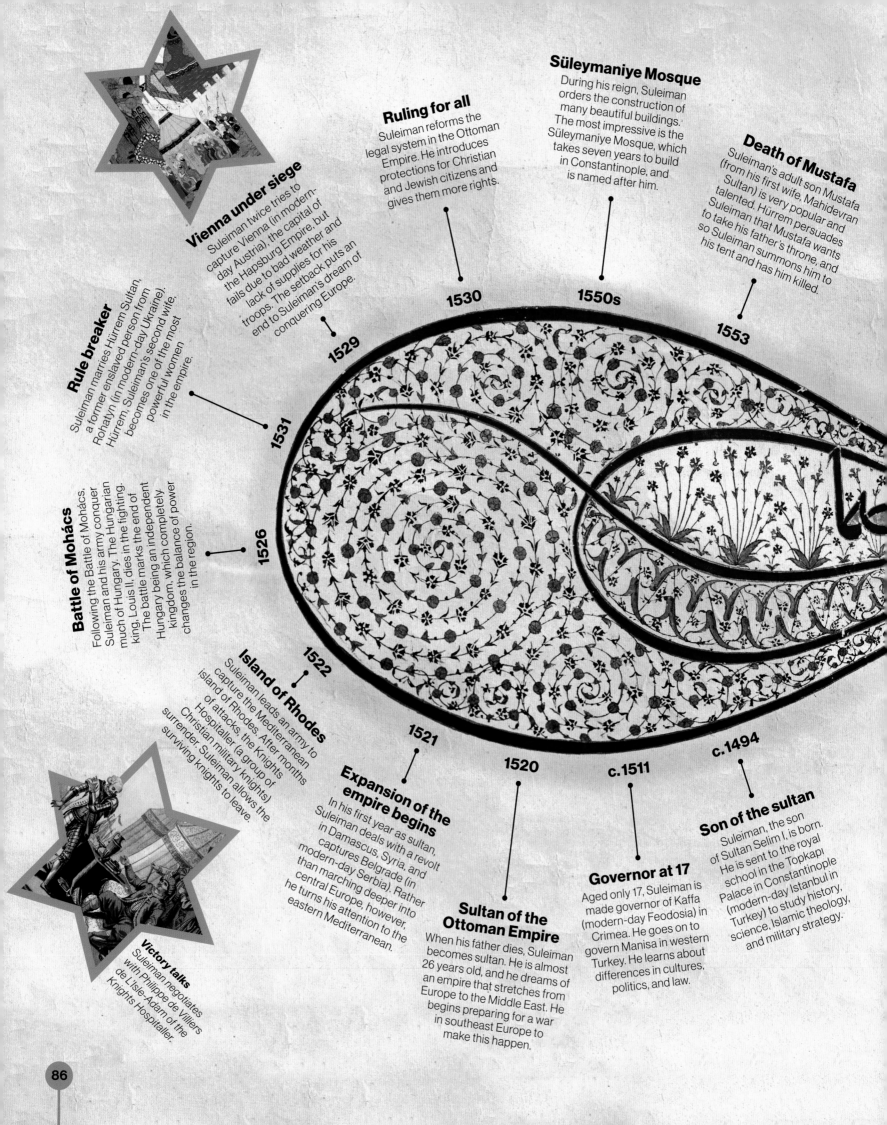

Süleymaniye Mosque
During his reign, Suleiman orders the construction of many beautiful buildings. The most impressive is the Süleymaniye Mosque, which takes seven years to build in Constantinople, and is named after him.

Ruling for all
Suleiman reforms the legal system in the Ottoman Empire. He introduces protections for Christian and Jewish citizens and gives them more rights.

Death of Mustafa
Suleiman's adult son Mustafa (from his first wife, Mahidevran Sultan) is very popular and talented. Hürrem persuades Suleiman that Mustafa wants to take his father's throne, and so Suleiman summons him to his tent and has him killed.

Vienna under siege
Suleiman twice tries to capture Vienna (in modern-day Austria), the capital of the Hapsburg Empire, but fails due to bad weather and lack of supplies for his troops. The setback puts an end to Suleiman's dream of conquering Europe.

Rule breaker
Suleiman marries Hürrem Sultan, a former enslaved person from Rohatyn (in modern-day Ukraine). Hürrem, Suleiman's second wife, becomes one of the most powerful women in the empire.

Battle of Mohács
Following the Battle of Mohács, Suleiman and his army conquer much of Hungary. The Hungarian king, Louis II, dies in the fighting. The battle marks the end of Hungary being an independent kingdom, which completely changes the balance of power in the region.

Island of Rhodes
Suleiman leads an army to capture the Mediterranean island of Rhodes. After months of attacks, the Knights Hospitaller (a group of Christian military knights) surrender. Suleiman allows the surviving knights to leave.

Victory talks
Suleiman negotiates with Philippe de Villiers de L'Isle-Adam of the Knights Hospitaller.

Expansion of the empire begins
In his first year as sultan, Suleiman deals with a revolt in Damascus, Syria, and captures Belgrade (in modern-day Serbia). Rather than marching deeper into central Europe, however, he turns his attention to the eastern Mediterranean.

Sultan of the Ottoman Empire
When his father dies, Suleiman becomes sultan. He is almost 26 years old, and he dreams of an empire that stretches from Europe to the Middle East. He begins preparing for a war in southeast Europe to make this happen.

Governor at 17
Aged only 17, Suleiman is made governor of Kaffa (modern-day Feodosia) in Crimea. He goes on to govern Manisa in western Turkey. He learns about differences in cultures, politics, and law.

Son of the sultan
Suleiman, the son of Sultan Selim I, is born. He is sent to the royal school in the Topkapı Palace in Constantinople (modern-day Istanbul in Turkey) to study history, science, Islamic theology, and military strategy.

1553
1550s
1531
1530
1529
1526
1522
1521
1520
c.1511
c.1494

Suleiman's *tughra*

The ruler of the Ottoman Empire had an official signature called a *tughra*. It was applied by a special court artist to all official documents and letters. It could not be easily copied, because it was a unique symbol. When translated, Suleiman's *tughra* reads "the one who is always victorious," which is fitting for the many achievements of his long reign.

Ottoman rulers

Established about 1300, the Ottoman Empire became one of the largest empires the world has ever seen. It lasted for more than 600 years.

Osman I (c.1258–c.1326)
Known as the father of the Ottoman Empire, Osman I set up a small state made up of lands he had seized from the Byzantine Empire. This would grow in time into the Ottoman Empire.

Hürrem Sultan (c.1505–1558)
Hürrem Sultan held a prominent position during Suleiman's rule. She discussed matters of state with foreign leaders, and commissioned new buildings. She was accused of plotting the downfall of others to ensure her sons would succeed to the throne.

Abdul Hamid II (1842–1918)
The last powerful Ottoman sultan, Abdul Hamid was removed from the throne after an uprising. He had tried to reform the empire, but ended up being a harsh and violent leader.

Poet

Suleiman writes about 2,000 *ghazals* (short love poems), showing his skills as a poet. Many of them are dedicated to his wife, Hürrem. A beautifully illustrated copy of his work is published shortly before his death.

1566

A final mission

Aged 71, Suleiman leads his army to fight the Hapsburgs in Hungary, but he dies of a heart attack before the battle. News of his death is kept quiet, so his troops do not lose their focus. His heart is buried in his last battlefield, and his body is buried in Constantinople.

1566

Suleiman I

Sultan of the Ottoman Empire, Suleiman I (c.1494–1566) ruled over much of southeast Europe, the Middle East, and North Africa. Known as Suleiman the Lawgiver to his own people, and as Suleiman the Magnificent to those outside the Ottoman lands, he is remembered today as an intelligent ruler who promoted literature, the arts, and architecture throughout his empire.

ATAHUALPA

The last emperor of the Inca Empire

Atahualpa (c. 1501–1533) seized power from his brother to make himself Inca emperor, only to find himself immediately facing an invading force of Spanish soldiers. That meeting between the Spanish and the Inca soldiers, high in the Andes of Peru, turned out to be the beginning of the end for the once-powerful Inca Empire.

Brothers at war

In about **1525**, Huayna Capac, ruler of the vast Inca Empire that stretched from Ecuador to Chile in South America, suddenly died. Huáscar, the elder of his two sons, became emperor. Atahualpa, the younger of Huayna Capac's sons, was said to be his favorite, and Huáscar saw him as a threat. While Huáscar ruled from the capital, Cuzco, in southern Peru, Atahualpa established a northern power base for himself in Quito, in modern-day Ecuador. In **1529**, the two brothers began fighting a violent and destructive civil war. In **April 1532**, Atahualpa's forces won a crushing victory over Huáscar's army. After capturing Huáscar and taking control of Cuzco, Atahualpa was proclaimed *Sapa Inca* (Inca emperor) in **May**.

The Spanish arrive

A few months earlier, the Spanish soldier and adventurer Francisco Pizarro lands on the coast of Peru. He is on his third expedition to discover a new land that some people believe to be rich in gold. Pizarro begins marching inland in **September 1532** with a force of 106 soldiers and 62 cavalry (soldiers on horses). When Atahualpa hears that a group of strangers is approaching, he sends some of his troops to investigate. They report back that the Spanish force is too small to pose a threat. Atahualpa invites Pizarro and his troops to Cajamarca, a small town close to where he is camped, with his own army of 80,000 soldiers.

Invitation to a feast

Pizarro arrives in Cajamarca on

deserted, as most of its inhabitants are in Atahualpa's camp. Pizarro sends a message inviting Atahualpa to a feast the next day. Atahualpa accepts. Leaving most of his army behind, Atahualpa is carried into the town on a litter (a ceremonial chair) lined with parrot feathers. He is accompanied by 5,000 soldiers carrying ceremonial battle-axes. The central square, or plaza, where the meeting is due to take place, is empty. Pizarro has hidden his troops, armed with muskets (guns) and four cannons, in the surrounding buildings.

Caught in a trap

Vincente de Valverde, a Catholic priest, appears with an interpreter. He urges Atahualpa to become a Christian and hands him a prayer book. Atahualpa examines it briefly, before throwing it to the ground. He angrily tells the Spanish to leave. Pizarro

orders his soldiers to open fire from their hiding places around the plaza. The Incas have never encountered firearms or seen horses charge before, and are terrified. The battle lasts less than an hour. Most of the Incas are killed or flee, and Atahualpa himself is taken prisoner. No Spanish soldiers are killed. On **November 17**, the Spaniards ransack Atahualpa's camp, stealing his gold, silver, and emeralds.

Prison and execution

Pizarro holds Atahualpa hostage, but allows him to keep the title of emperor. Fearing that Pizarro will use Huáscar to remove him from power, Atahualpa has his brother executed. In return for his own life and freedom, he makes an offer to the Spaniards—he will have his followers fill a large room with gold and silver. It takes about three months to collect the treasure from across the empire. After it has been collected, Pizarro has no intention of freeing the Inca emperor. Instead, he

HUÁSCAR

organizes an unofficial trial. Atahualpa is found guilty of stirring up rebellion and murdering his brother. He is sentenced to death. The usual method of execution for a heathen (non-Christian) is to be burned at the stake. At the last moment, Atahualpa agrees to become a Christian, but his conversion is not enough to save him from the death sentence. He is strangled on **August 29, 1533**.

Aftermath

In **1535**, Pizarro establishes a new capital at Lima. It will take about 40 years for the Spanish to fully conquer the Inca Empire. The language and culture of the Inca people survives the Spanish conquest, and continues to play an important role in modern-day Peru, Ecuador, and Bolivia.

Ivan the Terrible

Czar Ivan IV of Russia (1530–1584) is known to history as Ivan the Terrible, though his nickname in Russian, *Grozny*, is closer in meaning to "formidable." At first, Ivan ruled fairly and well, and he introduced much-needed reforms. He later became suspicious, unpredictable, and violent, ultimately leaving Russia with an uncertain future.

St. Basil's Cathedral

Famous for its colorful onion domes, St. Basil's Cathedral is Moscow's best-known landmark. A popular (though untrue) legend says Ivan IV had the architect blinded so he could not build another like it. Each of its dome-topped chapels honor a battle in Ivan's five-year struggle against Kazan.

Livonian War

Ivan invades Livonia (modern-day Estonia and Latvia). He starts a war with neighboring Sweden, Poland, and Lithuania, which lasts until 1582. This drains Russia of money and soldiers.

1558

St. Basil's Cathedral

Work begins on St. Basil's Cathedral in Moscow, built on Ivan's orders to commemorate his victory over Kazan.

1555

Reforming czar

Ivan introduces a parliament called the Zemsky Sobor ("Assembly of the Land"). He makes a number of reforms to the legal system, and orders the first printing press to be set up in Moscow.

c. 1549

1552

Wars of conquest

Ivan conquers the khanates (kingdoms) of Kazan and Astrakhan, surviving parts of Genghis Khan's Mongol Empire. His conquests double the size of Russia, extending its control as far as the Caspian Sea.

Czar of All the Russias

When he is 16, Ivan is crowned as the "Czar of All the Russias"—the first time the title is used ("czar," meaning "emperor," is the Russian form of "caesar"). He marries Anastasia Romanovna.

1547

Grand Prince

Ivan is born just outside Moscow, the son of Basil III, Grand Prince of Moscow. When the Duchy of Moscow. Ivan becomes Grand Prince at the age of three. Basil dies in 1533, Ivan becomes Grand Prince.

1530

Personality change

With Russia facing the problems of drought and famine, as well as foreign invasions, the pressure begins to mount on Ivan. His wife Anastasia dies, possibly by poisoning. This loss affects Ivan deeply, and, along with the other stresses in his life, causes him to become more suspicious and irrational.

The Time of Troubles

After Feodor I's death, Russia was plunged into a period of political chaos known as the "Time of Troubles." Stability returned when the first Romanov czar took the throne.

Boris Godunov (c.1551–1605)

A former bodyguard to Ivan IV, Boris Godunov seized the throne on Feodor I's death in 1598. His enemies accused him of murdering Ivan IV's youngest son, Prince Dmitri. Just before Godunov's death from a stroke, a man claiming to be Dmitri appeared on the scene.

The False Dmitris

Dmitri became czar but didn't last long—he was an impostor. As rival noble families fought for power, a second False Dmitri emerged but failed to win the throne. Polish and Swedish armies invaded Russia, and occupied Moscow. Russia was in chaos.

Michael I (1595–1645)

Order returned in 1613. An army of nobles and merchants expelled the invaders, and 16-year-old Michael Romanov, related through marriage to Ivan IV, became czar. He was the first czar of the House of Romanov, which ruled Russia until 1917.

Reign of terror

Ivan takes a large area of Russia under his direct rule and orders his bodyguards to terrorize and execute anyone suspected of disloyalty. They wear black and carry a dog's head emblem as a symbol of their loyalty to Ivan and their ability to sniff out enemies and rip them to shreds.

Murderous attack

After a family dispute with his eldest son, Prince Ivan, Ivan IV flies into a temper and attacks him with a piece of metal. His son dies from the blows a few days later to Ivan's intense grief. In one moment of madness, the country has increased the instability of the country by killing his son and heir.

Massacre of Novgorod

Ivan suspects that the leaders of the historic city of Novgorod are conspiring with Lithuania to leave Russia. He orders his army to destroy the city and execute its inhabitants. The attack and massacre last five weeks and leave thousands of citizens dead.

Death of Ivan

While playing chess, Ivan suffers a stroke, and dies. His second son succeeds him, as Feodor I, but he is a weak ruler and dies childless in 1598. This leads to a huge succession crisis known as the "Time of Troubles."

1560

1565

1570

1581

1584

Oda Nobunaga

A Japanese samurai (elite warrior) and *daimyo* (clan lord), Oda Nobunaga (1534–1582) used diplomacy as well as effective military tactics to take control of central Japan. His reign established strong government and paved the way for his successors to unite the entire country.

> "The nation under a single sword."
> **Oda Nobunaga's personal motto**

Oda clan crest
Many powerful samurai families had a crest or *mon*. The Oda clan *mon* was modeled on a quince fruit.

Born into power
Oda Nobunaga is born into a powerful family in the Owari Province of central Japan. His father, Oda Nobuhide, is a minor official of the *shogun* (military dictator). Nobunaga is nicknamed "*Owari no Ōutsuke*" ("The Great Fool of Owari") because of his rebellious personality.

1534

Marriage
In spite of a long-standing feud between Nobuhide and Saitō Dōsan (*daimyo* of a neighboring province), Nobunaga marries Dōsan's daughter Nōhime. Nobunaga describes Nōhime as having "the mind of a genius."

1549

Eliminating rivals
When Nobuhide dies suddenly, Nobunaga faces rivalry from within the Oda clan for power. He sets about eliminating his opponents, and shows his ruthlessness in 1557 when he has his younger brother murdered in order to seize power.

1551

A daring attack
Now in control of a united Owari Province, Nobunaga sets about extending his power. He leads an army of just 2,000 in a surprise attack on the 25,000-strong army of Imagawa Yoshimoto, a rival *daimyo*, as it marches on Kyoto, the Japanese capital. The attack is a success. Yoshimoto is killed, and his army weakened.

1560

Forming alliances
After the Kyoto success, many rival *daimyo* pledge allegiance to Nobunaga. The powerful warlord Tokugawa Ieyasu joins forces with Nobunaga, ending decades of hostility between their two clans.

1562

March on Kyoto
Nobunaga's armies enter Kyoto, and place the weak Ashikaga Yoshiaki as a *shogun* under Nobunaga's control. Nobunaga soon falls out with Yoshiaki, and five years later drives him from Kyoto.

1568

Battle of Anegawa
An attempt by Nobunaga to take lands from the Azai and Asakura infuriates them. A battle ensues, with terrible bloodshed. Using massive firepower, the allied forces of Nobunaga and Ieyasu emerge triumphant.

1570

Economic development

As he gains control, Nobunaga sets about economic reform. He promotes business by breaking up powerful associations that had restricted it. He also builds roads and bridges, making it easier to transport armies and goods.

Takeda Shingen

The formidable warlord Takeda Shingen is the only *daimyo* capable of halting Nobunaga. Shingen's cavalry overruns Ieyasu's army at Mikatagahara, but Shingen dies soon afterward.

Battle of Nagashino

Nobunaga clashes again with the Takeda armies at Nagashino Castle, but this time Nobunaga's ingenious use of fighters armed with arquebuses (portable, long-barreled guns) destroys the enemy. Nobunaga emerges all-powerful.

A cultural age

At Azuchi near Kyoto, Nobunaga starts building an exquisite, state-of-the-art castle to impress his enemies. He also takes a great interest in European culture, becoming one of the first Japanese people to wear Western clothes, and allows the first Christian church in Kyoto to be built.

Death

One of Nobunaga's allies, Akechi Mitsuhide, betrays him. While Nobunaga is holding a tea ceremony in a Kyoto temple, Mitsuhide's soldiers set fire to the building. Nobunaga kills himself rather than fall into enemy hands.

Warriors of the shogun era

After Nobunaga's death, two former allies completed his goal of uniting Japan's warring clans. The *shogun* era came to an end after imperial rule was restored in 1868. The samurai class was soon abolished.

Toyotomi Hideyoshi (1537–1598)
Nobunaga's successor, Hideyoshi was Japan's second "great unifier." Many of the temples still standing in Kyoto date from his rule.

Tokugawa Ieyasu (1543–1616)
Ieyasu completed the unification of Japan and set up the Tokugawa shogunate, which ruled Japan from 1600 until 1868. He established Edo (now called Tokyo) as its new capital.

Saigō Takamori (1828–1877)
After helping to overthrow the Tokugawa shogunate, Saigō led dissatisfied samurais in the failed Satsuma Rebellion. He is often called "the last true samurai."

1570 **1573** **1575** **1576** **1582**

Mr. WILLIAM
SHAKESPEARE

Generally considered to be the greatest writer in the English language, English playwright, poet, and actor William Shakespeare (1564–1616) wrote 37 plays, 154 sonnets, and two narrative poems. His work introduced the world to numerous unforgettable characters, and even shaped the way we use English to this day.

LONDON
Printed by Isaac Jaggard, and Edward Blount. 1623.

Opening scene 1564

William Shakespeare is born in Stratford-upon-Avon, England. He is one of eight children born to Mary Arden, an heiress from a wealthy family, and John Shakespeare, a well-off glove-maker.

c.1571 Education

William begins his education around age six or seven. He attends grammar school, where he studies Greek classics and dramas in Latin. He leaves school at about the age of 15.

Marriage and children 1582

When he is 18, William marries Anne Hathaway. They have three children within a few years—a daughter Susanna, and twins, Judith and Hamnet. We do not know when William begins writing and acting, but we do know that he moves to London at some point during the 1580s.

1592 "Upstart crow"

William's writing is beginning to make waves in London, but perhaps not the ones he wants. He receives his first review from rival playwright Robert Greene who insults him by calling him an "upstart crow," and accuses him of not being at the same level as university-educated playwrights, such as Greene himself.

Tragedy and comedies 1596

William's 11-year-old son Hamnet dies. The death devastates him, but back in London, his career is really beginning to take off. His early plays about English history, and his comedies *The Comedy of Errors* (1594) and *A Midsummer Night's Dream* (1595) are huge hits.

1598 Becoming famous

Some of William's plays are published, including his hit historical dramas *Richard II* (1595–1596) and *Richard III* (1592), as well as *Love's Labour's Lost* (1595–1596). His work attracts royal attention and he even acts in several performances before Queen Elizabeth I.

The Globe 1599

William's theater company builds its own theater called the Globe in London to stage his plays. He begins work on what will become *Hamlet* (1600), perhaps his most famous work, about a young prince seeking revenge on his uncle for killing his father.

1603 Royal approval

William's theater company is awarded a royal patent by the new king, James I, an indication of how well they are known and how highly regarded they are. William writes several plays, notably *King Lear* (1605–1606) and *Macbeth* (1606).

Sonnets 1609

William publishes 154 sonnets (poems of 14 lines, with a rhyming scheme). They cover topics such as love, time, and death. Many are addressed to either a "dark lady," a "fair youth," or a rival poet. It is not clear if these are real people, and if the "I" in the poems represents William's own feelings.

1613 Catastrophe

The Globe burns to the ground after a prop cannon sets fire to the thatch roof. The company rebuilds the theater. The lost play *Cardenio* (1611–1612) and *The Two Noble Kinsmen* (1613–1614) are Shakespeare's last contributions to the stage, co-written with another famous playwright of the time, John Fletcher.

Death 1616

William makes his will a month before he dies, in which he states he is in "perfect health," and leaves most of what he owns to his daughter Susanna. There is no record of what caused his death, but it is likely that it was the result of a short illness.

Trailblazers

Actors have trod the boards for centuries bringing Shakespeare's work to new audiences, but some stand out and are remembered for their talent and personalities, and for challenging the conventions of their day.

Margaret Hughes (c.1645–1719)
During Shakespeare's time, women were not allowed to act, so female roles were played by boys or young men. That said, there were a few ground-breaking women who ignored the standards of the times. English actor Margaret Hughes was one of the first to enjoy a successful stage career.

Ira Aldridge (1807–1867)
African American actor Ira Aldridge was one of the 19th century's best actors. He was primarily a Shakespearean actor, performing in many of the playwright's roles in his 43-year career. He won more awards and honors than any other actor of his time.

Paul Robeson (1898–1976)
Paul Robeson blended his interests in singing, acting, and activism together throughout his life. In 1943, he became the first African American to lead a Broadway production, when he took the lead role in *Othello*. It became the most successful Shakespeare production in Broadway history.

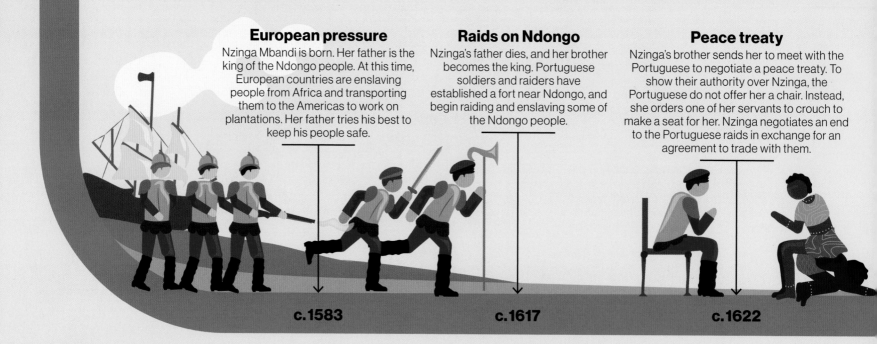

European pressure

Nzinga Mbandi is born. Her father is the king of the Ndongo people. At this time, European countries are enslaving people from Africa and transporting them to the Americas to work on plantations. Her father tries his best to keep his people safe.

c. 1583

Raids on Ndongo

Nzinga's father dies, and her brother becomes the king. Portuguese soldiers and raiders have established a fort near Ndongo, and begin raiding and enslaving some of the Ndongo people.

c. 1617

Peace treaty

Nzinga's brother sends her to meet with the Portuguese to negotiate a peace treaty. To show their authority over Nzinga, the Portuguese do not offer her a chair. Instead, she orders one of her servants to crouch to make a seat for her. Nzinga negotiates an end to the Portuguese raids in exchange for an agreement to trade with them.

c. 1622

African rulers

Africa has produced many great leaders with compelling stories that often do not get as much attention as they deserve.

King Ezana of Axum (c. 303–c. 350)

Ezana ruled over Axum (a region made up of parts of modern-day Ethiopia and Eritrea). He converted to Christianity as a child, and Axum became the first Christian kingdom in Africa as a result. He had numerous stone pillars called stelae made that recorded his achievements.

Queen Amina of Zazzau (c. 1533–1610)

Queen Amina was a skilled military leader who expanded the city-state of Zazzau (in modern-day Nigeria). To protect Zazzau from its enemies, Amina built huge walls around each of her military camps. Some of these walls are still standing today.

Shaka Zulu (c. 1787–1828)

Shaka Zulu emerged as a strong and skilled chief of the Zulu Empire (in modern-day South Africa). Shaka added land from conquered tribes into his empire. He got along with the European powers in the area, but many of his people grew tired of his rule. He was eventually assassinated by his half-brother.

Nzinga Mbandi

Queen Nzinga Mbandi (c. 1583–1663) ruled the kingdoms of Ndongo and Matamba (in modern-day Angola). Mbandi spent most of her reign defending her land from Portuguese colonization, and from raiders trying to enslave her people.

c. 1647

c. 1646

Unlikely allies

Nzinga's forces, along with her Dutch allies, claim a huge victory against the Portuguese. The following year, Portugal calls in reinforcements from their colony in Brazil, and fight back by expelling the Dutch. Nzinga's forces must fight on, without Dutch help.

Warrior queen

With the help of the Imbangala and the Dutch, Nzinga has a better chance against the Portuguese. Even though she is well past fighting age, Nzinga personally leads her troops into battles.

Regent

Nzinga's brother dies. As his heir is too young to rule, Nzinga rules in his place as regent. Some of her tribespeople disagree with this decision.

1624

Becoming queen

The heir to the throne dies, and Nzinga decides to rule herself. Some believe that she had a hand in the heir's death and others feel that a woman should not rule, but she has support from many of her people.

c.1624

c.1626

Dutch alliance

Nzinga allies with the Dutch, Portugal's European rival in the area. Nzinga begins to prepare for an attack on the Portuguese with Dutch help, which she hopes will help her reclaim Ndongo.

1641

Military moves

In Matamba, the Imbangala, a group of African soldiers who had been trained by the Portuguese, join Nzinga. She declares herself the queen of Matamba after conquering the region.

1630

Betrayal

The Portuguese break the treaty, and attack Nzinga's people, who are forced to flee Ndongo to the nearby kingdom of Matamba. This marks the beginning of what will be a 30-year war between Nzinga and Portugal.

War continues

The back-and-forth war between the Portuguese and Nzinga's forces rumbles on. Though both sides win important victories, neither is able to beat the other completely and to bring the war to an end.

1648

Peace again

Nzinga's refusal to back down eventually tires the Portuguese armies. They sign a peace treaty with Nzinga to end the war and return Ndongo to her. She rules both Ndongo and Matamba until her death in 1663.

1656–1663

"A teardrop on the cheek of time."

Indian artist and poet Rabindranath Tagore describing the Taj Mahal

Joy
Shahab ud-Din Muhammad Khurram, or Khurram (meaning "joy") for short, is born in Lahore (in modern-day Pakistan). He is the third son of Emperor Jahangir of the Mughal Empire—an Islamic dynasty that holds power in regions that today are parts of northern India, Pakistan, and Afghanistan.

1592

A love match
Arjumand Banu Begum is born into a Persian noble family in Agra in India. She becomes engaged to Prince Khurram when she is 14 and he is 15— it is love at first sight.

1593

Children
The couple have their first child, a daughter named Jahanara. Dara Shikoh, a son, is born the following year, and another son—the future emperor Aurangzeb—is born in 1618. In total, they will go on to have 14 children, though only seven will survive into adulthood.

Glory of the World
Emperor Jahangir sends Prince Khurram to put down a rebellion on the southern border of the empire. The prince is victorious, and his father grants him the name "Shah Jahan," meaning "Glory of the World."

Marriage
Court astrologers counsel the prince to wait five years for a particular favorable date before marrying Arjumand. When the day arrives, in 1612, she becomes Prince Khurram's second wife. He all but forgets his other wife, and gives Arjumand the name Mumtaz Mahal, which means "Jewel of the Palace."

1612

Close couple
The couple are inseparable. Mumtaz travels with her husband on military campaigns throughout India, despite often being pregnant. Her husband values her opinion, and often consults her on state matters.

1616

1617

1614

Shah Jahan and Mumtaz Mahal

Shah Jahan (1592–1666) was the fifth Mughal Emperor of India. His marriage to Mumtaz Mahal (1593–1631) was a love story uncommon for the time. Devastated by her early death, he built the Taj Mahal as a monument to her.

Game of thrones
Jahan becomes the next Mughal Emperor upon the death of his father. He sets about eliminating his chief rivals, imprisons his stepmother, and has his brother and two nephews executed.

Mumtaz's home
Beautiful architecture adorns Agra Fort, where Mumtaz had her quarters.

Ill health
Shah Jahan never fully recovers from the death of Mumtaz. Military losses and poor economic choices lead to huge debts. He can no longer afford to pay his troops and generals, and each of his four sons move in for a chance to rule the vast Mughal Empire themselves.

Last years
Shah Jahan is imprisoned in Agra from July 1658, as a civil war rages between his sons. From there he can see the Taj Mahal. When he dies in 1666 he is buried in the monument, next to Mumtaz.

1658

Vast wealth
Shah Jahan showers Empress Mumtaz with great riches. Her home is decorated with gold, precious stones, and rosewater fountains. No other Indian empress received as much money for her own expenses as Shah Jahan gives to Mumtaz Mahal.

Death of Mumtaz
Mumtaz dies giving birth to their 14th child. Grief-stricken, Shah Jahan orders a beautiful mausoleum made of shimmering white marble to hold her remains, and names it in her honor: the Taj Mahal. It will take about 20 years to complete.

1628

1629

1658

1631

1575 | 1600 | 1625 | 1650 | 1675 | 1700

Artemisia Gentileschi (1593–c.1656)

Pocahontas (c.1595–1617)

Aphra Behn (c.1640–1689)

Isaac Newton (1642–1727)

Juana Inés de la Cruz (c.1648–1695)

Artemisia Gentileschi to Ada Lovelace

In science, politics, and the arts, the period between Artemisia Gentileschi and Ada Lovelace was one of revolutionary change. George Washington led the armies that won the American Revolution and became the first president of the United States of America. Simón Bolívar fought to liberate much of South America from Spanish colonial rule. And the fossil-hunting work of Mary Anning shook up the way people thought about prehistoric life.

1725	1750	1775	1800	1825	1850	1875

Catherine the Great (1729–1796)

George Washington (1732–1799)

Toussaint L'Ouverture (c.1743–1803)

Jean-Paul Marat (1743–1793)

Olaudah Equiano (1745–1797)

Olympe de Gouges (1748–1793)

King Louis XVI (1754–1793)

Queen Marie Antoinette (1755–1793)

Wolfgang Amadeus Mozart (1756–1791)

Maximilien Robespierre (1758–1794)

Mary Wollstonecraft (1759–1797)

Wang Zhen Yi (1768–1797)

Napoleon Bonaparte (1769–1821)

Daniel O'Connell (1775–1847)

Ching Shih (c.1775–1844)

Elizabeth Fry (1780–1845)

Simón Bolívar (1783–1830)

Sacagawea (c.1788–1812)

Charles Babbage (1791–1871)

Policarpa Salavarrieta (c.1795–1817)

Mary Anning (1799–1847)

George Sand (1804–1876)

Ada Lovelace (1815–1852)

Artemisia Gentileschi

Italian painter Artemisia Gentileschi (1593–c.1656) made a successful career for herself at a time when it was extremely difficult for women to become professional artists. Though she was well-known in her own day, she was forgotten for centuries. Her work is beginning to receive praise again.

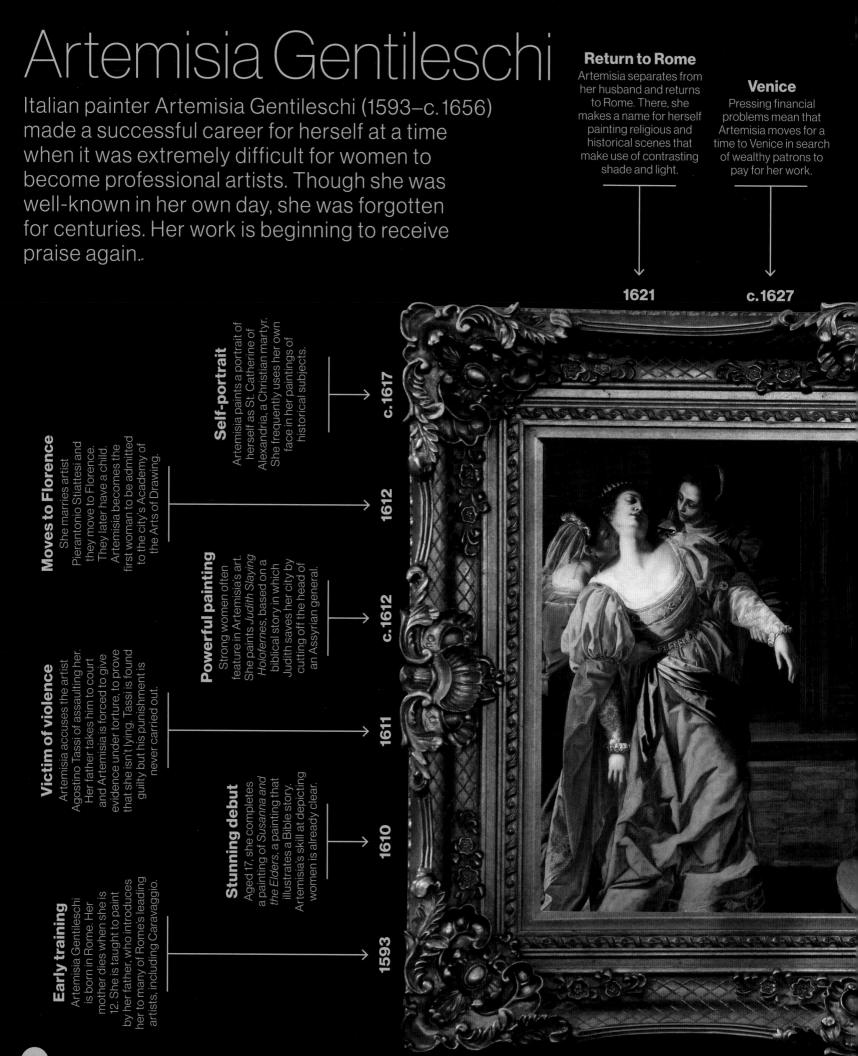

Return to Rome
Artemisia separates from her husband and returns to Rome. There, she makes a name for herself painting religious and historical scenes that make use of contrasting shade and light.

1621

Venice
Pressing financial problems mean that Artemisia moves for a time to Venice in search of wealthy patrons to pay for her work.

c.1627

Self-portrait
Artemisia paints a portrait of herself as St. Catherine of Alexandria, a Christian martyr. She frequently uses her own face in her paintings of historical subjects.

c.1617

Moves to Florence
She marries artist Pierantonio Stiattesi and they move to Florence. They later have a child. Artemisia becomes the first woman to be admitted to the city's Academy of the Arts of Drawing.

1612

Powerful painting
Strong women often feature in Artemisia's art. She paints *Judith Slaying Holofernes*, based on a biblical story in which Judith saves her city by cutting off the head of an Assyrian general.

c.1612

Victim of violence
Artemisia accuses the artist Agostino Tassi of assaulting her. Her father takes him to court and Artemisia is forced to give evidence under torture, to prove that she isn't lying. Tassi is found guilty but his punishment is never carried out.

1611

Stunning debut
Aged 17, she completes a painting of *Susanna and the Elders*, a painting that illustrates a Bible story. Artemisia's skill at depicting women is already clear.

1610

Early training
Artemisia Gentileschi is born in Rome. Her mother dies when she is 12. She is taught to paint by her father, who introduces her to many of Rome's leading artists, including Caravaggio.

1593

Rome and Naples

After living in Rome for a time, Artemisia settles in Naples. She sets up her own successful workshop there— and she receives many commissions to produce new works.

Travels to England

She travels to England to join her father, who is employed as court painter to King Charles I. *Self-Portrait as the Allegory of Painting*, from around this time, shows her painting at her easel, palette in one hand, and her paintbrush in the other.

Death in Naples

The date of her death is uncertain, but Artemisia may have died in the devastating plague that swept through the city of Naples in 1656, killing much of the population.

c.1630

1638

c.1656

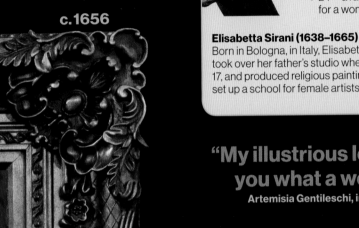

Out of the shadows

Artemisia was not the only artist whose work was influenced by Caravaggio, the master of light and shade.

Caravaggio (1571–1610)
Caravaggio was the most influential painter of his time. Originally from Milan, his work made him famous in Rome, but he had to flee in 1606 after killing a man in a fight.

Judith Leyster (1609–1660)
Judith Leyster was noted for her varied scenes of daily life. Born in Haarlem (in the modern-day Netherlands), she was admitted to the town's guild of painters at the age of 24—a rare achievement for a woman of that time.

Elisabetta Sirani (1638–1665)
Born in Bologna, in Italy, Elisabetta Sirani took over her father's studio when she was 17, and produced religious paintings. She set up a school for female artists in the city.

> "My illustrious lordship, I'll show you what a woman can do."
>
> **Artemisia Gentileschi, in a letter to a client (1649)**

POCAHONTAS

The Native American woman who helped end a war

Daughter of the chief of the Native American Powhatan people, Pocahontas (c.1595–1617) lived in what is modern-day Virginia (in the eastern US). During a time of great hostility between Native Americans and English settlers, her friendship with some of the settlers helped to bring about a short period of peace.

Jamestown colony

In **1607**, 500 English colonists arrived in Virginia with the intention of building a fort on the James River. Led by a soldier and explorer named John Smith, the settlers established a colony called "Jamestown". The area was already occupied by the Powhatan alliance, made up of about 30 different Native American tribes who had lived there for many years. Tensions soon arose because the local tribes felt threatened by the colonists. Most of the colonists were not adventurers or explorers, but skilled workers, such as blacksmiths or carpenters. The majority did not know how to farm, fish, or hunt for themselves. When the colonists demanded food and supplies from the Powhatan people, the Powhatan began to resent the presence of the colonists.

Pocahontas and John Smith

Pocahontas (birth name Matoaka), the daughter of Chief Powhatan, befriends the settlers, forming a friendship with John Smith. However, relations between the Powhatan people and the settlers break down. When the English colonists begin to kidnap members of the Powhatan tribes, the tribes retaliate. They capture some of the colonists and steal their weapons. According to Smith's own account, in **1607**, Pocahontas saves his life when he is captured by Chief Powhatan and is about to be executed. However, many historians doubt Smith's account and suggest that Chief Powhatan's intention is, in fact, to make Smith a sub-chief of the Powhatans. The "execution" is part of a ceremony, and not an attempt to kill him. It is also possible that Smith makes up the story to portray himself as a heroic settler facing up to a dangerous situation.

War breaks out

In **1609**, Chief Powhatan offers Smith the title of chief of one of his villages. Smith refuses, declaring his allegiance to King James I of England. Attempting to win Chief Powhatan's favour, Smith gives the chief a crown, signifying that the chief would be a subject of the king. Chief Powhatan rejects this deal and decides to stop trading with the colonists. They suffer starvation without access to corn and other food supplies. By spring **1610** their numbers have shrunk to around 100. More English soldiers and colonists arrive. They are more aggressive and have been commanded to be less diplomatic. They wage war against the Powhatan people and over the next four years, kill or capture entire tribes. The conflict becomes known as the First Anglo-Powhatan War.

Peace of Pocahontas

In **1613**, midway through the war, the settlers kidnap Pocahontas for ransom. While she is imprisoned, she meets John Rolfe, a tobacco farmer, and they form a relationship. Pocahontas is freed in **1614** after her father pays a ransom, and she then returns to Jamestown with Rolfe and lives with the colonists. There, Pocahontas is baptised a Christian, and dresses in an English manner. She is given a Christian name, Rebecca.
In **1614**, Pocahontas marries Rolfe, and the following year gives birth to a son, Thomas. Some historians think the marriage between Rolfe and Pocahontas only takes place because the English colonists want to set up an alliance with the Powhatan people, and the marriage is used later to justify the conquest of North America by Europeans. In any case, Pocahontas helps to bring the fighting between the settlers and the Powhatan people to an end, and the following eight years become known as the "Peace of Pocahontas". As a result of his marriage to Pocahontas, Rolfe learns how to cure tobacco and soon establishes a lucrative tobacco trade in Virginia.

In England

In **1616**, Pocahontas, who is now known as Lady Rebecca Rolfe, travels to England with some of the colonists. There, she is presented as proof of good relations between the colonists and the Native Americans. During her stay, Pocahontas is given the status of a visiting ambassador, and she meets important figures, such as King James I, Queen Anne, and the Bishop of London. As she sets off on her journey home in **1617**, Pocahontas falls ill and dies, aged only 21. Her sister and brother-in-law, who had accompanied her on the trip, insist she has been poisoned by the English.

The aftermath

Following Pocahontas' death, the Powhatan people find themselves under growing pressure from the colonists to abandon their traditions and become Christians (because the colonists believe their culture is superior to that of the Powhatan tribes). When Chief Powhatan dies in **1618**, relations between the settlers and the Native Americans once again become strained. In **1622**, the Powhatan people lead an attack on the English colonists that kills a quarter of the settler population. War continues intermittently for another ten years before a peace treaty is called in **1632**. An uprising in **1644** leads to a third war that lasts two years. In **1646**, a peace treaty is signed that relegates the Powhatan people to small areas (reservations) and makes them subjects of the English king. Many Powhatan tribes die out, and most of the remaining tribes are forced to sell their land in the 19th century, as a result of poverty. Two tribes refuse – the Pamunkey and Mattaponi – and continue to this day to control the small reservations that they were granted by the colonists in the 17th century.

Saving John Smith

John Smith wrote that Pocahontas saved his life by placing her own head on his at the moment he was about to be executed by the Powhatan people.

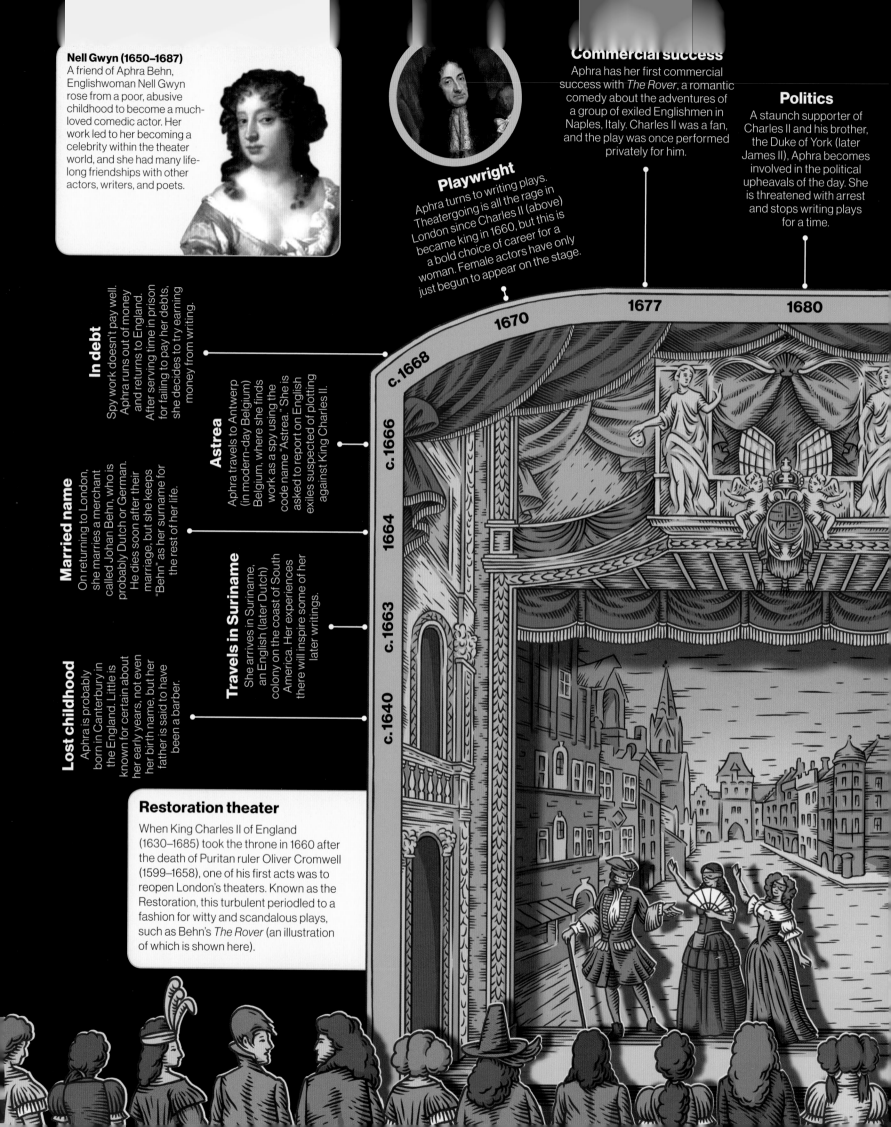

Nell Gwyn (1650–1687)
A friend of Aphra Behn, Englishwoman Nell Gwyn rose from a poor, abusive childhood to become a much-loved comedic actor. Her work led to her becoming a celebrity within the theater world, and she had many life-long friendships with other actors, writers, and poets.

Commercial success
Aphra has her first commercial success with *The Rover*, a romantic comedy about the adventures of a group of exiled Englishmen in Naples, Italy. Charles II was a fan, and the play was once performed privately for him.

Politics
A staunch supporter of Charles II and his brother, the Duke of York (later James II), Aphra becomes involved in the political upheavals of the day. She is threatened with arrest and stops writing plays for a time.

Playwright
Aphra turns to writing plays. Theatergoing is all the rage in London since Charles II (above) became king in 1660, but this is a bold choice of career for a woman. Female actors have only just begun to appear on the stage.

In debt
Spy work doesn't pay well. Aphra runs out of money and returns to England. After serving time in prison for failing to pay her debts, she decides to try earning money from writing.

Astrea
Aphra travels to Antwerp (in modern-day Belgium) Belgium, where she finds work as a spy using the code name "Astrea." She is asked to report on English exiles suspected of plotting against King Charles II.

Married name
On returning to London, she marries a merchant called Johan Behn, who is probably Dutch or German. He dies soon after their marriage, but she keeps "Behn" as her surname for the rest of her life.

Travels in Suriname
She arrives in Suriname, an English (later Dutch) colony on the coast of South America. Her experiences there will inspire some of her later writings.

Lost childhood
Aphra is probably born in Canterbury in the England. Little is known for certain about her early years, not even her birth name, but her father is said to have been a barber.

c.1640 **c.1663** **1664** **c.1666** **c.1668** **1670** **1677** **1680**

Restoration theater
When King Charles II of England (1630–1685) took the throne in 1660 after the death of Puritan ruler Oliver Cromwell (1599–1658), one of his first acts was to reopen London's theaters. Known as the Restoration, this turbulent period led to a fashion for witty and scandalous plays, such as Behn's *The Rover* (an illustration of which is shown here).

Aphra Behn

Aphra Behn (c. 1640–1689) was the first Englishwoman to earn her living as a professional writer. She wrote poems, novels, and 19 plays, and championed the right of women to make their voices heard. Her views were considered scandalous at the time, but today she is recognized as an important figure in literature.

Freezing times
During a very harsh winter, the Thames River freezes solid for two months. Aphra, who publishes several volumes of poetry around this time, commemorates the event in a comic poem.

"All women ... ought to let flowers fall upon the tomb of Aphra Behn ... for it was she who earned them the right to speak their minds."

Virginia Woolf, *A Room of One's Own* (1929)

1684

1684

A story in letters
The book *Love-Letters Between a Nobleman and His Sister* is published anonymously. Many believe Aphra is its author, and if so, it is her first novel. Some see it as the first novel written in English.

1687

The Emperor of the Moon
One of the last plays Aphra writes is *The Emperor of the Moon*. Played for laughs with noisy comic effects, it is a forerunner of modern pantomime, and is one of her greatest successes.

Oroonoko
Aphra's last great work, *Oroonoko*, is set in Suriname and tells the story of an African enslaved person. It explores the injustices and hardships of slavery, and is inspired by Aphra's travels through Suriname.

1688

OROONOKO: OR, THE Royal Slave. A TRUE HISTORY. By Mrs. A. BEHN. LONDON, Printed for Will. Canning, at his Shop in the Temple Cloyster, 1688.

Death and burial
Though she suffers from ill health, Aphra continues to write right until her death at the age of 49. She is buried with other famous writers in Westminster Abbey in London.

1689

Young Isaac

Isaac Newton is born in the village of Woolsthorpe, England. His father died three months earlier. Isaac has a sickly and unhappy childhood. He excels at school, however, and earns a place at Cambridge University.

Light experiments

Isaac devises an experiment using a prism to split light. He proves that white light is made up of all the colors of the rainbow mixed together. He publishes his findings.

1642

1665

1672

1684

First reflector telescope

Isaac is forced home from Cambridge after an outbreak of bubonic plague. He invents a new kind of telescope, which uses a mirror, rather than a lens, to collect and focus light rather than lenses. It is much more powerful than existing telescopes.

Defining gravity

Isaac is inspired to think about forces when he sees an apple fall from a tree in his grandmother's orchard. He develops his theory of gravity—which suggests that there is an invisible force that pulls all objects together, which is why the apple falls to the Earth.

Isaac Newton

English mathematician and scientist Isaac Newton (1642–1727) was a key figure in the Scientific Revolution, a period of great scientific progress in the 16th and 17th centuries. He is most famous for his theory of gravity, but he also carried out experiments with light and motion. He often kept his ideas quiet, waiting years before publishing them.

Scientific advances

From the 16th to the 19th centuries, European scientists challenged established ideas and introduced new methods of experimentation. Many of the breakthroughs they made have stood the test of time.

Robert Boyle (1627–1691)

Irish-born Robert Boyle is often considered to be the first modern chemist. His greatest legacy is Boyle's law, which explains how the pressure of a gas increases as the space it occupies decreases. Newton was familiar with Boyle's work, and often provided mathematical proof of Boyle's discoveries in his own work.

Alessandro Volta (1745–1827)

The inventor of the voltaic pile, the first electric battery, and also the discoverer of methane, Italian physicist and chemist Alessandro Volta's work led to huge advances. His experiments showed that electricity could be generated chemically, and debunked the idea that it was produced solely by living things.

Mary Somerville (1780–1872)

Though largely ignored by the scientific community, prolific Scottish writer Mary Somerville became one of the foremost authors on science of her time. Her book *On the Connexion of the Physical Sciences* was a huge hit. She was also a key campaigner for more rights, and better education, for women.

1685

Laws of motion

Isaac begins to think about motion, and works out three laws of motion. These explain what makes an object move or stop; what makes it move faster or slower or change direction; and how for every action there is an equal and opposite reaction.

1687

Principia Mathematica

Isaac publishes his laws of motion, and his theory of gravity in *Philosophiæ Naturalis Principia Mathematica*. The book wins him instant fame and transforms people's understanding of the world.

1696

Warden of the Mint

Isaac becomes the Warden of the Mint, a job he holds until his death. It is the most senior job in the Royal Mint, where coins are made. The role requires him to reform England's currency, including rooting out people making fake coins.

1703

The Royal Society

Isaac is elected President of the Royal Society, the most prestigious scientific institution in the world, and runs it until his death. A difficult man, he gets involved in many disputes with fellow scientists.

1705

Sir Isaac

Isaac is made a knight by Queen Anne. He becomes only the second scientist (after Sir Francis Bacon) to receive a knighthood.

1727

Isaac dies

At the age of 84, Isaac dies in his sleep. He is buried among royalty at Westminster Abbey in London, and celebrated as a national hero.

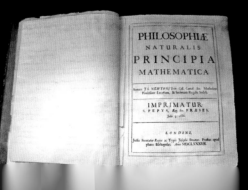

Published in Latin
The Philosophiæ Naturalis Principia Mathematica *was published in Latin. The title means "Mathematical Principles of Natural Philosophy."*

Juana Inés de la Cruz

A Mexican scholar, poet, and nun, Juana Inés de la Cruz (c.1648–1695) devoted her life to study, choosing to enter a convent rather than marry. In the convent, she had the time and a peaceful space in which to work on her studies. During her lifetime, she was recognized as one of the greatest thinkers in Mexico. Today, Juana is championed as an early feminist and someone who struggled for women's rights.

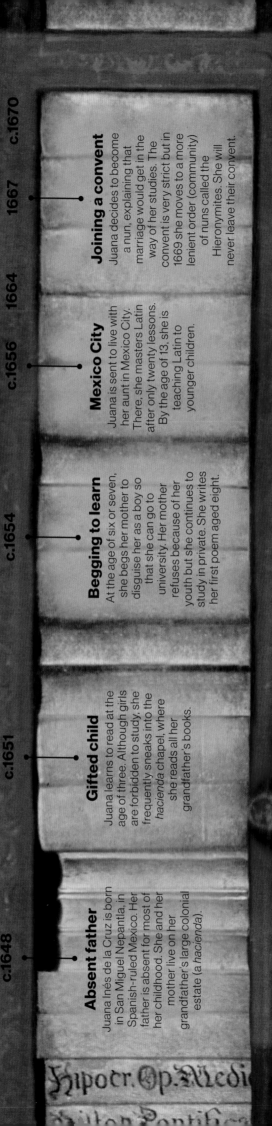

Marriage proposals

Juana's aunt introduces her to the viceroy (the most important official in Spanish-ruled Mexico). She gets a job as a lady-in-waiting to his wife. Here, her reputation for her brilliant mind grows. Many men propose marriage to her, but Juana prefers to focus on her studies.

Freedom to study

At the convent, Juana has the freedom she desires to study. She has her own apartment, she collects a huge library of books, and she is able to teach music and drama to the girls at the convent's school.

c.1648

c.1651

c.1654

c.1656

1664

1667

c.1670

c.1675

1680

1690

1691

Absent father

Juana Inés de la Cruz is born in San Miguel Nepantla, in Spanish-ruled Mexico. Her father is absent for most of her childhood. She and her mother live on her grandfather's large colonial estate (a *hacienda*).

Gifted child

Juana learns to read at the age of three. Although girls are forbidden to study, she frequently sneaks into the *hacienda* chapel, where she reads all her grandfather's books.

Begging to learn

At the age of six or seven, she begs her mother to disguise her as a boy so that she can go to university. Her mother refuses because of her youth but she continues to study in private. She writes her first poem aged eight.

Mexico City

Juana is sent to live with her aunt in Mexico City. There, she masters Latin after only twenty lessons. By the age of 13, she is teaching Latin to younger children.

Joining a convent

Juana decides to become a nun, explaining that marriage would get in the way of her studies. The convent is very strict but in 1669 she moves to a more lenient order (community) of nuns called the Hieronymites. She will never leave their convent.

Celebrated poet

Despite remaining in the convent, Juana keeps in touch with educated and powerful members of the elite. She writes poetry, plays, and religious works. She also collects musical and scientific instruments.

Patrons

The viceroy and vicereine, who she had worked for as a lady-in-waiting, become her patrons (financial supporters). They make sure that her writings are published. Her works include love poems—very unusual for a nun. They leave Mexico for Spain in 1688.

Public shaming

The departure of her patrons leaves Juana vulnerable to criticism by people who disapprove of her work. The Bishop of Puebla tries to damage her reputation. Pretending to be a nun, he writes a letter stating that she should focus on religion rather than studying secular (non-religious) topics.

Self-defence

In reaction to the bishop, Juana writes an amazing defence of her work. She writes that women should have the right to learn, and that studying secular topics is essential to gain an understanding of religion.

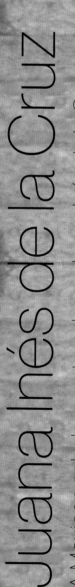

Hipocr. Op. Medic

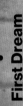

1694

Retirement and death

Authorities in the Catholic Church continue to criticise Juana. In 1694, she gives up writing, sells her books, and dedicates herself to prayer. While looking after fellow nuns during an epidemic in Mexico the following year, she becomes infected and dies at the age of 46.

1692

First Dream

Juana publishes her most important poem, *First Dream*, in which she describes the soul leaving the body at night on a quest for knowledge. When the soul is reunited with the body in the morning, the body reawakens but the soul's desire to learn remains.

Nun's shields

This painting of Juana Inés de la Cruz depicts her wearing a nun's shield (*escudo de monja* in Spanish), fastened to her habit just below the neck. Nuns often wore shields like this in Spanish-ruled Mexico. The shields often displayed images of saints, angels, or scenes from the Bible. A nun wore a shield as an expression of her devotion to God.

Russia

The Russian kingdom (and later, Empire) spanned two continents. Russia's size was its greatest strength, but it also made it difficult for the country to modernize. As a result, it has had a unique history, with many twists and turns.

Peter the Great (1672–1725)

Peter immediately set about modernizing Russia upon becoming ruler in 1696. He traveled through Europe, picking up ideas on many things—from shipbuilding to government—which he then brought home. He established the city of St. Petersburg in 1703, and made it the capital city in 1713.

Yekaterina Vorontsova-Dashkova (1743–1810)

Catherine's closest friend was a crucial figure in the spread of Enlightenment ideas in Russia. She was the first female head of a national academy of sciences anywhere in the world, and helped set up the Russian Academy, which protected the Russian language.

Alexandra Feodorovna (1872–1918)

A German princess, Alexandra entered into Russian royalty when she married Nicholas II in 1894. They proved to be the last royals of Russia, as a revolution removed them from power in 1917. They were executed in 1918.

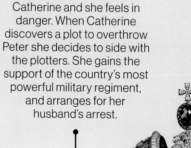

Enlightenment

Catherine sets about strengthening her position. She institutes reforms inspired by the Enlightenment—a philosophical, intellectual, and cultural movement in the 17th and 18th centuries—which help modernize the Russian Empire.

Disharmony

Peter threatens to divorce Catherine and she feels in danger. When Catherine discovers a plot to overthrow Peter she decides to side with the plotters. She gains the support of the country's most powerful military regiment, and arranges for her husband's arrest.

Sophie

Sophie von Anhalt-Zerbst is born, the eldest daughter of a poor but well-connected prince from Prussia (a German kingdom). She would later comment that nothing of interest happened in her childhood.

Unhappy marriage

Sophie takes the name Catherine when she converts to Russia's Christian Orthodox religion. She marries Peter, but the marriage is unhappy—they despise each other. They lead separate lives and have only one child, Paul.

CATHERINE'S CROWN

Visit to Russia

Sophie is invited to Russia by its ruler, Empress Elizabeth. Elizabeth has chosen her nephew Grand Duke Peter as heir to the throne of Russia, and for political reasons, she approves Sophie to be his bride.

Peter III

Upon the death of Empress Elizabeth, Peter becomes emperor, with Catherine as his empress. His political ideas and reforms are deeply unpopular. He alienates the Russian nobility, the Church, and even the Russian people.

Empress of Russia

Peter is overthrown and Catherine is proclaimed sole ruler. While in prison, Peter is murdered. This casts a shadow over Catherine's reign, as many believe she is involved in her husband's death— to this day, no one knows the truth.

Female education

Catherine advances state education for women. She writes a guide for the education of young noble women, and establishes the Smolny Institute (above)— Russia's first educational establishment for women.

1729   **1744**   **1745**   **1761**   **1762**   **1762**   **1762**   **1764**

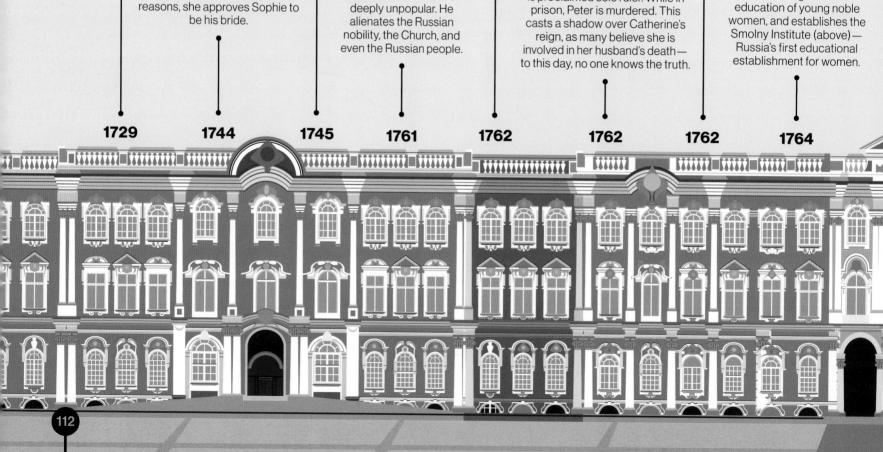

Hermitage Museum

The Hermitage Museum is one of the oldest, largest, and most respected art institutions in the world. For its galleries Catherine gathered 38,000 books, 10,000 drawings, countless engraved gems, and hundreds of priceless paintings by key European artists, giving Russia a lasting artistic legacy.

Catherine the Great

Born neither a Catherine, nor expected to be great, Catherine the Great (1729–1796) went on to become Russia's longest-ruling female leader. An outstanding political figure, intelligent and cultured, she is regarded as one of the most important people in world history. She modernized her beloved adopted country, improved its education system, and expanded its borders.

Art collection

Art and culture flourish during Catherine's reign. She collects a vast amount of art. She has buildings constructed that will become the Hermitage Museum in the Winter Palace, St. Petersburg, to house her treasures.

Russo-Turkish war

Catherine helps the King of Poland suppress a revolt. The rebels bring in the Ottoman Empire as an ally, and the Ottoman Turks declare war on Russia. Russia emerges victorious in 1774.

Expansion

Poland, weakened after a series of wars and poor leadership, begins to be swallowed up by its more powerful neighbors. Catherine seizes the largest share, while Prussia and Austria take other parts. By 1795, Poland is gone.

Uprising

A group of armed fighters led by army officer Yemelyan Pugachev rebel against the harsh conditions endured by Russia's lowest class, the serfs. Pugachev claims to be Peter III, which, if true, would question Catherine's right to rule.

Execution

Pugachev gains thousands of supporters and captures a large amount of territory. Catherine responds with massive force and Pugachev is captured and executed. Catherine's authority is once more unquestioned.

Vicious rumors

Catherine suffers a stroke and dies in her bed. She is buried in a gold coffin at the Peter and Paul Cathedral in St. Petersburg. After her death, Catherine's enemies go on to spread gossip about her private life in an attempt to damage her reputation.

1764   **1768**   **1772**   **1773**   **1775**   **1796**

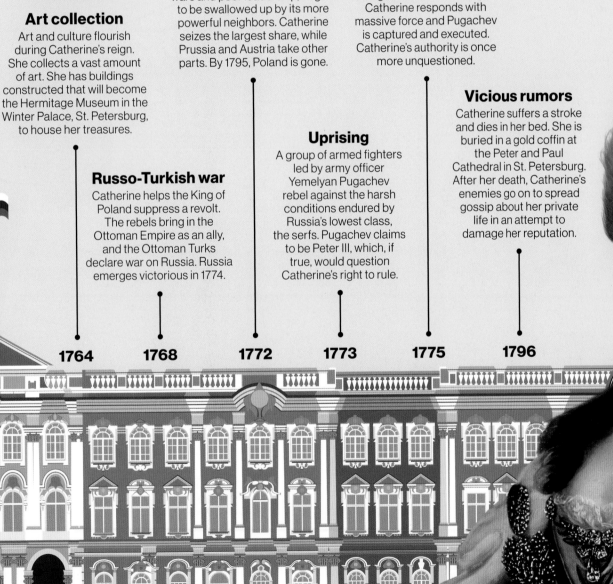

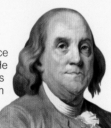

Crossing the Delaware

In July, the colonies issue their Declaration of Independence, stating that they are now a separate country from Britain. On Christmas night, George leads his army of 5,000 troops across the icy Delaware River to launch a surprise attack on a British-led force at Trenton, New Jersey. Though George's army lacks weapons and reinforcements, they capture the town. His unconventional attack proves the army's potential for victory.

Valley Forge

George sets up a winter training camp for his troops at Valley Forge, Pennsylvania. Here he transforms the inexperienced Continental Army into a highly efficient fighting force.

1777

American Revolution

Angry that they lack the same rights as other British subjects, the 13 American colonies revolt against British rule. George's experience in battle leads him to be appointed to command the American Continental Army for the coming war against the British.

1776

1775

> "Observe good faith and justice to all Nations; cultivate peace and harmony with all."
>
> **George Washington,** *Farewell Address as President* **(1796)**

Marriage

George marries Martha Custis, and they live at Mount Vernon. To maintain their part of the estate, the Washingtons have about 100 enslaved people.

1759

Call to arms

After the French seize land in the Ohio Valley that was claimed by the British, George is ordered to lead an attack on the French. He secures the help of the native Iroquois people, and with them, successfully defeats the French. His handling of this dispute earns him a lot of praise in the American colonies and in Britain.

1753

1752

Joining the army

Inspired by Lawrence's service in the Colonial Army, George signs up for the military. He is appointed a major and commander.

Young George

George Washington is born in Virginia, then a British colony. His father dies when he is 11, and George goes to live with his half-brother Lawrence at the large estate called Mount Vernon that Lawrence inherited in their father's will.

1732

Founding Fathers

Among the leaders of the American Revolution were thinkers, lawyers, soldiers, business leaders, and farmers. Known as the "Founding Fathers," they oversaw the birth of the United States.

Benjamin Franklin (1706–1790)

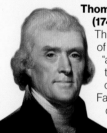

A leading author, scientist, and diplomat, Franklin traveled to France to win support for the Revolution. He helped negotiate the Treaty of Paris (1783), which brought the American Revolution to an end.

Thomas Jefferson (1743–1826)

The main author of the Declaration of Independence, which states that "all men are created equal." Even at the time, this phrase attracted criticism as many of the Founding Fathers were themselves slave owners. Jefferson became the 3rd US president in 1801.

Alexander Hamilton (1757–1804)

As a penniless teenager, Hamilton emigrated from the Caribbean to New York. As US treasury secretary in Washington's government, Hamilton set up the national bank and helped create the US financial system.

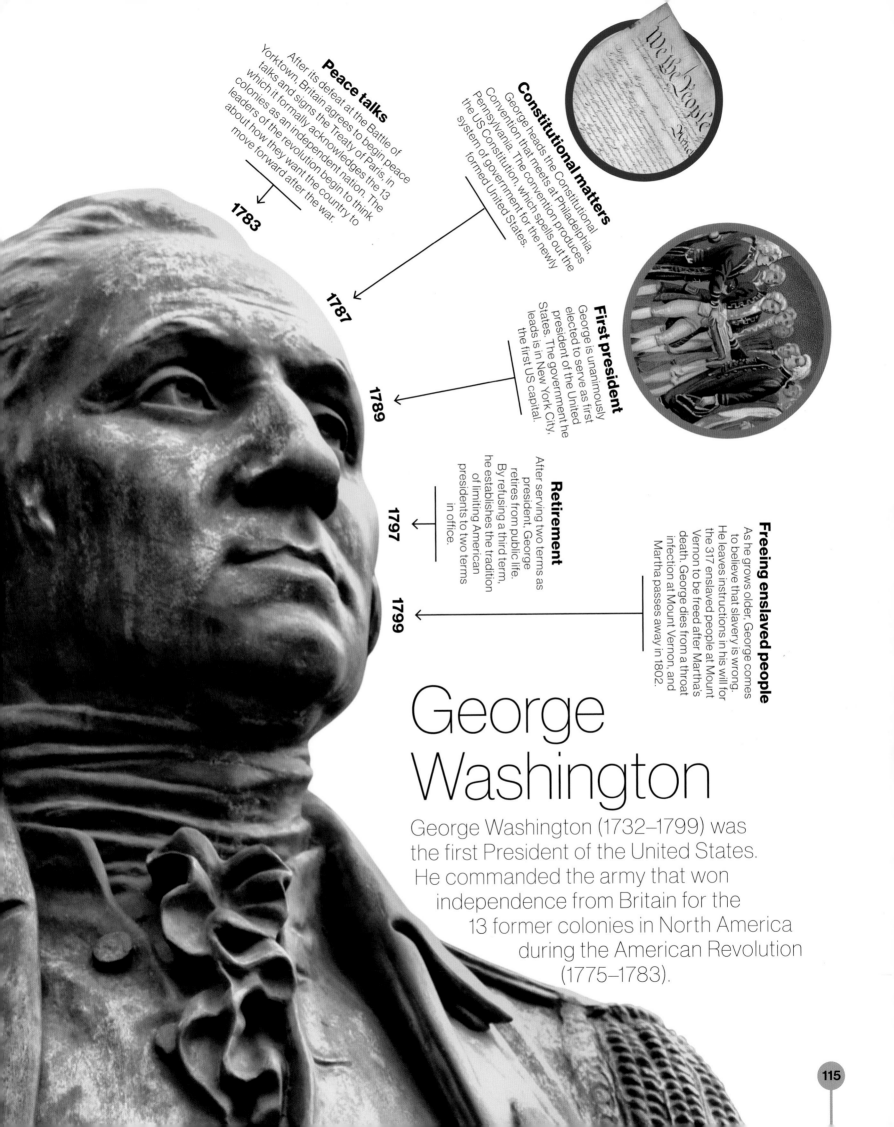

Peace talks

After its defeat at the Battle of Yorktown, Britain agrees to begin peace talks and signs the Treaty of Paris, in which it formally acknowledges the 13 colonies as an independent nation. The leaders of the revolution begin to think about how they want the country to move forward after the war.

1783

Constitutional matters

George heads the Constitutional Convention that meets at Philadelphia, Pennsylvania. The convention produces the US Constitution, which spells out the system of government for the newly formed United States.

1787

First president

George is unanimously elected to serve as first president of the United States. The government he leads is in New York City, the first US capital.

1789

Retirement

After serving two terms as president, George retires from public life. By refusing a third term, he establishes the tradition of limiting American presidents to two terms in office.

1797

Freeing enslaved people

As he grows older, George comes to believe that slavery is wrong. He leaves instructions in his will for the 317 enslaved people at Mount Vernon to be freed after Martha's death. George dies from a throat infection at Mount Vernon, and Martha passes away in 1802.

1799

George Washington

George Washington (1732–1799) was the first President of the United States. He commanded the army that won independence from Britain for the 13 former colonies in North America during the American Revolution (1775–1783).

Shamans

Many tribal communities, such as the San people of southern Africa, believe that illness is caused by evil spirits entering a person's soul. Healers, or shamans, perform ritual dances in order to enter the spirit world and plead for a patient's recovery.

Harsh punishments

Practicing medicine in Ancient Babylon can be a risky business. A code lays out the penalties if surgery goes wrong. If a patient dies during an operation, the surgeon risks having his or her hands cut off.

Manure medicine

In Ancient Egypt, ointments made from animal and human dung are used as remedies for various illnesses and injuries. Though disgusting, they are useful because we now know some types of animal dung contain helpful antibiotic substances.

Hippocratic Oath

At Greek doctor Hippocrates' medical school, students have to swear an oath promising to give patients the best treatments. The oath establishes medicine as a profession regular people can trust, and is still sworn in the 21st century.

c. 1750 BCE **c. 1500 BCE** **c. 400 BCE**

Healers through time

In the past, healers relied on remedies that often seem strange today to cure illnesses and diseases. Healers used treatments that were often useless or even dangerous, but some of their cures worked and are still used by medical practitioners today.

Leech mania

Used since ancient times, the practice of placing leeches (bloodsucking worms) on the skin for bloodletting reaches a peak. In the Val-de-Grâce military hospital in Paris, France, each new patient is given a treatment of 30 leeches regardless of their symptoms.

1820s

Female doctors

In Britain, women are banned from studying at medical school. A group of pioneering women, including Elizabeth Blackwell (the first woman to receive a medical degree in the US) and Elizabeth Garrett Anderson (who qualified in France), set up Britain's first medical school training female doctors.

The first X-rays

The discovery of X-rays by a German physicist, Wilhelm Röntgen, changes the way doctors diagnose and treat diseases. Doctors can now see inside the body to detect broken bones or serious illnesses.

Frontline nurses

Though banned from frontline conflict, many women serve on the World War I battlefields as volunteer nurses. They work in field hospitals, carrying out lifesaving procedures in appalling conditions, while others drive ambulances to rescue injured troops from the front line.

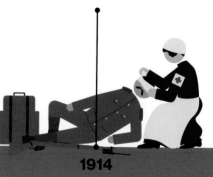

1874 **1895** **1914**

Acupuncturists

Chinese healers develop the practice of acupuncture to ease pain and suffering. An acupuncturist skillfully inserts very tiny needles into a patient's skin in order to restore their *qi*—the energy stream believed to flow through the body.

Monks and nuns

In medieval Europe, monks and nuns provide health care in monastic hospitals. They have only basic medical knowledge, and believe a patient's spiritual welfare is as important as his or her medical needs. Lepers and those suffering from contagious diseases are excluded from treatment.

Barber-surgeons

In Europe, the Christian Church forbids monks, nuns, and priests from performing any operation that sheds blood. Barbers take over many surgical tasks, from tooth extractions to amputations. Most have no formal training.

Bloodletting

The Roman physician Galen popularizes the ancient practice of bloodletting—bleeding patients to treat disease. Surgeons wrongly believe that bloodletting drains "stagnant" blood from the body, restoring the natural balance of its four fluids, or "humors."

Bimaristans

In the Islamic world, qualified medical staff look after patients in hospitals called *bimaristans*. Treatment is provided regardless of race, religion, or gender. Patients are treated in separate wards depending on their illness.

c.100 BCE   **c.200 CE**   **1000s**   **1000s**   **1163**

Plague doctors

European physicians believe that plague epidemics are caused by bad air. To protect themselves from infection, doctors in France and Italy wear a long overcoat covered with wax, and a mask. A "beak" on the mask is filled with dried herbs and spices to keep bad air away.

The Canon of Medicine

After it is translated into Latin, medical scholars in Europe begin to use *The Canon of Medicine* written by Persian scholar Ibn Sina, or Avicenna, as their standard textbook. First published in 1025, Ibn Sina's book collects medical knowledge from Europe, Persia, India, and China.

Trepanation

Trepanation—drilling a hole in a patient's skull for medical reasons—has been practiced around the world for thousands of years. The process is highly risky, but Inca surgeons in Peru master the skill, with up to 80 percent of patients surviving surgery.

1600s   **c.1400s**   **1200s**

Surgical robots

A robot guided by a human surgeon is used to assist an operation for the first time. These machines are able to use tools too small for human hands, with pinpoint precision. Surgical robots are now used to perform hundreds of thousands of operations worldwide every year.

Aspirin

Aspirin is made available to buy without a prescription for the first time, giving pharmacists a new way to offer pain relief. The drug was first made in 1899 by German scientist Felix Hoffman. Its most important ingredient, found naturally in willow bark, was known as a painkiller to the ancient Egyptians.

Universal health care

In the United Kingdom, the government brings together more than 400,000 doctors, nurses, dentists, and other staff to form the National Health Service. It is the first universally free health care system in Europe.

1915   **1948**   **1985**

Tensions rise

Simmering tensions lead to a slave rebellion in Saint-Domingue. Plantation houses are set on fire and slaveholders are killed. Toussaint helps his former slaveholder and wife escape. He secures his own family's safety, before joining the rebellion.

1791

Joining forces

As fighting between the rebels and the plantation owners continues, Toussaint joins the rebels under the leader of the revolt, Georges Biassou. Toussaint becomes his military secretary.

1791

War

War breaks out between French colony Saint-Domingue and Spanish colony Santo Domingo, both fighting to control the island. Britain fears the rebellion will spread to its colony, Jamaica, and sends troops to end the revolt.

1793

Becoming L'Ouverture

Commanders of the rebellion join the Spanish to fight against the French. Toussaint successfully leads a 4,000-troop army. He adopts the surname L'Ouverture (meaning "the one who opened the way"), from the French word for "opening."

1793

Seeking equality

Inspired by the French Revolution, formerly enslaved people speak out about inequality. When local plantation owners fail to grant citizenship to wealthy formerly enslaved people, fighting breaks out.

1790

Marriage

Toussaint marries Suzanne Simone Baptiste, his godfather's daughter. He adopts Suzanne's son, Placide, and they have two sons together, Isaac and Saint-Jean.

1782

A free person

At the age of 33, Toussaint is freed, but it is the slaveholder and keeper of the plantation who later frees: whom the plantation people frees: is freed. Toussaint is now for work, for himself, on the plantation land and keeps.

1776

Educated

He grows up on a slave plantation, where he works as a coachman and a manager. Toussaint's godfather, a freed slave, teaches him to read and write. He learns some French, as well as Creole.

1763

Born into slavery

Toussaint is born into an enslaved family in Saint-Domingue, on the Caribbean island of Hispaniola. According to a family story, he is the grandson of a prince from the West African kingdom of Arada.

c.1743

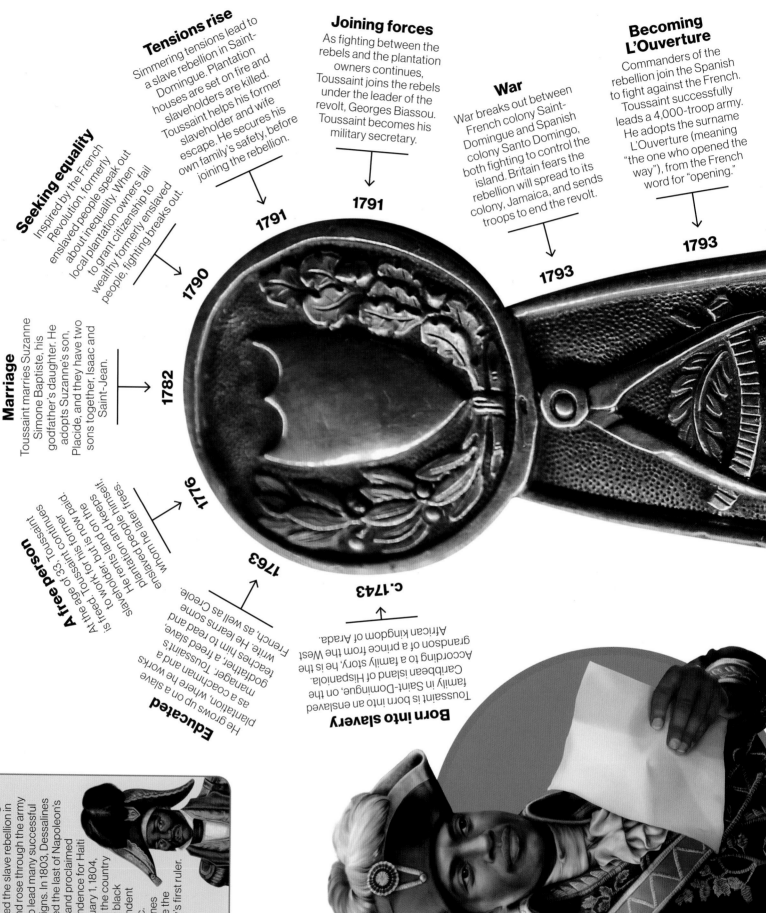

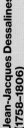

Jean-Jacques Dessalines (1758–1806)
Like Toussaint L'Ouverture, Jean-Jacques Dessalines was born into enslavement in Saint-Domingue. He joined the slave rebellion in 1791, and rose through the army ranks to lead many successful campaigns. In 1803, Dessalines defeated the last of Napoleon's forces, and proclaimed independence for Haiti on January 1, 1804, making the country the first black independent republic. Dessalines became the country's first ruler.

Toussaint L'Ouverture

Born enslaved in the French colony of Saint-Domingue (modern-day Haiti), Toussaint L'Ouverture (c. 1743–1803) led a successful slave rebellion against colonial rule. His actions paved the way to establishing Haiti as an independent black-governed state, and inspired others in the Americas to resist colonial rule.

Switching sides

With its rule over Saint-Domingue threatened, the French abolish enslavement across their empire. Spain and Britain refuse to do the same, leading Toussaint to change his allegiance to France. He inspires his troops to follow him.

1794

Leading the way

Toussaint forces the French to declare him Lieutenant Governor of Saint-Domingue. He expels the British and gains territory from Spain. He introduces a constitution, guaranteeing rights for black people.

1796

War with Napoleon

When French ruler Napoleon Bonaparte announces his plan to restore direct rule to the island, Toussaint prepares his troops for war. Napoleon dispatches his brother-in-law with troops to Saint-Domingue.

1802

Death

After much fierce fighting against French forces, Toussaint signs a peace treaty. However, he is seized by the French and sent to prison, where he is tortured and dies. In 1804, Saint-Domingue proclaims independence from France.

1803

French colonialism

France began to colonize North America in the 16th century, taking control of much of modern-day Canada, the midwestern United States, and the Caribbean. The colony of Saint-Domingue, on the Caribbean island of Hispaniola, was established in 1659. Its slave plantations provided sugar and coffee to France. In the 18th century, slave rebellions and conflicts with colonial rivals led to France losing most of its colonies in North America and the Caribbean.

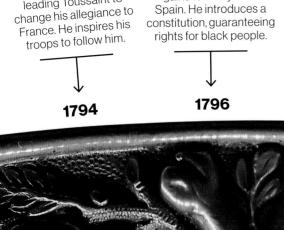

TOUSSAINT L'OUVERTURE'S SWORD

Olaudah Equiano

Kidnapped and enslaved as a child from the Kingdom of Benin (modern-day Nigeria), Olaudah Equiano (1745–1797) dedicated his life to abolishing slavery. After settling in Britain, he wrote about his experiences as an enslaved person in his autobiography, which went on to have a powerful impact on public opinion. Equiano did not live to see the abolition of the slave trade, but his story deeply influenced the abolitionist cause, and encouraged other formerly enslaved people to tell their stories, too.

The Atlantic slave trade

Between the 16th to the 19th centuries, English, French, Dutch, Spanish, and Portuguese traders took goods to Africa, which they exchanged for enslaved people. These people were transported to the Americas in ships like the one shown below, where they were forced to work without pay or freedom in plantations growing crops. These crops were then sold at high prices to buyers in Europe.

Ownership

In the British colony of Virginia, Olaudah is sold to Michael Pascal, an officer in the British Royal Navy. It is common practice for owners of enslaved people to rename their captives, as a way of further stripping their identity away. Pascal renames Olaudah "Gustavus Vassa."

Life at sea

Olaudah spends several years at sea as Pascal's valet (personal servant) during the Seven Years' War between Britain and France. He becomes an experienced seafarer, and carries gunpowder onto ships' decks during battles.

Cheated

While enslaved to Pascal, Olaudah is baptized as a Christian and later learns to read and write. Having fought for the British, Olaudah is led to believe that he should gain his freedom, but Pascal cheats him and Olaudah remains enslaved.

Enslavement

Olaudah is born in the Igbo region of modern-day Nigeria—then part of the Kingdom of Benin. At the age of 11, he and his sister are kidnapped, enslaved, and taken across the Atlantic Ocean to the Americas.

1745

1756

1758

1759

Slave ship

This model shows the appallingly cramped conditions inside the *Brookes*, a British slave ship. The model was widely reproduced to raise awareness of the evils of the slave trade.

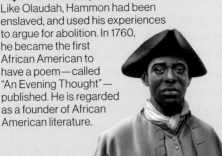
Freedom

Olaudah works as a deckhand and valet for King, and earns money as a trader, selling sugar and fruit. After three years, he has earned enough to pay King the exact sum of money he was bought for. By the age of 21 he is free.

Zong massacre

The captain of a British slave ship, the *Zong*, throws 133 enslaved people overboard in the mid-Atlantic so the ship owner can claim insurance for what is considered the loss of "human cargo." The barbarism of this act helps Olaudah and other abolitionists to alert the public to the cruelty of the slave trade.

Sons of Africa

In London, Olaudah joins with 11 other leaders of the black community to form the Sons of Africa, a group that campaigns for slavery to be abolished.

Sold

Olaudah is sold twice, and ends up enslaved to Robert King, a wealthy merchant, on the Caribbean island of Montserrat. Witnessing the torture of other enslaved Africans reignites Olaudah's desire to gain his freedom as soon as possible.

Exploring the world

Olaudah uses the skills he has learned as a sailor to explore and discover the world. One voyage, led by English explorer Constantine Phipps, takes him to the Arctic on a mission to find out if the seas there are navigable.

Settling in Britain

On his voyages, Olaudah runs the risk of being re-enslaved. He decides to settle in London, England, where his right to be free is most likely to be protected, even though slavery is still legal there.

Leading voice

By now, Olaudah is the leading voice on African issues in London, and his comments on issues such as slavery are reported in the newspapers.

1762 **1766** **1773** **1781** **1784** **1786** **1788** **1789** **1797**

Autobiography

Olaudah describes the horrors of slavery in his book *The Interesting Narrative of the Life of Olaudah Equiano, or Gustavus Vassa, the African*. It is a huge success, and profoundly influences public opinion. Olaudah spends many months publicly speaking about his life and enslavement.

Death

Olaudah dies at the age of 52. His work, and the work of other abolitionists, results in the slave trade being made illegal in the British Empire in 1807. Slavery itself was abolished completely in most British colonies in 1833.

Wolfgang Amadeus Mozart

One of the greatest composers in history, Wolfgang Amadeus Mozart (1756–1791) began writing music at the age of five. He amazed audiences across Europe with his expert playing of the piano and violin as a child, and went on to compose more than 600 pieces, including some of the most famous works of classical music.

Great composers

Since the 1600s, composers have given classical music particular structures and styles. Some composers, including Mozart, are seen as geniuses.

Ludwig van Beethoven (1770–1827)
Perhaps the most influential composer of all time, Beethoven created music that explored the depths of the human heart. His symphonies and later concertos are unrivaled masterpieces.

Pyotr Ilyich Tchaikovsky (1840–1893)
The first Russian composer to gain fame in Europe and the US, his most famous works include the ballets *Swan Lake*, *The Nutcracker*, and *The Sleeping Beauty*.

Louise Farrenc (1804–1875)
A brilliant concert pianist and music professor from France, Farrenc battled to gain recognition for her compositions among her male colleagues. Her work began to receive attention and interest in the late 20th century.

First symphony
On his travels, Wolfgang meets many influential composers. Inspired by German composer Johann Christian Bach, he writes his first symphony in London, England, at the age of eight.

Travels in Italy
Wolfgang writes his first opera at the age of 11. He is accepted into a prestigious music academy in Bologna, Italy. The Mozart family tour Italy, giving concerts and attending opera performances.

Music lessons
When Leopold starts teaching Nannerl to play the piano, three-year-old Wolfgang is also desperate to learn. He takes to it instantly, and soon makes speedy progress with the violin, too.

Child prodigy
As their skills blossom, Leopold takes the two children on a series of concert tours across Europe, where they perform to royalty in cities such as Brussels, Vienna, and Paris.

Early childhood
Born in Salzburg in Austria, Wolfgang and his elder sister Maria Anna ("Nannerl") are the only two of seven Mozart children to survive infancy. Their father, Leopold, is a violinist, composer, and music teacher.

1767

1764

1762

1759

1756

Success

Wolfgang's years in Vienna are very productive. He performs regularly and composes dozens of works. Wolfgang and Constanze move into an expensive apartment.

Death

Wolfgang produces some of his greatest work in the final year of his life, including *The Magic Flute*. But after the opera's premiere, he is bedridden with a mysterious illness. He dies on December 5 at the age of 35.

1791

Vienna

Wolfgang's opera *Idomeneo* is a success. He moves to Vienna in Austria, and later meets Emperor Joseph II, who goes on to support his career. Wolfgang lives in Vienna for the rest of his life.

The Marriage of Figaro

He begins to focus on opera. His new works, *The Marriage of Figaro* and *Don Giovanni* (1787), are masterpieces, but war causes him to lose his financial support. He struggles for money and becomes depressed.

1786

Marriage

Aloysia's family move to Vienna and take Wolfgang as a lodger. He falls in love with and marries Aloysia's younger sister Constanze, who is also a singer. They have six children.

1782

1782

First love

While traveling, Mozart meets and falls in love with a professional singer named Aloysia Weber in the German city of Mannheim. Their relationship ends as Aloysia's career takes off, but Wolfgang finds it difficult to get work.

1781

1777

Mary Wollstonecraft

Mary Wollstonecraft (1759–1797) is regarded as England's first feminist. A supporter of the French Revolution, she argued that women deserved the same rights as men. The Victorians of her day were scandalized by her life, and so her writings lay forgotten for almost a century, until she became an inspiration for the feminist movement.

Published author

After moving to London, Mary decides to try supporting herself through writing. Her first published book, *Thoughts on the Education of Daughters*, is a self-help book for middle-class parents. She also writes a novel, *Mary: A Fiction*, and a book of stories for children.

1787

Governess in Irelan[d]

Mary finds work in Ireland a[s] a governess (teacher) to th[e] children of the noblewoman L[ady] Kingsborough. She does not [get] along with her employer, an[d is] fired within a year.

1759

Unhappy childhood

Mary Wollstonecraft is born in Spitalfields, London. Her family are well off, but her father falls into debt and is often drunk and abusive. Her brother receives a better education than Mary and her sisters, which she resents.

1785

1784

Schoolteacher

With her two sisters and a frie[nd,] Mary opens a small school for g[irls] in Newington Green, in north [London.] The experience helps f[orm] her ideas on education, but th[e] school closes after two years[.]

Radical circles

In London, Mary contributes to the *Analytical Review*, a journal edited by her publisher, Joseph Johnson. He is a radical (someone who wants to change society) and introduces Mary to influential writers and intellectuals.

1790

Rights of Men

Mary is enthusiastic about the French Revolution, seeing it as an opportunity for greater equality. In answer to a pamphlet written by leading politician Edmund Burke, which attacks the revolution's aims, she writes *A Vindication of the Rights of Men*, a vigorous defense.

1792

ghts of Woman

ws this up with *A Vindication ghts of Woman*, in which she hat if women are educated n the same opportunities as ey will be able to contribute more to society.

92

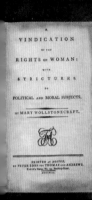

olutionary France

ravels to France to study the ution for herself. Arriving in she witnesses King Louis XVI way to trial. As the Reign of or—in which thousands of e are guillotined—takes hold, nce becomes dangerous for foreigners.

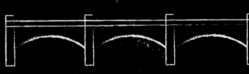

"Strengthen the female mind by enlarging it, and there will be an end to blind obedience."

Mary Wollstonecraft, *A Vindication of the Rights of Woman* (1792)

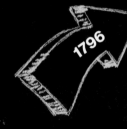

1796

William Godwin

A friendship develops between Mary and William Godwin, an English journalist and philosopher. They fall in love and marry.

1797

Desperate act

Mary returns to London, but is rejected by Imlay. Crushed, she attempts to end her life by leaping from Putney Bridge into the Thames River. A boatman pulls her out of the water, saving her life.

Tragic death

Mary dies of an infection 10 days after giving birth to a daughter. The baby is named Mary after her, and will grow up to become a famous author herself.

1794

Birth of Fanny

While in Paris, Mary falls in love with Gilbert Imlay, an American businessman and diplomat. She gives birth to their daughter, Fanny, in Le Havre in France. Imlay returns to London soon afterward, leaving Mary on her own.

1795

Female voices

With few opportunities for work outside the home, some women in the 19th century made a name for themselves by becoming novelists.

Jane Austen (1775–1817)

Jane Austen's six novels are among the best-loved works of fiction in English. They feature strong-minded, intelligent women, and offer witty, critical observations of family life.

Mary Shelley (1797–1851)

Mary Wollstonecraft's daughter Mary wrote *Frankenstein*, her first and most successful novel, at the age of just 20. The novel follows Victor Frankenstein, a scientist who creates a monster as an experiment.

Louisa May Alcott (1832–1888)

Louisa May Alcott was raised in Concord, Massachusetts. She began writing magazine stories to support her family. She is best known for the novel *Little Women*, based on memories of her childhood.

Wang Zhenyi

Chinese scholar Wang Zhenyi (1768–1797) dedicated her life to writing poetry and studying mathematics and astronomy, despite, as a female, being excluded from receiving a formal education. She became a respected thinker in Qing dynasty China, explaining complicated ideas in a simple way so regular people could understand them.

Early life

Wang Zhenyi is born in eastern China to an educated family. Her grandfather is an astronomer, her father writes about medicine, and her grandmother is a poet.

1768

Math made easy

Her first mathematics book, *The Simple Principles of Calculation*, is published. It revises and simplifies mathematical and scientific theories. Because she was denied a formal education, Zhenyi tries to make science and mathematics accessible to all people.

1792

Trigonometry

Zhenyi teaches herself mathematics. She masters trigonometry (the study of triangles) and Pythagoras' theorem. She writes an article explaining these in simple language.

c.1790

Pioneers of astronomy

Women have made important discoveries that have increased our understanding of the night sky, often despite facing prejudice and discrimination.

Maria Margaretha Kirch (1670–1720)
In 1702, German astronomer Maria Margaretha Kirch discovered a comet, an achievement which was at first credited to her husband. She wrote a lot about the passing of Venus, Jupiter, and Saturn in front of the Sun between 1709 and 1712. Because she was a woman, she was denied a position at the Royal Academy of Sciences.

Caroline Herschel (1750–1848)
German astronomer Caroline Herschel discovered many comets and was the first female to receive a salary as a scientist. She became the first woman in Britain to hold a government position.

Huang Lü (1769–1829)
Chinese astronomer Huang Lü's family supported her wish to gain an education. She studied astronomy and arithmetic, and used her knowledge to build a telescope and an early type of camera.

Marriage

Zhenyi meets Zhan Mei, who is also from a family of scholars, and they marry. She continues to write poetry, and study mathematics and astronomy. The couple never have children.

1793

Knowledge

Zhenyi believes that it is important to study both Chinese and European ideas, and she uses both to support her findings.

1795

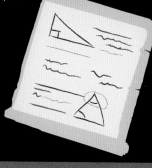

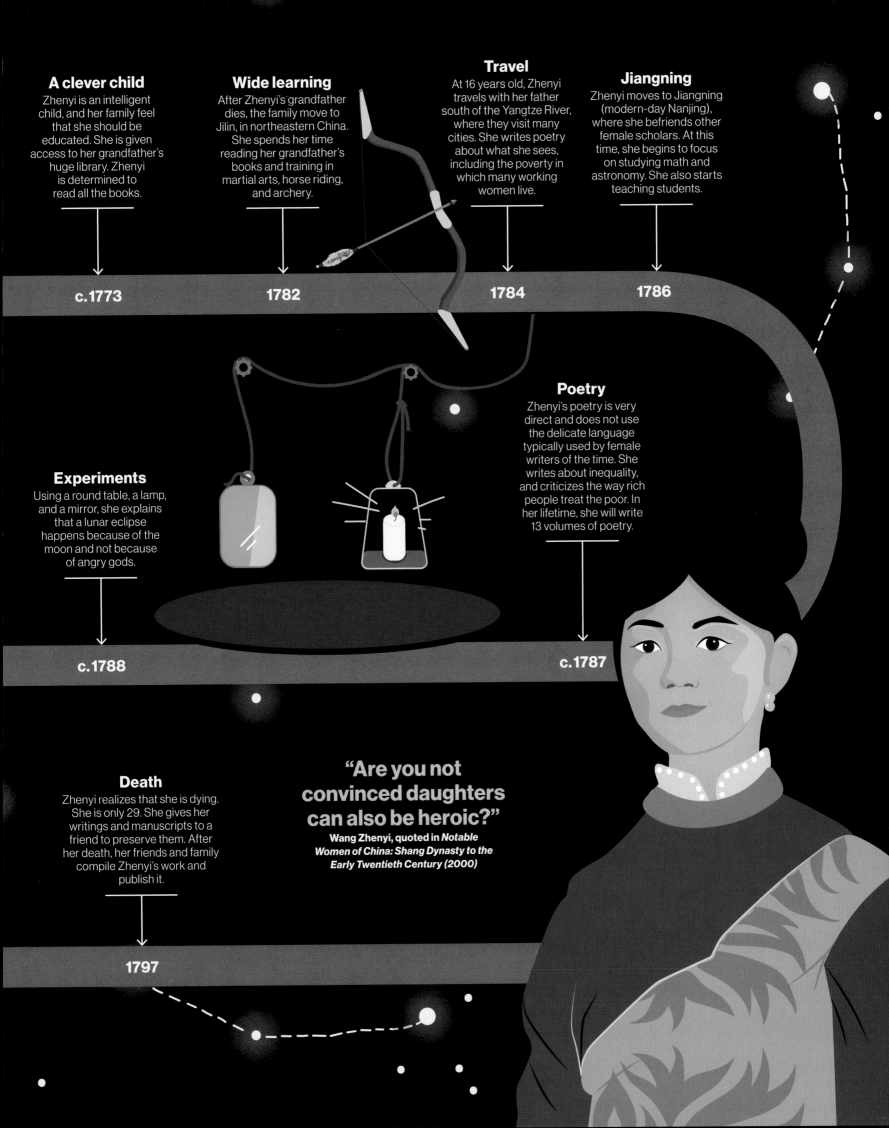

A clever child

Zhenyi is an intelligent child, and her family feel that she should be educated. She is given access to her grandfather's huge library. Zhenyi is determined to read all the books.

c.1773

Wide learning

After Zhenyi's grandfather dies, the family move to Jilin, in northeastern China. She spends her time reading her grandfather's books and training in martial arts, horse riding, and archery.

1782

Travel

At 16 years old, Zhenyi travels with her father south of the Yangtze River, where they visit many cities. She writes poetry about what she sees, including the poverty in which many working women live.

1784

Jiangning

Zhenyi moves to Jiangning (modern-day Nanjing), where she befriends other female scholars. At this time, she begins to focus on studying math and astronomy. She also starts teaching students.

1786

Experiments

Using a round table, a lamp, and a mirror, she explains that a lunar eclipse happens because of the moon and not because of angry gods.

c.1788

Poetry

Zhenyi's poetry is very direct and does not use the delicate language typically used by female writers of the time. She writes about inequality, and criticizes the way rich people treat the poor. In her lifetime, she will write 13 volumes of poetry.

c.1787

Death

Zhenyi realizes that she is dying. She is only 29. She gives her writings and manuscripts to a friend to preserve them. After her death, her friends and family compile Zhenyi's work and publish it.

1797

"Are you not convinced daughters can also be heroic?"

Wang Zhenyi, quoted in *Notable Women of China: Shang Dynasty to the Early Twentieth Century* (2000)

Daniel O'Connell

Irish political leader Daniel O'Connell (1775–1847) peacefully campaigned on behalf of Irish Catholics living within the British Empire. His work centered on two concerns—removing the discrimination that Irish Catholics were subjected to, and increasing the level of independence that Ireland had within the British Empire.

1775
Large family
The oldest of 10 children, Daniel is born into a Catholic family in County Kerry, Ireland. His wealthy uncle pays for him to study in France at 15 years old.

1790
Anti-violence
Revolution breaks out in France. A witness to the ferocity of the events, Daniel develops a lifelong hatred of violence. He returns to Ireland to study law, but his future career opportunities are limited due to British anti-Catholic laws.

1798
Rebellion
The Society of United Irishmen rebels against British rule in Ireland. The rebellion is quickly quashed and many of its leaders are arrested and executed. Daniel is not involved with the rebellion because he believes that Irish rights should be secured through politics rather than violence.

1801
Act of Union
After the failed rebellion, British Prime Minister William Pitt passes the Act of Union, which merges the Irish and British parliaments. Daniel argues that the change means that Irish Catholic issues will not be properly represented in Parliament.

1802
Family Life
Daniel spends the next decade practicing law in Ireland. He marries, and he and his wife have 11 children. They have a happy marriage, although Daniel is frequently in debt.

1811
The Catholic Board
For years, laws are passed that discriminate against Irish Catholics. These laws stop Catholics from voting, getting jobs, owning land, holding public office, or teaching. Daniel sets up the Catholic Board to campaign for legal rights and freedom for Catholics—known as Catholic emancipation.

1815
Duel
Daniel criticizes the government for its prejudice against Catholics. Politician John D'Esterre challenges him to a duel. Reluctantly, Daniel agrees and in the duel, he kills D'Esterre. Horrified by his actions, Daniel vows never to fight again.

Irish Independence

Ireland had been ruled by Britain since the 12th century. Many Irish groups tried and failed to gain independence from Britain over the centuries, before succeeding in 1921.

Theobald Wolfe Tone (1763–1798)

Tone was a founding member of the United Irishmen, who wanted to end British rule in Ireland. He was one of the leaders of the 1798 United Irishmen rebellion. It failed, and Tone was captured, but he killed himself before he could be executed.

Constance Markievicz (1868–1927)

Constance Markievicz fought in the 1916 Easter Rising—a rebellion against British rule that broke out in Dublin. In 1918, she became the first woman elected to the UK Parliament, but she did not take her seat.

Michael Collins (1890–1922)

A soldier, politician, and revolutionary, Collins played a crucial role in the Irish War of Independence (1919–1921), which freed Ireland from British rule. He led the Irish side of the peace treaty negotiations that followed after the war.

1824 Catholic Rent

Daniel sets up the Catholic Rent, a fee of one penny a month (a sum that the Catholic poor can afford). Daniel uses these donations to fund the Catholic Association, an organization that fights for Irish Catholic rights. Support for his campaign is growing.

1829 Emancipation

The Roman Catholic Relief Act is passed, abolishing many of the restrictions on Catholics. It allows Catholics to sit as MPs, vote in elections, and hold senior political positions. Daniel is reelected to Parliament, and is the first Irish Catholic to sit in the House of Commons in 1830.

1840 Repeal Association

Daniel sets up the Repeal Association to reverse the 1801 Act of Union, which binds Ireland and the United Kingdom together. Daniel holds huge "Monster Meetings" all over Ireland to argue the case for Irish independence. He is arrested, charged with conspiracy, and imprisoned for three months.

1828 Deadlock

In an election for Parliament, Daniel wins the County Clare seat. He is unable to take his seat as the oath that Members of Parliament (MPs) take had essentially excluded Catholics from Parliament. The British prime minister is concerned that if Daniel does not take his seat for this reason, the people of Ireland will revolt.

1831 The Tithe War

Daniel leads a nonviolent campaign against tithes—taxes paid to the Protestant Church of Ireland, not to the Catholic Church. The tithes foster unrest among Irish Catholics. Daniel's campaign causes the taxes to be cut by a quarter in 1838, and fully lifted in 1869.

1847 Genoa

At 71 years of age, Daniel takes a pilgrimage to Italy. Weak from the journey, he dies. His heart is buried in Rome and the rest of his body is taken back to Ireland. He is often called "The Liberator" in recognition of his work to liberate Irish Catholics.

During the repeal campaign, racist images from the British press often depicted Ireland as an uncivilized monster.

Ching Shih

One of the most feared pirate lords in history, Ching Shih (c.1775–1844) led a band of outlaws that was powerful enough to fight battles against the Chinese navy. At the height of her reign, she controlled most of the waters off the coast of China.

A pirate's life

Much of Ching Shih's early life is shrouded in mystery, including the name she is born with. When she is around the age of 26, Zheng Yi, commander of the Red Flag Fleet of pirate ships, asks her to marry him. It is believed that she accepts his proposal on the condition that she gets an equal share of the fleet's plunder.

c.1775

Pirate coalition

On her marriage to Zheng Yi, she gains the name Ching Shih, meaning "Zheng's wife". The couple unite to build a formidable pirate fleet in the South China Sea. By 1804, they command 40,000 junks (Chinese sailing ships) and 70,000 pirates.

1801

Unusual tactics

As the usual tactics to defeat Ching Shih are not having any effect, the Chinese government sends flaming boats towards her fleet. Ching Shih orders her pirates to put out the flames, repair the boats, and absorb them into her fleet.

c.1808

Lantau attack

Ching Shih's fleet sails into harbour on Lantau island (in Hong Kong). Chinese naval ships block the harbour entrance to trap them inside, and begin a bombardment. Ching Shih's fleet sinks many of the Chinese ships in their way, and sails out without any major damage.

c.1808

Amnesty

The Chinese government asks for help from the British and Portuguese navies to regain control, but still Ching Shih remains unstoppable. The Chinese government offers an amnesty (an official pardon) to all pirates in an attempt to break her coalition.

1809

Terms of retirement

Ching Shih walks unarmed into the office of Chinese government official Zhang Bai to negotiate her retirement. She arranges to keep her money, and organizes naval posts for her pirates, and a pardon for herself and nearly all of her pirates.

1810

Military advisor

Even though she has retired, Ching Shih's notorious reputation leads her to be asked to advise Lin Zexu, a Chinese government official, on battle tactics when fighting the British navy. She dies in 1844, at the age of 69, one of the few pirate lords to survive into old age.

1839–1844

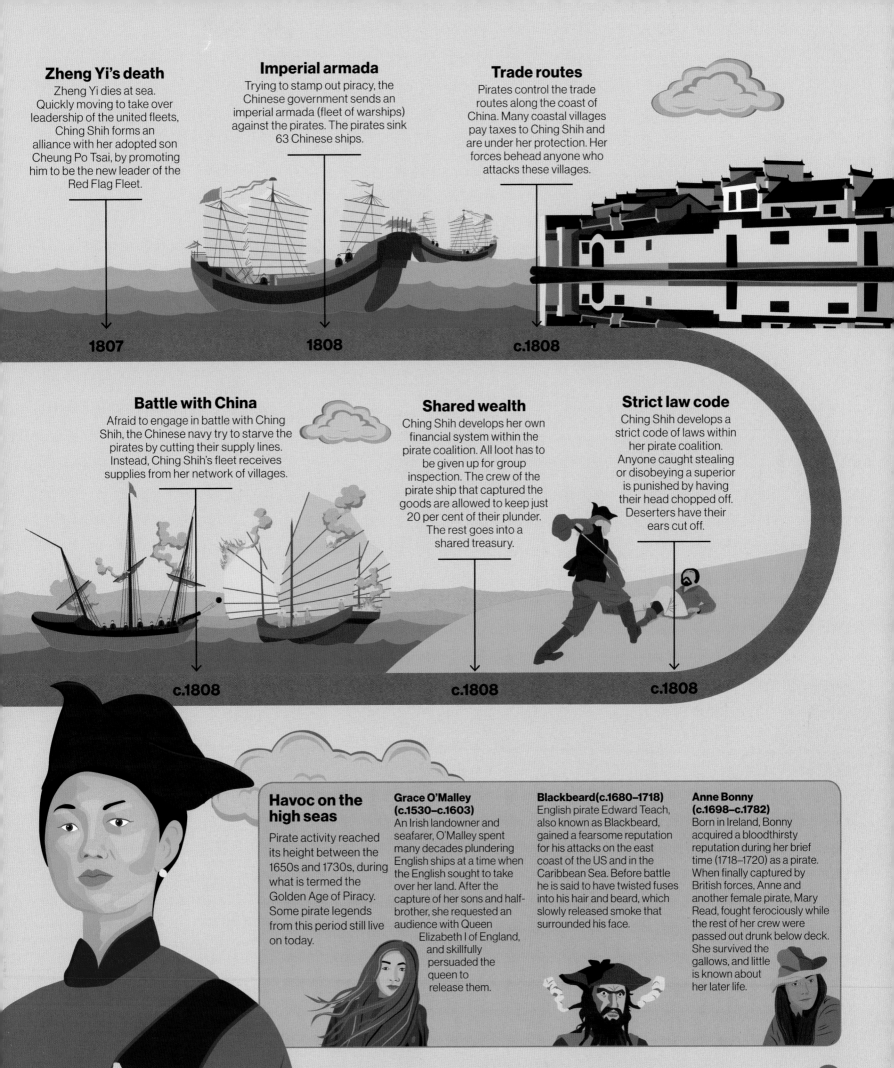

Zheng Yi's death

Zheng Yi dies at sea. Quickly moving to take over leadership of the united fleets, Ching Shih forms an alliance with her adopted son Cheung Po Tsai, by promoting him to be the new leader of the Red Flag Fleet.

1807

Imperial armada

Trying to stamp out piracy, the Chinese government sends an imperial armada (fleet of warships) against the pirates. The pirates sink 63 Chinese ships.

1808

Trade routes

Pirates control the trade routes along the coast of China. Many coastal villages pay taxes to Ching Shih and are under her protection. Her forces behead anyone who attacks these villages.

c.1808

Battle with China

Afraid to engage in battle with Ching Shih, the Chinese navy try to starve the pirates by cutting their supply lines. Instead, Ching Shih's fleet receives supplies from her network of villages.

c.1808

Shared wealth

Ching Shih develops her own financial system within the pirate coalition. All loot has to be given up for group inspection. The crew of the pirate ship that captured the goods are allowed to keep just 20 per cent of their plunder. The rest goes into a shared treasury.

c.1808

Strict law code

Ching Shih develops a strict code of laws within her pirate coalition. Anyone caught stealing or disobeying a superior is punished by having their head chopped off. Deserters have their ears cut off.

c.1808

Havoc on the high seas

Pirate activity reached its height between the 1650s and 1730s, during what is termed the Golden Age of Piracy. Some pirate legends from this period still live on today.

Grace O'Malley (c.1530–c.1603)

An Irish landowner and seafarer, O'Malley spent many decades plundering English ships at a time when the English sought to take over her land. After the capture of her sons and half-brother, she requested an audience with Queen Elizabeth I of England, and skillfully persuaded the queen to release them.

Blackbeard (c.1680–1718)

English pirate Edward Teach, also known as Blackbeard, gained a fearsome reputation for his attacks on the east coast of the US and in the Caribbean Sea. Before battle he is said to have twisted fuses into his hair and beard, which slowly released smoke that surrounded his face.

Anne Bonny (c.1698–c.1782)

Born in Ireland, Bonny acquired a bloodthirsty reputation during her brief time (1718–1720) as a pirate. When finally captured by British forces, Anne and another female pirate, Mary Read, fought ferociously while the rest of her crew were passed out drunk below deck. She survived the gallows, and little is known about her later life.

Elizabeth Fry

Elizabeth Fry (1780–1845) campaigned for the better treatment of British prisoners after she witnessed the dreadful conditions that they had to live in. Throughout her life, Fry helped the neediest in society, believing that everyone, even those who had committed a serious crime, deserved to be treated fairly.

Elizabeth's family
Elizabeth Gurney is born in Norwich, England. Her family are Quakers (followers of a Christian group that believes in peace and equality). Both sides of her family work in banking, which has brought them great wealth.

A family tragedy
When her mother dies, Elizabeth is devastated. She has to take care of her younger siblings. Elizabeth starts reading books that discuss making England a fairer place for all.

Marriage
Aged 20, Elizabeth meets Joseph Fry, who is a merchant and a Quaker, like Elizabeth. They marry and move to London. They will have 11 children together over the following 22 years.

A caring child
Known as Betsy to her family, Elizabeth is a curious and imaginative child, and enjoys collecting shells with her mother. But what she wants most is to help people in difficult situations.

Devotion
Elizabeth takes her religion more seriously. Quakers believe in living simply, so she rejects the rich lifestyle of her family. She visits the sick and teaches deprived children how to read. She will devote the rest of her life to helping others.

Newgate Prison
Elizabeth visits Newgate Prison in London because she wants to help the prisoners there. The conditions she finds are disgusting. Women, many with children, are crammed into filthy cells, where they have to wash clothes, cook, and sleep on straw on the floor.

1780

c. 1788

1792

1798

1800

1813

Newgate Prison
Newgate Prison, in central London, opened in the 12th century. By the late eighteenth century, the prison had become notorious as the place where criminals were held before they were executed. After more than 600 years, Newgate closed in 1904.

Helping others

We call people who try to help those who find themselves in difficult situations "humanitarians."

Queen Victoria (1819–1901)
The second-longest reigning monarch of the UK, Queen Victoria supported more than 150 different organizations that promoted welfare or improvements in citizens' lives. Most notably, she was the first patron (financial supporter) of the Royal National Institute of Blind People (RNIB).

Henry Dunant (1828–1910)
Swiss humanitarian Henry Dunant was shocked when he witnessed the horrors of war after the Battle of Solferino in 1859. This led to him cofounding the Red Cross, an organization that helps victims of war. For this work, he won the first Nobel Peace Prize in 1901.

Princess Diana (1961–1997)
After marrying into the British Royal Family, Princess Diana took on many public duties. She brought the public's attention to a number of causes, such as charities helping people suffering from HIV/AIDS, and also organizations that worked toward removing dangerous land mines from war-torn areas.

Rules for prisoners
Elizabeth writes a set of rules for Newgate Prison. Only guards who are women can take charge of female prisoners. The prisoners receive work (such as needlework) which will help them find employment when they are released.

Night shelter
After seeing a young boy sleeping on the street, Elizabeth creates an organization to help homeless people. Volunteers provide them with support and a place where they can find shelter at night.

School for nurses
Elizabeth opens a training school for nurses in London. At the school, nurses learn about hygiene, and provide the same care to patients, whether they are rich or poor.

Good in everyone
Elizabeth decides to try to improve the lives of prisoners, believing that there is good in everyone. She teaches basic hygiene and sewing to prisoners. She comforts those inmates who are waiting to be executed.

Spreading her message
Elizabeth visits the British Parliament to talk about her prison work. She argues that prisons should rehabilitate people (help them become better citizens) rather than simply punish them. She speaks out against the death penalty.

Prison tour
Elizabeth's reforms have made her famous. Princess Alexandrina Victoria – later to become Queen Victoria – is among her admirers. Elizabeth goes on tours of the UK and Europe, introducing her ideas to prisons in other cities.

Death
Following a short illness, Elizabeth dies. More than 1,000 people stand in silence during her burial to honor her life's work. In 1849, a shelter for women who have just been released from prison is opened in her memory.

1816

1817

1818

1824

1827

1840

1845

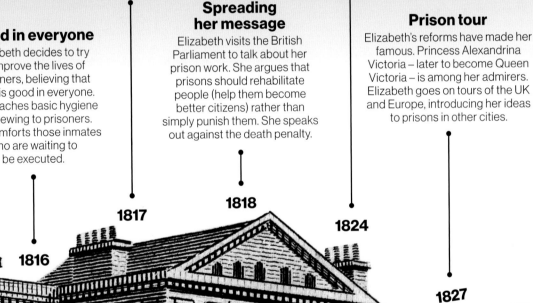

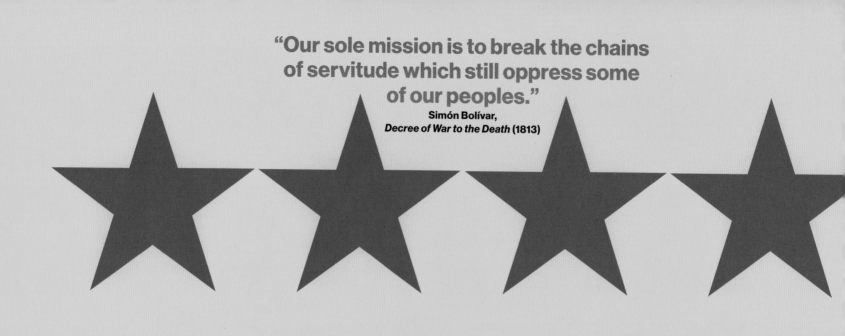

1783

Privilege

Simón Bolívar is born in Caracas (in modern-day Venezuela) to an elite creole (American-born white) family. At the time, Venezuela is under the colonial rule of Spain and Portugal.

1785

Orphaned

His father dies when Simón is just two and his mother passes away when he is about nine. His uncle hires tutors to educate him. One, Simón Rodríguez, introduces Simón to ideas of liberty and freedom. They become lifelong friends.

1797

Military academy

Simón enters an academy, where he studies military strategy and tactics. South America is simmering with political and economic tension, and many feel that a revolution against colonial rule is coming.

1799

Love and loss

Aged 15, Simón is sent to Spain to complete his education. He meets María Teresa del Toro, the daughter of a Spanish nobleman. They marry and return to Venezuela. In 1803 Maria dies of yellow fever and Simón goes back to Europe, devastated. He vows never to marry again – and he keeps his vow.

1804

Liberty

Simón is in Paris at the time of the coronation of Napoleon Bonaparte as Emperor of France. Though he disagees with Napoleon's politics, the idea of revolution interests him. He returns to Venezuela in 1807.

1810

First Republic

Napoleon's invasion of Spain and Portugal severs those countries' contact with their colonies in South America. The Spanish colonial authorities are overthrown in Venezuela, and rebels declare Venezuela an independent republic. This marks the start of the Venezuelan War of Independence.

1811

Colonial rule

Spain reasserts control over its rebellious colony. Going into exile in New Granada (in modern-day Colombia), Simón joins that country's independence movement and leads an army of 200 troops in numerous victories against the Spanish.

Simón Bolívar

Venezuela's most famous leader, Simón Bolívar (1783–1830) is remembered across Central and South America as *"El Libertador"* ("The Liberator"). His success in battle against the Spanish Empire helped to bring about the end of colonialism in South America, achieving independence for his own country as well as the modern-day nations of Bolivia, Colombia, Ecuador, Panama, and Peru.

Liberators of South America

In the 19th century, several key South American figures fought for liberation from Spanish and Portuguese rule.

Francisco de Miranda (1750–1816)

A Venezuelan military leader, Miranda fought in battles in Africa and North America. In 1810 he took part in the establishment of the First Venezuelan Republic.

1813   **1817**   **1824**   **1828**   **1830**   **1830**

Third Republic

Exiled to Jamaica, Simón writes of the struggles of people in the South American colonies – likening them to slaves. He returns to Venezuela to fight once more, proclaiming the Third Republic. It unites with New Granada, Ecuador, and what is now Panama to form a new state, Gran Colombia.

Manuela Saenz

Simón works to liberate other countries from Spanish rule. An attempt to assassinate him is stopped by Manuela Sáenz, who has been his romantic companion since 1822.

Last days

Ill with tuberculosis, Simón intends to exile himself to Europe, but he dies during the journey there. Though he found it hard to hold on to and manage the areas he liberated, his stunning victories are still celebrated in the region.

Second Republic

Simón's fame spreads, which him to recruit more soldiers to his army. He successfully marches on Caracas, and liberates Venezuela. He sets up, and is made ruler of, the Second Venezuelan Republic, but it is soon defeated and reclaimed by Spain.

Peru and Bolivia

Next, Simón sets about liberating Peru. Peruvian politicians declare him dictator of the region, and in under a year, he achieves his aims by defeating the Spanish there. In 1825 a part of Peru declares independence, calling itself "Bolivia" after Simón.

Splitting up

Internal arguments erupt in Venezuela and the great state of Gran Colombia splinters into the separate states of Ecuador, Venezuela, and New Granada. Simón's hopes of a united Spanish America lie in ruins.

José Francisco de San Martín (1778–1850)

A native Argentinian, San Martín assembled a force he named the "Army of the Andes". After Argentina declared independence in 1816, he campaigned against the colonial Spanish. An inspirational leader, he crushed Spanish power in southwestern South America, which also led to independence for Chile.

Juana Azurduy (1780–1862)

Juana Azurduy de Padilla fought in the Bolivian wars for independence. Her husband was killed early on in the war, but Azurduy continued to fight against the Spanish forces until they were finally overthrown in 1826, making Bolivia an independent republic. However, she died in poverty, largely forgotten.

Flag of the Third Republic

Simón Bolívar and his troops fought under this flag during the struggle for the Third Republic of Venezuela. The yellow represented wealth, the blue courage, and the red independence from Spain. The eight stars stood for the eight provinces of Venezuela.

Kidnapped

Aged about 12, Sacagawea is kidnapped by a group of Hidatsa – a rival tribe of the Shoshones. She is enslaved and later sold to a French-Canadian fur trader, Toussaint Charbonneau, who marries her. They live together in a Hidatsa village.

c.1788

Northern Shoshone

Sacagawea is born in land that is in modern-day Idaho, near the Rocky Mountains. She is born into the Agaidika ("Salmon Eater") band of the Northern Shoshone tribe.

c.1800

Corps of Discovery

US President Thomas Jefferson creates an army unit called the Corps of Discovery to explore the American northwest and search for a route to the Pacific Ocean. The unit, led by two explorers, William Clark and Meriwether Lewis, arrives in the Hidatsa village where Sacagawea lives.

Winter 1804

Sacagawea

Native American guide, interpreter, and explorer Sacagawea (c.1788–1812) helped explorers Meriwether Lewis and William Clark to map and explore North America. She translated local languages, found food, made clothes, and prepared medicines for the expedition. Without Sacagawea, the Lewis and Clark expedition would surely have failed.

Eating candles

The expedition across the Rocky Mountains is extremely hard and the explorers are close to starving. Sacagawea and the group are forced to eat candles to survive.

September 1805

Pacific coast

Sacagawea votes on where the explorers should build a fort for the winter. They build Fort Clatsop and stay there until spring. In January, Sacagawea sees the Pacific Ocean for the first time, and also a beached whale.

1805

A symbol of peace

The presence of Sacagawea with her baby helps to ease any tensions that suspicious tribes might have upon seeing the Lewis and Clark expedition.

"Monstrous fish"
The whale had died by the time the explorers got to it. Sacagawea was fascinated by what she called the "monstrous fish".

November 1805

Meriwether Lewis (1774–1809)

Lewis joined the armed forces aged 20. President Jefferson offered him a leading role on the expedition for his knowledge of the "Western country". Lewis became the Governor of the Upper Louisiana Territory in later life.

Toussaint Charbonneau

Hired

Lewis and Clark hire Charbonneau as an interpreter on their route to the Pacific Ocean. He does not speak Shoshone, so the explorers agree to take Sacagawea (who is pregnant) with them.

c.1804

William Clark (1770–1838)

Clark became friends with Lewis while in the army. As co-leader of the expedition, he oversaw the training of men and acted as the mapmaker. After the expedition, Clark governed the Missouri Territory.

Newborn

Sacagawea gives birth to her son, Jean Baptiste Charbonneau, in a fort built by the explorers. Sacagawea decides to take her son with them on the expedition.

February 11, 1805

Capsized boat

Charbonneau almost capsizes their boat. Sacagawea calmly saves important valuables and the explorers' papers, books, medicines, and instruments, which would have been lost.

May 14, 1805

Reunited

The explorers meet a group of Shoshone. Sacagawea is delighted to discover that their leader is a long-lost relative, Cameahwait. She helps Lewis and Clark buy horses and obtain a guide from him.

August 1805

River

A week after Sacagawea saves their belongings, Lewis and Clark name a tributary of the Musselshell River in Montana after her. It is known as the Sah-ca-gah-weah, or Bird Woman's, River.

May 1805

Moving to St. Louis

Clark invites Sacagawea and her husband to St. Louis, Missouri, and suggests they settle there. Clark enrols her son, Jean Baptiste, at a boarding school. A year or two later, Sacagawea gives birth to a daughter and names her Lizette.

Jean Baptiste Charbonneau (1805–1866)

After finishing school, Jean Baptiste worked as a fur trader. He impressed Duke Paul Wilhelm of Württemberg, Germany, on an expedition and was invited to live in Europe. When he returned, he worked as a guide and as a gold miner.

Death

Sacagawea dies at Fort Manuel Lisa from a fever, aged only 24. Clark becomes legal guardian to both her children after her death.

No payment

Sacagawea, her son, and her husband return to their village after the expedition. Her husband is paid $500, but Sacagawea receives nothing despite her crucial role in the expedition.

August 1806

1809

1812

The French Revolution

Queen Marie Antoinette (1755–1793)

Initially loved by the French people, Marie Antoinette gradually became a symbol of everything they felt was wrong with French society.

1755
Maria Antonia is born into the Austrian royal family at Hofburg Palace, in Vienna.

1770
She marries Louis-Auguste, the future king of France, and adopts the French version of her name to become Marie Antoinette.

c.1780s
Poor harvests cause food prices to increase.

1788
The royal family are in massive debt. Many regular people become angry that, as they struggle to survive, the queen is spending the country's money on luxuries such as fine dresses and parties.

1789
The Revolution begins. Louis turns to Marie Antoinette for advice, but neither of them are sure what to do. It is unclear what role the royal family will have in France's future.

October 1793
The new government is unsure what to do with Marie Antoinette, but eventually settles on a trial. She is found guilty of offenses, including treason (betraying France), and is executed by the guillotine (a machine with a sharp blade that is used to behead a person).

Jean-Paul Marat (1743–1793)

Jean-Paul Marat became a very influential figure before and during the early days of the French Revolution. He often wrote about the poor people of France, who he felt had been forgotten by the wealthy and powerful.

1743
Jean-Paul is born in Boudry, Prussia (in modern-day Switzerland). He is one of the nine children born to Jean-Paul Mara and Louise Cabrol.

1765
After receiving medical training in France, Jean-Paul moves to England to work as a doctor.

1774
Jean-Paul begins writing about the rights of the regular people. In *The Chains of Slavery*, he attacks the ruling classes for being tyrants opposed to freedom.

1789
Jean-Paul establishes the newspaper *L'Ami du Peuple* ("The Friend of the People"). In it, he writes that all French citizens should be equal. He believes this is only possible through political and legal reform. These ideas influence many people within France.

May 5, 1789
The Revolution begins.

1790
Jean-Paul becomes critical that the Revolution has done nothing to combat the inequality he sees in French society. Fearing his life is in danger, he goes into hiding several times.

1792–1793
After King Louis XVI is arrested, Jean-Paul is elected as a deputy to the new government of France. He argues with other politicians about the future of the country. One of his political enemies assassinates him while he is taking a bath.

King Louis XVI (1754–1793)

King Louis XVI led France before the Revolution. After it began, the new government eventually decided that he would be the country's last king.

1754
Louis-Auguste is born at Versailles. His older brother, Louis, is expected to become the next king, but he dies at the age of nine.

1774
Louis-Auguste becomes King Louis XVI of France. He inherits a massive financial crisis that has the country on the edge of bankruptcy.

May 1789
The Estates General—an assembly of representatives from across the country—are called to help with the crisis. They make suggestions to fix the problem. Louis fails to make a decision, which angers the Estates General. They declare that they are now the government of France. The Revolution has begun.

July 1789
Rumors spread that Louis plans to stop the Estates General. Revolutionaries attack the Bastille prison, looking for ammunition and gunpowder to fight the monarchy. The chaos forces Louis to accept the Revolutionary government's power—he is no longer in charge.

1791
With the Revolutionary government in power, the royal family try to flee France. They are captured and placed under house arrest by the government. The event further angers many of the revolutionaries.

January 1793
The Revolutionary government abolishes the monarchy—meaning that Louis is no longer the king. The revolution enters a bloody stage, with thousands killed because they are accused of treason. Louis, once king of France, is publicly guillotined in Paris.

The French Revolution (1789–1799) began as a struggle for power between the royal family and the regular people of France. It erupted into violence, instability, and war. The following people are just a few of the many who shaped the story of the Revolution.

Maximilien Robespierre (1758–1794)

A lawyer and politician, Maximilien Robespierre became one of the leaders of the French Revolution during its most violent period.

1758
Maximilien is born in Arras, in the north of France. He later moves to Paris to study law. He is a gifted student, and achieves good grades.

1789
He is elected as a deputy (representative member) of the Estates General, and later serves in the newly formed Revolutionary government. Maximilien openly criticizes the monarchy and supports the reform of the government, views which lead to him becoming increasingly popular with the French people.

1790
Maximilien is elected president of the Jacobin club—one of the political factions in the government. Elected to the government in 1792, Maximilien helps abolish the monarchy and put Louis XVI on trial for treason. France is declared a republic, a form of government in which power is held by elected representatives, not kings or queens.

1793
The execution of the king causes tension between the Girondins and the Jacobins—the two main political parties in the government. After a power struggle, Maximilien's party—the more extreme of the two—seizes control of the government.

September 1793

Now in charge of the government, Maximilien believes that the success of the Revolution is under threat by traitors. He begins the "Reign of Terror"—an incredibly violent series of executions and massacres. In less than a year, nearly 17,000 people are officially executed.

1794
As the Reign of Terror spins out of control, opposition to Maximilien's power grows. His rivals accuse him of ruling with absolute power—much like a king—and have him arrested. He is guillotined, and the Reign of Terror ends.

Olympe de Gouges (1748–1793)

The playwright, essayist, and activist Olympe de Gouges wrote in support of equal rights for women and enslaved people during the French Revolution.

1748
Marie Gouze is born into a middle-class family in southwestern France.

1765
She is forced into a marriage at the age of 16. Her husband dies a year later, and she decides to never marry again.

1770
Marie moves to Paris, and adopts the name "Olympe de Gouges." She makes friends with many people from the artistic and political worlds of Paris.

1789
Originally written in 1784, her play L'Esclavage des Noirs ("Black Slavery") is finally staged in Paris. The play attacks slavery, and the French monarchy's support of it in their colonies. It is shut down after a few performances.

1791
Olympe's essay Déclaration des droits de la femme et de la citoyenne ("Declaration of the Rights of Woman and the Female Citizen") is published. In it, she calls for equal rights for men and women in the new France that will emerge from the Revolution. It influences many revolutionaries, but it also gains Olympe some powerful enemies, who feel a woman should not speak out in this way.

November 1793

Olympe's criticism of the execution of the king, support of the Girondin party of the French government, and political writings lead her to be convicted of treason. She is tried and executed by guillotine during the Reign of Terror for her beliefs.

Napoleon Bonaparte (1769–1821)

Napoleon Bonaparte rose to fame during the French Revolutionary Wars that followed the execution of the king.

1769
Napoleon is born and educated in Corsica, an island off the coast of France.

1784
He attends a military academy in Paris and joins the army in 1785.

1793
After the king's execution, many of his supporters, both inside and outside the country, gather armies to attack France. Napoleon helps stop one such attack. For many, he instantly becomes a hero of the Revolution.

1794
Napoleon's reputation is tarnished as a result of his friendship with Robespierre. He is arrested for treason, but is eventually acquitted and released.

1796
By now a famous and respected military officer, Napoleon is given command of the French Army in Italy. He leads the troops in numerous victories in France's wars against Austria.

November 1799

Napoleon overthrows the government of France, and seizes power, calling himself First Consul (head of government). The Revolution is over.

1804–1821
After a string of military victories, and some clever political moves, Napoleon becomes emperor of France. When he starts losing battles, opinion in France turns against him. He is removed from power in 1814, and he dies in exile in 1821.

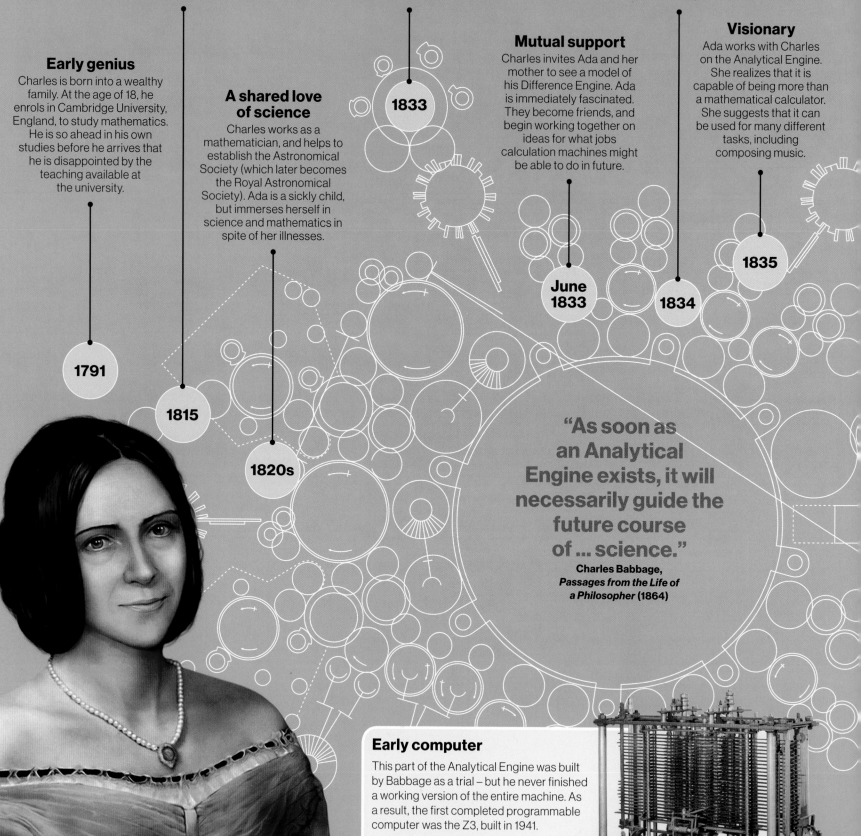

Maths and poetry

Ada is born to Lady Annabella Byron (a mathematician) and Lord George Byron (a famous poet). Her parents soon separate, and Ada never sees her father again. He dies in Greece when she is eight years old.

Calculating machine

Charles spends years developing a machine – called the "Difference Engine" – that can do calculations on its own. When Ada and Charles meet at a party in London, Ada is fascinated by his plans to build an ambitious new machine, which he calls the "Analytical Engine".

Analytical Engine

Charles sends Ada detailed notes about the Analytical Engine. The Difference Engine is designed to do one particular task. Charles hopes the Analytical Engine can be instructed to do any mathematical task – just like modern computers.

Early genius

Charles is born into a wealthy family. At the age of 18, he enrols in Cambridge University, England, to study mathematics. He is so ahead in his own studies before he arrives that he is disappointed by the teaching available at the university.

A shared love of science

Charles works as a mathematician, and helps to establish the Astronomical Society (which later becomes the Royal Astronomical Society). Ada is a sickly child, but immerses herself in science and mathematics in spite of her illnesses.

Mutual support

Charles invites Ada and her mother to see a model of his Difference Engine. Ada is immediately fascinated. They become friends, and begin working together on ideas for what jobs calculation machines might be able to do in future.

Visionary

Ada works with Charles on the Analytical Engine. She realizes that it is capable of being more than a mathematical calculator. She suggests that it can be used for many different tasks, including composing music.

1791

1815

1820s

1833

June 1833

1834

1835

> ### "As soon as an Analytical Engine exists, it will necessarily guide the future course of … science."
>
> **Charles Babbage,**
> *Passages from the Life of a Philosopher* **(1864)**

Early computer

This part of the Analytical Engine was built by Babbage as a trial – but he never finished a working version of the entire machine. As a result, the first completed programmable computer was the Z3, built in 1941.

Charles Babbage and Ada Lovelace

Charles Babbage (1791–1871) designed the "Analytical Engine" – a machine that was the ancestor of modern computers. Ada Lovelace (1815–1852), a mathematician with an artist's imagination, understood and explained what Babbage's invention might be able to do. Together they were pioneers in the field of computer science.

Computer scientists

Ada Lovelace was the first in a long line of women who played critical roles throughout the history of computer science, the field of science she helped to kick-start.

Grace Hopper (1906–1992)

Grace Hopper was an American computer pioneer and naval officer. She is best known for her contributions to the development of computer languages – the way humans tell computers what they want them to do. She also found the first computer "bug" – an actual moth that flew into Harvard University's Mark II computer, and caused a malfunction. The word "bug" has been used for a computer error ever since.

Annie Easley (1933–2011)

Annie Easley was an American computer programmer, mathematician, and rocket scientist for NASA, the US space agency. She worked on programs that were crucial to spaceflight and space exploration. Easley was one of the first African Americans to work at NASA.

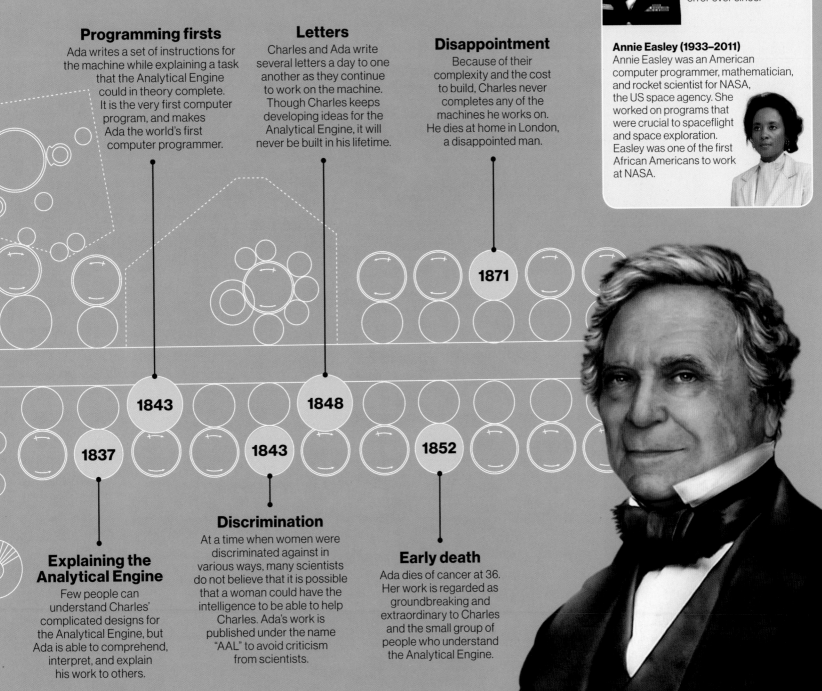

Programming firsts

Ada writes a set of instructions for the machine while explaining a task that the Analytical Engine could in theory complete. It is the very first computer program, and makes Ada the world's first computer programmer.

Letters

Charles and Ada write several letters a day to one another as they continue to work on the machine. Though Charles keeps developing ideas for the Analytical Engine, it will never be built in his lifetime.

Disappointment

Because of their complexity and the cost to build, Charles never completes any of the machines he works on. He dies at home in London, a disappointed man.

1871

1843

1848

1837

1843

1852

Explaining the Analytical Engine

Few people can understand Charles' complicated designs for the Analytical Engine, but Ada is able to comprehend, interpret, and explain his work to others.

Discrimination

At a time when women were discriminated against in various ways, many scientists do not believe that it is possible that a woman could have the intelligence to be able to help Charles. Ada's work is published under the name "AAL" to avoid criticism from scientists.

Early death

Ada dies of cancer at 36. Her work is regarded as groundbreaking and extraordinary to Charles and the small group of people who understand the Analytical Engine.

Policarpa Salavarrieta

A daring spy and revolutionary, Policarpa Salavarrieta (c.1795–1817) supported the struggle to free what is today the country of Colombia from the Spanish Empire. Working undercover as a seamstress, Salavarrieta entered the homes of her enemies to search for documents and information to help the revolutionary cause.

c.1795

Childhood

Policarpa is one of nine children born to a middle-class family in Guaduas (in modern-day Colombia). She has a comfortable childhood, and learns to read and write (unlike most girls at this time in the Spanish Empire).

c.1798

Move to Bogotá

Policarpa and her family move to a new house in Bogotá, the capital of New Granada, a Spanish colony that includes modern-day Colombia, Panama, Ecuador, and Venezuela.

c.1802

Smallpox

An outbreak of smallpox, a highly infectious disease, sweeps across Bogotá. Policarpa's mother, father, and two of her siblings die. Policarpa returns to Guaduas with her brother and sister, where they live with their godmother.

c.1805

New skills

Policarpa becomes a seamstress (someone who sews and makes clothes), and finds work in the homes of wealthy local families. Meanwhile, people throughout Spanish-ruled South America begin to campaign for their independence.

c.1810

Struggle for independence

Policarpa meets Alejo Sabaraín, a revolutionary fighting against the Spanish Empire. They plan to marry, but only after Colombia has won its independence.

Fighting for freedom

During the wars and rebellions of the 19th century, women often risked their lives working as spies or soldiers.

Luisa Recabarren (1777–1839)
A supporter of Chile's struggle for independence from the Spanish Empire, Luisa Recabarren was married to one of the country's leading revolutionaries. When her husband was forced into exile in Argentina in 1814, Recabarren wrote to him, passing on information about the political situation in Chile. Recabarren was arrested for sharing this information, and imprisoned.

Manuela Sáenz (1797–1856)
A revolutionary from what is now Ecuador, Manuela Sáenz fought against Spanish rule in New Granada. As well as hosting political meetings in Peru, Sáenz campaigned for women's rights, and worked alongside Simón Bolívar, one of the leaders of the South American independence movement. Sáenz organized troops during battle, and was given the rank of colonel in the rebel army.

Pauline Cushman (1833–1893)
Originally an actress, Pauline Cushman became one of the most successful spies for the Union Army during the US Civil War. Cushman pretended to be a supporter of the Confederate Army, and used this to gain important information that she passed to the Union side. She later went undercover dressed as a Confederate soldier.

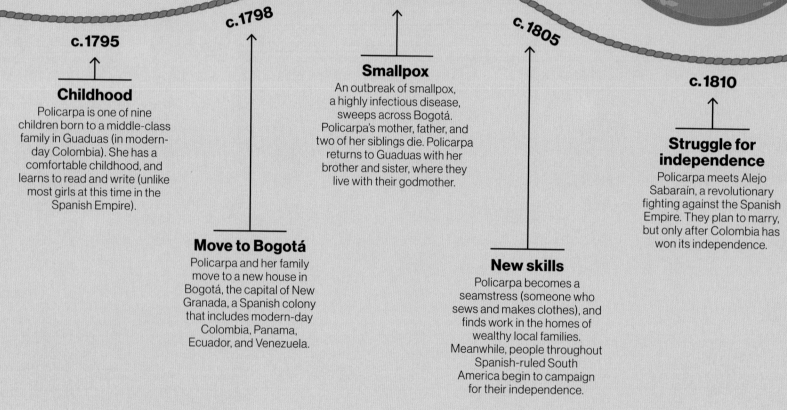

Working undercover

After pro-Spanish forces win back control of New Granada, Policarpa and Sabaraín have to work undercover. Because she has become a well-known revolutionary in her hometown, Policarpa has to move to Bogotá (which is under Spanish control again).

Arrested

Policarpa has become a leading spy and revolutionary. However, when Sabaraín is captured by pro-Spanish forces, they find documents connecting Policarpa to the rebels. This quickly leads to her arrest.

1816

September 1817

July 1810

1817

November 14, 1817

Rebellion in Bogotá

A rebellion against Spanish rule breaks out in Bogotá. Policarpa supports the uprising, and helps recruit people to the movement. She passes on any information she discovers about the Spanish to the rebels.

Back in Bogotá

Using a fake identity, Policarpa is able to enter and leave Bogotá. Policarpa works as a seamstress for pro-Spanish families, listening and looking for important information. She befriends enemy soldiers and persuades them to join the revolutionaries.

Execution

Policarpa refuses to give away the names of her fellow rebels to the Spanish authorities. As a result, she is sentenced to death by public execution. Policarpa's death turns her into one of the great heroes of the struggle for Colombian independence, which is achieved in 1819.

> "Although I am a woman and young, I have more than enough courage to suffer this death and a thousand more."
>
> **Policarpa Salavarrieta, speaking just before her execution (1817)**

MARY ANNING

The fossil hunter who shook up our knowledge of prehistoric life

Mary Anning (1799–1847) made revolutionary discoveries in the new field of paleontology—the branch of science dealing with the fossilized remains of living things. Her fossil-hunting work often came into conflict with the religious views of the time, and she was regularly shunned by scientists because she was a woman. Yet she carried on, and completely changed the way we think about the history of the Earth, as well as prehistoric life.

"Her history shows what humble people may do, if they have just purpose and courage enough, toward promoting the cause of science."

Charles Dickens, *Mary Anning, the Fossil Finder* (1865)

Extinction

In the early **19th century**, French scientist Georges Cuvier wrote about his ideas on the theory of extinction (the dying out of species). At this time, the majority of Europeans believed that God created the universe in seven days, and that everything had remained the same since then. Known as "Creationism," this view also stated that Earth was just a few thousand years old. Cuvier's work discussed the idea that species could become extinct as a result of great disasters—such as volcanic eruptions, or changes in the climate. The remains of these animals then became fossils—a remnant or an impression of an animal or plant preserved in the Earth's crust. His work opened up the new field of paleontology.

Curiosity hunting

Mary Anning is from a poor family. To make some extra money for their household, Mary and her brother Joseph help their parents search the beaches near where they live in Dorset, UK. The Annings hunt the rocks and cliffs for strange "curiosities"—rocks with mysterious impressions on them, or in shapes that look like animals that they do not recognize. Mary's father, Richard, teaches her and Joseph how to safely chip these curiosities off the rocks, and how to clean them without damaging them. They then sell the curiosities to local collectors. Over time, Mary discovers that the curiosities the Anning family have been finding and selling are actually prehistoric fossils.

Ichthyosaurus

In **1810**, Richard Anning dies from tuberculosis (an infection that affects the lungs), leaving the family in severe debt. Mary becomes increasingly skilled at identifying the curiosities she finds on the cliffs of Dorset, and begins studying fossils and paleontology. In **1811**, Mary and her brother come across the fossilized skull of a creature that they cannot identify. Mary unearths the rest of the skeleton in **1812**. It is more than 16 ft (5 m) long. The Annings sell the fossil, and it is sold a further two times. In **1819**, it ends up with a German naturalist, Charles Konig, who works for the British Museum. Konig suggests the name "*Ichthyosaurus*," meaning "fish lizard," for the fossil: the Annings had found the fossilized remains of a creature that had lived 200 million years ago.

Plesiosaurus

Mary often sells ammonite and belemnite (both closely related to modern-day squid) shells, which are very common on the Dorset coast. In **1823**, she discovers something larger, and more mysterious. It has a small head; a long, slender neck; a wide body with two pairs of paddle-like fins; and a short tail. Mary unearths the entire creature so quickly that the scientific community doubt that it is a real fossil, and Georges Cuvier even calls the discovery a fake. He eventually takes his comments back at a meeting of the Geological Society of London, admitting that it is an entirely unknown species. Despite having more knowledge and having spent more time working with fossils than many of the experts in the field, Mary is not invited to the debate, nor is she properly credited for her discovery, which is given the name "*Plesiosaurus*" meaning "near to reptile."

Dimorphodon

Mary's finds improve her wealth, and in **1826**, she buys a home with a storefront to display and sell her fossils. She is often mentioned in newspapers when she makes a new discovery, but official scientific groups, such as the Geological Society,

DIMORPHODON

ignore her because she is a woman. As a result, the men who move her fossils to be cleaned and preserved take the praise for her work themselves. In **1828**, she finds the first *Dimorphodon* fossil (a type of winged dinosaur) discovered outside of Germany, and it creates a huge sensation when it is displayed in the British Museum. In **1829**, Mary also discovers the fossil of a *Squaloraja*—a type of marine dinosaur similar to modern-day sharks.

Lasting legacy

The areas where Mary and her family hunted for fossils are eventually called the "Jurassic Coast," the name given to the period of time when ichthyosaurs, plesiosaurs, and dimorphodon roamed this part of Earth. She found many more notable fossils before her death in **1847**. Her discoveries were revolutionary in many different ways. They shook up the traditional teachings on the creation of Earth—demonstrating that the planet is much older than people had thought, and that many different kinds of animals once lived on it. Though she did not receive enough recognition for her work, Mary inspired others to discover more about the natural world and how it has changed over time. She spurred others on to find fossils across the world—helping us understand prehistoric animals such as dinosaurs, and even prehistoric humans.

ICHTHYOSAURUS

Aurore is born

Amantine-Aurore-Lucile Dupin (known as "Aurore") is born in Paris. Her father, Maurice, is a soldier and a descendant of the king of Poland. Her mother, Sophie-Victoire, comes from a working-class family.

1804

A countryside childhood

When she is four, Aurore's father dies. She leaves Paris with her mother and moves to Nohant, a small country town in central France. They move in with her father's mother, the Contesse de Horn, who owns a country estate there.

1808

Paris convent

Aurore is sent to Couvent des Augustines Anglaises, a convent (a community of Christian nuns) in Paris. Although she is described as rebellious at first, she gradually becomes more religious.

1817

Chopin

George's new partner, the Polish composer and pianist Frédéric Chopin, is ill. To help his health, the couple stay in Majorca, Spain, where the weather is warmer. She writes about the trip in her novel *A Winter in Majorca*. The two separate in 1847.

1838

George Sand

Amantine-Aurore-Lucile Dupin (1804–1876) was a French novelist and feminist best known by her pen name "George Sand". During her lifetime, she was one of the most popular writers in Europe. Her books mirrored her unique and eventful life in a way that kept readers hooked.

Aurore's story

Aged 50, George's autobiography, *The Story of my Life*, is published. In it, she tells the story of her family history, her own early life, her quest to be independent, and how she became a writer.

Country roots

After moving back to Nohant, George begins writing novels about the countryside. She draws inspiration from life on her country estate, and the lives of the working people there. These books are highly regarded by critics, who think they are her finest works.

1846

Fairy tale

George publishes a book for children called *The Mysterious Tale of Gentle Jack and Lord Bumblebee*. It is the story of a gentle child born into a wicked family. Its message is that it is important to be kind and humble.

1851

1854

Elderly years

George spends her final years in Nohant, often living with her grandchildren, for whom she writes *Tales of a Grandmother*, one of her last books. She dies from cancer at the age of 71.

1873–1876

Rebellious years

Aurore returns from the convent. Back home, she develops a passion for studying nature, practising medicine, and reading philosophy. She is a rebel, and even wears men's clothes in public (something that is illegal for women in France at this time).

c.1820

Mistress of Nohant

When Aurore's grandmother dies, Aurore inherits the estate. Soon after, she marries Casimir Dudevant. They will have two children together.

1822

Scandal

Aurore's marriage starts to decay, and she begins having relationships with other men. She develops a close bond with a lawyer, Aurélien de Sèze. This causes a scandal, because she is married, and he is engaged to be married.

1825

Back to Paris

Aurore leaves her family and escapes to Paris. She starts writing articles to earn money. She meets and falls in love with Jules Sandeau, a young writer. The two write a novel together, *Rose et Blanche*.

Becoming successful

George finds fame with *Indiana*. Her next four novels are also commercial successes. A few years later, George and Dudevant are legally separated.

1833

George Sand

Aurore works alone on her next novel. *Indiana* is a story about a woman seeking an escape from her unhappy marriage. She writes under the pen name George Sand. Like many female writers of the time, she uses a man's name, believing that male authors are taken more seriously.

1832

1831

French authors

In the 19th century, France produced many authors whose works were read all over the world.

Honoré de Balzac (1799–1850)

A novelist and playwright, Honoré de Balzac embarked on his most famous work, *La Comédie humaine* ("*The Human Comedy*") in 1831. It is a collection of novels that explore the different ways in which people lived in France at the time.

Victor Hugo (1802–1885)

Victor Hugo was a novelist, playwright, and poet. His novels *Les Misérables* and *Notre-Dame de Paris* ("*The Hunchback of Notre Dame*") are full of compassion for people in desperate situations.

Elizabeth Ann Ashurst Bardonneau (1813–1850)

English translator and activist Elizabeth Ann Ashurst Bardonneau translated many of Sand's books into English, helping them to find an audience there. She admired Sand's independent lifestyle.

1770 1785 1800 1815 1830 1845

Ranavalona I (c.1788–1861)
Mary Seacole (1805–1881)
Charles Darwin (1809–1882)
Abraham Lincoln (1809–1865)
Elizabeth Cady Stanton (1815–1902)
Karl Marx (1818–1883)
Frederick Douglass (c.1818–1895)
Harriet Tubman (c.1822–1913)
Louis Pasteur (1822–1895)
Cetshwayo kaMpande (c.1826–1884)
Rani Lakshmibai (c.1828–1858)
Emily Dickinson (1830–1886)
Rebecca Lee Crumpler (1831–1895)
Sitting Bull (c.1831–1890)

Ranavalona I to Nellie Bly

In the time between Queen Ranavalona I and Nellie Bly, injustice and inequality in societies across the world led many people to attempt to make things better. Harriet Tubman made daring raids to free African Americans from slavery. In India, the warrior queen Rani Lakshmibai led her people to stand up to colonial oppression by the British. And in Europe and the US, campaigners such as Emmeline Pankhurst and Elizabeth Cady Stanton helped secure the right to vote for women.

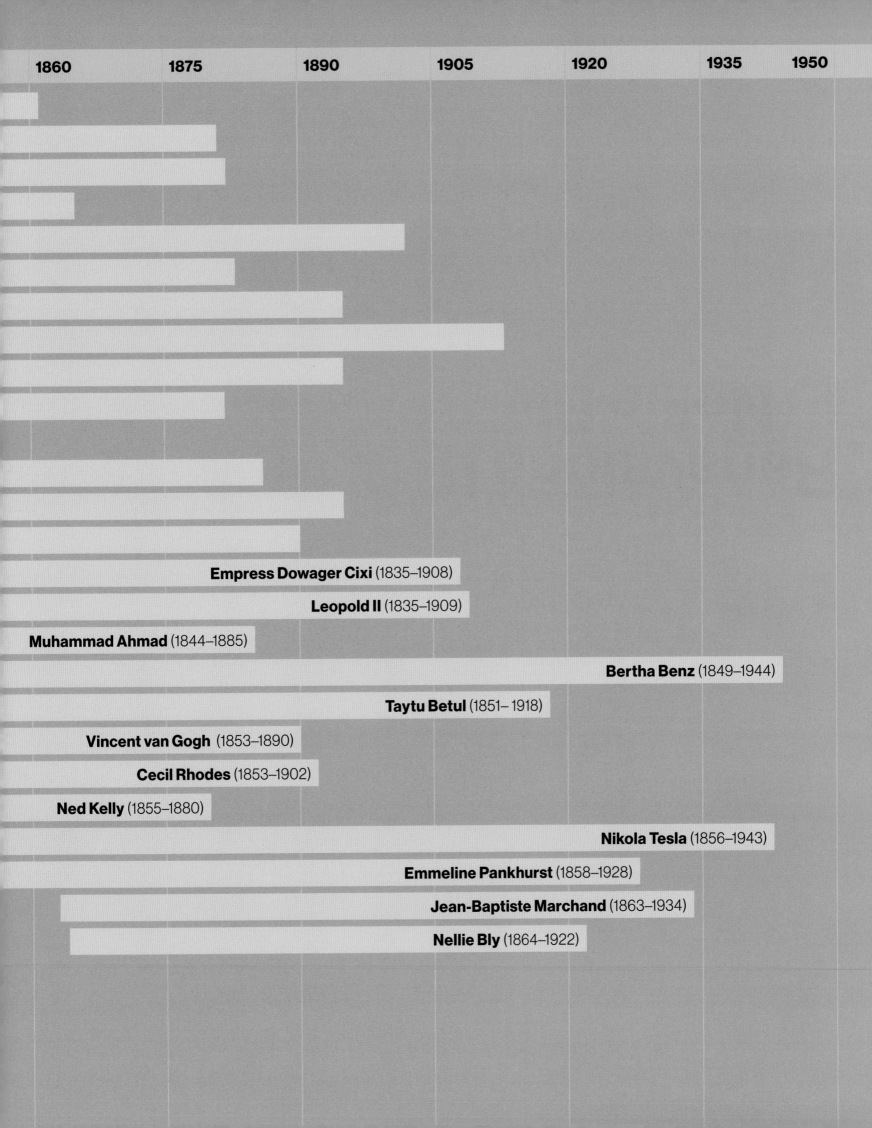

1860 1875 1890 1905 1920 1935 1950

Empress Dowager Cixi (1835–1908)

Leopold II (1835–1909)

Muhammad Ahmad (1844–1885)

Bertha Benz (1849–1944)

Taytu Betul (1851– 1918)

Vincent van Gogh (1853–1890)

Cecil Rhodes (1853–1902)

Ned Kelly (1855–1880)

Nikola Tesla (1856–1943)

Emmeline Pankhurst (1858–1928)

Jean-Baptiste Marchand (1863–1934)

Nellie Bly (1864–1922)

Mary Seacole

Jamaica-born nurse Mary Seacole (1805–1881) dedicated her life to caring for the sick. After her offer to help save lives as a nurse during the Crimean War (1853–1856) in eastern Europe was rejected by the British government, she funded her own trip to the battlefields. There she became known as "Mother Seacole" by the grateful soldiers she cared for. After her death, her remarkable achievements were forgotten for more than a century, but now she is once again recognized as a hero.

> **"The grateful words ... which rewarded me for binding up a wound ... was a pleasure worth risking life for."**
>
> **Mary Seacole,**
> ***Wonderful Adventures of Mrs Seacole in Many Lands (1857)***

Pioneering health workers

The 19th century was a time of great development in health care. Thanks to pioneers such as Florence Nightingale and Mary Eliza Mahoney, nursing standards radically improved, ultimately saving millions of lives.

Florence Nightingale (1820–1910)
British social reformer Florence Nightingale brought huge changes to the profession of nursing. Like Mary Seacole, she served as a nurse in the Crimean War, where her promotion of good hygiene in hospitals dramatically reduced the number of deaths. In 1860, she set up the world's first nursing school in London.

Mary Eliza Mahoney (1845–1926)
Born to formerly enslaved parents, Mary Eliza Mahoney was one of the first African American women to become a registered nurse. She established an organization to help promote African Americans in the nursing profession. She fought for women's equality and for women to be able to vote.

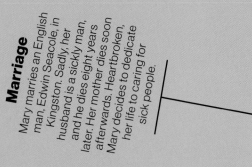

Yellow fever
Mary returns to Jamaica just as an epidemic of yellow fever, an often fatal disease, hits the island. The medical authorities ask her to supervise nursing services for the British Army.

1853

Treating cholera
While Mary is visiting her brother in Cruces, Panama, a cholera epidemic sweeps through the town. Using herbal medicine, she successfully nurses many of the patients back to health.

1851

Marriage
Mary marries an English man, Edwin Seacole, in Kingston. Sadly, her husband is a sickly man, and he dies eight years later. Her mother dies soon afterwards. Heartbroken, Mary decides to dedicate her life to caring for sick people.

1836

Travelling
Eager to explore the world, Mary sails twice to London, to visit family, and England, to visit family, and later travels around the Caribbean. In all the places she visits, she boosts her knowledge by studying local medicines and treatments.

c.1821

Mary the nurse
By the age of 12, Mary is care for her mother of her patients. Because of her father's army connections, helping her community to she has military profession practise their their profession She combined with her knowledge gained from watch experience and African remedies.

1817

Early life
Mary Seacole is born Mary Grant, to a Jamaican mother and a Scottish father in Kingston, Jamaica. Her mother, a nurse and a healer, treats sick people using traditional herbal remedies. Her father is a British army officer.

1805

British Hotel

In the Crimea, Mary and her friend Thomas Day build the British Hotel, a makeshift restaurant and shop where soldiers can rest, and buy food and medical supplies. She treats the wounded, and delivers rations to the front line. The troops call her "Mother Seacole".

Crimean War

The Crimean War, a conflict in eastern Europe between Britain and its allies and the Russian Empire, breaks out. When Mary hears about the British military's poor medical facilities, she travels to England and asks to be sent to the area as an army nurse. Refused by the British government, she decides to fund her own trip.

Back to England

Mary returns to England with little money and declares herself bankrupt. She survives at first on donations from the public.

Telling her story

Mary's autobiography, The Wonderful Adventures of Mrs Seacole in Many Lands, is published. In it, she gives her account of caring for the sick and coping with the constant barrage of missiles during the war.

WONDERFUL ADVENTURES of Mᵣˢ SEACOLE

LONDON
JAMES BLACKWOOD

Royal connections

As Mary's celebrity grows, she becomes known in royal circles. A nephew of Queen Victoria carves a statue of her, which is later exhibited at the Royal Academy. She becomes a nurse to Alexandra of Denmark, the Princess of Wales and wife of the future King Edward VII.

Death

Mary spends her last years living quietly. She dies in her home in London.

1853

1855

July 1856

July 1857

1871

1881

STATUE OF MARY SEACOLE BY SCULPTOR MARTIN JENNINGS OUTSIDE ST THOMAS' HOSPITAL IN LONDON

Charles Darwin

For millennia, people have tried to answer the big questions of where we come from, and why there is life on Earth. In 1859, English naturalist Charles Darwin (1809–1882) unveiled his theory of natural selection, which explained how life developed through evolution. His book *On the Origin of Species*, would prove to be one of the most influential scientific works in history.

1850s
"The mystery of the beginning of all things is impossible to solve by us."
The Life and Letters of Charles Darwin (1887)

Although Charles is convinced that he is right, he is troubled by his conclusion, as it contradicts the Christian belief that living things have remained unchanged since their creation by God. Disturbed by ill health and the death of his beloved daughter Anne, he sets aside his work on evolution and spends eight years studying barnacles.

1831
"Nothing can be more improving to a young naturalist, than a journey in distant countries."
The Voyage of the Beagle (1839)

After graduating from Cambridge University, where he develops a passion for natural history, 22-year-old Charles is offered a place aboard HMS *Beagle* as resident naturalist on a voyage around the world. The trip lasts five years. Charles later felt it to be the most important event of his life.

1840s
"I am convinced that Natural Selection has been the main ... means of modification."
On the Origin of Species (1859)

Charles develops his principle of "natural selection." He believes that the living things that survive long enough to pass on their characteristics to the next generation are those that adapt best to their environment. This natural selection causes "modification," or slow changes that happen through the generations. He later terms this "evolution."

1835
"The natural history of these islands is eminently curious, and well deserves attention."
The Voyage of the Beagle (1839)

Going ashore as often as possible, Charles carefully makes records of the plants and animals he finds. On the remote Galápagos Islands, 621 miles (1,000km) off the South American mainland, Charles is intrigued to learn that the shells of giant tortoises vary subtly from island to island, and notes differences between mockingbirds, too.

1838
"As many more individuals of each species are born than can possibly survive ... there is a frequently recurring struggle for existence."
On the Origin of Species (1859)

Charles is inspired by an essay by English economist Thomas Malthus, which predicts that the rapid growth in the human population will outstrip the supply of food, causing famine and disease. He wonders whether this "struggle for existence" might apply to all plants and animals.

1836
"A man who dares to waste one hour of time has not discovered the value of life."
Letter to Susan Elizabeth Darwin, The Life and Letters of Charles Darwin (1887)

Back in England, Charles starts the huge task of organizing his notes and cataloging specimens. As well as writing an account of the voyage, he keeps a notebook in which he speculates that "one species does change into another." He keeps his ideas secret as he knows they will challenge Christian thinking—which states that everything was made by God, and does not evolve.

1858

"Every species has come into existence coincident ... with a pre-existing closely allied species."

Alfred Russel Wallace, *On the Law which has Regulated the Introduction of New Species* (1855)

When British naturalist Alfred Russel Wallace proposes a similar theory of natural selection, Charles is spurred into publishing his own more detailed and thoroughly researched work.

1859

"I would rather be the offspring of two apes than be a man and afraid to face the truth."

T.H. Huxley, *Oxford evolution debate* (1860)

Charles's groundbreaking *On the Origin of Species* eventually hits the bookshelves in 1859. It divides the scientific community and causes uproar among many Christians. The author's illness keeps him away from public debates, but one of his friends, English scientist T.H. Huxley passionately argues his case.

1871

"There is **no fundamental difference** between man and the higher mammals."

The Descent of Man (1871)

Charles expands his ideas in *The Descent of Man*, proving that humans are animals descended from apes. People make fun of his theories—a famous drawing shows him with the body of chimpanzee—but few disagree with him. He dies in 1882 after a long illness, and is buried with great ceremony at Westminster Abbey in London.

Abraham Lincoln

Born into a poor family, lawyer and politician Abraham Lincoln (1809–1865) went on to become the 16th president of the United States. He led the country through the difficult years of the Civil War, and is now regarded as one of the greatest presidents in US history.

Humble beginnings
Abraham is born in a one-room log cabin in Kentucky. His family move to rural Indiana in 1816. Though he lacks regular schooling, Abraham teaches himself to read.

Local politics
Settling in New Salem, Illinois, Abraham becomes a shopkeeper and a popular member of the community. He gets involved in local politics and is elected to the Illinois State Legislature.

Marriage and family
He meets Mary Todd, an upper-class Kentucky woman, and they marry. They lose their second son Edward to tuberculosis in 1850, and typhoid fever kills their third son William, known as "Willie," in 1862.

Return to politics
Slavery—legal in many of the southern states, but illegal in the northern states—has become a huge political issue. Abraham reenters politics, joining the anti-slavery Republican party.

On the move
The family move to Macon County, Illinois, and Abraham gets a job on a riverboat. He observes slavery for the first time while working on the Mississippi River.

Lawyer
Abraham qualifies as a lawyer after teaching himself law. He moves to Springfield, Illinois, and for the next few years works as a lawyer.

Government
Abraham is elected to the US House of Representatives—the lower house of the US government. He serves for two years, before returning to Springfield to continue practicing law.

"A house divided"
Abraham delivers a powerful speech making it clear that slavery is immoral and that the US cannot be a country when it is "half slave and half free" or "a house divided."

1809

1830

1834

1836

1842

1846

1856

June 1858

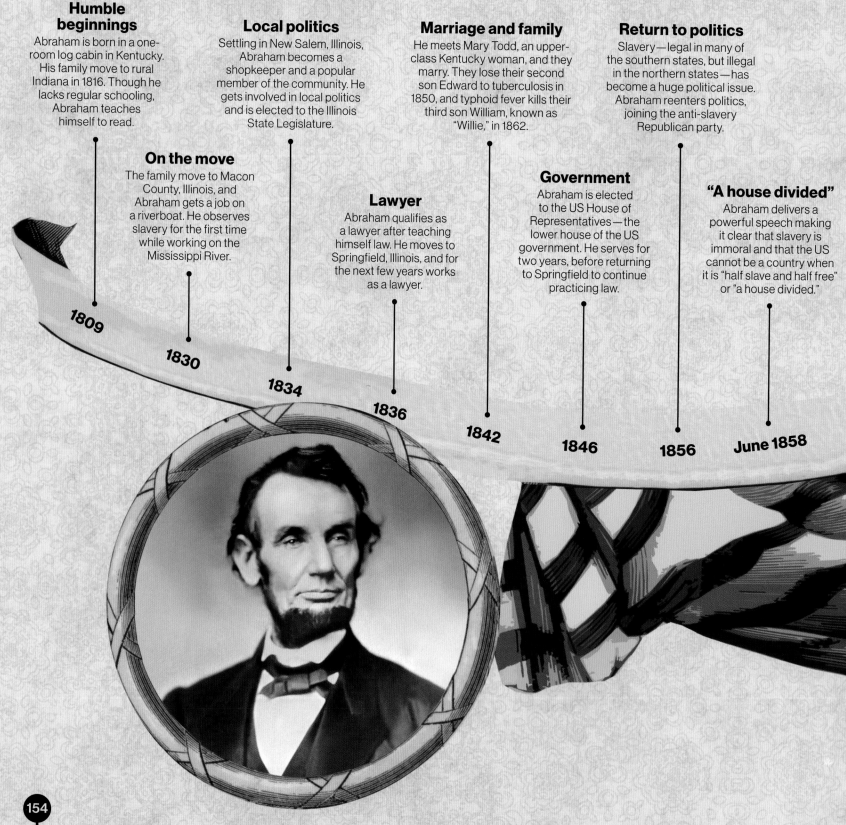

> **"Government of the people, by the people, for the people, shall not perish from this earth."**
> Abraham Lincoln, *Gettysburg Address* (1863)

American Civil War (1861–1865)

In the Civil War, the 23 Union states of the north and west fought the 11 Confederate states of the south. The Confederacy was forced to surrender for a variety of reasons, including exhaustion and lack of resources. The war led to long-term bitterness between north and south.

Breaking away

The southern states, which depend on slave labor, do not want Abraham to be president. They fear he will abolish slavery, which will wreck their economy. They secede (break away) and together form the Confederate States of America, in opposition to the northern Union states.

Emancipation

At a crucial point in the Civil War, Abraham issues the Emancipation Proclamation, which frees all 3.5 million enslaved people in the Confederate states. Many of these join the ranks of the Union army and fight against the Confederate forces.

Gettysburg Address

At a ceremony in Gettysburg, Pennsylvania, Abraham summarizes that the Civil War is essentially about the freedom granted to every American in the Declaration of Independence. It becomes the most quoted speech in US history.

Assassination

Five days after the Confederates surrender, John Wilkes Booth, a Confederate supporter, shoots Abraham in the head as he watches a play at a theater. Abraham never regains consciousness, and dies the next morning.

US president

Abraham decides to run for president. His humble origins, opposition to slavery, and gentle personality are all highlighted in the campaign. He wins the election thanks to strong support in the north and west of the country.

Civil War

Although Abraham hopes to avoid a war, fighting breaks out between the Confederate and the Union armies, which leads to a civil war (a war between people of the same country).

Reelected

Abraham is reelected as president, and his second term starts the following March. In April 1865, the Confederate forces surrender. More than 600,000 soldiers have died during the war.

1860

1861

April 1861

January 1, 1863

November 1863

November 1864

April 14–15, 1865

Two friends and a foe

The people who played a role in Lincoln's life (and death) have themselves become well-known figures in US history.

Mary Todd Lincoln (1818–1882)
Abraham Lincoln's wife, Mary, was a great support to her husband, but was unpopular with the public, who criticized her for her outspoken opinions and her overspending in the White House. After her husband's death, Mary fell into a deep depression.

William H. Seward (1801–1872)
Secretary of State in Abraham's cabinet, Seward became one of his closest advisers during the Civil War. After the war, he helped to reintegrate the south into the US. He later negotiated the purchase of Alaska from the Russian Empire.

John Wilkes Booth (1838–1865)
A rising actor, Booth believed that the abolition of slavery would destroy his country. He hoped to keep the war going by killing Lincoln. After shooting the president, he managed to escape, but he was pursued and was himself shot dead by a soldier two weeks later.

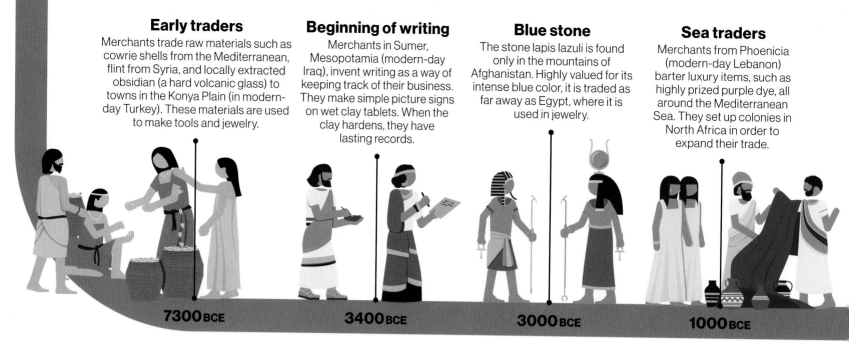

Early traders

Merchants trade raw materials such as cowrie shells from the Mediterranean, flint from Syria, and locally extracted obsidian (a hard volcanic glass) to towns in the Konya Plain (in modern-day Turkey). These materials are used to make tools and jewelry.

Beginning of writing

Merchants in Sumer, Mesopotamia (modern-day Iraq), invent writing as a way of keeping track of their business. They make simple picture signs on wet clay tablets. When the clay hardens, they have lasting records.

Blue stone

The stone lapis lazuli is found only in the mountains of Afghanistan. Highly valued for its intense blue color, it is traded as far away as Egypt, where it is used in jewelry.

Sea traders

Merchants from Phoenicia (modern-day Lebanon) barter luxury items, such as highly prized purple dye, all around the Mediterranean Sea. They set up colonies in North Africa in order to expand their trade.

7300 BCE **3400 BCE** **3000 BCE** **1000 BCE**

Merchants through time

Merchants trade (buy and sell) goods. Trade goes back to early human history when the first merchants transported useful materials they found in plentiful supply to places where they were scarce. Later, merchants exchanged goods by bartering—swapping a sheep, say, for a piece of cloth.

Plague port

A ship arriving in the port of Messina, Sicily, from Constantinople (Istanbul) brings the Black Death (a deadly bubonic plague) to Europe. It rapidly spreads along trade routes, killing 30–50 percent of the European population in four years.

1347

Merchant spies

In the Aztec Empire (in modern-day Mexico), merchants called *pochteca* travel long distances in search of exotic bird feathers, jaguar pelts, jade, and cocoa. The *pochteca* work as spies, too, gathering information that they pass on to the Aztec army.

Spicing things up

Portuguese explorer Vasco da Gama discovers a sea route from the Atlantic Ocean around the tip of southern Africa to Asia. Soon after, European merchants begin trading in pepper, cinnamon, and other spices from Indonesia.

Food exchange

Foods such as potatoes, maize (corn), and tomatoes are introduced to Europe from the Americas. Sugar cane, originally from Southeast Asia, is now grown in Brazil. It is farmed on plantations worked by enslaved people brought there from Africa.

1450 **1498**

1550

First money

The world's first known coins are produced in the kingdom of Lydia (in modern-day Turkey). Trading coins for goods gradually replaces bartering. They are made of electrum, a mixture of gold and silver. (Chinese people start using paper money in around 1000 CE.)

The Silk Road

Silk from China is taken westward to Europe along an overland trade route through Central Asia using camel trains. Ideas spread along the Silk Road, too, as missionaries and pilgrims from India bring Buddhism to China.

Trading empire

The city of Rome is the hub of a vast trading network stretching from Arabia to Britain. Cargo ships transport grain from Egypt. Other imported goods include silk from China, spices from India, and amber from Scandinavia.

600 BCE   **130 BCE**   **100 BCE**

Merchant guilds

In Europe, craftspeople form merchant guilds. These organizations set standards for their work and grant permits to trade. There is a guild for almost every trade. Trainees known as apprentices have to follow strict rules. They must work for their masters for at least five years before they can become full guild members.

Hanseatic League

Merchants in several North German cities form a powerful trade association called the Hanseatic League. It dominates long-distance trade in northern Europe until the 1500s.

Crossing the Sahara

In Africa, merchants lead caravans of camels across the Sahara, linking Mediterranean ports with West Africa. The camels are loaded with salt, metal armor, and beads, which are exchanged for gold, ivory, and enslaved people.

1300   **c.1260**   **1000 CE**

Trading companies

English investors establish the East India Company to trade in the Indian Ocean region. In 1602, Dutch merchants set up the Dutch East India Company with the same purpose. Rivalry between the two companies leads to bitter trade wars.

Japan expels merchants

To stop the spread of Christianity, the Tokugawa Shogunate (military government) of Japan forbids Europeans from entering the country. This dramatically reduces trade. Japan does not resume trading relations with the West until 1853.

Atlantic slave trade

The brutal trade in enslaved people from Africa is at its height. British and other European traders transport thousands of men, women, and children across the Atlantic from West Africa to the Americas, to be sold to plantation owners. The slave trade is outlawed by Britain and the US in 1807 but in the US enslavement itself is not abolished until 1863.

Trade speeds up

More goods than ever are carried around the world by sea. The opening of the Suez Canal, connecting the Red and Mediterranean seas, vastly shortens the time taken for cargo to reach its destinations.

Buying online

Companies such as Amazon and eBay are set up to take advantage of e-commerce—buying and selling products and services over the internet. Today, people can browse, buy, sell, and review goods, wherever they are.

1600   **1638**   **1780**   **1869**    **1994**

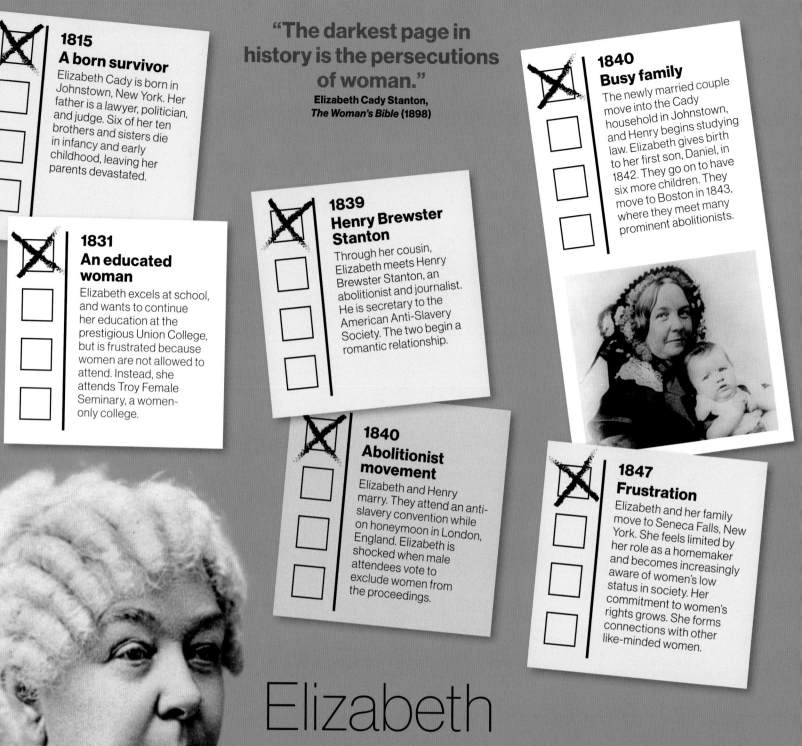

1815
A born survivor
Elizabeth Cady is born in Johnstown, New York. Her father is a lawyer, politician, and judge. Six of her ten brothers and sisters die in infancy and early childhood, leaving her parents devastated.

"The darkest page in history is the persecutions of woman."
Elizabeth Cady Stanton,
***The Woman's Bible* (1898)**

1840
Busy family
The newly married couple move into the Cady household in Johnstown, and Henry begins studying law. Elizabeth gives birth to her first son, Daniel, in 1842. They go on to have six more children. They move to Boston in 1843, where they meet many prominent abolitionists.

1831
An educated woman
Elizabeth excels at school, and wants to continue her education at the prestigious Union College, but is frustrated because women are not allowed to attend. Instead, she attends Troy Female Seminary, a women-only college.

1839
Henry Brewster Stanton
Through her cousin, Elizabeth meets Henry Brewster Stanton, an abolitionist and journalist. He is secretary to the American Anti-Slavery Society. The two begin a romantic relationship.

1840
Abolitionist movement
Elizabeth and Henry marry. They attend an anti-slavery convention while on honeymoon in London, England. Elizabeth is shocked when male attendees vote to exclude women from the proceedings.

1847
Frustration
Elizabeth and her family move to Seneca Falls, New York. She feels limited by her role as a homemaker and becomes increasingly aware of women's low status in society. Her commitment to women's rights grows. She forms connections with other like-minded women.

Elizabeth Cady Stanton

US activist Elizabeth Cady Stanton (1815–1902) was a pioneering campaigner in the battle for women to be granted the same rights as men. She organized one of the first women's rights conventions in the US, and argued passionately for women's suffrage—the right for women to vote.

Suffrage activists

The suffrage movement in the US was made up of many women from different backgrounds and cultures.

Maria W. Stewart (1803–1879)
After losing both her parents at the age of five, Maria W. Stewart went on to become a teacher, journalist, and activist. In the 1830s, she became the first African American to lecture for the causes of abolition and women's rights.

Lucy Stone (1818–1893)
A brilliant orator (public speaker) on abolition and women's rights, Lucy Stone became a close associate of Elizabeth Cady Stanton. She was the first woman in Massachusetts to earn a college degree, and caused controversy by refusing to take her husband's surname after marriage.

Susan B. Anthony (1820–1906)
Susan B. Anthony's ceaseless work alongside her friend Elizabeth Cady Stanton paved the way for the 19th Amendment to the US Constitution, which is sometimes named after her.

1848
Seneca Falls

With her friend Lucretia Mott and other activists, Elizabeth organizes a women's rights convention in Seneca Falls. She drafts the "Declaration of Sentiments," based on the US Declaration of Independence, which demands women's suffrage because men and women are equal.

1854
New York speech

Elizabeth makes a speech to the New York State Legislature. Her speech helps secure a law that gives married women the right to keep their wages—previously the property of their husbands.

1880s
Writing

In her 60s, Elizabeth shifts her focus from public speaking to writing. She contributes to a six-volume *History of Woman Suffrage*. She causes controversy with her book, *The Woman's Bible*, in which she challenges the traditional Christian view that women should obey men.

1851
Susan B. Anthony

Now a popular public speaker on women's rights, Elizabeth meets Susan B. Anthony, who shares her passion. The two become firm friends. Their contrasting personalities—Elizabeth is lively and talkative, while Anthony is quiet and studious—make them a powerful team.

1863 13th Amendment

During the US Civil War, Elizabeth and Anthony present a petition to Congress. It has nearly 400,000 signatures in support of banning slavery. The 13th Amendment (law change) to the US Constitution, outlawing slavery, is passed in 1865.

1902
Death and legacy

At the age of 86, Elizabeth dies of heart failure. Eighteen years later, her dream of women's suffrage finally comes true in the US. The 19th Amendment is passed, finally giving American women the right to vote.

1852
Temperance

As well as their work on women's suffrage, Elizabeth and Anthony establish the Woman's New York State Temperance Society, to draw attention to the harmful effects of alcohol. Elizabeth remains committed to promoting temperance her whole life.

1869
Women's suffrage

The two women form the National Woman Suffrage Association (NWSA), arguing that the 15th Amendment, which gives African American men the right to vote, should also include women. The amendment comes into effect in 1870, excluding women, but they fight on.

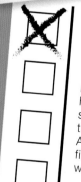

Karl Marx

The writings and ideas of Karl Marx (1818–1883), a German-born philosopher and economist, have had a huge impact on world history. His belief in "class struggle," a prediction that the poor would rise up against the wealthy to create a fairer society, has inspired political movements around the world.

Communism

Marx's revolutionary ideas were used as the foundation for communism, a political belief that all people should share wealth and land equally. It is considered to be the opposite of capitalism, which promotes individual wealth and can lead to inequality.

German thinkers

Huge changes in 19th-century life led many across Europe to question the way society worked. Many of the new breed of thinkers on these issues came from Germany.

Friedrich Engels (1820–1895)

The key architect of Marxist theory, alongside Marx, Engels finished off the second and third volumes of *Das Kapital* after his friend's death.

Friedrich Nietzsche (1844–1900)

A brilliant intellectual, Nietzsche attacked the ideas of religion, arguing that individuals should take charge of their own destiny. He also disliked communism.

Rosa Luxemburg (1871–1919)

A Marxist philosopher and writer, Luxembourg was born in Poland but moved to Germany in 1898. She was executed after leading a failed communist uprising.

University

To please his father Karl studies law, but his passion is for philosophy and literature. In 1836 he gets engaged to the aristocratic Jenny von Westphalen. Their partnership is controversial because of their different classes and religious backgrounds.

Journalism

Karl completes his studies and moves to Cologne, where he works as a journalist for a radical newspaper. The paper faces heavy censorship by the authorities, and is banned after publishing an unflattering article about the Russian royal family.

Meeting Engels

Karl and his wife move to Paris, where he writes for *Forward!*, a German-language newspaper. He meets a fellow German, Friedrich Engels, and the pair begin to collaborate.

Early life

The eldest of nine children, Karl is born in Trier, Prussia (in modern-day Germany), into a middle-class Jewish family. Shortly before his birth, his family converts to Christianity because of discrimination against Jews.

1818   **1835**   **1842**   **1844**

Move to Brussels
Karl is forced to leave France after the government shuts down *Forward!*. He is allowed to move to Belgium as long as he stops writing about politics.

1845

1847

The Communist Manifesto
Marx and Engels write *The Communist Manifesto*. In it, they encourage the proletariat (poor people) to rise up against the bourgeoisie (wealthy people) in revolution, in order for the world to be more fair.

1848

Expulsions
Across Europe, protestors start rebellions demanding freedom and democracy. Karl writes in support of the uprisings, causing him to get kicked out of the country. He returns to Cologne but is soon expelled from there, too.

1849

Move to London
Karl's wife is expecting their fourth child as the family seek refuge in London. He makes little money from his writing, so Engels (who is from a wealthy family) provides for his friend.

1852

Regular writer
The *New-York Daily Tribune* hires Karl to write regular articles, satisfying the growing US interest in European news about politics.

First International
Karl becomes a leading figure in the International Working men's Association (often called the "First International"), which aims to promote interest in other International class struggle. His lack of view leads points of to conflict.

1864

1867

Das Kapital
After many years of research, Marx publishes the first volume of *Das Kapital* ("Capital"). This book on economics focusing on the negatives of capitalism, becomes a huge "communist bible."

Family tragedies
Karl's health is failing, and the death of his beloved wife Jenny leaves him devastated. Caroline, his eldest daughter, dies two years later. Karl falls into despair.

1881

1883

Death in London
Karl dies of bronchitis and pleurisy. Only a few people (including Engels) attend his funeral. These days, his tomb in Highgate Cemetery, London, is visited by hundreds of people every day.

1826

"I set out ... at whatever cost of trouble, to learn how to read."

Narrative of the Life of Frederick Douglass, An American Slave (1845)

Aged eight, Frederick is sent to a new slaveholder in Baltimore. The slaveholder's wife teaches him to read, but her husband stops the lessons, worried that reading will lead Frederick to demand his freedom.

1838

"I prayed for freedom for twenty years, but received no answer until I prayed with my legs."

Narrative of the Life of Frederick Douglass, An American Slave (1845)

Two years after a failed attempt, Frederick successfully escapes by hopping on a train heading north, to the anti-slavery states. He is helped by his fiancée, a free African American woman named Anna Murray, and they marry. He changes his surname to Douglass to divert attention from himself. He becomes a preacher, and begins to campaign against slavery.

1845

"You have seen how a man was made a slave; you shall see how a slave was made a man."

Narrative of the Life of Frederick Douglass, An American Slave (1845)

Having delivered his first anti-slavery speech in 1841, Douglass is now an established public speaker. He writes the first of three volumes of his autobiography. It's a huge success, but Douglass worries that this old slaveholder will find him and claim him back. He decides to leave the US, and travels around Ireland and the UK. Two years later, two Englishmen "purchase" his freedom by paying off his former slaveholder.

1847

"Right is of no sex — Truth is of no color."

Slogan of The North Star newspaper

Returning to the US, Douglass sets up a weekly anti-slavery newspaper, *The North Star*, in New York. The paper advocates women's rights, as well as the abolition of slavery.

1861

"Let the slaves be ... formed into a liberating army, to march into the South and raise the banner of Emancipation."

"How To End the War," Douglass' Monthly (1861)

The Civil War breaks out in the US, with slavery as a central point of difference between the anti-slavery Union in the north and pro-slavery Confederacy in the south. Douglass argues that African Americans should be allowed to fight for their freedom for the Union.

1864

"[Lincoln] did not let me feel for a moment that there was any difference in the color of our skins."

About Abraham Lincoln (1864)

President Abraham Lincoln's Emancipation Proclamation declares the freedom of all enslaved people in Confederate-held territory. Douglass is critical of Lincoln's late conversion to abolition but recognizes his hatred of slavery, and the two become friendly.

Frederick Douglass

A formerly enslaved person, African American Frederick Douglass (c. 1818–1895) was the leading campaigner against slavery of his time. He was a brilliant public speaker and wrote a best-selling autobiography, which powerfully described the effect of slavery on the enslaved. In his later years, he acted as an advisor to President Abraham Lincoln during the US Civil War, and campaigned for equal rights for all people right up to the end of his life.

c. 1818

"I do not recollect ever seeing my mother by the light of day ... She would lie down with me, and get me to sleep, but long before I waked **she was gone**."

Narrative of the Life of Frederick Douglass, An American Slave (1845)

Frederick Bailey is born into slavery in Maryland, the son of an enslaved woman and an unknown white man. He is separated from his mother as an infant, and lives with her parents.

1867

"Let no man be kept from the ballot box because of his color."

From a speech (1867)

The passage of the Thirteenth Amendment to the US Constitution brings slavery in the US to an end forever. Douglass switches his attention to African American rights. He supports Ulysses S. Grant as president in the 1868 election. Grant wins, and he supports guaranteeing African Americans the right to vote, which is granted in 1870 in the Fifteenth Amendment.

1883

"No man can put a chain about the ankle of his fellow man without at last finding the other end fastened about his own neck."

From a speech at Civil Rights Mass Meeting, Washington, D.C. (1883)

Douglass continues giving powerful speeches well into old age, lecturing and writing in support of civil rights. He dies in 1895 after giving a speech to the National Council of Women.

Harriet Tubman

In the South, Harriet Tubman (c. 1822–1913) battled enslavement and disability to help more than 70 enslaved people escape captivity. She achieved this through a secret network known as the Underground Railroad. In later years, she became a passionate speaker for women's right to vote.

Harsh conditions

Harriet is born Araminta ("Minty") Ross in Maryland, into an enslaved family. She endures cruel beatings by slaveholders as a child. Aged around 12, she is hit on the head with a heavy metal weight. The injury causes her lifelong seizures and hallucinations.

1822

Harpers Ferry

Harriet's success gains her respect among other abolitionists (people looking to end slavery). She helps leading abolitionist John Brown recruit for a planned raid on an arsenal at Harpers Ferry, Virginia, which he hopes will start a slave revolt. However, the raid fails and Brown is executed.

Civil war

Civil war breaks out between the slaveholding Confederate states of the south and the antislavery Union states of the north. Harriet welcomes the war as an opportunity to advance the abolitionist cause. She works as a nurse, but is soon helping recruit African American soldiers to fight for the Union.

Moses

Harriet mounts 13 successful missions in total. She uses her growing network of trusted friends and contacts to rescue many family members, as well as 50-60 additional people. She earns the nickname "Moses," after the biblical prophet who led the Hebrews to safety.

1861　　　　**1859**　　　　**1851**

Female activists of the 19th century

Before the 19th century, women's opinions on how society should work were rarely taken into account. As the abolition cause grew, female activists began to speak out about slavery and women's issues.

Sojourner Truth (1797–1883)

African American activist Sojourner Truth was born Isabella Baumfree to enslaved parents. After escaping and gaining freedom in 1826, she campaigned passionately for abolition and women's rights, delivering heartfelt speeches across the nation. Truth would often point to her own muscles, gained during her years of slave labor, to demonstrate a woman's strength.

Harriet Beecher Stowe (1811–1896)

Shocked by the cruelty of the Fugitive Slave Act, American writer Harriet Beecher Stowe was inspired to write *Uncle Tom's Cabin*. It vividly described the suffering that enslaved people endured and firmly convinced many people of slavery's evil. Although criticized today for its portrayal of African Americans, the novel was so successful in the 19th century that only the Bible sold more copies.

Combahee River Raid

Harriet leads a group of armed scouts through South Carolina's swamps and marshes, providing key army intelligence. She becomes the first woman in charge of an armed assault during the Civil War when she guides Union steamboats along the Combahee River safely past the Confederate fire. Once ashore, Union troops set several plantations ablaze, liberating more than 700 enslaved people.

Humanitarian work

The Union Army wins the Civil War, and slavery is finally abolished across the US. Harriet starts a new career helping formerly enslaved people and the poor, but struggles for money, having been denied compensation for her role in the war.

1863　　　　**1865**

Dreams of freedom

She is allowed to marry a free black man, John Tubman, and around this time she decides to name herself "Harriet," which was her mother's name. She sets her heart on escaping slavery by fleeing to the north (where slavery is illegal), but her husband does not share her dream.

1844

Underground Railroad

When Harriet's slaveholder dies, she fears she will be sold and separated from her family. While "loaned" out to another plantation, she escapes by using a network of trusted people and safe houses known as the Underground Railroad. She reaches the free state of Pennsylvania.

1849

Underground Railroad

The Underground Railroad was not a literal railroad. Instead, it was a network of secret routes and safe houses organized by black and white abolitionists along which fleeing enslaved people (or "passengers") could travel to reach safety in the northern US or Canada. Small bands of runaways, led by a guide or "conductor," kept away from towns, crossing forests, swamps, and mountain trails to escape detection by slave catchers. In total, the Underground Railroad is estimated to have taken about 100,000 enslaved people to freedom.

Growing confidence

After successfully rescuing her brother, Harriet returns to Maryland to find her husband, only to discover he has married another woman. Instead, she leads a group of 11 people safely to Canada, her most daring mission yet.

1851

First rescue

Congress passes the Fugitive Slave Act, which punishes those helping enslaved people escape. Despite the risks, Harriet vows to return to Maryland to rescue her family. Using her knowledge of the swamps and forests, she leads her niece and her niece's two children to safety.

1850

This was the slogan of the National Association of Colored Women, which fought for women's rights.

LIFTING AS WE CLIMB

Home for the aged

Harriet donates land to open a home for elderly and poverty-stricken African Americans. She dies there of pneumonia in 1913, surrounded by friends and family.

Women's rights

Harriet becomes actively involved in the movement to give women the vote. She is finally granted an army pension in 1899.

Biting the bullet

Harriet undergoes brain surgery in an attempt to treat the head trauma she has suffered since childhood. She refuses an anesthetic, choosing instead to bite on a bullet, as Civil War soldiers had during their operations.

1890s

1898

1903–1913

Louis Pasteur

Regarded as one of the world's greatest scientists, Louis Pasteur (1822–1895) made important discoveries that uncovered how tiny, microscopic life-forms spread disease and contaminate things. His work led to improved hygiene standards, medicines, and vaccines, and many other things we take for granted today, which have helped save millions of lives.

Cholera

Cholera is an infection of the small intestine that results in severe diarrhea. It is caused by eating or drinking food or water that contains the microscopic bacterium *Vibrio cholerae*. Through a microscope, we can see that this bacteria has an elongated head, and a long tail.

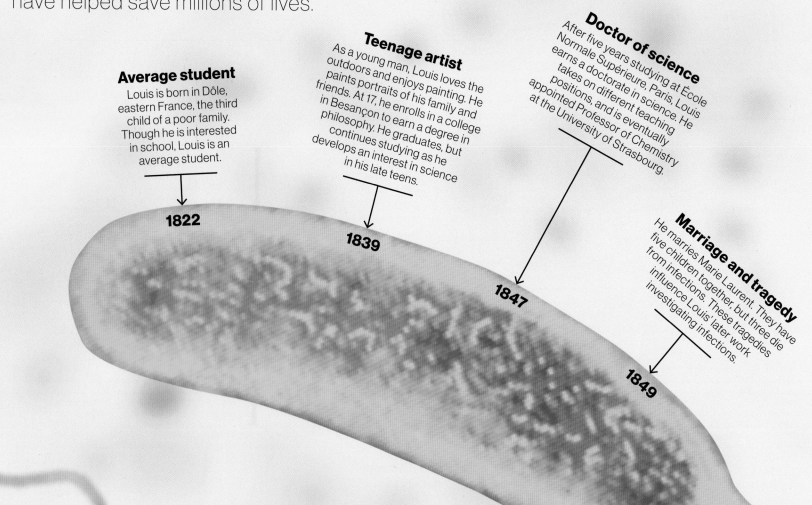

Average student

Louis is born in Dôle, eastern France, the third child of a poor family. Though he is interested in school, Louis is an average student.

1822

Teenage artist

As a young man, Louis loves the outdoors and enjoys painting. He paints portraits of his family and friends. At 17, he enrolls in a college in Besançon to earn a degree in philosophy. He graduates, but continues studying as he develops an interest in science in his late teens.

1839

Doctor of science

After five years studying at École Normale Supérieure, Paris, Louis earns a doctorate in science. He takes on different teaching positions, and is eventually appointed Professor of Chemistry at the University of Strasbourg.

1847

Marriage and tragedy

He marries Marie Laurent. They have five children together, but three die from infections. These tragedies influence Louis' later work investigating infections.

1849

Pioneers of medicine

Some of the world's most dangerous diseases have been brought under control by pioneering scientists who discovered the causes of these deadly infections and how to treat them.

Edward Jenner (1749–1823)

Experimental vaccinations by English physician Jenner provided protection against the killer disease smallpox. His vaccination procedures spread around the world.

Alexander Fleming (1881–1955)

Scottish scientist Fleming discovered penicillin's potential to kill bacteria in 1928. Mass production of the drug helped protect soldiers from wound infections during World War II.

To Youyou (b. 1930)

Chinese chemist To Youyou discovered a new treatment for malaria. Her work has saved millions of lives, and earned her the Nobel Prize in 2015.

Death

Louis' work on vaccines saves countless lives. In 1888, he sets up the Pasteur Institute in Paris, which is committed to the investigation of microbes, diseases, and vaccines. In 1894, he suffers a second stroke, which he never fully recovers from. He dies the following year.

1888–1895

Rabies

Louis works on a vaccine for rabies—a contagious disease—using rabbits, then dogs, as test subjects. As an unlicensed doctor, Louis is not allowed to test it on humans. However, a desperate father pleads with him to help his infected son, who recovers after the use of the vaccine.

1885

Cholera epidemic

Louis suffers a stroke and is partially paralysed, but continues to work. He begins to apply his knowledge of how microbes behave to the study of cholera and other diseases.

1868

Vaccines

Louis believes that the weakened cholera microbes gave immunity (resistance to infection) to the chickens. He develops a weak form of the cholera infection, which, once injected, helps animals and humans fight the infection. This is known as a vaccine.

1879

October 1879

Weakened microbes

He starts culturing (growing) fresh cholera microbes. But his research is interrupted by a long summer holiday. When he returns home, he injects the old and weakened microbes into some chickens. They become ill, but do not die.

1865

Silkworms

Louis explains that harmful microbes attack silkworm eggs, causing the silk to be ruined. His advice on how this can be prevented saves the silk industry from huge financial losses.

1854

Souring

Now a chemistry professor at Lille University, Louis studies why drinks sometimes "spoil" (turn sour). He learns that tiny microbes (microscopic organisms) of bacteria contaminate them. He then realizes that heat kills these microbes, and prevents the drink from spoiling. In time, this process becomes known as "pasteurization."

"I will not give up my Jhansi."
Rani Lakshmibai, to an official of the British East India Company (1853)

RANI LAKSHMIBAI

Warrior queen of the Indian Rebellion

Lakshmibai, the Queen of Jhansi (c. 1828–1858), was an extraordinary Indian leader. During the Indian Rebellion of 1857, she showed outstanding bravery in defending her beloved state of Jhansi against British forces. She died in battle but became an inspirational figure for many Indians for her resistance to British colonialism.

The British in India

In the **early 1850s**, India was under the control of the East India Company, a powerful British trading corporation with its own huge army. The prosperous state of Jhansi, in north India (in modern-day Uttar Pradesh), was not ruled directly by the East India Company but by its own raja (king), Gangadhar Rao, with the corporation's approval. In **1851**, Gangadhar Rao and his wife, Lakshmibai—the rani (queen) of Jhansi—had a son, but the boy died when he was only three months old. The British had a policy called the "doctrine of lapse," which allowed them to take control of an Indian ruler's lands if he died without a male heir. By **November 1853**, the raja was very ill. The couple adopted a son. They asked the British authorities to accept the boy as the raja's heir, and for Lakshmibai to take over as ruler on the raja's death. However, when he died the next day, the British ignored the request, and moved to take control of Jhansi.

Unconventional queen

Lakshmibai is now a widow. As a child, she received a good education, and learned to sword fight, ride horses, and shoot. She challenges the British decision but is rejected. In **March 1854**, she is given a pension (a regular payment for those unable to work), and told to leave the royal palace. Meanwhile, resentment in India against British rule is growing. In **April 1857**, sepoys (Indian-born soldiers) serving in the East India Company in the town of Meerut, 300 miles (500 km) away, refuse to go on parade and are imprisoned. This sparks protests and riots, which quickly spread to other towns and cities. It is likely that Lakshmibai sees this as an opportunity to regain control. In **June**, she gathers supporters, takes control of Jhansi Fort, and reestablishes order. She offers safe haven for British families, but they are massacred by rebels. The British authorities blame her, and make plans to capture Jhansi.

Freedom fighter

Lakshmibai moves quickly to defend her city. She gathers large stores of food and orders the manufacture of ammunition and gunpowder in preparation for a long siege. She calls for men and women to join her army. Major-General Hugh Rose, a senior British officer, is put in charge of the campaign against Jhansi. Around **March 21, 1858**, British forces surround the city, and they start firing on Jhansi around **March 25**. The rani takes up her sword, and gathers her officers. She urges her soldiers to hold their nerve and discipline. Riding a horse, she supervises the city's defenses, but the Jhansi army is unable to withstand superior British firepower. Around **April 3**, Rose orders his soldiers to storm the city. Many citizens are massacred. Lakshmibai, it is believed, collapses with mental and physical exhaustion, but recovers to resume the fight.

Daring escape

During the night of **April 4**, Lakshmibai is persuaded to escape. She leaves on horseback, with her son strapped to her back in a shawl. The British are in hot pursuit. Covered in dust, she arrives at Kalpi, 100 miles (150 km) northeast, where she joins with another rebel group. They occupy Kalpi until **May 22** when the British take the town. Forced to flee again, the rebels move on to Gwalior (in modern-day Madhya Pradesh), where they join Indian forces in the city's fort. On **June 17**, the British attack Gwalior Fort. In the thick of the fighting, the queen is wounded, probably by a saber (sword), and falls from her horse. She slips into unconsciousness, and dies two days later. Three days after her death, the British retake the fort. Recalling one of his greatest adversaries, Sir Hugh Rose describes her as "remarkable for her bravery, cleverness, and perseverance ... the most dangerous of all the rebel leaders."

Immortal

By the **fall of 1858**, the Indian Rebellion has been crushed. The British government closes down the East India Company and brings India under its direct control. Statues of Lakshmibai on horseback, with her son strapped to her back, are erected in cities throughout India. She continues to be a subject of books, films, and songs today.

mid-1850s
"I do not go out at all ... Mother is much as usual. I know not what to hope of her."
Letter to Mrs. Haven (1858)
Emily's mother becomes bedridden with illness. Emily helps with all the work required to maintain a large household, rising before dawn to make the fires, preparing the family breakfast, and looking after the garden.

1856
"To own a Susan of my own Is of itself a Bliss—."
Letter to Susan Huntington Gilbert (1870)
Emily's brother Austin marries her friend, the writer Susan Huntington Gilbert. Susan becomes a lifelong supporter of Emily's poetry, and the two women exchange hundreds of letters over the years.

1854
"I'm so old fashioned, Darling, that all your friends would stare."
Letter to Abiah Root (1854)
Emily becomes increasingly reclusive, preferring to avoid interacting with other people in person. At the age of 23, she declines an invitation from Abiah Root, a close friend, to visit Boston. Withdrawing into her inner world, she rarely leaves the house.

Emily Dickinson

Although she was not widely known during her lifetime, and her work was rarely published, Emily Dickinson (1830–1886) is now recognized as one of the most innovative and important poets ever. The majority of her vast collection of poems were discovered only after her death.

1852
"Good bye Sir, I am going My country calleth me."
Sic transit gloria mundi (1852)
Having started to write poetry as a teenager, Emily has her first work—a playful poem called "Sic transit gloria mundi" ("Thus passes earthly glory") published in the local newspaper, the Springfield Daily Republican, though she does not supply her name when she submits it.

1830
"I have a Brother and Sister—My Mother does not care for thought— and Father—too busy with his Briefs—to notice what we do."
Letter to T. W. Higginson (1862)
Emily Elizabeth Dickinson is born into a well-to-do family in the college town of Amherst, Massachusetts. She is the second of three children to Edward and Emily Norcross Dickinson. Her father is a lawyer.

1850
"... the tears come, and I cannot brush them away."
Letter to Abiah Root (1852)
Leonard Humphrey dies suddenly, aged 25. Emily is devastated at the loss of her inspirational friend and finds it difficult to adjust to life without him.

1848
"'Faith' is a fine invention When Gentlemen can see— But Microscopes are prudent In an Emergency."
"Faith" is a fine invention (c.1860)
As a student at Mount Holyoke Female Seminary she rebels against the school's religious teachings. She is fascinated by the idea of scientific study, which she sees as essential to understanding the universe.

1846
"I went to school ... but had no education."
Letter to T. W. Higginson (1862)
She studies at Amherst College. She finds it dull at first, but things change when Leonard Humphrey takes over as principal. Emily grows close to him as a friend and mentor.

1862

"Are you too deeply occupied to say if **my Verse is alive?**"

Letter to T. W. Higginson (1862)
The early 1860s are a very productive period for Emily. After reading an essay by literary critic Thomas Wentworth Higginson in *The Atlantic Monthly*, a literary magazine, she writes and asks him to review her work. They strike up a correspondence that lasts for many years.

1870

"Forgive me if I am **frightened**; I never see strangers, and hardly know what I say."

T. W. Higginson, recalling Emily's comments at their first meeting (1891)
After many years of corresponding, Emily and Higginson finally meet. She talks constantly, and he finds a lot of what she has to say to be wise.

1874

"**Wild nights**—Wild nights! Were I with thee Wild nights should be Our luxury!"

***Wild nights—Wild nights!* (c.1861)**
After her father's death, Emily develops a close relationship with her father's friend Judge Otis Phillips Lord. Letters to Lord suggest she considers marrying him.

1886

"Because I could not stop for **Death**— He kindly stopped for me—."

***Because I could not stop for Death* (published 1890)**
Emily dies of a stroke. Before she died, she had requested that her coffin be carried through fields of buttercups, and then buried in West Cemetery in Amherst.

1890

"I have had a '**Joan of Arc**' feeling about Emilies [*sic*] poems from the first."

Lavinia Dickinson, Letter to T. W. Higginson (1890)
After Emily's death, her sister Lavinia discovers hundreds of unpublished poems. Family members argue over what to do with them, but eventually they are published. Emily's poems become an overnight sensation, and are now held in high regard as a unique and fascinating collection of work.

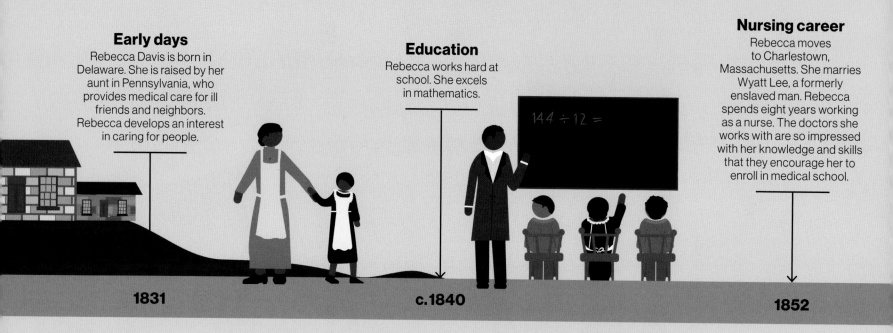

Early days
Rebecca Davis is born in Delaware. She is raised by her aunt in Pennsylvania, who provides medical care for ill friends and neighbors. Rebecca develops an interest in caring for people.

1831

Education
Rebecca works hard at school. She excels in mathematics.

$144 \div 12 =$

c.1840

Nursing career
Rebecca moves to Charlestown, Massachusetts. She marries Wyatt Lee, a formerly enslaved man. Rebecca spends eight years working as a nurse. The doctors she works with are so impressed with her knowledge and skills that they encourage her to enroll in medical school.

1852

Rebecca Lee Crumpler

Rebecca Lee Crumpler (1831–1895) was the first African American woman to qualify as a doctor. She dedicated herself to treating women and children who lived in poverty. She treated patients regardless of their ability to pay, and often took no money for her work.

African American pioneers

These trailblazing African Americans inspired future generations with their groundbreaking achievements in the 19th century.

Alexander Twilight (1795–1857)
Born in Vermont, Alexander Twilight is believed to have been the first African American to graduate from college. He went on to become principal of a school, and in 1836 became the first African American to serve in a US state legislature.

William Wells Brown (c.1814–1884)
William Wells Brown escaped enslavement at the age of 20. An activist and writer, he became famous for his powerful speeches arguing for an end to enslavement. His novel *Clotel* (1853) was the first by an African American to be published.

Sarah Jane Woodson Early (1825–1907)
An educator and author, Sarah Jane Woodson Early was the first African American woman to teach at a university. She taught English and Latin, and also lectured widely on the importance of education for women.

Back to Boston
Rebecca and Arthur move to Boston. She starts a medical clinic in the mainly African American neighborhood of Beacon Hill. She treats women and children even if they are not able to pay her for her work. The following year, she and Arthur have a daughter, Lizzie.

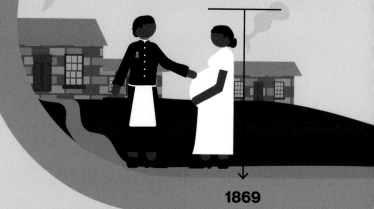

1869

Medical school

Rebecca wins a scholarship to train as a doctor at New England Female Medical College in Boston. Only 300 of about 55,000 doctors in the US at this time are women, and none are African American women.

1860

Graduation

When Rebecca graduates, she becomes the first African American woman to earn a medical degree. She battles several misfortunes to get there, including losing her funding when the Civil War breaks out, and suffering the death of her husband from tuberculosis.

1864

Racism

Though she is valued by her patients, Rebecca is often shunned by fellow doctors because of her ethnicity and gender. They sometimes refuse to supply medicine to her patients.

1865

Move to Virginia

After the Civil War ends, Rebecca and Arthur move to Richmond, Virginia. She works for an organization that helps formerly enslaved people rebuild their lives after slavery. She treats people who would otherwise receive no medical care.

1865

Marriage

After graduating, Rebecca marries Arthur Crumpler, a man who escaped from enslavement. She starts a medical clinic in Boston, caring for poor African Americans.

1864

A Book of Medical Discourses

Now living in Hyde Park, New York, Rebecca turns the journal notes she has kept during her years of medical practice into a book. *A Book of Medical Discourses* gives advice to women on how to care for themselves and their children.

1883

Death

Long after retiring from practicing medicine, Rebecca dies in Fairview, Massachusetts. Despite the many obstacles placed in her way, she has achieved much in her career, and is an inspiration to many who came after her.

1895

Sitting Bull

Tatanka Iyotanka, more commonly known as Sitting Bull (c.1831–1890) was a Native American chief and holy man of the Hunkpapa Lakota people, a Teton Sioux tribe. He spent much of his life struggling against white Americans who sought to take over land his people had lived on for centuries.

Strong Heart Warrior Society
Sitting Bull rises to become leader of the Strong Heart Warrior Society, a group of elite warriors that seeks to ensure the welfare of the Sioux tribe.

Becoming a leader
Through a series of battles against US forces, Sitting Bull demonstrates qualities that the Sioux value, including bravery and wisdom. After visions of the future he receives come true, the Sioux come to see him as a spiritual leader, too.

c.1831	1840	1844	1854	1856	c.1863	c.1868

Birth
The child who will later be known as Sitting Bull is born into a Hunkpapa Lakota community on land that is now part of South Dakota.

"Slow"
Early in his life, he shows no great interest in warfare. He is given the nickname "Slow", perhaps as he takes his time before answering any question. He learns how to hunt buffalo about the age of 10.

"Sitting Bull"
During a raid on an enemy tribe, Slow knocks a warrior off his horse. His father is so impressed by his bravery that he gives him his own name. Slow will now be known as Tatanka Iyotanka, which means "Sitting Bull".

War begins
In retaliation for the killing of 30 US soldiers, the US Army massacre 86 Lakota Sioux warriors in the Battle of Ash Hollow. It is the beginning of a 36-year war in which Sitting Bull will play an important role.

Fighting back
Sitting Bull's people are attacked by the US Army, who are retaliating against a different Sioux tribe. This is Sitting Bull's first experience of fighting against US troops.

Native American warriors
Despite lacking numbers and firepower, Native American warriors used the tactics of guerrilla warfare – such as ambushes and raids – to inflict several major defeats on the US Army.

Geronimo (1829–1909)
An Apache war leader and healer, Geronimo gained a fearsome reputation for repelling Mexican, and later, US, invasions of Apache land. Towards the end of his life, he dictated his life story to a translator, and the book was published before he died.

Crazy Horse (c.1840–1877)
Remembered for his life-long resistance against the US government, Crazy Horse led the annihilation of the US cavalry at Little Bighorn in 1876. He was killed a year later in battle.

Buffalo Calf Road Woman (c.1844–1879)
Buffalo Calf Road Woman is famous as the only woman who fought at the Battle of the Little Bighorn. Some also believe that she knocked General Custer off his horse during the battle.

Treaty

Many of the Sioux leaders sign the Treaty of Fort Laramie with the US government. In exchange for an end to the fighting, these leaders agree to live on a reservation – an area of land set aside for them. Sitting Bull does not sign the treaty, and feels no obligation to respect its terms.

Defiance

Sitting Bull and his people decide to stand their ground and not leave their land. As US troops move into the area, Sitting Bull gathers a big force of Sioux, Cheyenne, and Arapaho warriors.

Battle of the Little Bighorn

The US Army, led by General George Custer, attacks the Native American camp by the Little Bighorn River. Sitting Bull is now too old to fight, but he provides spiritual leadership and strong medicines for the warriors. The Native Americans defeat the US forces, killing more than 250 soldiers, including Custer himself.

Surrender

With food and resources scarce, Sitting Bull and his followers are forced to return to the US and surrender. They are imprisoned for almost two years.

Death

Local police fear Sitting Bull is planning to join a rebellion, and go to arrest him. In the tussle that follows, Sitting Bull is shot and dies immediately.

1868 **1874** **1876** **June 1876** **June 1876** **1877** **1881** **1885** **1890**

Gold Rush

The discovery of gold in the Black Hills of Dakota – within the Sioux reservation territory – sparks a rush of American miners to the area. The US government ignores the Treaty of Fort Laramie, and orders Sioux tribes off their reservation.

Sitting Bull's vision

During a sun dance ritual, one of the most important spiritual events of the year, Sitting Bull has a vision of US soldiers falling into the camp "like grasshoppers from the sky". He interprets this as an omen of a coming war.

Pursued

The defeat at Little Bighorn shocks the US public. The US Army recruits more troops to pursue the Native American warriors. Sitting Bull leads his people across the border to safety in Canada.

Wild West show

Sitting Bull finally rejoins his tribe on the reservation. He reluctantly tours for four months with *Buffalo Bill's Wild West* theatrical show, earning money for performing to crowds.

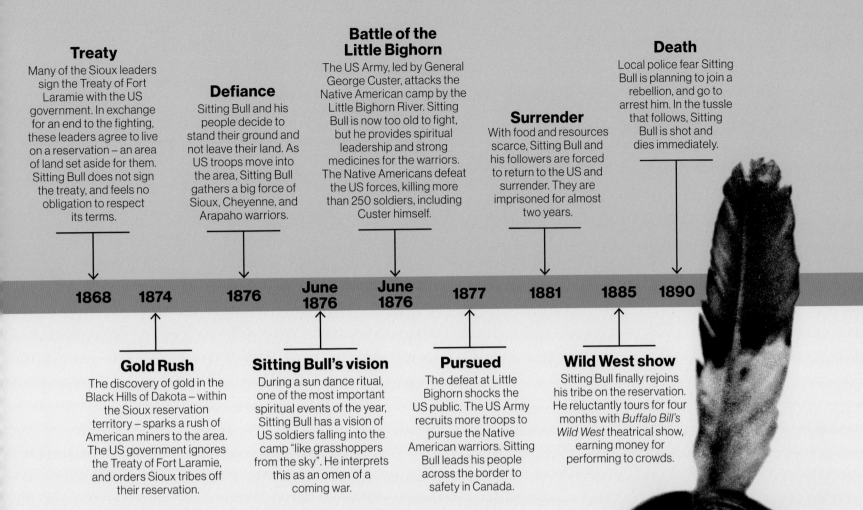

Battle of the Little Bighorn

This painting of the US cavalry retreat at the Battle of the Little Bighorn is by Amos Bad Heart Buffalo (c.1868–1913), a Lakota artist. Amos was 8 years old at the time of the battle, and later fled to Canada with his family and Sitting Bull.

Empress Dowager Cixi

Strong-willed and often ruthless, Empress Dowager Cixi (1835–1908) was the unofficial ruler of China during the reigns of two emperors. She controlled the country for 47 years from behind the scenes, during the difficult final years of the Qing Dynasty (1644–1911). Her reign saw China struggle to keep its power and influence.

Childhood

Little is known of Cixi's childhood, not even her birth name. Her father is probably a government official belonging to the Manchu people from northwestern China.

1835

Move to Beijing

Aged 16, Cixi is chosen to become one of Emperor Xianfeng's concubines (unofficial wives). She leaves her family to live in the Forbidden City, the imperial palace in Beijing. She is now known as Yi.

1851

Birth of a son

Yi's status at court rises when she gives birth to a boy, Zaichun, who is emperor Xianfeng's only surviving son. When he is five years old, Zaichun succeeds his father and becomes Emperor Tongzhi.

1856

Empresses seize control

Yi is now the Empress Dowager (mother of the Emperor). She seizes control of the palace alongside Empress Zhen, Xianfeng's principal wife. Adopting the names Cixi and Ci'an, the two become co-regents (rulers of China until Tongzhi is an adult).

1861

Behind the screen

Supported by Prince Gong, Xianfeng's brother, Cixi supervises the meetings of ministers from behind a screen. As a woman, she is not allowed to show her face, but instead tells Emperor Tongzhi what to do until he is mature enough to rule in 1873.

c.1865

Fall of the Qing Dynasty

The Qing Dynasty (1644–1911) saw China reach the peak of its power, before the country entered a period of decline. In 1911, a revolution put an end to the dynasty, and China became a republic.

Emperor Qianlong (1711–1799)
Qianlong ruled Imperial China at the height of its power. Under his rule, it was the richest country in the world. He was a lover of the arts and poetry. Qianlong gave up the throne in 1795 after reigning for 60 years.

Soong Ching-ling (1893–1981)
Soong Ching-ling was married to Sun Yat-sen, leader of the 1911 revolution. She championed the liberation of Chinese women and became a Communist Party supporter after her husband's death in 1925.

Emperor Puyi (1906–1967)
The last emperor of China, Puyi was forced from the throne in 1912 when China became a republic. During World War II, he became emperor of Manchuria, in northeastern China, for three years. In later years, he worked as a gardener in the botanical gardens in Beijing.

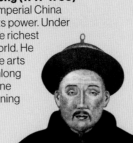

Swift action
Tongzhi dies suddenly. He does not have any children. Cixi quickly adopts her four-year-old nephew, who becomes the Emperor Guangxu. Cixi and Ci'an once again act as co-regents. Ci'an dies in 1880, leaving Cixi in sole charge.

Sweeping reforms
Now realizing the need for reforms, Cixi sends officials to Japan and Europe to discover how the countries there are governed. She goes on to introduce reforms, such as a modern police force. The reforms are more radical than those she opposed in 1898.

Two deaths
Guangxu (who is still under house arrest) dies suddenly. The next day Cixi also dies, possibly of a stroke. Cixi may have had Guangxu poisoned because she knew she was ill, and did not trust Guangxu to rule. His nephew Puyi becomes emperor at the age of two.

Summer Palace
When Guangxu becomes an adult, Cixi retires to her luxurious Summer Palace just outside the Forbidden City. The palace even has its own railroad that runs between Cixi's apartments and her dining hall.

Boxer Rebellion
Cixi supports the Boxer Rebellion, a violent uprising against Christians and people from other countries living in China. When an international force invades Beijing to restore order, she is forced to flee the Chinese capital.

Back in charge
Emperor Guangxu announces a series of reforms to modernize China. Fearing he is changing things too quickly, Cixi places Guangxu under house arrest and takes charge once again.

Exam system ends
The ancient exam system used to recruit government officials has become corrupt. Bribery and cheating have become widespread. Cixi abolishes the old system and makes plans to introduce a fairer system of choosing new recruits.

1875

1889

1898

1900

1902

1905

1908

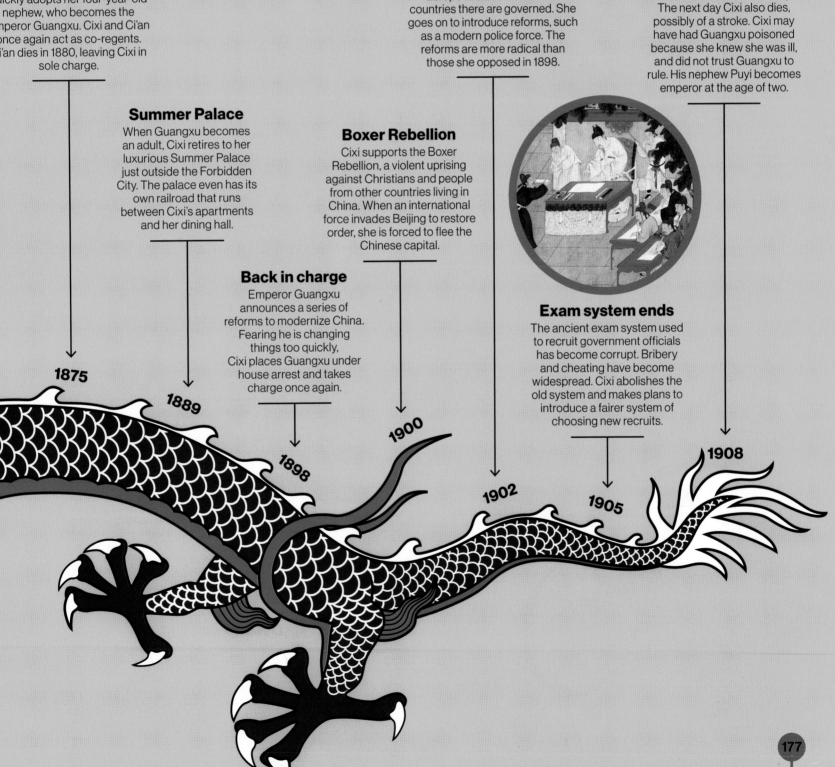

BERTHA BENZ

A *pioneer of motoring*

German transport pioneer Bertha Benz (1849–1944) was tenacious and ambitious. Bertha was the business partner and loyal supporter of her husband, Karl Benz (1844–1929), and became the first person to take a long-distance drive when she took Karl's invention—the world's first car—for a spin. It was an event that revolutionized the automobile industry.

> "Only one person remained with me [when the] ship of life seemed destined to sink. Bravely and resolutely [my wife] set the ... sails of hope."
>
> **Karl Benz, *The Life of a German Inventor* (1925)**

A new patent

Growing up in a well-to-do family in Pforzheim, southwest Germany, Bertha Ringer was interested in technology from a young age. In **1869**, she met a young engineer called Karl Benz. Talented but penniless, Karl dreamed of building a "horseless carriage"—the world's first motorized passenger vehicle. Bertha was fascinated by Karl's ambition and fell in love with him. In **1871**, against her father's advice, she invested in Karl's business in Mannheim, allowing him to continue his research. They married in **1872**. After many years of hardship, setbacks, and lots of failed attempts, Karl finally finished the prototype of his *Motorwagen* (motor car) in **October 1885**. The new invention was an odd-looking contraption: it had just three wheels—one in the front and two in the back—no roof, and could reach a maximum speed of just 10 mph (16 kmh).

THE BENZ PATENT-MOTORWAGEN

Stalled attempts

The first few tryouts of Karl's motor car do not go well. The vehicle is hard to control, and during one test on a track near his workshop, Karl crashes it into a brick wall in front of gathering witnesses. Both he and Bertha emerge unhurt. Karl applies for a patent for the car—the Benz Patent-Motorwagen—on **January 29, 1886**. He continues to improve the design, and on **July 3** the car has its first public demonstration in Mannheim. Always a perfectionist, Karl is still not happy with the design, and returns to his workshop for nearly two years. He produces a new version, Model No.2, with a bigger engine, and a third in **1887**. The Model No.3 is a big improvement, and Karl makes his first sale. However, he refuses to advertise his car, and becomes disheartened by poor sales.

Woman on a mission

Bertha refuses to give up. She is convinced that Karl's invention can be a huge success, if only people get to see it and hear about it. To make this happen, she decides to perform a publicity stunt, without letting Karl know. She hatches a plan to drive the car from Mannheim to Pforzheim in the Black Forest, where her mother lives—a distance of 65 miles (105 km). At **dawn** on **August 5, 1888**, she leaves a note on the kitchen table for Karl, and creeps out of the house to the workshop with her two teenage sons, Eugen and Richard. They push the car out of the garage, and when they are far enough away not to wake Karl, Bertha gives the massive flywheel at its rear a spin to start the engine. It cranks into action immediately. Bertha and the two boys hit

the road, which—designed for horses, and not cars—is rocky, rutted, and dusty. With no clear road signs, Bertha is not sure of the way, so she sticks to places and roads that she knows. They head at first toward the town of Weinheim, passing through Heidelberg, where they stop for a snack. By **late morning**, 22 miles (36 km) into the journey, the car is running low on fuel and she stops at a pharmacy in Wiesloch to buy 2.6 gallons (10 liters) of ligroin (gasoline). The car breaks down around **noon**. Ever resourceful, Bertha clears a fuel blockage with her hatpin, and uses one of her garters to insulate an ignition wire that has short-circuited. An even bigger worry is keeping the engine from overheating. The engine needs to be cooled by having water regularly poured over it, so they find some—at public houses, shops, streams, and even a ditch—whenever they stop. As they approach Pforzheim in the **early evening**, the steep hills of the Black Forest prove too much for the car's two gears, and Bertha and her sons have to push the vehicle uphill. This effort is interspersed with the adrenaline rush of driving downhill along the twisting roads, which requires the boys to cling on to the hand-operated brake lever with all their strength to avoid losing control of the car. It is getting dark when the three weary and dirty, but triumphant, travelers finally reach the home of Bertha's mother around **dusk**, 12 hours after they set off.

Daring road trip

Bertha drives back home a few days later along a different route. When the car's brakes begin to wear out, she asks a shoemaker to line them with leather—the world's first brake pads. They are just one of several ideas and solutions Bertha contributes to make the car better. She returns home in triumph. Her daring trip has proved to Karl—and to all doubters—that a car is not a toy and can travel long distances. The feat attracts huge publicity, and gives Karl the confidence to display the car at the Munich Engineering Exposition in **September**, where it wins a gold medal. In **1889**, the car gains worldwide attention at the Paris Exposition, and orders begin to flow in. In **1890**, Benz & Co start production of a four-wheel model, and by **1898** it has grown to become the world's largest car company.

The Scramble for Africa

Ranavalona I of Madagascar (c.1788–1861)

In the decades before the Scramble for Africa began, Queen Ranavalona I of Madagascar was able to fend off European invasion.

c.1788
Ranavalona is born into the royal family of Madagascar, an island nation off the coast of Africa.

1828
When her husband, King Radama I, dies, Ranavalona becomes the ruler of the country. She reverses all of the pro-European policies that Radama had made with the British Empire.

1829
France tries to gain territory in Madagascar by sending ships to attack the country. Queen Ranavalona's forces are able to defeat them.

1835

To distance her kingdom from European influences Ranavalona bans Christianity, and expels all Christian missionaries from Madagascar.

1845
British and French warships attack the Madagascan fortress of Tamatave. The European forces fail to capture it, and suffer many casualties in the process.

1861
Queen Ranavalona dies, and her son Radama II becomes king. Madagascar holds onto its independence until the Scramble for Africa. It becomes a French colony in 1897.

Cetshwayo kaMpande (c.1826–1884)

To block the expansion of British colonial rule in southern Africa, Zulu chief Cetshwayo kaMpande and his warriors fought the British army in the Anglo–Zulu war of 1879.

c.1826
Cetshwayo is born into the royal family of the Zulu Kingdom (in modern-day South Africa).

1856
Cetshwayo defeats his younger brother in battle to become the official heir to the kingdom.

1872
After the death of his father, Cetshwayo is crowned king. He establishes a new capital, called Ulundi, and expands his army.

1879

Britain begins to attempt to claim the land of the Zulu Kingdom, which leads to the Anglo–Zulu War. Equipped with shields and spears, Cetshwayo and his men inflict a crushing defeat on the better-supplied British army at Isandhlwana. After a series of battles, the British eventually defeat the Zulus.

1879
Cetshwayo is imprisoned in Cape Town (in modern-day South Africa). Ulundi is destroyed by the British.

1882
After his release from prison, Cetshwayo visits Britain to negotiate for the return of his kingdom. This is granted, but with most of his powers removed, and large parts of the Zulu Kingdom under British control.

1883
Cetshwayo returns to the Zulu Kingdom. Cetshwayo is unable to prevent tribal fighting, which leads to a civil war. He seeks refuge in a British-controlled reservation (an area set aside for tribal people to live on).

1884
Cetshwayo dies on the reservation.

Muhammad Ahmad (1844–1885)

Islamic religious leader Muhammad Ahmad resisted European colonization by unifying many tribes in Sudan. As a result, he managed to create one of the few independent African countries of the 19th century.

1844
Muhammad is born in northern Sudan.

1881
Ahmad declares himself the al-Mahdi, the "Right-Guided One" who, according to some Islamic traditions, will rid the world of evil before the Day of Judgement.

1883

Muhammad and his growing number of supporters begin to attack European forces in the area. They defeat British Colonel William Hicks and an army of 8,000 soldiers in the Battle of El Obeid. Most of Sudan is now under Muhammad's rule.

January 1885
After a nine-month siege, Muhammad's forces take the capital city of Sudan, Khartoum, from British control. The British withdraw completely from the country.

1885
Muhammad begins to set up an Islamic religious empire, with a new capital very close to Khartoum.

June 1885
Muhammad dies, possibly from typhus.

From about 1881 and 1914, empire-building European nations competed to seize land in the resource-rich continent of Africa. After the "Scramble for Africa," more than 90 percent of the continent came under European control. Here are just some of the people involved.

King Leopold II of Belgium (1835–1909)

In 1885, King Leopold II took personal control of the central African region of Congo. A brutal leader, he enslaved the Congolese people and plundered the land for its resources, killing millions of people in the process.

1835
Leopold is born into the Belgian royal family, and becomes king in 1865 .

1876
King Leopold creates the International African Association. This claims to be a charitable organization to help Africans, but is in fact a cover to help him take over African territory.

c.1878
King Leopold hires British explorer Henry Morton Stanley to help him start a colony in central Africa. Having already explored Congo, Stanley has considerable knowledge of the region.

1884
The Berlin Conference is set up by major European nations to establish rules for the colonization of Africa. It grants the territory of Congo to King Leopold. No African countries are consulted or involved.

1894
King Leopold signs a treaty with Britain, giving the British a strip of land on the eastern border of Congo. In exchange, the British will allow Leopold access to the Nile River.

1908
Under King Leopold II's rule, many of the Congolese people are enslaved, mutilated, and killed. Following international pressure, the colony is taken from Leopold's control and given to the Belgian parliament to rule.

1909
King Leopold II dies.

Cecil Rhodes (1853–1902)

English-born Cecil Rhodes was determined to lead Britain's colonization of southern Africa. As the prime minister of Cape Colony (in modern-day South Africa), he brought most of southern Africa under British control.

1853
Cecil is born in Hertfordshire, England. He is a sickly child, and suffers from acute asthma.

1870
Instead of going to college, Cecil is sent to Natal, a British colony in southern Africa, in the hope that the climate will improve his health.

1871
Cecil decides to set off for the diamond fields of Kimberley, north of Natal, to try to make his fortune.

1880
Cecil establishes the huge De Beers diamond mining company. It still operates today.

1890
Cecil becomes prime minister of the Cape Colony. He introduces various laws that reduce the rights of African people.

1895
Cecil claims territory to the north of the Cape Colony for the British Empire, and calls it Rhodesia (modern-day Zimbabwe). He also orders the invasion of the Dutch Republic of the Transvaal in order to build the Cape to Cairo Railway, a transportation line through British-controlled African territory.

1896
After the Transvaal raid fails, Cecil resigns as prime minister of the Cape Colony.

1902
Cecil dies at the age of 48 in the Cape Colony.

Jean-Baptiste Marchand (1863–1934)

French explorer and military officer Jean-Baptiste Marchand played a key role in expanding France's empire from the west coast of Africa through to the east.

1863
Jean-Baptiste is born in Ain, France.

1888
Jean-Baptiste arrives in Senegal, France's colony on the west coast of Africa, to serve in the French army.

1889
He takes part in the French army's attack to capture the stronghold of Koundian (in modern-day Mali), followed by the fortress of Segu in Sudan a year later.

1890
Jean-Baptiste leads a group of troops to explore the Niger and Nile rivers. Later, Jean-Baptiste explores western Sudan and parts of the Ivory Coast.

1897
Jean-Baptiste and his troops set out on a grueling trek to Fashoda, Sudan. He claims the region for France.

1898
Controlling Fashoda means France can join its African colonies together, but Britain wants control of Fashoda for the same reason. A dispute ensues. After diplomatic discussions with Britain, France agrees to give up control of Fashoda.

1914
Jean-Baptiste takes part in World War I.

1919
Jean-Baptiste is awarded the Grand Cross of the Legion of Honor, France's highest order of merit for his service.

1934
Jean-Baptiste dies in Paris, France.

TAYTU BETUL

The warrior empress who fought off colonial invasion

As European countries greedily seized huge parts of Africa, Ethiopia was the only African country that was able to resist. Taytu Betul (1851–1918), the empress of Ethiopia, helped give her nation the hope and strategy it needed to overcome much better-supplied Italian armies. Her story, and in particular her brave and intelligent leadership during the war with Italy, have been celebrated by Ethiopians ever since.

The Scramble for Africa

For centuries, European countries exploited the natural resources of the African continent. They tended to stay in the coastal areas, though, and rarely ventured inland because they lacked decent maps, reliable ways of getting there, and the ability to deal with the diseases they came into contact with in the interior, such as malaria. Things began to change in the **19th century**, when technological and medical advances in Europe made it easier to deal with the challenges of the African continent. From **1881**, European countries rushed to seize large parts of the continent for themselves, a period historians call the "Scramble for Africa." In fewer than 50 years, European countries took 90 percent of the continent. The European powers ruled the African lands they seized as colonies.

Ethiopia and Italy

King Menelik II is the ruler of Shewa, a central region of Ethiopia, a country in East Africa. In **1883**, he marries Taytu Betul. The daughter of an aristocratic family in northern Ethiopia, Taytu is a confident scholar, poet, musician, and chess player. She has strong political ideas, including a desire to resist the spread of European power in Africa. In **1887**, she establishes and names the city of Addis Ababa (meaning "new flower"), which becomes Ethiopia's capital city. Menelik gradually brings more territory under his rule,

and is proclaimed emperor of Ethiopia in **1889**. Almost immediately, he signs the Treaty of Wichale with Italy. In it, the emperor agrees not to attack Italian-ruled territories to the north of Ethiopia (in modern-day Eritrea). However, the Italian version of the treaty gives Italy control over Ethiopia, something that is not in the version in Amharic, Menelik and Taytu's language.

War looms

When the Ethiopians discover the deception, Taytu's worries about European control are confirmed. The relationship between the two countries begins to fall apart. According to some sources, Italy tries to get Menelik and Taytu to accept the treaty. When they refuse, Italy threatens to invade. Knowing that their country's independence is at stake, Menelik and Taytu stand their ground. In **1895**, as war looms, the couple call their people together from across the country. Ethiopians from every tribe, culture, and community gather together to form the army. Though they have inferior weapons to the Italians, their army of 100,000 is larger, and more determined, than Italy expected.

Leading her people

The war begins when Italy invades Ethiopia from the north. The Italians initially make a lot of progress. They get deep into Ethiopian territory before the Ethiopians are able to

turn them back. As the war rages, Taytu becomes one of the key people on the Ethiopian side. Her ability to organize the Ethiopian forces and strategize during battles is a huge asset. She also uses spies to gain information about the Italian forces. During one part of the war, the Italians occupy a secure fort at Mekelle. Taytu gets them to surrender by surrounding the fort and cutting off its water supply—a clever plan that avoids any loss of life on either side.

The Battle of Adwa

The final event of the war takes place at the Battle of Adwa on **March 1, 1896**. With supplies running low for both sides, the Italians prepare a surprise attack by marching over the mountain tracks of Adwa. They soon become separated and disorganized. When the Ethiopians realize the Italians are attacking, they quickly prepare themselves. Knowing the land better than their enemies, they are able to take up better positions and expose flaws in the Italian army's tactics. Taytu personally leads a battalion of 5,000 infantry and 600 cavalrymen to the battlefront. She instructs more than 12,000 women in the camps to fill jugs of water for the soldiers, whom she inspires to fight until the end. It takes just a few hours for Taytu and Menelik's forces to destroy the Italian invasion.

Special empress

The Battle of Adwa ends the war. In a new peace treaty, Italy accepts it does not control Ethiopia. Taytu is celebrated as a hero of the conflict. Her leadership and bravery were crucial at a time when her country perhaps faced its end. As a result, Ethiopia becomes the only African country to successfully resist colonization by a European power. Menelik suffers a stroke in 1909, and Taytu takes over as ruler for a short while. Menelik dies in 1913, and Taytu follows him in 1918.

The Battle of Adwa

This painting (by an anonymous artist) of the Battle of Adwa hangs in Addis Ababa, Ethiopia. Taytu Betul and Menelik II look on from horseback as the Ethiopian and Italian armies clash in the field.

Vincent is born

Vincent van Gogh is born in Zundert, in the Netherlands. His father is a Christian minister. His mother is from a wealthy family.

1853

Brother Theo

Theo, Vincent's brother, is born. As they get older, the two brothers become close friends.

1857

Art dealer

Vincent does not enjoy school. When he is 16, he moves to The Hague. In the city, he works for his uncle as a trainee art dealer, buying and selling works of art.

1869

Vincent van Gogh

During his lifetime, Dutch artist Vincent van Gogh (1853–1890) struggled with mental health problems and a lack of buyers for his works. Since his death, his vivid and unique oil paintings, bursting with energy and colour, have become some of the most expensive paintings ever.

A new style

Vincent moves to Paris to live with Theo, who introduces him to the works of French artists. Vincent is fascinated by Japanese prints, and his painting style becomes much more colourful.

1886

The beginning of modern art

During the late 19th century, artists experimented with different ideas and techniques, creating new ways of reflecting the world.

Auguste Rodin (1840–1917)
French sculptor Auguste Rodin created marble and bronze figures. His sculptures went against the respected classical style of the time, but by the time he died, he was one of the most famous artists in France.

Edvard Munch (1863–1944)
Norwegian painter Edvard Munch is best known for his dark and intense works that deal with complicated emotions. Like Vincent Van Gogh, his work made use of bright colours and swirling patterns.

Camille Claudel (1864–1943)

Born in France, Camille Claudel created sculptures of human bodies that many found shocking at the time. She was influenced by Auguste Rodin, and worked as his studio assistant for a time.

Sunny Arles

Having moved to Arles, a city in sunny southern France, Vincent rents rooms in a place he calls the "Yellow House". He plans to open his own *atelier* there, and is thrilled when painter Paul Gauguin decides to join him. Mirroring the warm colours of Arles, Vincent's work becomes vivid and colourful.

Artist's studio

In Paris, Vincent joins an *atelier* (a studio where artists work alongside each other and share ideas). He dreams of one day starting his own *atelier*. He paints scenes of cafés, parks, and city life.

1887

1888

A year in London

After finishing his training, Vincent works as an art dealer in London, England. Vincent becomes depressed after his attempts to attract his landlady's daughter are rejected.

1873

Friend to the poor

Vincent gradually becomes more religious. He moves to a mining region in Belgium, where he helps the sick and needy, and reads to them from the Bible. He gives away all of his belongings to the poor.

1880

Artistic guidance

Vincent begins painting with oil paints, and is excited with the results. He studies different artistic techniques with Dutch painter Anton Mauve.

1881

Rejected

Vincent creates more paintings that show the lives of poor people. Theo works hard to find buyers for his brother's paintings in Paris, France, but their dark colours fail to attract customers. In his lifetime, very few of Vincent's paintings will be sold.

1885

The Potato Eaters

Vincent moves into his own studio in the town of Nuenen, where he continues to develop his own painting style. He produces his first major work, *The Potato Eaters*. It shows a poor family sharing a meal. Unlike Impressionist paintings, it is dark and realistic.

1885

Impressionism

Vincent throws himself into painting. He takes inspiration from nature and the lives of regular people. He begins to paint in the Impressionist style. This involves making quick and light brushstrokes to give an "impression" of a scene, rather than a completely realistic image on the canvas.

1883

Death

Vincent spends time in a hospital for people with mental health problems. When he leaves, he continues to suffer from depression. He shoots himself in the chest. He suffers for two days before dying.

Mental illness

Vincent and Gauguin work well together, but they often argue. When Gauguin threatens to leave, Vincent is devastated. In an agitated state, Vincent cuts off part of his ear. It is not clear why he does this, but Vincent has suffered from mental health problems for years.

1888

1890

NED KELLY

A bushranger's last stand

Argument still rages over whether Ned Kelly (1855–1880) was a hero or a villain. Kelly was a bushranger (bandit), thief, and convicted murderer. Yet he was also fearless, charismatic, and took a stand against prejudice. The story of his brief life, and final battle against the authorities, has passed into Australian legend.

> "A day will come, at a bigger court than this, when we shall see which is right and which is wrong."
>
> **Ned Kelly, speaking at his trial (October 30, 1880)**

Petty criminal

In **1851**, the discovery of gold in the British colony of Victoria in Australia sparked a huge gold rush. Unable to cope with the influx of new people, the local police recruited extra forces from the UK. Mostly Protestant, many were prejudiced against poor Irish Catholic settlers—including John ("Red") Kelly, Ned's father, who was sent to Australia for stealing pigs. Growing up in the small town of Greta, Victoria, Edward "Ned" Kelly was a tall and athletic youngster. He excelled at sports but, like his father and uncles, was often in trouble with the police. In **1871**, aged 16, he was arrested for riding a stolen horse and served a three-year prison sentence with punishment labor. He returned to the family home in **1874**, but continued to get into scrapes. On **April 15, 1878**, a drunken police officer decided to "fix the Greta mob" once and for all, and went to the Kelly house to arrest Ned's brother, Dan. He assaulted their sister, Kate, and sparked a brawl, from which he escaped. When he returned to the police station, he accused the boys and their mother, Ellen, of attempted murder. Ned and Dan went into hiding. Ellen was given a three-year jail sentence.

V. R.
£1,000 REWARD!!!
FOR THE KELLY GANG.

GO AND SEE
THE GREAT PICTURE
OF THE
NOTORIOUS BUSHRANGERS.
Painted by Fry from a photograph taken on the ground
where the Murder of Sergeant Kennedy was committed.
Every Visitor will be presented with a photograph of
the Notorious Ned Kelly
Now on View opposite Theatre Royal.

Dead or alive

Out in the bush, the brothers are joined by two friends, Joe Byrne and Steve Hart, and they form "the Kelly Gang." On **October 26**, a group of police officers mount a search, camping at Stringybark Creek near the gang's retreat. The outlaws decide to disarm them, but in the exchange of gunfire that follows, three officers are shot dead. The Kelly Gang are declared outlaws, with a reward for their capture—wanted dead or alive.

Daring raids

The gang emerge from the bush to mount two robberies in the towns of Euroa (**December 9**) and Jerilderie (**February 10, 1879**). They gain support among the public. Many view them as heroes who are standing up for regular people against injustice and police corruption. Ned feels his outlaw reputation is unfair, and composes a 56-page letter criticizing the police for their treatment of Irish Catholics. He sees himself as a revolutionary, and calls for Australia to become a republic. He tries to get the letter published in the local newspaper, but fails. Frustrated, the gang lie low, hiding with friends and family for the next 18 months.

An outrageous plan

Desperate to capture the Kelly Gang, the authorities deny the Kelly family the right to farm their land. Outraged, Ned makes a plan to start a rebellion. The gang will derail and attack a police train in Glenrowan, mobilize an army of sympathizers, and raise funds by robbing the bank in the town of Benalla. To lure the police train from Benalla to Glenrowan, they plan to kill Aaron Sherritt, Joe Byrne's best friend, who they suspect of betraying them and who now lives under police protection.

Attack at Glenrowan

On the night of **June 26, 1880**, Joe Byrne and Dan Kelly ride to the Sherritt homestead and kill their former associate, while Ned and Steve Hart force laborers to blow up the train tracks. Terrified, the officers hiding at Sherritt's don't escape to alert their colleagues until the next day. In the early hours of **June 27**, carrying suits of homemade armor, Ned and Steve Hart arrive in Glenrowan and force at gunpoint more than 60 townspeople from their homes into a local inn. There they lie in wait for any surviving police officers from the

train crash. But Ned has miscalculated. The police train takes far longer to arrive than he expects. As the gang wait uncertainly, the hostages become difficult to control. Ned releases 21 of them, including a local teacher, Thomas Curnow. Curnow thwarts the derailment plan by flagging down the train, which stops safely.

The final shoot-out

At **3 a.m. on June 28**, 46 officers surround the inn. Realizing their plan has failed, the sleep-deprived Kelly Gang don their heavy steel armor and prepare to fight. The police open fire, killing Joe Byrne and three hostages caught in the crossfire. Ned is shot in the arm and foot. At **dawn**, bleeding profusely, he staggers out into the mist and takes cover in the bush behind the inn. The officers shoot a barrage of fire at his unprotected legs. He collapses, and is captured. Dan Kelly and Steve Hart continue to shoot but at **10 a.m.**, officers halt the siege and the remaining hostages are released. At **3 p.m.**, in front of a large crowd, police set fire to the inn. The bodies of Steve Hart and Dan Kelly are later recovered.

Aftermath and execution

News of the Kellys' last stand soon spreads. The next morning, Hart's dead body is tied to a door and photographed as a warning to Kelly's supporters. Ned is taken to Melbourne Gaol (jail) and slowly recovers from his wounds in the prison hospital. On **October 28**, on the false statement of a police officer, Ned is found guilty of the murders at Stringybark Creek, and sentenced to death. Despite a massive public petition asking for mercy, at **10 a.m. on November 11, 1880**, Ned is executed at Melbourne Gaol and buried in an unmarked grave. His last words before facing the gallows are "Such is life."

Nikola Tesla

Serbian-American inventor and engineer Nikola Tesla (1856–1943) was one of the pioneers of modern electrical power. He developed a new type of motor essential for the alternating-current (AC) power systems that are used around the world today. He also achieved breakthroughs in the development of radio technology and X-rays, though his genius was perhaps not fully appreciated during his time.

The AC motor
The idea for a new type of AC (alternating current) motor comes to Nikola in a vision. The magnetic fields rotate within his motor, making the motor more efficient and practical.

College
Nikola enrolls at a college at Graz, in Austria, and is a hard-working student. During his second year, he gets into an argument with a professor over a dynamo that works with DC (direct current) electricity.

Working for Edison
He moves to Paris, France, and works for the Edison Electrical Company—the company of American inventor Thomas Edison. Nikola's works on improving generators (that convert mechanical energy into electrical energy), and motors that run on electricity.

Tragedy
Nikola's elder brother is killed in a riding accident. The tragedy stays with Nikola, who suffers from lifelong mental-health issues.

Move to Prague
Nikola turns to gambling because he is running out of money. He moves to Prague (in modern-day Czech Republic) to finish his studies, but does not qualify for the classes he wants to take. Instead, Nikola decides to take up philosophy.

Cholera
After he catches cholera (a dangerous infection), Nikola is in hospital for nearly a year. He almost dies, but his father promises him that if he recovers, he will send him to the best engineering school he can afford.

A child of light
Nikola Tesla is born in Smiljan (in modern-day Croatia), during a thunderstorm. The midwife says Nikola will be a child of darkness. His mother insists he will be a child of light.

1856

1863

1873

1875

1880

February 1882

1882

Tesla coil experiment

In 1891, Nikola developed a new induction coil—now known as the Tesla coil—that produced high-frequency alternating currents. He used it in experiments to produce electric lighting, X-rays, and wireless power, and it was used in early radios and televisions. Today, the coils, which produce bright arcs of lightning, are mostly used to entertain people.

Bright sparks

Nikola Tesla was just one of the people working on electricity. Each generation built on the discoveries of the previous one, leading to the electrification of the modern world.

Humphry Davy (1778–1829)

One of the most influential people of his time, English scientist Humphry Davy used electricity to discover many elements, including sodium and potassium. He took on an assistant named Michael Faraday, whom Davy would later claim was his greatest discovery.

Michael Faraday (1791–1867)

English scientist Michael Faraday discovered many of the fundamental laws of how electricity works. His work led to the transformer, which converts high voltage electricity to low voltage, making it safer to work with. Faraday's work paved the way for many of Thomas Edison's inventions.

Thomas Edison (1847–1931)

Best known as the inventor of the first practical electric light bulb, American Thomas Edison held the patents (legal rights) for more than 1,000 inventions. Tesla and Edison disagreed about which system would be more efficient and safer—direct-current (DC) or alternating-current (AC) electric power. In the end, the world adopted both systems, each for specific needs.

American dream

One of Nikola's managers asks him to move with him to the US. He starts work at Edison Machine Works, a company that makes mechanical parts for Edison's DC electrical system in New York. Edison is producing and selling DC technology, and he has no place for Nikola's AC motor.

Wireless power

Interest grows in Nikola's AC system and he attracts new investors. He sets up a laboratory in New York, where he researches ways of transmitting power without the use of wires. He develops the "Tesla coil," a machine that can send high-voltage electricity through the air.

Wild experiments

He moves his lab to Colorado Springs. There, he produces artificial lightning. He becomes well-known to his neighbors for his experiments—which cause sparks, thunder, and the occasional blackout.

First solo venture

Disgruntled, Nikola leaves Edison, and sets up his own company. Investors task him with developing an improved lighting system. However, he is forced out of the venture and has to work digging ditches to earn a living.

Niagara Falls

Nikola helps design an AC hydroelectric power plant at the Niagara Falls on the US-Canada border. The following year, the power plant is used to power the city of Buffalo, New York. He also performs a number of experiments with X-rays.

Final years

Nikola dies penniless in New York City. Though Nikola raised money to fund his experiments, he spends more, with little to show for his work. His dream of finding a workable way of delivering wireless electricity never comes to pass.

1884 1885 1891 1895 1899 1943

Emmeline Pankhurst

At a time when many of the freedoms enjoyed by women today were unthinkable, Emmeline Pankhurst (1858–1928) dedicated her life to achieving political and economic equality for women. One of the most renowned of the activists who strove to extend the right to vote—also known as suffrage—to women, Pankhurst is considered one of the most influential people of the 20th century.

1894
Poor Law Guardian
After returning to Manchester with her family, Emmeline joins the new Independent Labour Party (ILP). She becomes one of the first women to run for, and win, a public job when she becomes Poor Law Guardian—a role which includes researching the living conditions of the poorest people in society, especially those in government-provided workhouses.

1898
Widowed
Richard dies from a stomach ulcer. Emmeline takes work as a registrar of births and deaths, and serves on a school board—both positions give her more insight into the terrible effects of inequality on women's lives.

1903
DEEDS NOT WORDS!
Emmeline cocreates the Women's Social and Political Union (WSPU), a women-only group focused on gaining voting rights for women. With the motto "deeds not words," their intention is to use nonviolent but militant (confrontational) protest and speeches to have their cause recognized. The women are arrested, laughed at, and, on occasion, attacked, by men who oppose their cause.

1858
Bright child
Emmeline Goulden is born in Manchester, England. She is a smart child who is a regular reader from the age of three. Despite her intelligence and being born to liberal parents, Emmeline does not receive the same education as her brothers.

1872
An important meeting
At 14, Emmeline attends a talk by Lydia Becker, the editor of the Women's Suffrage Journal. Excited by the meeting, she declares herself a suffragist (a supporter of women's right to vote). In 1873, she studies chemistry and finance in Paris.

1878
Marriage and politics
Emmeline begins a relationship with Richard Pankhurst, a barrister and supporter of women's rights. She marries him in 1879, becoming Emmeline Pankhurst, and turns their London home into a meeting place for radical political debate.

1888
Radical rights
The National Society for Women's Suffrage (the first national suffrage group in the UK) splits up. A member of the society, Emmeline creates the Women's Franchise League (WFL) as a replacement, to advocate voting rights for women. The League is seen as radical as it calls for equal divorce and inheritance rights for women.

1908
IMPRISONMENT
After a clash with the police attracts public attention, the WSPU grows more combative than other suffrage groups. Emmeline is arrested and imprisoned seven times. Prison conditions are disgusting, so the women go on a hunger strike and are force-fed by prison staff through their noses or mouths, which is very painful.

Feminist ideas

Emmeline Pankhurst developed her campaign for women's rights based on the ideas of women who came before her and those fighting alongside her.

Laura Cereta (1469–1499)
An Italian feminist writer whose letters explore the importance of equality in a marriage and the requirement of mutual love and admiration between partners. She often wrote in defense of education for women and the damage caused by forced marriage.

Sophia Duleep Singh (1876–1948)
A British suffragette and the daughter of the last Maharaja (great king) of the Sikh Empire. Singh was a member of the WSPU and a leader in the Women's Tax Resistance League, which saw women refusing to pay taxes as long as they did not have the vote.

Sylvia Pankhurst (1882–1960)
Just like her mother Emmeline, Sylvia was very politically radical for her time. Taking interest in the Italian invasion of Ethiopia, she moved to Addis Ababa to establish the *Ethiopia Observer* journal.

1910
Suffragette action
Identified as "suffragettes" because of their violent protest methods, rather than "suffragists" (women pursuing equality through nonviolent methods), the women of the WSPU continue to be belittled and arrested. Suffragettes fight back by spitting at policemen and setting fire to property—one even throws an ax at a politician.

1914
War
World War I breaks out and Emmeline recommends that the WSPU stand down from their activities to support the war effort. Women take jobs in teaching, nursing, and in factories in order to make up the worker shortages caused by men being away at war. After seeing many women who have lost their men to the war struggle, Emmeline establishes an adoption home, and she adopts four children.

November 1918
CAMPAIGNING
A bill passes allowing women to run for Parliament. Instead of joining a political party with men, Emmeline campaigns for Christabel, who stands for The Women's Party. Unfortunately, she loses by a narrow margin.

1926
Conservative Party
Surprising many, Emmeline officially joins the Conservative Party and is chosen as a candidate for Parliament. Because this party has tended to form the government of the country, she believes working with them is the best way to secure the vote for all women.

1913
FAMILY POLITICS
As the WSPU's actions become increasingly violent, many women leave the group, including Emmeline's daughters Sylvia and Adela, who are pacifists (against violence). However, Emmeline's eldest daughter, Christabel, sticks by her mother.

February 1918
VOTES FOR WOMEN!
The crucial role women played during the war has changed the way women's rights are viewed. The government passes the Representation of the People Act, giving women over the age of 30 the right to vote, though many restrictions remain. By now, Emmeline is estranged from both Sylvia and Adela.

1928
Death
After years of protesting, imprisonment and hunger strikes, Emmeline is suffering from ill health. She dies at the age of 69, with Christabel by her side. She had not seen Adela again after 1914, and had never fully reconciled with Sylvia. Less than a month after Emmeline's death, the Conservatives finally gave the vote to all people in the UK—both women and men—over the age of 21.

1864
Pittsburgh childhood

Elizabeth Jane Cochran is born into a mill-owning family just outside Pittsburgh, Pennsylvania. Her father dies when she is about six, plunging the family into poverty. There is no money for her schooling.

1885
Angry young woman

Elizabeth helps her mother run a Pittsburgh boarding house. One day in 1885, she reads an article in the *Pittsburgh Dispatch* newspaper that says women are only good for housework and caring for children. It makes her so irritated that she writes an angry letter to the editor.

1885
Undercover reporter

Impressed, the editor offers her a job. Taking the pen name Nellie Bly, she writes a series of articles exposing the poor pay and working conditions of female factory workers. Several factory owners complain, and she is assigned to the "women's pages" to cover less controversial and exciting topics, such as fashion and gardening.

1885
Time in Mexico

Fed up with writing for the "women's pages," Nellie takes six months' leave from the *Pittsburgh Dispatch* to travel to Mexico. She sends back more than 30 letters describing the Mexican way of life, which are later published in book form.

1887
Mental asylum

Nellie leaves Pittsburgh for New York. She pretends to be mentally ill and has herself sent to an asylum (an institution for mentally ill people) for women. Her account of the shocking conditions she finds there is published in the *New York World* newspaper, rocketing her to fame.

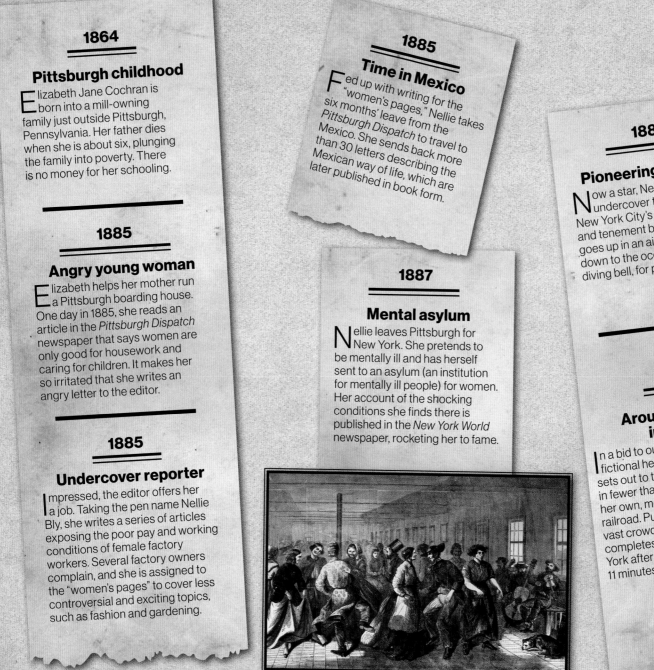

1888
Pioneering journalist

Now a star, Nellie goes undercover to investigate New York City's jails, factories, and tenement buildings. She goes up in an air balloon, and down to the ocean depths in a diving bell, for particular stories.

1889
Around the World in 72 Days

In a bid to outdo Jules Verne's fictional hero (see below), Nellie sets out to travel around the world in fewer than 80 days. She travels on her own, mostly by steamship and railroad. Public interest is huge and vast crowds greet her when she completes the journey in New York after 72 days, 6 hours, 11 minutes, 14 seconds.

Writing about the world

At a time of new ideas and political upheaval, journalists and novelists entertained, informed, and helped people understand the changes that were happening.

Jules Verne (1828–1905)
France's Jules Verne was the author of more than 60 highly popular fantasy adventure stories. In *Around the World in 80 Days* (1872), his fictional hero Phileas Fogg travels around the globe in 80 days to win a bet. Verne believed that recent technological advances in travel had made this feat possible. Nellie Bly proved him right.

Ida B. Wells (1862–1931)
African American Ida B. Wells embarked on a career as a journalist, writing about the racial politics in the southern states, and women's right to vote. Though she often received threats, she continued to write, organize protests, and speak up for her beliefs.

Dorothy Thompson (1893–1961)
One of the first foreign correspondents to warn against the rise of the Nazi Party in Germany, American journalist Dorothy Thompson dared to criticize Nazi leader Adolf Hitler in print. He immediately expelled her from the country.

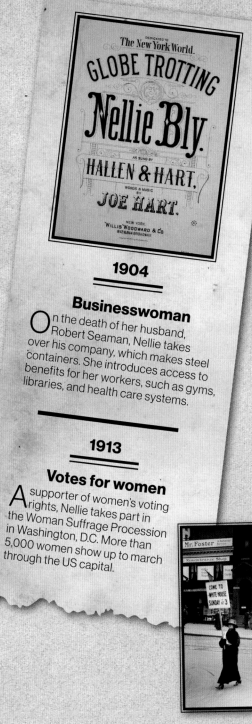

GLOBE TROTTING Nellie Bly.

DEDICATED TO The New York World.

AS SUNG BY

HALLEN & HART.

WORDS & MUSIC BY

JOE HART.

NEW YORK
WILLIS WOODWARD & Co
842 & 844 BROADWAY.

1914

War reporter

Nellie is on vacation in Vienna, Austria, when World War I breaks out. She is one of the first foreign reporters—and the first woman—to report on the war, writing a column called "Nellie Bly on the Firing Line" for the *New York Evening Journal*.

1918–1922

Back in New York

After the war, Nellie returns to the US, and she continues writing for the *New York Evening Journal* until the end of her life. She dies of pneumonia, aged 57, in St. Mark's Hospital in New York City. Her unique approach to journalism helped inspire many who came after her to follow her lead in order to get remarkable and groundbreaking stories.

1904

Businesswoman

On the death of her husband, Robert Seaman, Nellie takes over his company, which makes steel containers. She introduces access to benefits for her workers, such as gyms, libraries, and health care systems.

1913

Votes for women

A supporter of women's voting rights, Nellie takes part in the Woman Suffrage Procession in Washington, D.C. More than 5,000 women show up to march through the US capital.

Nellie Bly

American Investigative journalist Nellie Bly (1864–1922) did not want to write traditional "female interest" stories about fashion or gardening. She instead chose to go undercover, writing about prisons, factories, and hospitals. Her work often put her in uncomfortable situations and even danger at times, but it led to some groundbreaking stories and paved the way for modern journalists.

William Randolph Hearst (1863–1951)

Winifred Bonfils (1863–1936)

Marie Curie (1867–1934)

Sarah Breedlove (1867–1919)

Mahatma Gandhi (1869–1948)

Dadasaheb Phalke (1870–1944)

Qiu Jin (1875–1907)

Albert Einstein (1879–1955)

Helen Keller (1880–1968)

Lili Elbe (1882–1931)

Eleanor Roosevelt (1884–1962)

Charlie Chaplin (1889–1977)

Stan Laurel (1890–1965)

Zora Neale Hurston (1891–1960)

Oliver Hardy (1892–1957)

Fatma Begum (1892–1983)

Gavrilo Princip (1894–1918)

Amelia Earhart (1897–1937)

Golda Meir (1898–1978)

William Randolph Hearst to **Oodgeroo Noonuccal**

Newspapers, film, and new ways of communicating quickly spread the discoveries and achievements of this period's most brilliant people across the globe. Marie Curie changed how we identify and treat illnesses when she discovered radioactivity. Rachel Carson's research into the harmful effects of pesticides kick-started the environmental movement. And Tenzing Norgay and Edmund Hillary achieved what was once thought impossible when they became the first to climb Mount Everest in 1953.

Edmund Hillary (1919–2008)

Nelson Mandela (1918–2013)

Eva Perón (1919–1952)

Josephine Baker (1906–1975)

Rachel Carson (1907–1964)

Frida Kahlo (1907–1954)

Don Bradman (1908–2001)

Irena Sendler (1910–2008)

Alan Turing (1912–1954)

Rosa Parks (1913–2005)

Hedy Lamarr (1914–2000)

Tenzing Norgay (1914–1986)

Indira Gandhi (1917–1984)

Rosalind Franklin (1920–1958)

Oodgeroo Noonuccal (1920–1993)

Marie Curie

Polish-French physicist and chemist Marie Curie (1867–1934) is best known for her research into radioactivity—the loss of electrons by unstable elements. At a time when women faced many barriers to work and education, Curie managed to transform the understanding of science forever. She was the first woman to win a Nobel Prize and is still the only woman to have won the prize twice.

Meeting Pierre

Maria meets Pierre Curie, who is a scientist and teacher at the School of Physics and Chemistry in Paris. They marry a year later. She changes her first name to the French version, Marie, and adopts her husband's surname.

1894

Student in Paris

Maria enrolls at the Sorbonne university in Paris. She doesn't have much money, so she continues to work as a tutor at night. Her determination pays off—she obtains one degree in physics and another in mathematics.

1891

Flying University

Maria works as a tutor to earn money as a tutor to with her education. She continues to help her sister to the Flying University. She studies at education in Paris, then secret institution provides education in Polish (which is banned by the Russian authorities), and also accepts women students.

c. 1885

Deal with her sister

Women cannot study at the University of Warsaw, so Maria strikes a deal with her elder sister, Bronisława. Maria will work in Poland to support her sister's education in Paris, then Bronisława will return the favor.

1884

Gold medal

From a young age, Maria shows an interest in mathematics and physics (the subjects her father teaches at her father teaches at school). She later graduates from high school with a gold medal for her academic excellence.

1883

Young Maria

Born into a poor family in Warsaw, Poland (then part of the Russian Empire), Maria is the youngest of five children. Both of her parents are school teachers.

1867

Discoveries

Marie and Pierre work together. They do research into radioactivity (which was discovered by French physicist Henri Becquerel in 1896). The Curies discover a new radioactive element and name it "polonium" after Poland, Marie's homeland. A few months later, they discover another, radium.

1898

Nobel prizes

Their discoveries are groundbreaking, as radiation can be used for treating illnesses, such as cancer. Becquerel and the Curies are awarded the Nobel Prize in Physics in 1903—which makes Marie the first woman to win a Nobel Prize. In 1911, she becomes the first person to win two Nobel Prizes, this time in chemistry.

1903

Professor Curie

Pierre dies in an accident—he falls under a horse-drawn carriage. Marie is distraught. She is later appointed Professor of General Physics in the Faculty of Sciences in his place, becoming the first female professor at the Sorbonne.

1906

Saving lives

During World War I, Marie convinces the French government to set up mobile X-ray units within their military hospitals. The machines use technology based on Marie's research. They come to be known as "Little Curies," and are used on more than one million soldiers.

1914

Radium atom

The main timeline diagram shows the structure of a radium atom. The Curies noticed that radium could be used to destroy cancer cells. In 1932, Marie set up the Radium Institute in Poland to work on the element's healing properties and the treatment of cancer.

88
Ra
Radium
226

Radioactive notes

Marie's notebooks are still highly radioactive and cannot be handled without wearing protective clothing.

Death

Though nobody realizes at the time, exposure to high levels of radiation can be fatally dangerous. Marie's groundbreaking and life-saving work is sadly the cause of her own death—it leads to an immune system disease that kills her at the age of 66.

1934

NUCLEUS

ELECTRON

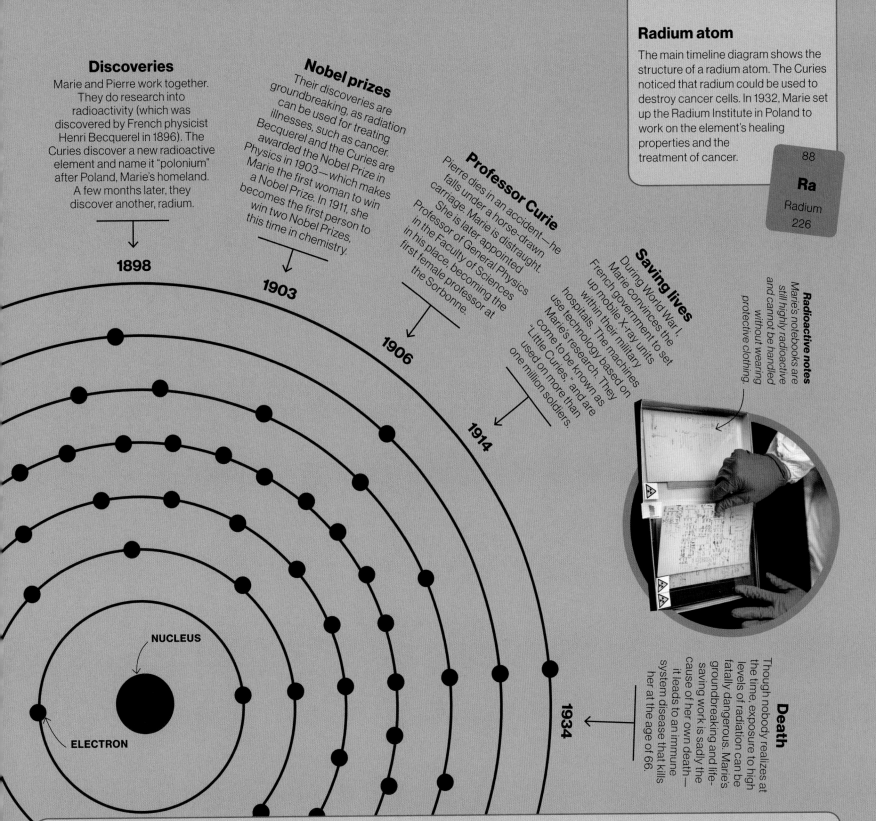

Nuclear scientists

In the early 20th century, scientists began to understand the structure of atoms. They also studied what happens when atoms lose electrons (decay). Their work provided the basis for modern nuclear physics.

Ernest Rutherford (1871–1937)

Known as the "father of nuclear physics," Ernest Rutherford worked out that an atom is made up of a nucleus with electrons circling it. He was the first person to split an atom.

Harriet Brooks (1876–1933)

The first Canadian woman to become a nuclear physicist, Brooks worked alongside Ernest Rutherford. She was one of the discoverers of the element radon, and also showed that radioactivity could be transferred between surfaces.

Irène Joliot-Curie (1897–1956)

Marie Curie's daughter Irène discovered how to make artificial radioactive elements. These are now used in many medical treatments. Irène and her husband won the Nobel Prize in Chemistry in 1935.

Early years

Hoping to build a happier and more stable life for herself, Sarah gets married. She gives birth to a daughter, Lelia, in 1885. Tragedy strikes again, however, when her husband dies six years later, leaving Sarah alone with the child to care for.

Developing an image

Sarah moves to Denver, and a year later marries Charles J. Walker. Her husband has experience in advertising, and helps Sarah promote her business. Sarah sells her products under the name "Madam C. J. Walker." They begin to sell in greater numbers.

Empowering women

Sarah opens a beauty college and factory in Pittsburgh, Pennsylvania. The college teaches African American women how to make and sell their own beauty products. This allows them to become more financially independent.

Business idea

After moving north to St. Louis, Sarah works as a laundress. She begins losing her hair due to stress, but there are few hair products available for African American people to use on their hair to help her. Sarah starts to experiment with making her own hair products, and sells them to her neighbors.

A growing business

Sarah travels across the South to market her products to new customers. She speaks to people in their homes, and even shows them how to use her products at schools and churches.

Childhood

Sarah Breedlove is born in Louisiana. She is the child of recently freed enslaved people Minerva and Owen Breedlove. By the time she is seven, Sarah has become an orphan, and lives with her sister Louvinia.

1867

1881

c.1904

1905

1907

1908

> "There is no royal flower-strewn road to success ... what success I have obtained is the result of many sleepless nights and real hard work."
>
> **Sarah Breedlove, in a speech made to her employees (1917)**

Big business

By now, Sarah's company employs about 3,000 African American men and women, who make and sell her hair products throughout the US.

1910

Speaking up

When Sarah attends a conference for African American businessmen, she is blocked from speaking because she is a woman. Undaunted, she interrupts events on the final day to tell the story of how she has become so successful.

1912

International reach

The business continues to succeed, and Sarah travels overseas to find new customers for her company's products. She visits Panama, Haiti, Cuba, and Jamaica. By 1916, her sales have reached an amazing $100,000 a year.

1913

Supporter of equality

Sarah supports organizations that campaign for the civil rights of African American people. She donates a large amount of money to the National Association for the Advancement of Colored People (NAACP).

1917

Giving back

Sarah donates money toward preserving the former home of Frederick Douglass, the great African American writer and campaigner against slavery.

1918

Death

Sarah dies at the age of 51. During her lifetime, she has overcome childhood poverty and racism to become the most successful African American businesswoman in the US. Sarah's daughter Leila inherits much of her fortune and takes over the company.

1919

Sarah Breedlove

At a time when most African Americans faced discrimination and limited business opportunities, inventor and businessperson Sarah Breedlove (1867–1919) became rich developing and selling beauty products. She later shared much of her wealth, donating it to causes which empowered the African American community.

Fighting for equality

Members of the African American community fought for the same civil rights, access to education, and business opportunities that white Americans had.

W. E. B. Du Bois (1868–1963)
Author and activist W. E. B. Du Bois was one of the most important leaders in the fight for full civil rights for African Americans. He helped set up the NAACP, which remains the most important African American civil rights organization.

Mary McLeod Bethune (1875–1955)
An African American educator and campaigner, Mary McLeod Bethune opened a boarding school for girls. In time, it became a college offering degree-level courses. After women won the right to vote in 1920, she strongly encouraged her students to register to vote.

Annie Turnbo Malone (1869–1957)
Businesswoman Annie Turnbo Malone became one of the first African American millionaires. Malone set up the Poro Company, which produced popular hair and beauty products for the African American community. She hired the young Sarah Breedlove as one of her door-to-door sales agents.

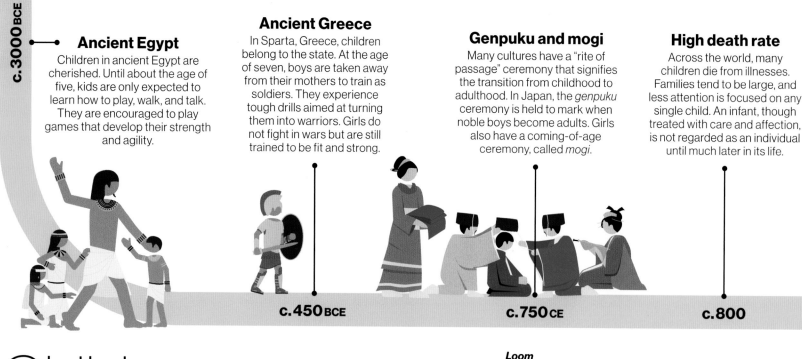

Ancient Egypt

Children in ancient Egypt are cherished. Until about the age of five, kids are only expected to learn how to play, walk, and talk. They are encouraged to play games that develop their strength and agility.

Ancient Greece

In Sparta, Greece, children belong to the state. At the age of seven, boys are taken away from their mothers to train as soldiers. They experience tough drills aimed at turning them into warriors. Girls do not fight in wars but are still trained to be fit and strong.

Genpuku and mogi

Many cultures have a "rite of passage" ceremony that signifies the transition from childhood to adulthood. In Japan, the *genpuku* ceremony is held to mark when noble boys become adults. Girls also have a coming-of-age ceremony, called *mogi*.

High death rate

Across the world, many children die from illnesses. Families tend to be large, and less attention is focused on any single child. An infant, though treated with care and affection, is not regarded as an individual until much later in its life.

c.450 BCE   **c.750 CE**   **c.800**

Children through time

Children have not always been allowed to just be children. Kids have often been treated as smaller adults: expected to work and sometimes even to fight in wars. The idea of children having their own rights, with time to play and learn, is a very modern one.

Loom
Children often helped operate machines, such as looms, during the Industrial Revolution.

Industrial Revolution

The Industrial Revolution leads to an increase in the number of factories across Europe and the US. Many children from poor backgrounds are employed in these factories, starting work as young as the age of four.

1800

Children's books

Grimm's Fairy Tales, written by two German brothers, is released. It leads to a whole new kind of book aimed at children, often featuring imaginative stories, wonderful illustrations, and strong moral messages. They aim to educate children through entertainment.

Protecting children

In the UK, the law begins to protect the well-being of children at work, school, and home. This shows a growing belief that children should be allowed to enjoy their childhood.

Education

Many countries begin to recognize that the education of children is extremely important for their well-being. Governments set curricula— the subjects and topics every child must learn at each stage of development in school.

"Children's Charter"

The UK parliament passes a law that outlaws cruelty to children. Known as the "Children's Charter," it enables the government to intervene to protect a child if someone is mistreating them.

1812   **1830s**   **1880s**   **1889**

Noble children

In western Europe, boys born to wealthy families are sent away to live in the castle or home of a rich lord. There, they begin training to become knights. Girls are taught how to run a household, including budgeting and making clothes.

Aztec toys

Aztec children play with bows and arrows and whistles, and they make dolls out of scrap materials. Some Aztec toys have wheels, though wheeled vehicles are not used as transportation by Aztec adults—so in some ways, these toys are more advanced!

Smaller adults

European artists usually depict a child as a smaller version of an adult. This mirrors how children are viewed more generally at this time. The idea of childhood as an important stage of life before becoming an adult does not exist.

Colonial America

Adults in the American colonies believe that play for children must have a purpose that helps the family or community. Any other kind of play—such as card games—is considered "idleness."

c.1000   **c.1300**   **c.1300**   **c.1650**

New toys

The first jigsaw puzzle—a map of Europe divided into its realms— is produced to help educate children. Dollhouses and other large toys are produced and marketed to the small number of families able to afford them.

Toy stores

Parents look for ways to increase their children's happiness by encouraging play and fun. The first toy store is opened by William Hamley in London, England. Stores that sells things just for kids soon open in other countries.

Playtime

The English philosopher John Locke writes that children should be treated differently than adults. He suggests that children are given toys to play with, and that they wear clothes more suitable for their bodies. In Europe and the US, the idea of a childhood as we understand it today gradually develops.

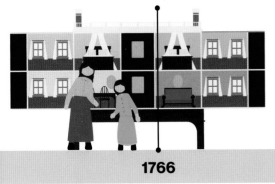

TOY STORE

1766   **1760**   **c.1693**

Childhood

The idea of childhood as an important life stage separate from adulthood is firmly established by this time in many places across the world. Children mix with each other; go to school; play with friends; and have their own games, books, toys, and clothes.

Child soldiers

In some parts of the world, children still work, and some are even forced to become soldiers to fight in armed conflicts.

Rights of the child

The United Nations sets out the basic rights that every child has from birth until the age of 18 in the "Convention on the Rights of the Child." It includes the right for children to be protected from abuse or exploitation.

Different times

Many adults worry about the effect that the internet and the rise of social media are having on children. Some fear that children are "growing up too quickly." At the same time, many children enjoy opportunities to learn and play— both online and offline—that would have been impossible for earlier generations.

c.1950s   **1980s**   **1989**   **2000s**

Marriage

Mohandas marries Kasturba Makhanji. Their families had arranged their marriage when Gandhi was younger, a traditional custom in India at the time.

Young Mohandas

Mohandas Gandhi is born in Porbandar, India. His mother is deeply religious, and his father is a political minister. Throughout his childhood and teenage years, Mohandas is timid and shy.

1869

Studying in England

Kasturba gives birth to a son, Harilal. Three months later, Mohandas leaves India and his family to study law at University College London, England. He stays there for three years.

1883

1888

South Africa

Mohandas passes his law exams. He returns to India to set up a law practice, but the business fails. He and Kasturba have another son. Mohandas moves to South Africa to work for an Indian law firm there. Kasturba remains in India until joining him in 1896.

1891

Racial discrimination

While working in South Africa, Mohandas faces a lot of racial discrimination. These experiences inspire him in the struggle for equality and justice.

c. 1893

The Green Pamphlet

In 1894, Mohandas sets up the Natal Indian Congress, an organization to protect Indians in South Africa. Later, he writes "The Green Pamphlet," which details the racism Indians living there face. Despite this, he himself makes racist remarks about black South Africans, showing his own prejudices.

Facing arrest

South Africa introduces a law that threatens to deport Indians working there, unless they register and produce identification when asked for it. Mohandas organizes a peaceful resistance against this law. In 1908, he is arrested, but he is soon released.

1896

1906

Mahatma Gandhi

Mohandas Karamchand Gandhi (1869–1948), later known as Mahatma Gandhi, was a leader in the Indian Independence Movement. Gandhi believed in using nonviolent ways to achieve his goals.

Return to India

Mohandas goes back to India. By now, many Indian people wish their country to no longer be part of the British Empire. Mohandas gets involved in the Indian Independence Movement, and gradually becomes one of its leaders.

1915

The Salt March

Britain enforces a tax on producing and selling salt, forcing Indians to buy expensive imported salt. In protest, Mahatma leads thousands of Indians on a 241-mile (388-km) march to Dandi, Gujarat, where salt is produced. The Salt March sparks a wave of protests. By the end of the year, more than 60,000 protestors are in jail.

Becoming Mahatma

Mohandas travels to Shantiniketan, India, where he meets Rabindranath Tagore, a poet and Nobel Laureate. Rabindranath calls him Mahatma, meaning "Great Soul" in Hindi. The two forge a friendship, writing to each other for years to come.

1915

Fasting

During an 18-month spell in prison, Mahatma begins a hunger strike in protest against a change in the electoral laws introduced by the British. A Hindu, Mahatma fears the change will cause division among India's Hindu population. His fast lasts six days before a solution is agreed.

1930

Independence

Britain finally grants India its independence. Despite Mahatma's opposition, the country is partitioned (split) broadly along religious lines into two countries—India (predominantly Hindu) and Pakistan (predominantly Muslim). Partition causes riots, mass migration, and between 200,000 and two million fatalities.

1920

1932

Death

While on his way to a prayer meeting, Mahatma is assassinated by a man who believed he had shown too much respect for India's Muslims. More than two million people attend his funeral. His birthday becomes an Indian national holiday and the International Day of Non-Violence.

Noncooperation

After several hundred Indian people are massacred by British troops in 1919, Mahatma organizes a nationwide noncooperation movement. He asks people to stop paying taxes and urges them to use only Indian-made goods. When the protest turns violent two years later, he calls it off. Despite this, he is soon arrested. He goes to prison for two years.

1942

Quit India

Mahatma launches the "Quit India" movement, demanding Britain immediately ends its rule in India. Mahatma and other leaders are imprisoned for their involvement in the movement. He is freed in 1944.

1947

Spinning wheel

To protest against Britain's control over India's textile industry, Gandhi spun his own thread with a *charkha* (spinning wheel). The *charkha* became a symbol of the nation, and was even on the first Indian flag.

1948

Writers and revolutionaries

Writers and revolutionaries like Qiu Jin wanted to bring about change in China. They also wanted the country to be strong and free from foreign control.

Sun Yat-Sen (1866–1925)
A revolutionary, philosopher, and politician, Sun Yat-Sen helped overthrow the Qing Dynasty in 1911. He was the first temporary president of the Republic of China, and later he became leader of the Chinese Nationalist Party.

Lu Xun (1881–1936)
One of the greatest Chinese writers of the 20th century, Lu Xun supported the revolutionaries and wrote articles for them. He criticized traditional Chinese culture, and wrote short stories using everyday language that regular people could understand, to get his ideas across.

Leaving China
Jin is increasingly unhappy with her husband, who does not understand why Jin wants China to change so much. She sells her jewelry, leaves her family behind, and sets off on a ferry to study in Japan.

Life in Japan
When Jin arrives in Tokyo, she finds there are more than a thousand Chinese students (including many Chinese women) in the city. In Tokyo, she dresses in men's clothes, carries a sword, and gives lectures on feminism (the idea that men and women are equal).

Beijing
Jin and her family move to Beijing. She meets a group of women who want to completely change the way China is governed. They want greater equality and freedom for women, and they want China to be treated with respect by other countries. Jin begins to agree with their ideas.

1904

Marriage and family
At this time, Chinese women are expected only to become good wives and to raise children. Jin's father arranges for Jin to marry Wang Tingjun, who is from a wealthy merchant family. They marry, and soon they have two children together. Jin feels unfulfilled in her life.

1902

1904

A young poet
Jin reads widely, and writes poetry. She loves stories about the heroes from the past. She particularly likes tales about women, such as Hua Mulan, who become warriors.

Bright pearl
Qiu Jin grows up in Shanyin, China. She has a comfortable childhood, and her parents ensure she has a good education, as they did. She does well in school, and her family often call her their "bright pearl."

Martial arts and horse riding
Her family move to Shaoxing, her father's hometown. Jin learns martial arts from an older cousin. She becomes an expert at sword fighting and horse riding—things Chinese girls are not normally allowed to do.

1896

1875

c.1888

1891

HUA MULAN

Qiu Jin

A poet, revolutionary, and campaigner for women's rights, Qiu Jin (1875–1907) is today recognized as a hero in China. Jin broke the rules that governed how Chinese women of her time should behave, learning martial arts, dressing in men's clothes, and leaving her family to study abroad.

Speaking out
In Japan, Jin joins a secret Chinese society that wants to overthrow the government in China. She writes articles that promote women's education.

1904

Crackdown
The government in China pressures the Japanese authorities to forbid Chinese students there from any political activity. Jin and other Chinese students protest against this, but they are ignored. She convinces many students to return to China with her.

1905

Return to China
After returning to China, Jin contacts local activists, and works with them to further her cause for women's equality. She gets a job teaching in a girls' school, and encourages teachers to educate students about gender equality, and the struggle for a strong Chinese nation.

1906

Campaigning journalist
Jin sets up a magazine that promotes feminism. In it, she encourages women to struggle for their own personal and financial freedom. She also asks them to work together to build a new China.

1907

Ready to fight
Jin becomes head teacher at a school in Shaoxing. The school is secretly training its students to be revolutionary activists. Jin teaches them how to use weapons.

1907

Betrayed
Jin organizes the Restoration Army, an alliance of secret societies wanting to overthrow the Chinese government. The group is betrayed, and the names of its leaders are passed to the local authorities.

1907

Death
Jin is captured by troops and tortured. She refuses to answer any questions. She is publicly executed. Over time, Jin becomes a hero within China for her struggle for women's rights, and her fight for a different kind of China.

1907

> **"Don't tell me women are not the stuff of heroes!"**
>
> **Qiu Jin, *Capping Rhymes with Sir Ishii from Sun's Root Land* (translated in 1937)**

Albert Einstein

German-American physicist Albert Einstein (1879–1955) remains one of the most important scientists of all time. His work completely changed the way we think about space, time, and gravity. As war loomed in Europe, and anti-Jewish persecution increased in Germany, he found a new life in the US, where he became known for his political activism as well as his scientific work.

1919
"One of the highest achievements of human thought."
J. J. Thomson, President of Royal Society, talking about Albert's theories (1919)

Albert, who is living in Berlin, Germany, hits the newspaper headlines. During a solar eclipse, his prediction that gravity can bend light is proved. He is applauded for his scientific genius, and becomes an overnight celebrity.

1879
"The important thing is to not stop questioning. Curiosity has its own reasons for existing."
***Life* magazine interview (1955)**

Born in Ulm, Germany, to Jewish parents, Albert is encouraged to be independent from a young age. He explores the local area on his own and when at the age of five his father gives him a compass to play with, the way it works fascinates him. This inspires his interest in science.

1916
"A thought struck me. If a man falls freely, he would not feel his weight ... This simple thought experiment ... led me to the theory."
From a speech delivered at Kyoto University, Japan (1922)

Albert announces his general theory of relativity, the result of eight years of research into gravity. His theory includes many fascinating and surprising observations about time and space. It challenges many of the accepted rules of physics.

1905
$E = mc^2$

***Annalen der Physik 18* (1905)**

In an extraordinary few months, Albert publishes his ideas in a science journal. These theories will transform the way scientists understand space, time, mass, and energy. They include his "special theory of relativity" (how space and time are linked), and "mass–energy equivalence." He comes up with an equation, $E = mc^2$, to explain this: "E" stands for energy, "m" stands for mass, and "c²" is the speed of light squared. The theory proves that anything with mass has an equivalent amount of energy, and vice versa.

1894
"He will never amount to anything."
From Albert's school report (1895)

After his parents move to Italy, Albert remains in Germany to continue his education. He is talented at science and math, but he finds the school curriculum quite restrictive. He speaks out about it from time to time, often resulting in bad school reports from his teachers.

1896
"The value of an education ... is not the learning of many facts, but the training of the mind to think."
Discussing the purpose of education, *The New York Times* (1921)

Albert completes high school in Aarau, Switzerland, and enrolls at Zürich Polytechnic. He is disappointed that they do not teach the latest theories. Albert often plays truant.

1901
"I am by heritage a Jew, by citizenship a Swiss, and by makeup a human being."
In a letter to Alfred Kneser (1918)

To avoid military service in Germany, Albert becomes a Swiss citizen and finds work in Schaffhausen, Switzerland, as a tutor. He marries Mileva Marić in 1903. They have a daughter and two sons together.

1921

"The **American** is friendly, self-confident, optimistic, and without envy."

My First Impressions of the USA **(1921)**

Albert visits New York. His distinctive appearance and friendly personality help him attract a lot of attention from the press. He enjoys his time in the US before traveling around Asia and Europe. While traveling, he finds out he has won the Nobel Prize in Physics for his work.

1933

"**Nationalism** is an infantile disease. It is the measles of mankind."

In an interview for *The Saturday Evening Post* **(1929)**

Adolf Hitler comes to power in Germany. His Nazi Party preaches the superiority of Germany—known as nationalism. They introduce anti-Semitic (anti-Jewish) policies, and attack Albert's theories. Fearing for his safety, Albert moves to the US, where he takes up a job at Princeton University in New Jersey.

1939

"**The power of the atom** has changed everything."

From a telegram sent by Albert to prominent scientists warning of nuclear war (1946)

Nazi Germany triggers World War II by invading Poland. Albert feels that physics can contribute to the fight against the Nazis. He writes to US president Franklin D. Roosevelt, urging the development of the nuclear bomb—a new kind of powerful weapon that uses atomic science to create a massive explosion. After two devastating bombs are dropped by the US on Japan, Albert begins to campaign against the use of nuclear weapons.

1955

"**Our death** is not an end if we can **live on in** our **children** and the younger generation."

From a letter sent by Albert to the widow of a friend who had recently died (1926)

Einstein dies at the age of 76. His final words are lost to history as he spoke them in German, a language his American nurse did not understand.

Helen Keller

Unable to see or hear from an early age, American Helen Keller (1880–1968) overcame her impairments to become an advocate for change—not just for deaf-blind people, but for disadvantaged people everywhere. A prolific author, she used her writing to call attention to a wide range of issues affecting disadvantaged people.

Ways of communicating

Helen begins to "hear" what people are saying by placing her hand on the speaker's lips and throat. She can understand what they are saying by the way their lips move, and the vibrations from their throat. She becomes skilled at reading Braille—a writing system that is read by touch.

College

She becomes a student at Radcliffe College, Boston. Anne remains by her side, as her interpreter. Academically brilliant, Helen graduates four years later, becoming the first deaf-blind person to earn a Bachelor of Arts degree.

Anne Sullivan

Anne Sullivan

Helen's father arranges for a teacher, Anne Sullivan, to come and live with the family. The first word Helen learns is "water": Anne makes a swirling motion across one of Helen's hands while running water over the other. Helen understands the connection and is eager to learn more.

Nonverbal speech

Unable to speak, Helen develops a simple method of communication with her childhood friend Martha Washington by using hand signs. Over the next few years, the two girls develop about 60 signs to communicate with each other.

A mysterious illness

Helen is born in Alabama. When she is 19 months old, she contracts an illness that her physician calls "brain fever." It may have been scarlet fever or meningitis. The illness causes her to lose her sight and hearing forever.

1880 **1883** **1887** **1890** **1900**

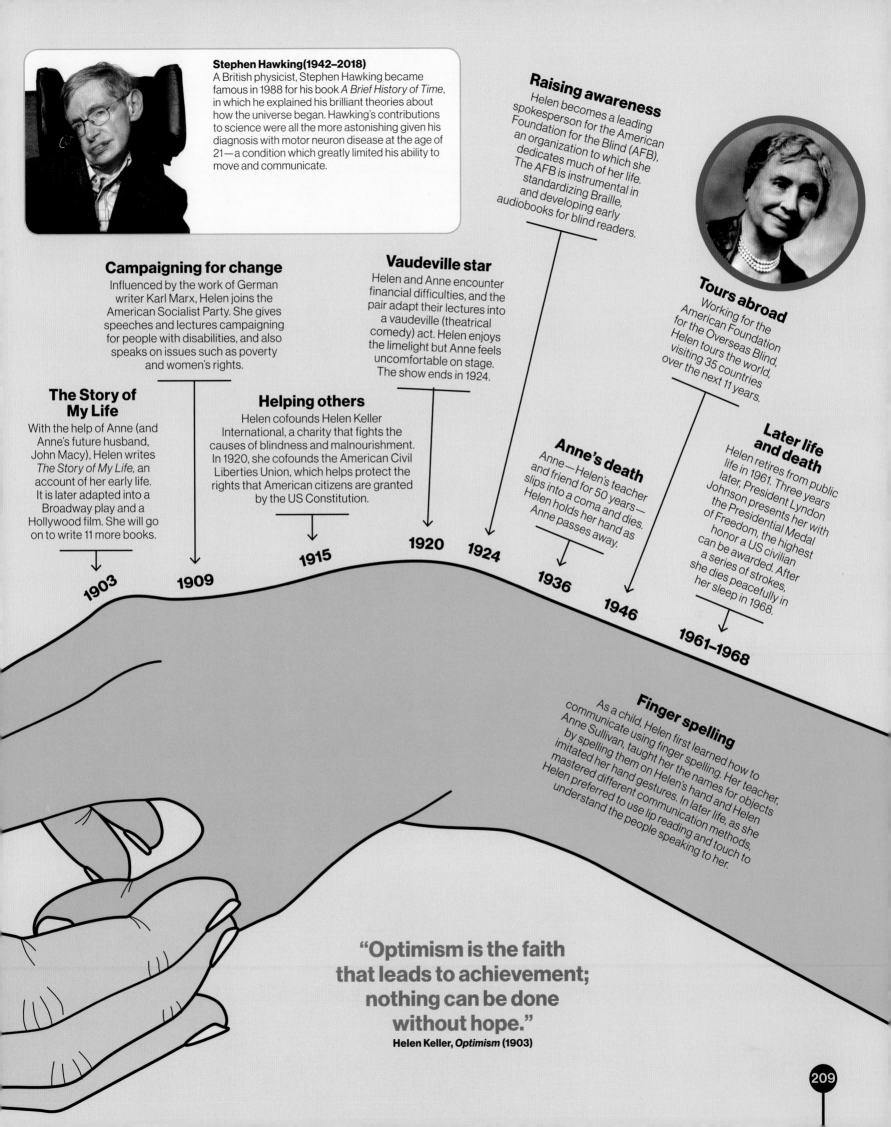

Stephen Hawking(1942–2018)
A British physicist, Stephen Hawking became famous in 1988 for his book *A Brief History of Time*, in which he explained his brilliant theories about how the universe began. Hawking's contributions to science were all the more astonishing given his diagnosis with motor neuron disease at the age of 21—a condition which greatly limited his ability to move and communicate.

Raising awareness
Helen becomes a leading spokesperson for the American Foundation for the Blind (AFB), an organization to which she dedicates much of her life. The AFB is instrumental in standardizing Braille, and developing early audiobooks for blind readers.

Campaigning for change
Influenced by the work of German writer Karl Marx, Helen joins the American Socialist Party. She gives speeches and lectures campaigning for people with disabilities, and also speaks on issues such as poverty and women's rights.

Vaudeville star
Helen and Anne encounter financial difficulties, and the pair adapt their lectures into a vaudeville (theatrical comedy) act. Helen enjoys the limelight but Anne feels uncomfortable on stage. The show ends in 1924.

Tours abroad
Working for the American Foundation for the Overseas Blind, Helen tours the world, visiting 35 countries over the next 11 years.

The Story of My Life
With the help of Anne (and Anne's future husband, John Macy), Helen writes *The Story of My Life,* an account of her early life. It is later adapted into a Broadway play and a Hollywood film. She will go on to write 11 more books.

Helping others
Helen cofounds Helen Keller International, a charity that fights the causes of blindness and malnourishment. In 1920, she cofounds the American Civil Liberties Union, which helps protect the rights that American citizens are granted by the US Constitution.

Anne's death
Anne—Helen's teacher and friend for 50 years—slips into a coma and dies. Helen holds her hand as Anne passes away.

Later life and death
Helen retires from public life in 1961. Three years later, President Lyndon Johnson presents her with the Presidential Medal of Freedom, the highest honor a US civilian can be awarded. After a series of strokes, she dies peacefully in her sleep in 1968.

1903

1909

1915

1920

1924

1936

1946

1961–1968

Finger spelling
As a child, Helen first learned how to communicate using finger spelling. Her teacher, Anne Sullivan, taught her the names for objects by spelling them on Helen's hand and Helen imitated her hand gestures. In later life, as she mastered different communication methods, Helen preferred to use lip reading and touch to understand the people speaking to her.

> **"Optimism is the faith that leads to achievement; nothing can be done without hope."**
>
> **Helen Keller,** *Optimism* (1903)

Growing up a boy

Einar Wegener is born in the town of Vejle, Denmark. Einar grows up as a boy, becomes a talented artist, and moves to Copenhagen as a teenager to study art at the Royal Danish Academy of Fine Arts.

1882

GERDA GOTTLIEB

Falling in love

At university, Einar meets fellow artist Gerda Gottlieb. They bond over their shared love of painting, and they fall in love. They marry two years later.

1902

EINAR WEGENER

Creative couple

Gottlieb becomes a successful illustrator, producing portraits for books and fashion magazines including *Vogue*. Einar's landscape paintings are shown in exhibitions.

1907

Lili Elbe

For many years, Danish artist Lili Elbe (1882–1931, born Einar Wegener) felt that she had been born into the wrong body. Elbe gradually realized that she was transgender. A transgender person feels that the gender they were assigned (given at birth) is not who they really are. Elbe became one of the first people to physically transition (change) from a "masculine" body to a more "feminine" body.

Lili

Anna Larssen, one of Gottlieb's models, fails to show up for a portrait sitting. Gottlieb asks Einar to step in by dressing as a woman. After first resisting, Einar agrees, and enjoys being in "this disguise." When Anna shows up, she suggests the name "Lili" for Einar when dressed as a woman, and Einar likes the name.

Gradual transition

Lili often feels as though she is two different people living in one body. She gradually realizes that she is more comfortable living as a woman than as a man, and that her true gender identity is female. She decides she wants to change her body to reflect how she feels inside, and to live her life completely as a woman.

A new identity

Lili undergoes three more operations at a clinic in Dresden, Germany. She is now legally recognized as a woman, and she changes her surname to "Elbe" after the river that flows through the city.

Death

Lili is joyful at forging a new life as her true self, and has a fifth and final operation in June to complete her transition. The surgery is initially successful, but soon leads to heart complications. She dies of cardiac arrest three months later.

1908 **1912** **c. 1925**

Paris

The couple move to Paris, where Lili feels more comfortable appearing in public as a woman. Lili becomes Gottlieb's favorite model. Gottlieb often introduces Lili as her sister to avoid the questions people might have. Lili spends many years dressing and appearing in public as both Einar and Lili.

Falling in love

Lili and Gerda's marriage is annulled (legally ended) as they are both women, and same-sex marriage is not legal at this time. Lili falls in love with an art dealer called Claude Lejeune, and dreams of having a family.

February 1930

1930

October 1930   **1931**

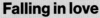

LILI WITH A FEATHER FAN
BY GERDA GOTTLIEB

Transitioning

Lili finally finds a doctor in Berlin, Germany, who can help her realize her dream of physically transitioning to a more feminine body. She sells many of her paintings in order to pay for an operation. The surgery is complicated, but it is a success.

"This human being was never intended to be anything but a woman."

Lili Elbe, *Man into Woman* (1933)

ELEANOR ROOSEVELT

Champion of human rights

At the end of World War II, many countries came together to form the United Nations (UN), which aimed to prevent such a terrible conflict ever happening again. One of the organization's early functions was to create the Universal Declaration of Human Rights. This document guaranteed freedom and equality to everyone, everywhere. American campaigner Eleanor Roosevelt (1884–1962) was a driving force behind the document's creation.

Respecting rights

Today, every human in the world has certain rights, which cannot be taken away from them. This was not always the case, however. In England, the *Magna Carta* of **1215**—an agreement between King John and his nobles—was the first document to grant some rights to all individuals. In the **17th century**, thinkers began to argue that there are certain freedoms that should be open to everyone. These ideas inspired revolutions in France and the US, and led to the French Declaration of the Rights of Man (**1789**) and the US Bill of Rights (**1791**). But each of these documents excluded certain groups of people, on grounds such as race, gender, or religion. After World War I, in **1919**, the newly formed League of Nations—an organization set up to prevent future conflicts—attempted to establish an international law of human rights. These attempts came to an abrupt end with the outbreak of World War II.

Campaigning First Lady

Since her teenage years, Eleanor Roosevelt has committed herself to public service. In the **1920s**, she devotes herself to the rights of women and children. In **1933**, her husband, Franklin D. Roosevelt, is elected president of the US. Eleanor uses the high profile she has as First Lady to fight for African Americans' civil rights. As the nation suffers from the Great Depression—a period of major economic downtown, during which many people go hungry or become homeless—she takes a leading role as a humanitarian activist. When World War II

breaks out in **1939**, she persuades her husband to allow people in Europe from persecuted groups, such as Jews, to take refuge in the US. She also supports greater roles for women and African Americans in the war effort.

The Four Freedoms

In **January 1941**, President Roosevelt delivers a speech to Congress in which he proposes "Four Freedoms" that everyone in the world should be allowed to enjoy: freedom of speech, freedom of worship, freedom from want, and freedom from fear. Recognizing the failure of the League of Nations to secure global peace, he persuades the leaders of his major allies to form an effective replacement. In **January 1942** representatives of the "Big Four" nations—the US, United Kingdom, China, and the Soviet Union—and 22 other countries come together at the White House to sign this "Declaration of United Nations." Over the next three years, as the war drags on, another 21 nations add their signatures.

United Nations Charter

As the war draws to a close, the atrocities committed by Nazi Germany—including the murder of more than six million Jews—become evident. Vowing that such crimes should never happen again, in **April 1945** delegates from 50 of the 51 signatories of the Declaration of United Nations come together in San Francisco and pledge to protect human rights around the world. One person missing is President Roosevelt, who died just two weeks earlier. The Charter of the United Nations, which established the UN, is signed in **June** and comes into force in **October**.

The drafting committee

In **December**, the new US president, Harry S. Truman, appoints Eleanor Roosevelt as the US' first representative (ambassador) to the UN. In **June 1946**, the UN establishes the Commission on Human Rights, made up of members from 18 countries. It is tasked with creating a new international bill of rights. Eleanor is appointed as the commission's first chair (person in charge). Six months later, in **January 1947**, the commission establishes a drafting committee for the document that will become the UN Declaration of Human Rights. When they meet in **June**, intense differences of opinion emerge between nations. In her

role as chair, Eleanor keeps the committee united with considerable skill. As she steers discussions forward, she helps ensure that the agreement respects all cultures, not just those of the dominant Western nations.

Adoption

The committee finishes its work in **May 1948**, but the document still requires UN member states to vote in its support. On **September 28**, Eleanor delivers a powerfully persuasive speech in Paris, France, and receives a standing ovation. Finally, after 81 meetings of the UN's General Assembly, the vote goes ahead in the Palais de Chaillot, Paris, at **11.56 pm on December 9**. The declaration is formally accepted in the early hours of the next day. Of the 58 UN members, 48 vote in favor and none against.

Aftermath

The Universal Declaration of Human Rights is a historic milestone. For the first time, the rights and freedoms to which

every human is entitled are universally agreed. In its 30 articles, the document covers the entire spectrum of human rights, and causes a revolution in international law. How a government treats its citizens is now a matter of international concern, and the UN now has the authority to step in to resolve human rights abuses. As the UN's most noted ambassador, Eleanor continues to travel the world on its behalf until she steps down from the role in **1953**. She dies in **1962**. After her death, in **1968**, she becomes one of the first people awarded the UN Human Rights Prize.

> "The world of the future is in our making. Tomorrow is now."
>
> **Eleanor Roosevelt,**
> *Tomorrow Is Now* (1963)

Zora Neale Hurston

Zora Neale Hurston (1891–1960) was one of the most significant African American writers of the 20th century. She was a leading figure in the Harlem Renaissance – a flowering of African American culture in the 1920s focused on Harlem, New York City. Hurston travelled widely, documenting the stories and traditions of black people across the US, the Caribbean, and Central America.

Tragedy strikes

Zora is just 13 when her mother dies. Her father remarries and sends Zora away to boarding school. In time, he stops paying the school fees, and Zora is forced to leave. At the age of 16, she joins a theatre company as a maid, and tours with them across the US.

1891   **1904**   **1917**

Early life

Zora is born in Notasulga, Alabama, but moves with the rest of her family to Eatonville, Florida, at the age of three.

Bending the truth

At the age of 26, Zora goes back to high school in Baltimore, Maryland. To gain admission, she fakes her age, pretending to be 10 years younger than she is. She keeps to this deception for the rest of her life.

American writers

The 20th century was a vibrant period for American literature. Many authors wrote about the difficulties of living in modern American society.

Alain LeRoy Locke (1886–1954)

The gifted scholar and teacher Alain LeRoy Locke was a major figure in the Harlem Renaissance of the 1920s. He brought together African American writers, musicians, and artists, and encouraged them to look to African culture for inspiration.

Langston Hughes (1902–1967)

A talented poet, playwright, and novelist, Langston Hughes was a key voice in the Harlem Renaissance. His works celebrated African American culture, spirituality, and humour, and addressed issues such as racism and poverty. Hughes loved the African American musical genre jazz, and often used jazz rhythms in his poetry.

Flannery O'Connor (1925–1964)

Considered one of the greatest 20th-century American writers of short stories, Flannery O'Connor set her works in the rural southern states of the US. Her stories often focus around the relationship between individuals and God.

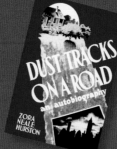

University studies

Zora continues her studies at Howard University, Washington, D.C. She co-establishes *The Hilltop*, a student newspaper. She also has her first short story, "John Redding Goes to Sea", published in a literary magazine.

Southern travels

Zora travels through the southern US states recording African American folk tales. She meets former enslaved person Cudjoe Kazoola Lewis, the last survivor of the final slave ship to cross from Africa to the US. She writes a book based on their conversations.

Travels to the Caribbean

Zora is given an award to research the rituals of voodoo (a West African religion) in Haiti, and *obeah* (spiritual healing) in Jamaica. She documents her findings in the book *Tell My Horse*.

Autobiography

Zora's autobiography, *Dust Tracks on a Road*, is published. She gains praise for the quality of her writing. She wins the Anisfield-Wolf Book Award for the book's contribution to the understanding of race relations.

Death

When Zora dies, she is buried in an unmarked grave because there is no money for a headstone. Much later, in 1973, the novelist Alice Walker locates Zora's grave and adds a headstone with the words "Zora Neale Hurston: A Genius of the South".

1921   1925   1927   1932   1936   1937   1942   1950s   1960

Harlem Renaissance

Zora earns a scholarship to study at Barnard College, New York City. She moves to Harlem, a vibrant, mainly African American neighbourhood which is the centre of an explosion of art and ideas called the Harlem Renaissance. She befriends the poet Langston Hughes and other rising stars. They launch a magazine called *Fire!!* in 1926.

Writing

Zora adapts her folk tale research into a play, *The Great Day*, which features African song and dance. Two years later, her first novel, *Jonah's Gourd Vine*, is published. Her work is well received, but does not give her mainstream success.

Literary classic

Her second novel, *Their Eyes Were Watching God*, is published. It becomes her most influential book, and many people today see it as a classic of the Harlem Renaissance.

Financial struggles

Zora finds it difficult to get her work published. She takes a job as a substitute teacher in a school, and writes occasional articles for newspapers. She is often underpaid because of her race and gender, and struggles with debt and poverty.

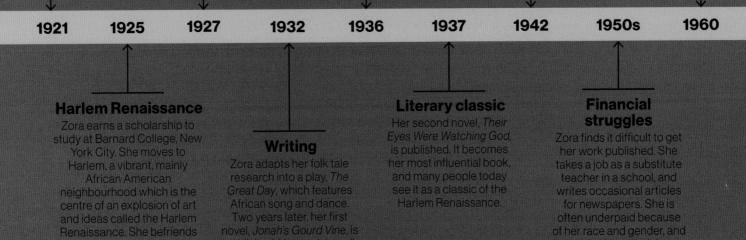

"Mama [told us] to 'jump at de sun'. We might not land on the sun, but at least we would get off the ground."

Zora Neale Hurston,
***Dust Tracks on a Road* (1942)**

GAVRILO PRINCIP
The assassin who started a war

The spark that exploded into World War I (1914–1918) was lit by a young Bosnian Serb revolutionary named Gavrilo Princip (1894–1918). Princip's assassination of the heir to the Austro-Hungarian throne on June 28, 1914, triggered a series of reactions that would lead to a full-scale European war within five weeks—a war that soon spread across the world.

A crisis builds

In **1908**, Austria-Hungary claimed the province of Bosnia-Herzegovina, infuriating the people from neighboring Serbia who lived there. Bosnian Serbs called for their own separate state to unite the region's Slavs (people who speak Slavic languages, such as Serbian and Bosnian). In **1913**, Emperor Franz Josef of Austria-Hungary sent his son, Archduke Franz Ferdinand, on a royal visit to Bosnia.

Warnings ignored

In **April 1914**, 19-year-old Gavrilo Princip is one of six revolutionaries recruited by the pro-separation Young Bosnia group in Belgrade, Serbia, to assassinate the

archduke. They practice shooting rounds of ammunition in a local park. Gavrilo and two accomplices arrive in Sarajevo, the Bosnian capital, on **June 4**, where they lie low, separately, to avoid police detection, and await further instructions. On **June 21**, the Serbian ambassador warns the Austro-Hungarian government that the archduke is in danger. No action is taken, and the archduke and his wife, Sophie, arrive in Bosnia on **June 25**. On **June 27**, the Young Bosnia group receive weapons, while the royal couple attend a banquet.

Failed attempt

An open-top motorcade through Sarajevo is planned for the royal couple's final day, **June 28**, which is also their 14th wedding anniversary. Crowds line the procession route as the royal couple arrive in Sarajevo by train at **9:50 a.m.** Meanwhile, the Young Bosnia group fans out along Appel Quay, to await the motorcade. After a meet and greet with local dignitaries and a troop inspection, the motorcade sets off for City Hall at **10 a.m.** Waiting on the quay, Gavrilo's accomplice, Nedeljko Čabrinović, spots the car and launches a hand grenade at **10:10 a.m.** The archduke's driver spots the bomb and accelerates—it bounces off his car and explodes beneath the vehicle behind, injuring two passengers and 18 spectators. Both the archduke and duchess are unharmed. Čabrinović tries to escape by jumping into the river, but he is hauled out by the police and arrested.

The assassin strikes

Gavrilo, thinking his chance has passed, ducks down a side street. The royal couple plan to continue the tour and speed to City Hall. After the reception, they decide that they would like to visit victims of the bombing. At **10:45 a.m.**, the motorcade travels back along Appel Quay, the fastest route to the hospital. The driver takes a wrong turn, driving down the same side street along which Gavrilo is positioned. Realizing his mistake, he stops to reverse, but the engine stalls. At **10:55 a.m.**, Gavrilo, seizing his chance, fires a shot into the archduke's neck. He aims again, but during the tussle, shoots the duchess by mistake. By **11:30 a.m.** the archduke and duchess are both dead.

Aftermath

Gavrilo tries to shoot himself but police and civilians wrestle the pistol from his hand, and he is arrested and imprisoned. The rest of the Young Bosnia assassins are rounded up in due course. News of the assassination quickly spreads across Europe. Within hours, riots break out across Sarajevo.

On **June 29**, anti-Serb demonstrations become more violent. Two Serbs are killed and hundreds of homes, schools, and businesses are destroyed. The governor declares martial (military) law. The bodies of the archduke and duchess are transported to Vienna, first by sea and then by train, and their funeral takes place on **July 4**.

Countdown to war

In Vienna, the Austro-Hungarian royal court is shocked by the assassination and holds the Serbian government responsible. Many want revenge. The court is split on how to respond—some prefer a diplomatic solution, while others want to declare an all-out war. On **July 5**, Germany assures Austria-Hungary of its full support, whatever action it chooses. On **July 28**, one month to the day after the assassination, Austria-Hungary declares war on Serbia. Russia sends troops to Serbia's defense, leading Germany to declare war on Russia. Within a week, as countries rush to defend their allies, war breaks out across Europe.

Trial and death

The trials of all the assassins, along with everyone who helped them along the way, are set for the middle of October. Gavrilo is found guilty, but at 19 years old, he is too young to be executed. On **October 28**, he is given a 20-year sentence and transferred to Terezín Military Prison (in modern-day Czech Republic) on **December 5**. Conditions are harsh, and he contracts tuberculosis, leading to the amputation of one of his arms. He dies in **April 1918**, convinced that his actions were not the cause of the world war that raged after the assassinations.

GAVRILO PRINCIP

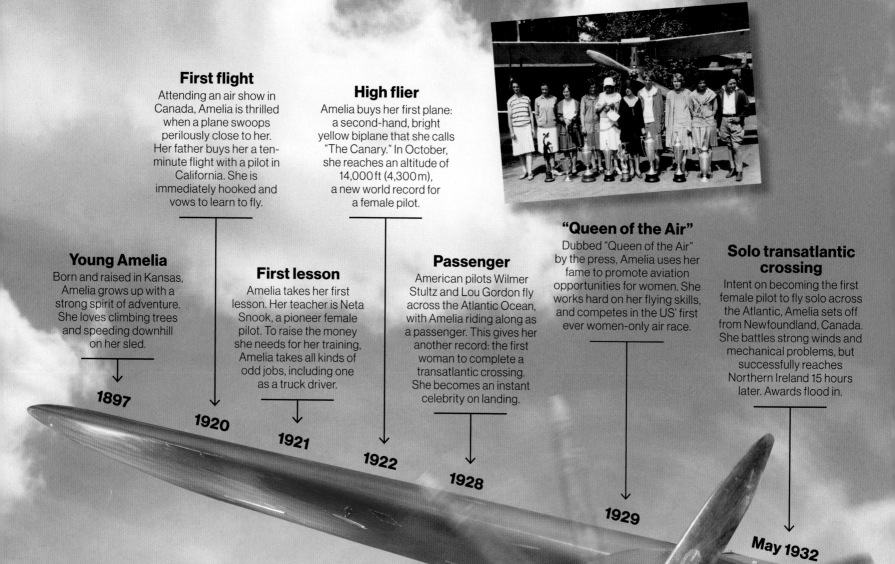

First flight

Attending an air show in Canada, Amelia is thrilled when a plane swoops perilously close to her. Her father buys her a ten-minute flight with a pilot in California. She is immediately hooked and vows to learn to fly.

High flier

Amelia buys her first plane: a second-hand, bright yellow biplane that she calls "The Canary." In October, she reaches an altitude of 14,000 ft (4,300 m), a new world record for a female pilot.

Young Amelia

Born and raised in Kansas, Amelia grows up with a strong spirit of adventure. She loves climbing trees and speeding downhill on her sled.

First lesson

Amelia takes her first lesson. Her teacher is Neta Snook, a pioneer female pilot. To raise the money she needs for her training, Amelia takes all kinds of odd jobs, including one as a truck driver.

Passenger

American pilots Wilmer Stultz and Lou Gordon fly across the Atlantic Ocean, with Amelia riding along as a passenger. This gives her another record: the first woman to complete a transatlantic crossing. She becomes an instant celebrity on landing.

"Queen of the Air"

Dubbed "Queen of the Air" by the press, Amelia uses her fame to promote aviation opportunities for women. She works hard on her flying skills, and competes in the US' first ever women-only air race.

Solo transatlantic crossing

Intent on becoming the first female pilot to fly solo across the Atlantic, Amelia sets off from Newfoundland, Canada. She battles strong winds and mechanical problems, but successfully reaches Northern Ireland 15 hours later. Awards flood in.

1897

1920

1921

1922

1928

1929

May 1932

Amelia Earhart

In 1932, American pilot Amelia Earhart (1897–1937) became the first woman to fly solo across the Atlantic Ocean. Her pioneering feat inspired generations of female aviators. She became an icon of the golden age of aviation, a time when pilots and planes captured the public imagination by flying faster, further, and higher than ever before.

Flying firsts

For centuries, humans dreamed of taking to the skies, but early attempts—such as simply strapping on wings to their arms—did not end well. The success of the first flight in 1903 paved the way for a string of amazing aviators.

Wilbur (1867–1912) and Orville (1871–1948) Wright

The age of aviation began when two US brothers, Wilbur and Orville Wright, completed the first powered flight on December 17, 1903. Made of wood and fabric, the *Wright Flyer* remained airborne for just 12 seconds on its first flight that day, but its success proved that the sky was now the limit.

Bessie Coleman (1892–1926)

Born in Texas, Bessie Coleman developed an interest in flying at a time when African Americans found opportunities in aviation few and far between. After earning her pilot's license in Paris, France, she returned to the US, where she became a professional stunt flier, performing dangerous tricks to an adoring crowd.

Valentina Tereshkova (b.1937)

In 1963, Soviet cosmonaut and engineer Valentina Tereshkova became the first woman to fly in space. She completed 48 orbits of Earth aboard the space capsule *Vostok 6*, in almost three days of continuous flying. She is the only woman to have been on a solo space mission.

First attempt

Flying a Lockheed Electra specially built for the trip, Amelia and her crew set out westward from Honolulu, Hawaii. After crashing on take-off, they decide it would be safer to fly eastward from Oakland, California.

> "Ours is the commencement of a flying age, and I am happy to have popped into existence at a period so interesting."
>
> **Amelia Earhart, *20 Hrs., 40 Min.* (1928)**

Hawaii to California

Amelia's trailblazing feats continue when she becomes the first pilot to fly solo from Hawaii to California. She starts dreaming of a new prize: a flight around the globe.

1935

Second attempt

Amelia and her copilot, Fred Noonan, begin a second attempt from Miami, Florida. After many stops, they reach New Guinea on June 29, having covered more than two-thirds of their journey.

March 1937

June 1, 1937

Disappearance

Visibly exhausted, Amelia sets off with Noonan on the 2,500-mile (4,000-km) leg to Howland Island, the next-to-last stop before California. They never arrive, and no trace of their bodies or their plane are ever found.

July 2, 1937

1898	1905	1913	1917	1921	1924	1938	1946	1948

Kiev
Born in Kiev (in modern-day Ukraine) to a Jewish family, Golda Meir grows up in poverty. Her father, a carpenter, boards up the doors of their home to protect them from a pogrom (an anti-Jewish attack).

New ideas
Golda moves in with her sister in Denver, Colorado. There, she is surrounded by thinkers and activists who teach her about socialism and women's rights. She meets her future husband, Morris Meyerson.

To Palestine
Now married to Meyerson, Golda moves to Palestine with him. They live on a *kibbutz* (a collective home on a farm, where everyone helps with cooking and domestic chores, and works together to farm the land).

Refugee crisis
Thousands of Jews flee Nazi Germany, where the government is persecuting them. Golda attends an international conference to help Jewish refugees, but most countries refuse to take in any Jews. The following year, World War II breaks out.

The State of Israel
The UN decides that Jewish people and Arab people should share Palestine (which is holy to both peoples). Golda helps set up the Jewish state, now called Israel. On May 14, Israel declares Independence. Many Arabs are expelled (or flee) from their homes.

Milwaukee
The family move to Milwaukee, Wisconsin, to escape persecution. Golda is top of her class at school, and she sets up the American Young Sisters Society. They collect money to pay for poor children's school supplies.

Zionist activism
Golda fundraises and campaigns for the Zionist cause. Zionists wish to set up a state where Jewish people can live in safety. Jewish people have faced hostility in Europe for centuries. Zionists look to set up a Jewish state in Palestine, in the Middle East.

Political beginnings
She leaves the *kibbutz* to work in politics. In 1928, Golda is elected secretary of the Women's Labor Council, an organization that stands up for the rights of women in the workplace. They send her to the United States for two years, where she builds links with the Jewish community there.

Keeping the peace
After World War II, Golda negotiates between Zionists (who are campaigning for a Jewish state) and the British authorities (who control Palestine). Britain ask the United Nations (UN) for help.

Golda Meir

A dedicated activist and no-nonsense politician, Golda Meir (1898–1978) was born into poverty in the Russian Empire. She became one of the leading figures in the creation of the State of Israel, and went on to serve as the country's first female prime minister in 1969.

Leading figures
Strong-willed politicians can make a huge impact on their nations but they can also divide opinions.

Yitzhak Rabin (1922–1995)
Yitzhak Rabin succeeded Golda Meir. He won the Nobel Peace Prize in 1994, but was assassinated by a terrorist opposed to his peace plan the following year.

Margaret Thatcher (1925–2013)
The first female prime minister of the United Kingdom, she was labeled "The Iron Lady" for her strong-willed leadership style.

Yasser Arafat (1929–2004)
The first president of the Palestinian National Authority, Yasser Arafat had previously fought in wars against Israel. He shared the Nobel Peace Prize with Yitzhak Rabin in 1994.

1948   **1949**   **1956**   **1969**   **1973**   **1973–1978**

Soviet Union
Golda is issued with the first ever Israeli passport. She travels to the Soviet Union (USSR) and attends the Moscow Choral Synagogue on *Rosh Hashanah* (Jewish New Year). About 50,000 Soviet Jews attend and chant her name. They see her as a hero.

Minister of Labor
Elected to the Knesset (the parliament of Israel), Golda becomes minister of labor and is in charge of the construction of new roads, hospitals, and schools. Thousands of new homes are built during this period.

Prime Minister
When Prime Minister Levi Eshkol dies suddenly, Golda is asked to take his place. During her time as prime minister, she meets many world leaders, and invites the West German leader, Willy Brandt, to Israel.

Yom Kippur War
Syria and Egypt launch an attack on Israel on the holiest day of the Jewish calendar, Yom Kippur. The Israeli forces repel the attack, but both Israel and Egypt begin to seek a path to peace.

Resignation and death
Golda's political party wins the Israeli elections in 1973, but she resigns the following year because some politicians blame her for the army's poor performance in the Yom Kippur war. She passes away aged 80 and is buried on Mount Herzl, in Jerusalem.

Foreign Minister
Golda becomes foreign minister. She changes her last name to its Hebrew version, Meir. The Second Arab–Israeli War breaks out when Israel, France, and the United Kingdom invade Egypt. The UN intervene and send troops to keep the peace on the Egypt–Israeli border.

> ## "It is true we have won all our wars, but we have paid for them."
> **Golda Meir, quoted in *LIFE* magazine (1969)**

Israeli–Palestine conflict
The conflict between Israel and Palestine began just before the creation of Israel in 1948 and continues today. As Jewish refugees from Europe settled in independent Israel, more than 700,000 Arabs had to leave their homes. Because of this, many Arabs refuse to recognize Israel as a proper independent country. The conflict between the two sides has led to many deaths. Despite decades of negotiation, a peaceful solution has not yet been reached.

Young performer

Born into poverty, Josephine grows up in St. Louis, Missouri. She leaves home as a teenager and earns a living as a street performer. By the age of 16, Josephine has toured the US with The Jones Family Band (a group of street performers) and The Dixie Steppers (an all-black traveling group).

1906

Broadway debut

Josephine auditions for a role in the musical comedy *Shuffle Along* on Broadway (the hub of the US theater world). Initially rejected for a role because she is "too dark" and "too skinny," she successfully auditions again, and dances in the show for a year.

1922

Living in harmony

In order to show that people from all walks of life can live in harmony, Josephine adopts 12 children from around the world, including Japan, Colombia, and Côte d'Ivoire (Ivory Coast). They live with her in her château (country house) in the Dordogne in southwest France. She calls her adopted children the "Rainbow Tribe."

1953

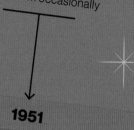

Protest

Though based in France, Josephine goes on several tours in the US. There, she boycotts (protests against) segregated clubs and concert venues. She refuses to perform in venues that stop black people from buying tickets, or that turn black ticket-holders away. She retires from the stage in 1956 but continues to perform occasionally

1951

1963

1973

1975

Grace Kelly (1929–1982)

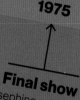

Grace Kelly was an American film actor who became friends with Josephine Baker after they met in a nightclub in New York in 1951. The club racially discriminated against Baker, and Kelly walked out in protest with her. Kelly later retired from acting and became Princess of Monaco when she married Prince Rainier III in 1956.

Civil Rights

Josephine is one of the only women to speak during the March on Washington, D.C., organized by African American groups seeking to end repression, segregation, and discrimination. The peaceful protests help spur the passing of the Civil Rights Act, which improves the lives of African Americans across the country.

Return to performing

Five years after her last appearance on stage, Josephine appears in a run of sold-out shows at Carnegie Hall in New York. She receives positive reviews for her performances.

Final show

Josephine celebrates 50 years since her first appearance in Paris by performing in a revue show at the Bobino Theater in Paris. She dies during the show's run. More than 20,000 people in Paris pay their respects and celebrate her life.

Follow-up shows

After the success of *Shuffle Along*, Josephine goes on to play a leading role as a clown in *The Chocolate Dandies*, a musical stage show about horse racing in a small town. She goes on to work as a performer at the Plantation Club theater restaurant in Harlem, New York.

1924

Moving to Paris

At the Plantation Club, she meets Caroline Dudley Regan, wife of a US diplomat in Paris, France. Regan invites her to join a theater group there. Josephine moves to Paris, where she performs with the dance group *La Revue Nègre*. She performs her most famous dance routine, *Danse Sauvage* ("Wild Dance").

1925

Movie success

Josephine's performances catapult her into roles in the French film industry. She is the first African American to star in major movies, including *Siren of the Tropics* (1927), a silent film telling the story of a young girl in love, and *Zou Zou* (1934), the tale of a man accused of murder.

A SCENE FROM *SIREN OF THE TROPICS* (1927)

1926

Back in America

Josephine returns to the US to perform with the Ziegfeld Follies (a music and dance act). Though she is a huge star in Europe, she finds life difficult in the US due to racism. While in the US, she resists racial segregation (enforced separation of people by race) by refusing to perform for audiences in theaters with segregated seating.

1936

Secret agent

While on tour during World War II, Josephine works as a spy. She passes on secrets about German troop movements, written on music scores, to the French Resistance (anti-Nazi movement). After the war, Josephine becomes the first American woman to be honored by the French government for her actions during the war.

1939

Superstar

Acting in films including *Princess Tam Tam* (1935), Josephine becomes one of the most famous black superstars in Europe. But during this period black actors have limited choices in the roles they play, and many of the roles she is offered portray negative stereotypes of black people.

1935

Josephine Baker

One of the first African American superstars, Josephine Baker (1906–1975) gained international fame through dancing, singing, and acting in Europe. Though she faced discrimination in both the US and Europe, Josephine used her fame to fight prejudice, and even worked as a spy during World War II.

Writer and editor
Rachel finds work with the US Bureau of Fisheries. Her job involves writing radio scripts and brochures on aquatic life aimed at educating the public. She works there for the next 15 years, eventually becoming chief editor.

1936

Under the Sea-Wind
Rachel's first book about the ocean, *Under the Sea-Wind*, is published. Combining poetic description and scientific information, it tells the story of three creatures—a wading bird, a mackerel, and an eel— that depend on the sea for survival.

1941

Best-seller
The Sea Around Us, her next book, is a history of the ocean. It gets wonderful reviews and becomes a best-seller, allowing her to resign from her job to become a full-time writer.

1951

Scientific studies
After graduating with a degree in zoology (the study of animals). Rachel begins to study for a doctorate (the highest level of study). After her father dies suddenly, she is forced to give up in order to support her family financially.

1932

Turning point
Rachel switches to biology. During a summer job at the US Marine Laboratory before starting a graduate degree, she develops a deep interest in the ocean. She is passionate about the conservation of its creatures and habitats.

1928

College
Rachel finishes high school at the top of her class, and goes on to study English literature at Pennsylvania College for Women. She wants to become a writer, and sends poems to several magazines, but without success.

1925

Country child
Rachel Carson is born on a farm in rural Pennsylvania. She develops a love of nature from her mother. She reads a lot, and enjoys writing stories. At the age of 10, she has her first story published in a children's magazine.

1907

Rachel Carson

A lifelong passion for the natural world led Rachel Carson (1907–1964), an American marine biologist, to write several best-selling books. Her most famous work, *Silent Spring*, drew attention to the damage humans do to the environment. It is now seen as the book that started the environmental movement.

"In nature nothing exists alone."

Rachel Carson,
Silent Spring (1962)

Maine cottage

The Sea Around Us is made into an award-winning documentary. Rachel uses the money she makes from its success to build a cottage by the coast in Maine. She spends many happy hours there researching her next book.

1953

The Edge of the Sea

In *The Edge of the Sea*, the third and last of Rachel's three books about the sea, she explores the complex natural life of the seashore. The book introduces the idea of ecosystems (interacting communities of organisms) to the general public.

1955

Research into pesticides

Using her connections with government scientists, Rachel begins investigating the damaging effects of DDT, an industrial chemical that is sprayed directly onto crops to destroy pests. She finds evidence it is killing birds and other animals as it spreads up the food chain.

1957

Silent Spring

Her research into DDT is published in the book *Silent Spring*, which details how the heavy use of pesticides pollutes soil and streams, damages animal populations, and poses risks to human health. The title symbolizes the death and decay—with no more birdsong—caused by the unlimited use of DDT.

1962

Facing her critics

Rachel's ideas are attacked by pesticide manufacturers. After she calmly presents the facts in a TV special report, public opinion turns massively in her favor. US president John F. Kennedy sets up a committee to look into the effects of pesticides.

1963

Death and legacy

Rachel dies of cancer at the age of 56, but *Silent Spring* helps launch the worldwide environmental movement. DDT is banned in the US in 1972.

1964

Frida Kahlo

One of the most outstanding artists of the 20th century, Mexican painter Frida Kahlo (1907–1954) was ill and in pain for much of her life. She is best known for her vivid self-portraits set among lush plants and exotic animals.

"I paint self-portraits because I am the person I know best."

Frida Kahlo, from an interview (1945)

Innovative artists

The early 20th century was a time of great innovation in art. Painters and sculptors experimented with ways of depicting modern life, leading to rapidly changing styles and movements such as Cubism, abstract art, and Surrealism.

Pablo Picasso (1881–1973)

Spanish-born Pablo Picasso, who spent most of his life in France, was probably the most important artist of the 20th century. Always working on new ideas, he helped develop Cubism, a way of representing objects as simple shapes that revolutionized Western art. His masterpiece is *Guernica* (1937), a huge painting depicting the horrors of war.

Salvador Dalí (1904–1989)

The flamboyant Spanish artist Salvador Dalí was a leading Surrealist painter. Influenced by the ideas of psychoanalyst Sigmund Freud (1856–1939), he studied the symbolism of dreams. One of his best-known paintings is *The Persistence of Memory* (1931), which shows mysterious melting clocks in a dreamlike landscape.

Death
1954

Eight days after completing a still life of watermelons, Frida dies in the "Blue House," the family home where she was born 47 years earlier. The house will become a museum dedicated to her life and works.

Final exhibition
1953

By this point, Frida's health is in serious decline. Her work is known worldwide. Though she is ill, she opens her first solo exhibition in Mexico from a four-poster bed specially set up for her in the gallery.

Paris visit
1939

Frida visits Paris. The influential French critic André Breton (1896–1966) acclaims her as a Surrealist—one whose work is inspired by the unconscious mind. She denies this, saying she paints reality, not her dreams.

Divorce
1939

Frida and Rivera divorce, and Frida throws herself into her work. She paints *Hummingbird* (1940), which some people feel displays her sadness at the end of the relationship. It becomes one of her best-known paintings. Frida and Rivera soon reconcile, and marry again in 1940.

New York exhibition
1938

Frida's first major New York solo exhibition in New York is a sign that she is recognized as an artist. It is also proof of a success, her becoming right and becoming her own wife of is an artist in her own right—not just as the wife of Diego Rivera.

Soviet guest
1937

A banished Soviet communist leader, Leon Trotsky (1879–1940), spends some time living with Frida and Rivera. In 1940, he is murdered in Coyoacán by agents acting on behalf of the Soviet Union.

American years
1930

Frida visits the United States with Rivera, who is commissioned to paint public murals in San Francisco, Detroit, and New York City. Homesick, she begins to paint astonishing self-portraits in a style based on Mexican folk art.

Marriage
1928

Frida meets Mexico's leading artist, Diego Rivera, at a party. She shows him her paintings, which he feels show a lot of artistic promise. They become a couple, and marry in 1929. He is 42 and physically imposing, while she is 22 and slight, which leads Frida's mother to call the pair "the elephant and the dove."

Bus accident
1925

A bus crash leaves Frida with severe injuries to her back and leg, and pain that will last for the rest of her life. Unable to study, her dreams of becoming a doctor come to an end. She is bed-ridden for several months, and takes up painting.

Childhood illness
1922

Frida Kahlo is born in her family's home in Coyoacán, near Mexico City. Aged six, she falls ill with polio, leaving her with one leg shorter than the other. She uses long, colorful skirts to hide this.

Bright future
1907

Frida is one of only 35 girls out of 2,000 students attending the National Preparatory School—an elite high school in Mexico City. She hopes to study medicine at university.

Monkeys often feature in Kahlo's Animals in work, such as *Self-Portrait With Monkeys*.

Homesick
Kahlo's *Self Portrait Along the Borderline Between Mexico and the United States* shows her rejecting the industry and pollution of the US, and yearning for a simpler life in Mexico.

227

William Randolph Hearst (1863–1951)

American entrepreneur and newspaper publisher William Randolph Hearst controlled Hearst, a massive American media company during the first half of the 1900s. He became successful by publishing "yellow journalism"—entertaining, sensational, but often untrue news stories.

1863
William is born into a wealthy family in San Francisco, California. His father, George Hearst, owned gold mines and a newspaper.

1882
William enrolls at Harvard College, where he becomes the business manager of the *Harvard Lampoon*—a funny paper published by students.

1887

William is put in charge of his father's failing newspaper, the *San Francisco Examiner*. He turns it around, and makes the newspaper into a success.

1895
William buys the *New York Morning Journal*. The *Journal* uses bold headlines, dramatic crime stories, and entertaining features about everyday life to attract thousands of readers.

1903
William gets involved in politics. He wins his first two-year term in the US House of Representatives. He wins another in 1905.

1935
William now controls more than 28 newspapers and 18 magazines. He is able to influence what is reported, and how it is reported, more than anyone else in the US.

1937
William's papers begin to fail during the Great Depression—a worldwide economic decline that began in 1929. He is forced to sell his priceless art collection to pay off his debts.

1940
William's financial problems mean he no longer leads Hearst.

1951
William dies at the age of 88. Hearst is still one of the largest media companies in the US.

Winifred Bonfils (1863–1936)

American investigative journalist Winifred Bonfils made her mark with her sensational style of reporting for William Randolph Hearst's newspapers.

1863
Winifred is born in Wisconsin.

1869
Her family moves, and Winifred spends her early years on a farm near Chicago, Illinois.

1890

Winifred starts work as a journalist for the *San Francisco Examiner*, Hearst's first newspaper. Her biggest story of this time is an investigation into the poor healthcare she receives while staying in one of the city's hospitals. It results in positive changes being made to hospitals in the city.

1895
Hearst sends Winifred to New York City to report for the *New York Morning Journal*.

1900
Winifred slips through a police cordon in Galveston, Texas, to report on the aftermath of one of America's deadliest hurricanes. She is the first reporter on the scene, and her eyewitness account of the disaster leads Hearst to help with the recovery effort.

1914
Winifred travels to Europe to report on World War I. She stays to cover the peace talks afterward.

1936
Winifred dies. She continued her newspaper work right up until her death.

Dadasaheb Phalke (1870–1944)

Indian film director and producer Dadasaheb Phalke produced the first film made in India. He started the Indian film industry, one of the largest in the world.

1870
Dhundiraj Govind Phalke, later known as Dadasaheb Phalke, is born in the town of Trimbakeshwar in British India (modern-day Maharashtra, India) into a relatively well-off family.

1885
Dadasaheb attends the Sir J. J. School of Art in Bombay (modern-day Mumbai), where he studies photography, art, and drawing.

1910
At the America-India Picture Palace in Bombay, he sees a European film. He starts thinking about making a film exploring Indian themes.

1912
Dadasaheb borrows money from a friend and sets sail for London, England, to buy film-making equipment. He also meets English film producer Cecil Hepworth, who shows him how to make films. After a successful trip, he returns to India.

1913

Desperately short of money, he sells family belongings to finance his first film, *Raja Harishchandra*. The story is about a king who sacrifices his kingdom and family to keep a promise. The film is a huge success. He continues making films in India.

1932
Following a short period of retirement, Dadasaheb returns to filmmaking. But, in the era of sound, his last silent film, *Setu-Bandhan*, is a box-office failure. Dadasaheb's attempt to add dialogue after the film had been shot does not work.

1944
Seven years after making his last film, *Gangavataran*, Dadasaheb dies.

The world of entertainment changed completely in the late 1800s. Newspapers became hugely popular. The invention of the camera led to silent films, and advances in recording sound resulted in "talkies" (movies with sound). Here are just some of the people involved.

Charlie Chaplin (1889–1977)

English actor Charlie Chaplin perfected the use of gestures and facial expressions to tell a story, in the era before films had sound. He featured in more than 80 films.

1889
Charlie is born in London, England, into a poor family. Both his parents are actors. His mother suffers from ill health, and his father dies when he is young. Charlie and his brother often have to look after themselves.

1894
At the age of five, Charlie makes his stage debut filling in for his mother when she loses her voice halfway through a performance. He impresses the audience with his singing and comedy skills.

1910
Determined to make it as an actor, Charlie heads to the US with a comedy troupe (group) led by Fred Karno, an English theater financier and organizer. Charlie is their main star.

1913
Charlie signs a contract with Mack Sennett, a film producer who had seen him performing in New York. He moves to California, where Sennet's studio is based.

1914

Charlie makes his film debut in *Making a Living*. This is followed by *Kid Auto Races at Venice*, a hugely successful film where he first plays "the Tramp," a friendly man with a funny walk and baggy trousers. This becomes his most famous character.

1916
Charlie stars in a series of successful films over the next decade, including *The Vagabond* (1916), *The Kid* (1921), and *The Gold Rush* (1925).

1936
Charlie makes his last silent film, *Modern Times*, which is set during the Great Depression.

1977
Charlie dies following a long spell of ill health. He is regarded a great comic actor, and one of the most important figures in early cinema.

Fatma Begum (1892–1983)

Starting her career as a film actress, Fatma Begum became India's first female director in 1926 with the film *Bulbul-e-Paristan*. She used visual techniques that she developed herself to make her films.

1892
Fatma is born into a Muslim family in the city of Surat (in the modern-day state of Gujarat).

1922
Fatma stars in her first silent film, *Veer Abhimanyu*. Though men usually played the role of women in Indian movies, her performance is an instant success.

1926

Fatma sets up her own film company, Fatma Films. She becomes the first Indian female director when she makes *Bulbul-e-Paristan*, a fantasy film that includes many special effects such as trick photography. She directs eight films in less than four years.

1929
Fatma's last film as a director, *Goddess of Luck*, is released. She continues to work as an actress.

1938
She stars in her last film, *Duniya Kya Hai*.

1983
Fatma dies at the age of 91. Though she spent only 16 years of her life working in films, she was a pioneer who showed a way forward for women in Indian cinema.

Stan Laurel (1890–1965) and Oliver Hardy (1892–1957)

Comedy duo Laurel and Hardy were stars of both silent movies and "talkies." During their careers, they made more than 100 comedy films together.

1890
Stan is born in Lancashire, England. Oliver is born two years later in Georgia.

1909
Stan joins Fred Karno's comedy troupe. He becomes Charlie Chaplin's understudy—learning Chaplin's lines so he can step in if ever needed.

1912
Stan travels to the US with Karno's troupe. He makes his first film *Nuts in May*. Chaplin is impressed by his acting.

1921
Stan appears in a film called *The Lucky Dog* alongside Oliver, who has already starred in numerous short films.

1927

Stan and Oliver appear together again in the silent film *Putting Pants on Philip*. The film is a success, and paves the way to stardom for the pair. They become known as Laurel and Hardy, and star in a string of successful films together. Stan's characters are usually silly fools, who frustrate the plans that Oliver's characters come up with.

1950
They make their last film, *Atoll K*. It is not a success. Afterwards, the pair tour England, giving live performances to packed theaters.

1957
Oliver dies in the US after three years of illness.

1965
Stan dies in Los Angeles, California.

Don Bradman

Australian cricket player Donald Bradman (1908–2001) was one of the greatest sporting legends of all time. Bradman was a prolific batsman who combined incredible natural skill with extraordinary stamina and intense determination to dominate his sport like no other player before or since. Bradman's impact extended beyond cricket. His success inspired the Australian nation during the dark days of the Great Depression in the 1930s, and helped put his country on the global stage.

Breaking records

Don is unstoppable. He blitzes a world-record 452 not out for New South Wales, and during the victorious test series of England clubs 334—another world record—in the third test match. He ends the series with a tally of 974 runs, a record that still stands.

1930

1928

Birth of a legend

Don is born in Cootamundra in Australia, the youngest of five children. His uncles teach him how to play cricket, and he is soon obsessed with batting. Young Don has extraordinary powers of concentration, and perfects his technique by hitting a golf ball against a water tank for hours on end, using a cricket stump as a bat.

1908   1925

1926

Youngest century

Don is asked to play on the Australian international cricket team, and achieves his dream of playing for Australia against England in the Ashes—the test series between the two teams. He initially struggles, but storms back to become the youngest player ever to score a century in a test match.

Teenage sensation

Don becomes a regular player for his local club, and quickly starts to rack up huge scores. One competition final stretches across five weekends because the opposition cannot get him out (dismiss him from batting).

A sparkling start

Don plays his first game for the state team, New South Wales, and smashes a hundred (known in the game as a "century"). His innings (his turn at batting) demonstrate his brilliance: crisp timing, fast footwork, and relentless determination.

Wedding crashers!

Don marries his childhood sweetheart, Jesse Menzies. Because of his celebrity status, hundreds of people gate crash the wedding. Don hates the attention, preferring to live a quiet life.

Aussie skipper

Don becomes Australian captain in the series against England. Initially the extra responsibility affects his form, but he grows into the new role. After losing the first two tests, the Australians win the series.

The Invincibles

On his final tour against England, Don captains one of the greatest cricket teams ever assembled. The Australians go through the entire summer unbeaten—which earns them the name "The Invincibles." Crowds welcome Don as a hero wherever he goes.

Final innings

Flags are lowered across Australia after Don dies from pneumonia at the age of 92. His memorial service is broadcast in cricket-loving nations around the world, and his ashes are buried at the cricket oval in Bowral, his home town.

1932   **1932**   **1936**   **1938**   **1948**   **1948**   **1971**   **2001**

Bodyline

To counter Don's brilliance, the English cricket team adopt the threatening strategy of "bodyline" bowling, targeting the bodies of the Australian batsmen. The tactic has some success, and Australia lose the Ashes, but it leads to public outrage and ill-feeling between the two nations.

Another Ashes win

Don is in the form of his life as his Australian team retain the Ashes yet again, recording a batting average of 115.66— the highest ever in an English season.

99.94

In his final test match at The Oval cricket ground in London, Don goes out to bat needing to score just 4 runs to achieve a career average of 100, but he is dismissed without scoring. Nevertheless, his final average of 99.94 far exceeds that of any other player in history.

Apartheid protest

After retiring, Don becomes a cricket administrator. He cancels a series against South Africa in protest at its policy of racial segregation, called "apartheid." When Malcolm Fraser, the Australian prime minister, visits South African anti-apartheid activist Nelson Mandela in prison 15 years later, Mandela's first question is: "Is Don Bradman still alive?"

> ## "He reminded Australians that they were capable of great things in their own right."
> **John Howard, former prime minister of Australia, on Don Bradman (2000)**

Sports heroes

Because of his astonishingly high batting average, mathematicians have rated Don Bradman as the greatest sportsperson who ever lived. Here are some more sports legends who outshone their peers.

Billie Jean King (b.1943)
Billie Jean King dominated women's tennis in the 1960s and 1970s, winning 39 Grand Slam titles. Her triumph over a male player in the famous "Battle of the Sexes" helped women's sports be taken more seriously. After retiring, she dedicated her life to campaigning for gender equality.

Wayne Gretzky (b.1961)
Nicknamed "the Great One," Wayne Gretzky is the leading scorer in NHL (National Hockey League) history. A superb athlete, the Canadian is universally agreed to have been the greatest ice hockey player of all time.

Simone Biles (b.1997)
Before she reached the age of 20, Simone Biles had won more gold medals in artistic gymnastics than any other gymnast. She dominated her sport at the 2016 Olympics, winning four golds for the US team.

Saving Jewish people

Many people made it their mission to help Jews escape persecution and death at the hands of the Nazis during World War II.

Henryk Sławik (1894–1944)

Polish politician Henryk Sławik lived in Budapest during World War II, where he helped thousands of Polish refugees, including about 5,000 Jews, escape from Nazi-controlled Europe. He helped these Jews by issuing them with false documents stating that they were Christians. Sławik was murdered by the Nazis when his work was discovered.

Ho Feng-Shan (1901–1997)

Ho Feng-Shan was a Chinese diplomat based in Austria who went against his bosses to save Jewish people during World War II. Jews were not able to leave Nazi-controlled Austria unless they received visas that were very hard to obtain. Ho saved lives by issuing at least 2,000 visas, allowing Jewish people to leave for Shanghai in China.

Emilie (1907–2001) and Oskar (1908–1974) Schindler

German factory owner Oskar Schindler employed thousands of Jews, declaring them to be essential workers so the Nazi authorities would not move them into death camps. His wife Emilie sold all of the couple's possessions to pay for medicine and food for their Jewish workers. The Schindlers saved more than 1,000 Jews.

Irena Sendler

A social worker and nurse living in Poland during World War II, Irena Sendler (1910–2008) is today remembered by the Jewish community as a great hero. In Nazi-occupied Poland, Irena risked her own life to save thousands of Jewish children. Her story is one of bravery and compassion, in the face of the most horrible circumstances.

This photograph shows some of the children that Irena Sendler managed to save from the Warsaw Ghetto.

1910
Small town upbringing
Irena Sendler grows up in Otwock, a small town on the outskirts of Warsaw in Poland. Her father is a doctor and humanitarian who mainly treats poor Jewish people in the local community.

1917
Father's death
Irena's father catches a contagious disease from a patient and dies. The Jewish community of Otwock are so grateful for his medical service that they offer to help Irena and her mother.

1930s
Student
While studying at the University of Warsaw, Irena openly disagrees with the common practice of segregating (separating) Jewish people on what were known as "ghetto benches" during lectures, which lands her in trouble from time to time.

1932
Free Polish University
Irena's first job is for the Free Polish University. While there, she makes friends with a group of female social workers, who she will later work alongside to rescue Jewish people.

1939
War breaks out
World War II erupts when Nazi Germany invades Poland. Irena is working at the Social Welfare Department, where the Nazi authorities ban all Jews from working. She begins to create false documents to make sure aid is given to wounded Jewish soldiers in the Polish army and her banned former colleagues.

1940
Warsaw Ghetto
More than 400,000 Jews are imprisoned in the ghetto (a small, walled area of Warsaw). Irena is given access to the ghetto to check for disease. She secretly sneaks in medicine and food. Helping Jewish people in this way is punishable by death.

1941
Socialist Party
Irena joins the underground (secret) Polish Socialist Party (PSP). The party plan to rescue Jews from the ghetto, where they are dying in huge numbers from starvation and Nazi violence. The PSP create fake documents to help Jews escape the ghetto.

1943
Żegota
Irena joins Żegota, another underground Polish resistance group, which aims to help save as many Jews as possible. She smuggles children and babies out of the ghetto — in bags, through sewers, or any other way she can think of — and hides them with families or orphanages.

1943
Arrest
The Gestapo (the Nazi secret police) raid Irena's home and arrest her. She is interrogated and viciously beaten, but she never divulges the names of the children Żegota has saved, as to do so would mean certain death for them all. Before she is to be executed, Żegota bribes the executioner, and Irena escapes.

1944
In hiding
Irena goes into hiding, but she continues to work for Żegota until the end of the war in 1945. Most of the parents of the children that Irena has saved are murdered in the Treblinka Nazi concentration camp.

1945
After the war
The war ends with the defeat of Nazi Germany. Irena takes on a number of important political positions in Poland. She continues to fight for justice and support the children she helped rescue. However, as time passes, her name begins to fade a little from history.

1991
Honors
Irena receives many awards and honors for her work in rescuing Jewish children during the war. She is made an honorary citizen of Israel — the Jewish state set up after World War II. She is honored by the Senate of Poland in 2007.

2008
Humanitarian hero
Irena passes away at the age of 98. She saved more than 2,500 Jewish children from death. She is now considered to be one of the great humanitarian heroes of the 20th century.

> "I was brought up to believe that a person must be rescued when drowning, regardless of religion and nationality."
>
> **Irena Sendler, from an interview (2007)**

Tim Berners-Lee (b. 1955)

English computer scientist Tim Berners-Lee was working at the physics research laboratory CERN, near Geneva, Switzerland, when he dreamed of improved communications between researchers. By 1989, he had invented the software for building web pages and linking them via the internet. He named the system World Wide Web (WWW).

World War II

Nazi Germany invades Poland, causing the UK to declare war. Alan joins the Government Code and Cypher School, located at Bletchley Park near London. Their mission is to break the codes that Nazi Germany uses to make communications between its headquarters and its troops secret.

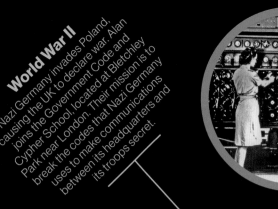

The "Bombe"

Alan and his colleagues develop a computerlike machine called the "Bombe" (so named because it makes an ominous ticking sound). It is capable of deciphering codes sent by Nazi Germany to its submarines in the North Atlantic in only an hour.

1940

1939

Princeton

Alan spends time studying at Princeton University in New Jersey. He receives his PhD for his work on logic and number systems. Though he has the option to stay in the US, he chooses to return to the UK to see if he can help in the impending war.

1936

Turing machine

Alan thinks up an imaginary machine (now known as a "Turing machine") that can carry out any algorithm (a set of instructions). This idea would eventually lead to programmable computers.

1936

Cambridge

After winning a scholarship to King's College, Cambridge, Alan studies Mathematics, where he is awarded first-class honors for his work. He enjoys life at Cambridge and remains there as a tutor after his undergraduate studies finish.

1931

1930

1929

1912

Tragedy strikes

Alan realizes that he has feelings for other boys when he falls in love with Christopher Morcom, a fellow student at his school. But it becomes a turning point because Christopher tragically dies of tuberculosis aged just 18. Alan is devastated. He studies these subjects and science remind him of his life's work. These subjects time will become the focus of his life's work.

School report

Alan is quiet, shy, and awkward, and somewhat of an average student. According to his school report, his mathematics work shows promise, but is somewhat spoiled by the untidiness of his writing.

Beginnings

Alan Turing is born in London, England. Alan and his older brother John spend most of their childhood separated from their parents, who live in India for work reasons. The boys stay with a retired Army couple.

Alan Turing

Though unrecognized during his lifetime, Alan Turing (1912–1954) is now famous for being a mathematical genius. His work was crucial to the development of modern computing and artificial intelligence (AI), and he was also a war hero who played a vital role in the Allied victory over Nazi Germany in World War II.

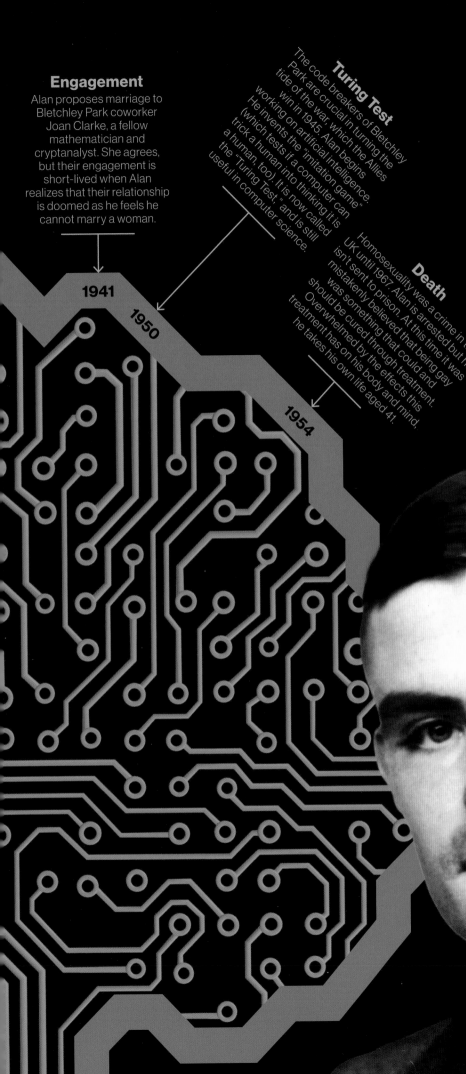

Engagement

Alan proposes marriage to Bletchley Park coworker Joan Clarke, a fellow mathematician and cryptanalyst. She agrees, but their engagement is short-lived when Alan realizes that their relationship is doomed as he feels he cannot marry a woman.

Turing Test

The code breakers of Bletchley Park are crucial in turning the tide of the war, which the Allies win in 1945. Alan begins working on artificial intelligence. He invents the "imitation game" (which tests if a computer can trick a human into thinking it is a human, too). It is now called the "Turing Test," and is still useful in computer science.

Death

Homosexuality was a crime in the UK until 1967. Alan is arrested but he isn't sent to prison. At this time it was mistakenly believed that being gay was something that could and should be cured through treatment. Overwhelmed by the effects this treatment has on his body and mind, he takes his own life aged 41.

1941

1950

1954

Royal pardon

After a long campaign supported by thousands of people, Turing was granted a royal pardon after his death, formally canceling his criminal conviction. An image showing him and his work will appear on the British £50 note from 2021.

"People always said that I didn't give up my seat because I was tired, but that isn't true ... No, the only tired I was, was tired of giving in."

Rosa Parks, *My Story* **(1992)**

ROSA PARKS

Started the Montgomery Bus Boycott

The Montgomery Bus Boycott was a nonviolent civil rights campaign that took place from 1955 to 1956 in Montgomery, Alabama. It followed the arrest of Rosa Parks (1913–2005), an African American woman who refused to give up her seat on a bus to a white man. Rosa's brave action inspired more than 40,000 African Americans to protest by refusing to take the city's buses. The protest ended when the US Supreme Court finally ordered Montgomery to integrate its bus system.

Abolition and the KKK

In **1865**, the 13th Amendment to the US Constitution was passed, abolishing slavery across the United States. Around 4 million enslaved people were freed. In the same year, a secret society called the Ku Klux Klan (KKK) formed. Believing white people to be superior, they terrorized black people, vandalizing schools and businesses, burning down homes, and violently attacking and murdering thousands of black people. Legislation was passed to crush the KKK in the early **1870s** but the society saw a huge resurgence in the 1920s and the 1950s.

Jim Crow and civil rights

In **1877**, the first of a set of laws that become known as the Jim Crow laws was introduced in the southern states. These laws legalized discrimination against black people—taking away the right to vote from many, and dictating where they can work, eat, and live. These laws eroded the few rights that black citizens enjoyed. In **1909**, the NAACP (The National Association for the Advancement of Colored People) was established by a group of African American activists to fight back. Over the next decades, the NAACP played a key part in the development of the civil rights movement. This movement campaigned to outlaw segregation, expand voting rights, and oppose discriminatory laws.

Rosa Parks

In **November 1943**, an African American seamstress named Rosa Parks joins her local NAACP branch in Montgomery, Alabama, as a secretary. She works with the branch president, Edgar Nixon, organizing equal justice campaigns and investigating cases of violence against black women. By the **1950s**, the growing US civil rights movement has begun to inspire a wave of protests across the southern states, as African American individuals start to defy segregation laws. One such protestor is Claudette Colvin, a teenage nurse and member of the local NAACP branch in Montgomery. The bus system in Montgomery is segregated by law—white people sit at the front of the bus, and black people have to sit at the back. On **March 2, 1955**, Colvin refuses to give up her bus seat to a white woman and is arrested. Some local civil rights leaders see the event as a chance to highlight the city's racist bus policy, but in the end they decide that Colvin is too young to represent the struggle. Nine months later, on **December 1**, Rosa Parks boards a bus and takes a seat behind a row filled with white passengers. When the bus stops, a white man boards and finds there are no free seats in the "whites-only" area. The bus driver, James Blake, orders Rosa to give her seat up for the man. She refuses. Two police officers board the bus and arrest Rosa. News spreads fast about her arrest. She is released in the evening when her NAACP colleagues bail her out.

Montgomery Bus Boycott

The case angers many. As Rosa is a respected member of her community, Edgar Nixon thinks that the incident could benefit the NAACP. On the night of her arrest, the Women's Political Council, a part of the civil rights movement, prints and circulates flyers to the black community in Montgomery urging them to boycott (stop using) bus services. On **December 2**, Rosa joins a meeting at the Mt. Zion Church, where they discuss how to implement a citywide boycott of public transportation. The mass boycott begins on **December 5**, with black taxi drivers lowering their prices to that of a bus ticket in solidarity. However, the boycott causes a backlash. In retaliation, groups of white thugs firebomb activists' houses and many black churches, and physically attack boycotters. The protest gains national attention and much support from the public. After mounting public pressure, on **November 13, 1956**, the US Supreme Court upholds a court ruling that segregation on public buses is against the law. The boycott ends, after 381 days, on **December 20, 1956**, as the city is finally forced to allow black people to sit anywhere on public transportation.

Life after the boycott

Although the Montgomery Bus Boycott has been successful, many white Americans do not agree with the new laws. Over the next few months, there are shootings of buses and bus passengers, as well as frequent attacks on other individuals. Despite this, the Montgomery Bus Boycott has been an important part of the civil rights movement, as it has shown how nonviolent protest can bring about change. The NAACP and the wider civil rights movement continues to fight racist laws. They successfully campaign for the passing of the Civil Rights Act of **1964**, which bans discrimination based on race. In **1965**, the Voting Rights Act is passed, which makes practices that prevent African Americans from voting illegal. Rosa Parks continues to campaign for and support civil rights causes right up to her death in **2005**.

Hedy Lamarr

Hedy Lamarr (1914–2000) was an Austrian-born actor who became a major Hollywood star in the 1940s and 1950s. She was also a groundbreaking inventor who designed technology that would one day form the basis for internet communication systems that we use today, such as Wi-Fi and Bluetooth.

Little Hedwig
Hedwig ("Hedy") Kiesler is born into a well-to-do Jewish family in Vienna, Austria. She is an only child.

Young mechanic
Hedy shows an interest in machines. At the age of five, she takes her music box apart and puts it back together again, to find out how it works.

Budding actor
At the age of 16, Hedy is eager to work in films, so she takes acting classes in Berlin, Germany—the center of the German film industry. There she embarks on a successful film career.

Unhappy marriage
She marries Friedrich Mandl, a wealthy Austrian weapons merchant. Mandl is cruel to Hedy, and she is very unhappy in the relationship. She flees their home disguised as a maid. Hedy makes her way to Paris, France, and then to London, England. The couple divorce in 1937.

Hollywood calls
In London, she meets Louis B. Mayer, the head of the big Hollywood movie studio MGM. He offers Hedy a contract to star in his films, and she leaves Europe for the US. At his suggestion, she changes her surname to Lamarr.

Hollywood debut
Hedy has her first starring role in a Hollywood movie, Algiers. She appears alongside the French actor Charles Boyer. Hedy goes on to make dozens more movies.

Wing design
She dates wealthy American film director Howard Hughes. He is also an aviator and has designed new planes in which he has broken several airspeed records. They share an interest in inventions, and she designs a new wing shape that makes his planes go even faster.

Frequency hopping
During World War II, Hedy teams up with Hollywood composer George Antheil to design a device that can help the war effort. The invention uses "frequency hopping" between radio waves to guide radio-controlled torpedoes to their targets. They call it the "Secret Communication System."

1914
1919
1930
1933
1937
1938
1940
1941

CHARLES BOYER · HEDY LAMARR
STRANGE LOVES
HIDING IN THE CASBAH
CITY OF SECRETS!
Algiers
with SIGRID GURIE

Hollywood's European stars

Hollywood has always attracted screen actors from Europe, especially during its classic years—often called its Golden Era—from the 1920s to the early 1960s.

Marlene Dietrich (1901–1992)
German-born Marlene Dietrich's career as an actor and singer spanned eight decades. She starred in German-language films before arriving in Hollywood in 1930. She became an American citizen in 1939, and in World War II entertained US troops on the frontline.

Greta Garbo (1905–1990)
Born in Sweden, Greta Garbo began starring in Hollywood silent films in the 1920s. Her popularity soared when she switched to "talkies" (movies with sound) in 1930. She made 28 films before retiring in 1941. In later life she was famous for being reclusive.

Ingrid Bergman (1915–1982)
Swedish-born Ingrid Bergman rose to fame in *Casablanca* (1942), her most famous movie. She went on to star in many more Hollywood movies, and won the Oscar—a Hollywood film industry award—for Best Actress three times.

Belated recognition
US Navy engineers rediscover Hedy and Antheil's invention, and update it. Over the decades, engineers develop the concept further into the frequency hopping system used in modern digital technology including Wi-Fi, Bluetooth, and GPS. Hedy and Antheil win an award for their work in 1998.

2000

Death
Hedy dies at her home in Florida at the age of 86. After her death, she is inducted into the American National Inventors Hall of Fame.

mid-1950s

1953

American citizen
Hedy becomes an American citizen. Five years later, she decides to leave the film industry. Her last film is *The Female Animal*. She stays out of the spotlight for the rest of her life.

Huge hit
Hedy stars as Delilah in *Samson and Delilah*, the blockbuster movie of the year. It is her most commercially successful film.

1949

> "The brains of people are more interesting than the looks, I think."
>
> Hedy Lamarr, interview with *Forbes Magazine* (1990)

1942

War bonds
Hedy and Antheil patent their Secret Communication System, but the US Navy decides not to develop it. Instead, Hedy helps the war effort in another way, by promoting war bonds—a way of raising money for the government—to the public.

SECRET COMMUNICATION SYSTEM PATENT

Hollywood star

This studio publicity photo features Hedy Lamarr in one of the many romantic comedy roles she played in the 1940s. Her good looks and dark hair are said to have been the inspiration for Snow White in Walt Disney's famous animated movie.

Indira Gandhi

The life of Indira Gandhi (1917–1984), from her childhood, through Indian independence, and up to her assassination, was dominated by politics. She served three terms as prime minister and became one of the world's most powerful women.

1917
Lonely childhood
Born in 1917, Indira is an only child. Her father, Jawaharlal Nehru, is a leader in the struggle for India's independence from Britain. Their family home serves as the headquarters for the independence movement, and her father is often away or imprisoned, so Indira has a lonely childhood.

1928
Letters
During one spell in prison, Nehru regularly writes to his daughter. Their messages to each other are published in a book, *Letters From A Father to His Daughter*. In the letters, Nehru seeks to inspire in his daughter an interest in and understanding of the world, its peoples, its history, and why things are the way they are.

1930s
High expectations
As Nehru's daughter, Indira finds that much is expected of her. She performs poorly at school and later at Somerville College, Oxford, England, which disappoints her father. She is also troubled by ill health, and her studies are interrupted by the death of her mother.

1942
Marriage
Indira marries Feroze Gandhi, an independence campaigner. Within six months, Feroze is imprisoned for a year for joining Mahatma Gandhi's Quit India Movement, which campaigns for Indian independence. Indira and Feroze have two sons, Rajiv and Sanjay, in 1944 and 1946.

1947
Experience
After India wins its independence, Indira's father becomes its first prime minister. Indira becomes his assistant, moving into the prime minister's residence, and getting firsthand experience of high office.

1950s
Fraught marriage
Feroze, who is a rising politician himself, resents Indira's decision to become her father's assistant. As a result, the couple separate. Indira is away a great deal, and she stands in for her father on tours abroad. Feroze Gandhi dies of a heart attack in 1960.

1959
PARTY PRESIDENT
Indira is elected as the president of the Indian National Congress (INC) party, which is led by her father. After Nehru's death in 1964, she becomes a member of parliament, and is appointed a minister in the government of Prime Minister Lal Bahadur Shastri.

1966
PRIME MINISTER
After Shastri's death, the party choose Indira as his successor, mistakenly thinking that she can be easily manipulated. The Indian nation faces food shortages, rising prices, and unemployment. After tackling these problems, Indira goes on to win the 1967 general election.

Remarkable leaders
South and Southeast Asian history is packed with charismatic queens and remarkable female leaders who rose to power despite the dominance of men.

Ratu Hijau (r. 1584–1616)
Ratu Hijau returned order and prosperity to the Malay kingdom of Patani (in modern-day Malaysia) during her 32-year reign. She governed with great skill, and opened the state to merchants from China and Europe.

Sirimavo Bandaranaike (1916–2000)
Sirimavo Bandaranaike became the world's first female prime minister when she took control of Sri Lanka in 1960. During her period in office, the country became a republic.

Corazon Aquino (1933–2009)
Elected president of the Philippines in 1986 on a wave of popular support, Corazon ("Cory") Aquino ended 21 years of brutal dictatorship, and restored democracy.

1971

POLITICAL HIGH

Indira wins a landslide victory in the 1971 general election. Her popularity reaches an all-time high when India emerges as decisive victors in the Indo-Pakistani War in December.

1975

State of Emergency

India's economic problems deepen. As Indira's popularity suffers, she is taken to court on a charge of using dishonest tactics during the 1971 election. The court bans her from office for six years. To stay in power, Indira declares a state of emergency, suspending basic freedoms, imposing strict press censorship, and imprisoning 160,000 opponents.

1977

OUT OF POWER

After extending the state of emergency twice, Indira eventually calls new elections. She is defeated, and even loses her seat in parliament. Many people remain sympathetic toward her, however, and she becomes prime minister again in 1980.

1984

Assassination

A Sikh militant group takes over the Golden Temple in Amritsar, the holiest shrine of the Sikh religion. In June, Indira sends in Indian troops to remove them, resulting in many deaths. In retaliation, her two Sikh bodyguards shoot her in her garden in Delhi. She dies within hours.

INDIRA WITH SATWANT SINGH, ONE OF THE BODYGUARDS WHO ASSASSINATED HER

> "I am not a person to be pressured—by anybody or any nation."
>
> **Indira Gandhi,**
> **Interview with *Time* magazine (1977)**

Desmond Tutu (b. 1931)
A South African religious leader, activist, and Nobel Peace Prize winner, Desmond Tutu used nonviolent methods to campaign against apartheid. He coined the term "Rainbow Nation" in reference to post-apartheid South Africa, which was to be for people of every color and ethnicity.

| 1918 | 1934 | 1948 | 1952 | 1961 | 1961 | 1964 |

Mvezo
Rolihlahla Mandela is born in Mvezo, a small village in eastern South Africa, and spends his boyhood herding cattle. His teacher gives him the English name "Nelson."

Apartheid
The government begins the apartheid ("separateness") policy. These are a series of racist laws that discriminate against black South Africans, who make up the vast majority of the population.

In disguise
Disguising himself as a chauffeur to avoid the police, Nelson drives around the country holding secret meetings and arranging for the ANC to strike.

Taking up arms
The government makes it impossible to peacefully protest against apartheid. Nelson helps set up a resistance group. He is arrested and imprisoned, and then sentenced to life in prison for further crimes in 1964.

Imprisonment
Prison conditions are terrible. Nelson sleeps on a straw mat and carries out hard physical labor. Global opposition to Nelson's imprisonment grows as many see him as an inspirational figure who stands against ingrained racist policies.

Education
Nelson studies English and law. In defiance of his headmaster's teaching of the superiority of British culture and government, he grows interested in African history and politics.

Arrest
Nelson becomes one of the leaders of the ANC (African National Congress) and the anti-apartheid cause, speaking at rallies to tens of thousands of people. He is arrested and put in prison for a short time.

Nelson Mandela

A revolutionary activist, Nelson Mandela (1918–2013) led the movement against apartheid—racist laws that discriminated against black South Africans. His struggle for equality for black South Africans resulted in him spending 27 years in prison, but when he was freed, he became South Africa's first ever black head of state.

Mandela's cell

Mandela spent 18 of his 27 years in jail imprisoned at Robben Island, off the coast of Cape Town in South Africa. This photo was taken when he revisited his old cell in 1994, the year he became president of the country.

1989 **1994** **1995** **1996** **1999** **2013**

Election

A multiracial general election is held—the first of its kind in South Africa. The ANC are victorious and Nelson becomes president—a result unthinkable during apartheid.

Truth and Reconciliation

As president, Nelson aims to bring peace to his nation. The Truth and Reconciliation Commission is set up so that both perpetrators and victims under the apartheid era can meet and talk openly. Nelson meets with, and forgives, senior apartheid-era politicians.

Retirement

After retiring, Nelson spends much of his time working on rural development, school construction, and bringing awareness to the HIV/AIDS crisis.

The end of apartheid

F.W. de Klerk comes to power in 1989 and ends the policy of apartheid. He also quashes Nelson's sentence, freeing him in February 1990. Nelson is awarded the Nobel Peace Prize in 1993.

Welfare

Nelson's government increases welfare spending to assist poor citizens, including grants for disability and child maintenance. Nelson donates a third of his monthly wage to help disadvantaged children.

Death

Nelson passes away at the age of 95. Three days after his death, South Africa dedicates a national day to mourn the leader referred to as "the Father of the Nation."

EDMUND HILLARY AND TENZING NORGAY

Conquerors of Mount Everest

At 8,850 m (29,035 ft), Mount Everest (known as *Zhumulangma* in Chinese) on the Nepal–Tibet border, is the world's highest mountain. For decades, all attempts to scale it ended in failure. Then in 1953, Edmund Hillary (1919–2008), a beekeeper from New Zealand, and Tenzing Norgay (1914–1986), a Nepali-Indian guide from the Sherpa community, achieved what was once thought impossible – the first successful ascent of Everest.

> **"Fear became a friend ...
> it added spice to the
> challenge and satisfaction
> to the conquest."**
> **Edmund Hillary, *Nothing Venture,
> Nothing Win* (1975)**

The Mallory mystery

When British surveyors identified Peak XV – soon renamed Mount Everest – as the world's highest mountain in **1856**, they believed it could never be climbed. In **1921**, an expedition led by George Mallory, an English mountaineer, proved that a route was feasible. Mallory's attempt on the summit in **1924** ended in disaster, however, when he and a fellow climber disappeared on the mountain's upper slopes. Five further attempts were made prior to World War II, each from the Tibetan side of the mountain. All failed.

The race is on

In the **late 1940s**, Nepal, closed to visitors for centuries, opened up to the outside world. This allowed the possibility of an alternative approach to Everest. In **1951**, Eric Shipton, a veteran of four previous Everest expeditions, led a survey of the mountain in Nepal. His team included Edmund Hillary, a super-fit and ambitious mountaineer who had achieved several climbing feats in his native New Zealand.

In **April 1952**, a well-equipped Swiss team attempted to scale the mountain. They opened a new route to the peak, and Tenzing Norgay, a highly experienced Himalayan climber, and Raymond Lambert were chosen to make the final ascent. The two men reached higher than anyone had ever reached before, but were forced to turn back about 250 m (820 ft) from the top. The race for the summit was on.

Assembling a team

A British expedition is confirmed for the following year. The organizing committee replaces Shipton with the more determined Colonel John Hunt, an army officer and mountain warfare expert. Under their new leader, the group source the latest equipment and spend **winter 1952** training in Wales. Hunt's team arrives in Kathmandu, the Nepali capital, in early **March 1953**. His team includes eight British climbers, a doctor, a filmmaker, and James Morris, a journalist from *The Times* newspaper. They are joined by two climbers from New Zealand – Edmund Hillary, a veteran of the 1951 expedition, and George Lowe. Hearing of his brilliance with the Swiss team, Hunt also invites Tenzing Norgay to become a team member.

The expedition begins

In Kathmandu, the team hire a small army of helpers. Over 400 people set off, in two parties, on **10 and 11 March**, including more than 350 porters carrying over 4,500 kg (10,000 lb) of baggage, as well as 20 Sherpa guides – people who are native to the region. On **12 April**, they reach Base Camp, and plan the rest of the climb. They intend a slow, careful ascent, establishing advance camps as they go. The treacherous Khumbu Icefall, a glacier where towers of ice tumble from above and huge crevasses (cracks) open up below, is the first major obstacle. Edmund calmly leads the team through the glacier. Using ladders and logs to bridge the drops, they forge a route through, and reach Camp 3 on **22 April**. The next major challenge is the Lhotse Face, a 1,200 m (4,000 ft) ice slope between Everest and Lhotse, its nearest neighbour. In dreadful weather, it takes the team 12 days to retrace the Swiss team's route up the face. With the imminent threat of the monsoon rains, they despair of reaching the summit.

A thwarted attempt

Finally, on **21 May**, the expedition reaches the desolate, wind-lashed South Col, a vital staging post. Hunt plans for two attempts on the summit, with a third if necessary. On **26 May**, his first-choice pair to make the ascent, Tom Bourdillon and Charles Evans, set off. They reach the South Summit, Everest's secondary peak, and get within 100 m (330 ft) of the true summit (highest point) but, with their oxygen tanks failing, are forced to turn back. Everything now depends on Edmund and Tenzing. Bad weather strikes again the next day, but on **28 May** the wind dies down. Tenzing and Edmund set off from the South Col camp, with a support party. At 8,320 m (27,300 ft), they collect supplies dumped by the earlier climbers. They stop and hack out a narrow ledge for their tent.

The final push

On **29 May**, Edmund and Tenzing awake at **4 a.m.**. Edmund discovers his boots are frozen solid. They take two hours to defrost. At **6.30 a.m.**, with the sun shining brilliantly on a crystal-clear morning, the climbers strap on their oxygen packs and set off in the snow. On a ledge below the South Summit, their confidence is boosted when they discover the oxygen cylinders, a third full, left by Bourdillon and Evans – these can be used for the descent. At **9 a.m.**, the pair reach the South Summit, Everest's secondary peak, but their progress to the top is blocked by a wall of vertical rock 12 m (40 ft) high. They find a snowy crack up the rock face and, risking a 3,000 m (9,800 ft) drop (and certain death!), wriggle up. Finally, at **11.30 a.m.**, the two men jubilantly step on to the summit. Edmund reaches out to shake hands but Tenzing grabs Edmund in an exuberant hug. Tenzing buries sweets and a pencil given to him by his daughter in the snow, while Edmund takes photographs and buries a cross. The men spend just 15 minutes at the summit, and then start the descent. Four hours later they arrive back at the South Col.

EDMUND HILLARY AND TENZING NORGAY

National heroes

The next day the men are reunited with the rest of their team at Base Camp. The team races down the icefall, and James Morris sends word of their triumph, via courier, to the British ambassador in Kathmandu. **2 June** is Coronation Day for the new British queen, Elizabeth II, and the news is announced to large crowds lining London's Mall. The British press claim it as a coronation gift, and Edmund is knighted. In Nepal, well-wishers put together money to fly Tenzing's family from their remote village to Kathmandu for a welcome party, where Tenzing is received like a god. The achievement of the two climbers has opened up a new chapter in mountaineering history. In **1954**, Tenzing becomes Director of Field Training at the Himalayan Mountain Institute, while in the **1960s**, Edmund sets up a charity to improve the lives of Nepali people. Hundreds now flock to Everest each year, though the ascent remains a formidable challenge.

Eva Perón

During her short life, Argentinian Eva Perón (1919–1952) rose from poverty to become a national icon. As well as being a successful actor, she became the First Lady of Argentina when her husband, Juan Perón, became president. In the years that followed, Eva Perón became a powerful political figure in her own right, campaigning for women's right to vote, and improving the lives of the poor.

Cristina Fernández de Kirchner (b.1953)
Cristina Fernández de Kirchner became the first female president of Argentina in 2007. She was influenced by many of the political ideas of Juan Perón. During her eight years in office, she was a champion of human rights and same-sex marriage.

> "I will soon be back in the struggle, with more strength and love, to fight for this people, which I love so much."
>
> **Eva Perón, from a speech at a rally in Buenos Aires (1951)**

Rural upbringing
Born María Eva Duarte, Eva is the youngest of four children. Her parents are unmarried, and her father leaves her mother when Eva is young because he has another family. Growing up in Los Toldos, a village in Argentina, Eva has a poor but happy childhood.

Move to Junín
Eva and her family move to the city of Junín, where her mother works as a seamstress. They rent rooms of their home to earn money and Eva's older siblings work to support the family. Eva dreams of becoming an actor, though it seems unlikely to happen.

Movie role
Eva lands her first major film role in ¡Segundos Afuera! ("Second's Out!"). The film is a success and helps launch her acting career.

Important meeting
Eva meets Juan Perón, an army general and politician, and they begin to develop a relationship. The story of her humble origins helps him win support from the public, which he builds on in his role as labor secretary. He passes reforms that improve the rights of laborers.

1919	1926	1930	1935	1937	1939	1944	1945	1946

Family tragedy
In a sad turn of events, Eva's father, Juan, dies in a car accident, leaving Eva's family struggling financially. They are shunned at her father's funeral by his other family.

Buenos Aires
At the age of 15 , Eva leaves her family and travels to the capital, Buenos Aires, to find work in the film industry. Despite her lack of experience, she finds work on the radio and is given some small parts in films.

Business
Eva establishes her own entertainment company, El Compañia de Teatro del Aire ("The Company of the Theater of the Air"), which specializes in producing radio shows. She uses it to showcase famous women in history such as Queen Elizabeth I of England and Catherine the Great of Russia.

Captured
Now vice president, Juan Perón is arrested in October by rivals within the government because of his outspoken views. Eva organizes and leads a mass protest which results in his release in just four days. Later that month, Eva and Perón marry.

First Lady
With widespread support, Juan Perón campaigns for, and wins, the presidential election. Now the First Lady of Argentina, Eva grows more politically active and begins speaking about social issues.

Huge support

As Eva launched her bid to become vice president on August 28, 1951, more than one million Argentinians flooded the streets of the capital, Buenos Aires, to demand that the Peróns lead the country. Eva's popularity with the regular people of Argentina ensured her a huge source of support throughout her life.

1947	**1948**	**1951**	**1952**

Women's suffrage
Eva campaigns for women's right to vote (suffrage). The campaign succeeds, ultimately changing the course of history for Argentinian women.

Charitable aid
Eva sets up the Eva Perón Foundation. Drawing upon her experience of poverty, the foundation provides support to disadvantaged people by building schools, hospitals, and orphanages.

Falling ill
Juan is due to run for president and Eva is thinking about running as vice president. Although widely supported by the working classes, she is forced to step down from the nomination when she falls ill.

Death
Eva's health declines and she discovers that she has cancer. She becomes the first Argentinian to undergo chemotherapy treatment, but she dies at the age of 33. Following her death, Argentina enters a period of mourning.

"X-ray studies ... show the basic molecular configuration has great simplicity."
Rosalind Franklin, from *Nature* (1953)

ROSALIND FRANKLIN

Discovering the structure of DNA

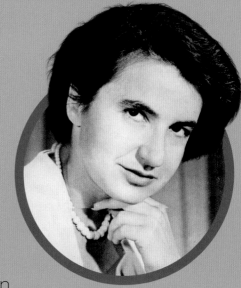

English chemist Rosalind Franklin (1920–1958) made a crucial discovery in 1952 that allowed scientists to understand the structure of DNA—the molecule that carries genetic information. This important find revealed how DNA works, and how it stores the information that determines how we look and function. Franklin's contribution to science was not appreciated in her lifetime, but today she is recognized as one of the great scientists of the 20th century.

What is DNA?

Deoxyribonucleic acid (DNA) is a complicated molecule that is able to store and copy information. It provides the instructions that allow our bodies to function properly. It also contains the information that allows a single fertilized egg to develop into a baby. Scientists have spent more than a century figuring out what DNA is and how it works.

Cracking the code

In **1869**, Swiss scientist Friedrich Miescher identified a chemical in the nucleus of a cell while researching white blood cells in Germany. He did not know it was DNA and named the mysterious substance nuclein after the nucleus of the cell. By the **1940s**, scientists had already figured out that instructions called genes control our development and traits such as hair color. In **1944**, Canadian-American physician Oswald Avery discovered that DNA carried genetic information and was responsible for which genes humans inherited. He did not understand how it worked, but his discovery inspired another scientist, Erwin Chargaff. In **1950**, Chargaff discovered that each animal or plant species had different DNA. Each of these discoveries paved the way for other scientists to make other important discoveries about how the human body works.

Photo 51

In **1951**, British scientist Rosalind Franklin begins work at Kings College in London, England. Here she studies the structure of DNA. Rosalind is an expert in X-ray crystallography (a technique used to figure out the structures of molecules), which she has studied in Paris, France. She works alongside another scientist, Maurice Wilkins, who has also been examining the structure of DNA. Maurice and Rosalind do not have a good working relationship. Using a machine that she develops herself, Rosalind and her assistant Raymond Gosling attempt to photograph DNA using X-rays. Each of their images is created by exposing the DNA to X-rays for 100 hours. In **May 1952**, they eventually produce a clear image of what DNA looks like. Rosalind produces *Photo 51* (as it is now known). She uses it to calculate the size of the strands of DNA, and realizes that DNA probably has a spiral (or helix) shape. She writes her findings in a report, but feeling that she needs more information to prove her findings, Rosalind does not publish it. Her research over the past two years has come close to discovering the structure of DNA, but unknown to her, there are others also competing in this scientific race.

Crick and Watson

At the University of Cambridge in England, British scientist Francis Crick has been working alongside American scientist James Watson, investigating the structure of DNA. In **January 1953**, Rosalind's colleague Maurice Wilkins shows Crick her findings without her permission, and James Watson immediately realizes what they have been missing. Francis Crick and James Watson recognize that the DNA molecule is made up of two connected strands in a shape similar to a spiral staircase, and that it can copy itself when the two strands divide. This process explains how living things are able reproduce their genes. They use Rosalind and Gosling's photograph, together with other discoveries, to solve what has puzzled scientists for years. In **April 1953**, they publish their discoveries in the important scientific journal *Nature*, and instantly become internationally famous. Rosalind's pioneering work that shone a light on the molecule's structure is not mentioned.

Aftermath

Rosalind goes on to carry out further important research into viruses. But in **1958**, she dies of cancer aged just 37. Having finally cracked the DNA riddle, Crick, Watson, and Wilkins are awarded the Nobel Prize for Physiology or

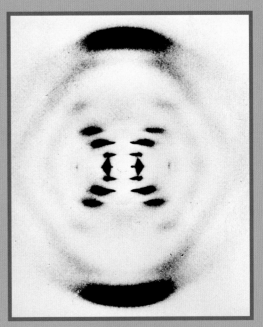

PHOTO 51

Medicine in **1962**. The Nobel committee (who choose the winners) cannot give the award to Rosalind, because they are not allowed to give the prize to people after they have died. As her role has been overlooked, it is likely she would not have been named even if she were alive. Rosalind's work is carried on by her colleague Aaron Klug, who wins the Nobel Prize for Chemistry in **1982** for his work on the molecular structure of viruses. In more recent times, people have begun to recognize the crucial role Rosalind played in the discovery of the structure of DNA. She is now seen as a pioneer who was not treated properly during her lifetime.

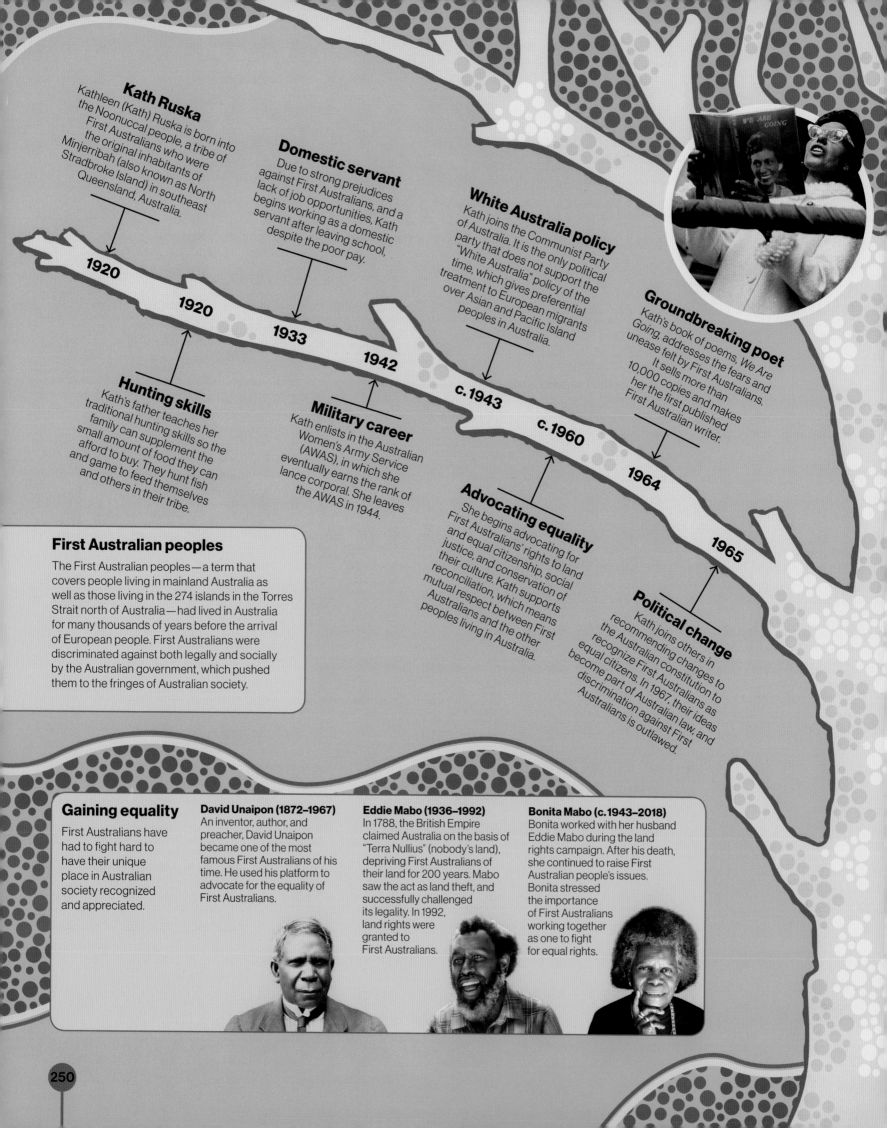

Kath Ruska
Kathleen (Kath) Ruska is born into the Noonuccal people, a tribe of First Australians who were the original inhabitants of Minjerribah (also known as North Stradbroke Island) in southeast Queensland, Australia.

1920

Domestic servant
Due to strong prejudices against First Australians, and a lack of job opportunities, Kath begins working as a domestic servant after leaving school, despite the poor pay.

1920

1933

Hunting skills
Kath's father teaches her traditional hunting skills so the family can supplement the small amount of food they can afford to buy. They hunt fish and game to feed themselves and others in their tribe.

1942

Military career
Kath enlists in the Australian Women's Army Service (AWAS), in which she eventually earns the rank of lance corporal. She leaves the AWAS in 1944.

White Australia policy
Kath joins the Communist Party of Australia. It is the only political party that does not support the time, which gives preferential "White Australia" policy of the treatment to European migrants over Asian and Pacific Island peoples in Australia.

c. 1943

Groundbreaking poet
Kath's book of poems, We Are Going, addresses the fears and unease felt by First Australians. It sells more than 10,000 copies and makes her the first published First Australian writer.

c. 1960

1964

Advocating equality
She begins advocating for First Australians' rights to land and equal citizenship, social justice, and conservation of their culture. Kath supports reconciliation, which means mutual respect between First Australians and the other peoples living in Australia.

1965

Political change
Kath joins others in recommending changes to the Australian constitution to recognize First Australians as equal citizens. In 1967, their ideas become part of Australian law, and discrimination against First Australians is outlawed.

First Australian peoples
The First Australian peoples—a term that covers people living in mainland Australia as well as those living in the 274 islands in the Torres Strait north of Australia—had lived in Australia for many thousands of years before the arrival of European people. First Australians were discriminated against both legally and socially by the Australian government, which pushed them to the fringes of Australian society.

Gaining equality
First Australians have had to fight hard to have their unique place in Australian society recognized and appreciated.

David Unaipon (1872–1967)
An inventor, author, and preacher, David Unaipon became one of the most famous First Australians of his time. He used his platform to advocate for the equality of First Australians.

Eddie Mabo (1936–1992)
In 1788, the British Empire claimed Australia on the basis of "Terra Nullius" (nobody's land), depriving First Australians of their land for 200 years. Mabo saw the act as land theft, and successfully challenged its legality. In 1992, land rights were granted to First Australians.

Bonita Mabo (c.1943–2018)
Bonita worked with her husband Eddie Mabo during the land rights campaign. After his death, she continued to raise First Australian people's issues. Bonita stressed the importance of First Australians working together as one to fight for equal rights.

Naming herself

Kath adopts the tribal name Oodgeroo (meaning "paperbark tree," pictured above) Noonuccal (the name of her tribe), which she is known by for the rest of her life. She feels her new name more closely aligns with her culture than her birth name did.

c.1988

Championing culture

Kath returns to Minjerribah to establish a cultural center. In it, she teaches people about First Australian culture. This period inspires a new direction for her work as she publishes several books on First Australian legends.

Rejected award

Kath returns the Member of the British Empire (MBE) award that she was given in 1970. She does this in protest against the Bicentennial Celebration of Australia, an event celebrating European settlement in Australia.

1987

Political realization

After attending the World Council of Churches Consultation on Racism, Kath realizes that First Australian activists should start their own political groups instead of working within white-dominated ones.

1969

1971

1972

International events

Kath tours Australia and other countries, giving lectures. In 1976, she acts as a senior advisor to the World Black Festival of the Arts in Lagos, Nigeria. Her flight home is hijacked by terrorists. Held captive for three days, the ordeal inspires Kath to write two poems on an airline vomit bag.

1990–1993

Participating in government

Oodgeroo is elected to the Southeast Queensland Regional Council after the creation of the Australian and Torres Strait Islander Commission (ATSIC). The commission is a governmental body through which First Australians can participate in the systems of government. Oodgeroo passes away in 1993.

Oodgeroo Noonuccal

The culture and rights of the First Australian peoples were a central part of author and political activist Oodgeroo Noonuccal's (1920–1993) life. She was the first person of her heritage to have a book of her poetry published. Her activism helped lead to changes to the Australian constitution that recognized First Australians as equal citizens of Australia.

1870
1885
1900
1915
1930
Winston Churchill (1874–1965)
Joseph Stalin (1878–1953)
Franklin Delano Roosevelt (1882–1945)
Benito Mussolini (1883–1945)
Adolf Hitler (1889–1945)
Michinomiya Hirohito (1901–1989)

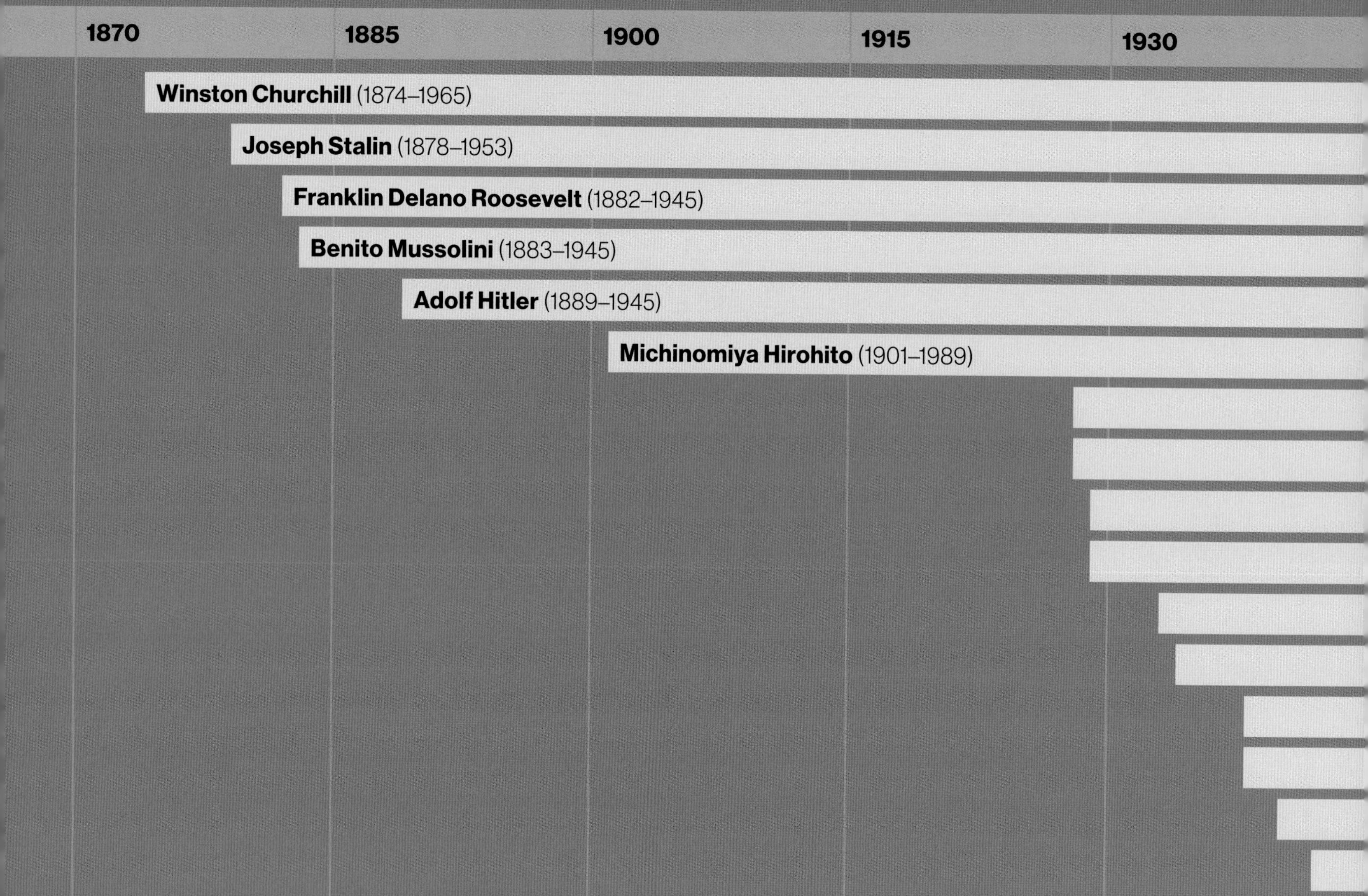

Winston Churchill to **Greta Thunberg**

In recent decades, famous figures have inspired huge changes for humankind that would have been unthinkable a few generations earlier. Russian cosmonaut Yuri Gagarin became the first person ever to leave Earth and travel into space in 1961. Martin Luther King, Jr. inspired millions of African Americans to resist racial oppression. And Kenyan environmentalist Wangari Maathai stood up to climate change by coordinating the planting of more than 50 million trees.

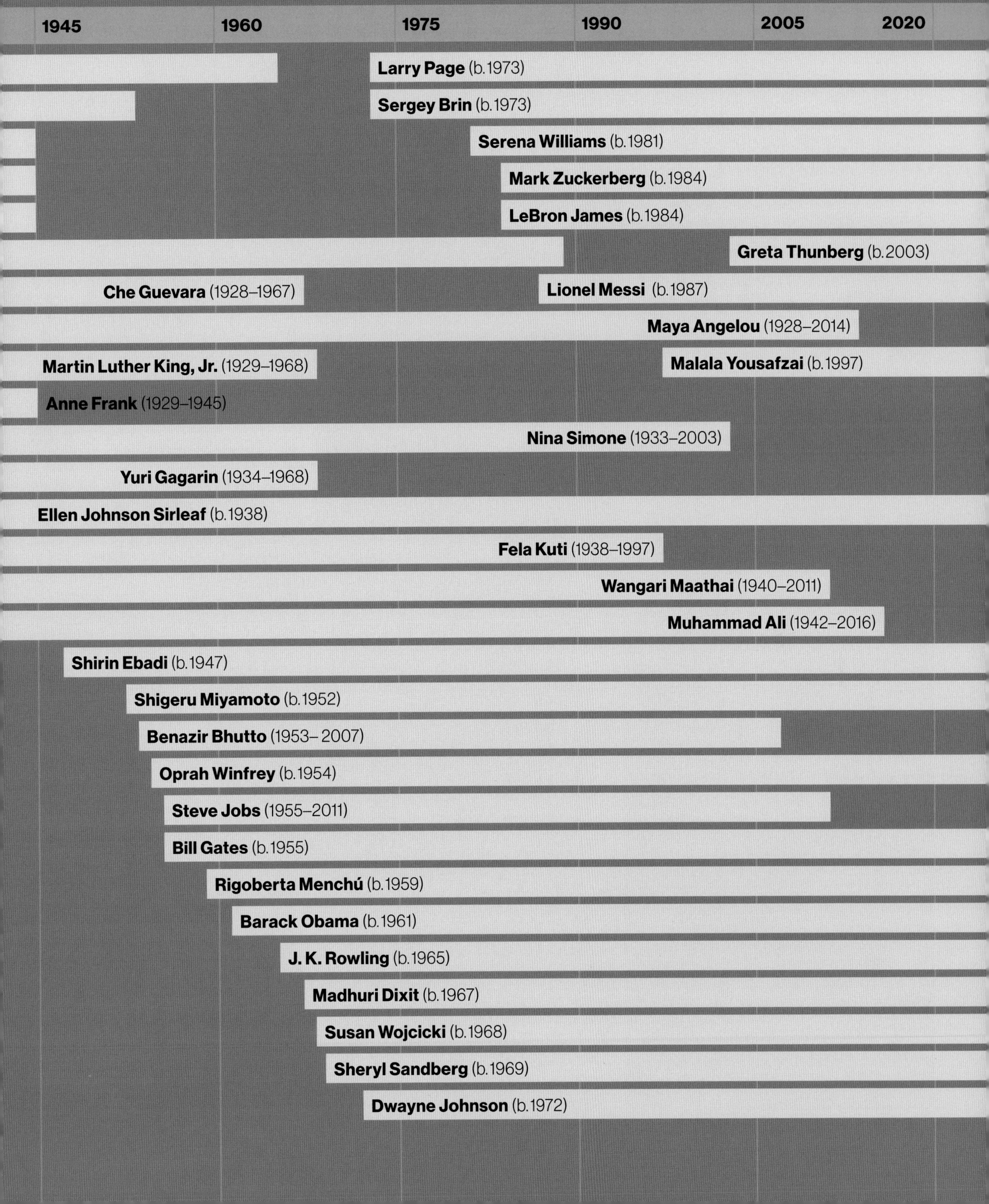

1945	1960	1975	1990	2005	2020

Larry Page (b.1973)

Sergey Brin (b.1973)

Serena Williams (b.1981)

Mark Zuckerberg (b.1984)

LeBron James (b.1984)

Greta Thunberg (b.2003)

Che Guevara (1928–1967)

Lionel Messi (b.1987)

Maya Angelou (1928–2014)

Martin Luther King, Jr. (1929–1968)

Malala Yousafzai (b.1997)

Anne Frank (1929–1945)

Nina Simone (1933–2003)

Yuri Gagarin (1934–1968)

Ellen Johnson Sirleaf (b.1938)

Fela Kuti (1938–1997)

Wangari Maathai (1940–2011)

Muhammad Ali (1942–2016)

Shirin Ebadi (b.1947)

Shigeru Miyamoto (b.1952)

Benazir Bhutto (1953– 2007)

Oprah Winfrey (b.1954)

Steve Jobs (1955–2011)

Bill Gates (b.1955)

Rigoberta Menchú (b.1959)

Barack Obama (b.1961)

J. K. Rowling (b.1965)

Madhuri Dixit (b.1967)

Susan Wojcicki (b.1968)

Sheryl Sandberg (b.1969)

Dwayne Johnson (b.1972)

Che Guevara

The poverty, hunger, and failed governments Che Guevara (1928–1967) encountered in his travels across South America inspired him to become a revolutionary. His most successful act was as one of the leaders of the 1959 Cuban Revolution. During his life, he was both admired and feared as a champion of violent revolution, and as an opponent of the US' power over developing nations.

Meeting Castro
In Mexico, Che meets Cuban revolutionary Fidel Castro, who is planning to overthrow the government in his home country. Che soon signs up to Castro's revolutionary 26th of July Movement, which is named after an attack on an army barracks that started the revolution.

1955

Becoming "Che"
The US intervenes to remove the government in Guatemala. Ernesto, who is now nicknamed "Che" (meaning "friend"), joins an armed group opposing this. He flees to Mexico when he finds his life is in danger.

1954

"We are the future and we know it."
Che Guevara, from a letter to his parents (1959)

Guatemala
Ernesto graduates as a doctor. When he hears that the president of Guatemala is giving private land to landless peasants, he decides to settle there.

1953

Journey around South America
While at university, Ernesto travels by motorcycle across South America. He is angered when he sees how North American companies make money from the land of the poor.

1950

Born in Argentina
Ernesto Guevara is born in Rosario, Argentina. His family's home is often visited by guests with different books and is full of different political opinions. Ernesto develops great sympathy for people living in poverty.

1928

Cuban revolutionaries

Che Guevara fought alongside revolutionary activists to bring about the changes they believed in for South America. Many of these activists went on to have political careers in communist Cuba.

Fidel Castro (1926–2016)
A revolutionary and politician, Castro was prime minister of Cuba from 1959–2008 and president from 1976–2008. He is viewed today by supporters as a socialist hero who helped free Cuba from its domination by the US. Critics, however, see him as a dictator who destroyed Cuba's economy.

Vilma Espín (1930–2007)
One of the most significant leaders of the Cuban revolutionary movement, Espín was a feminist, a spy, and a politician. She championed gender equality across every aspect of Cuban life, from the revolution right up until her death, including campaigning for female literacy and a woman's right to work.

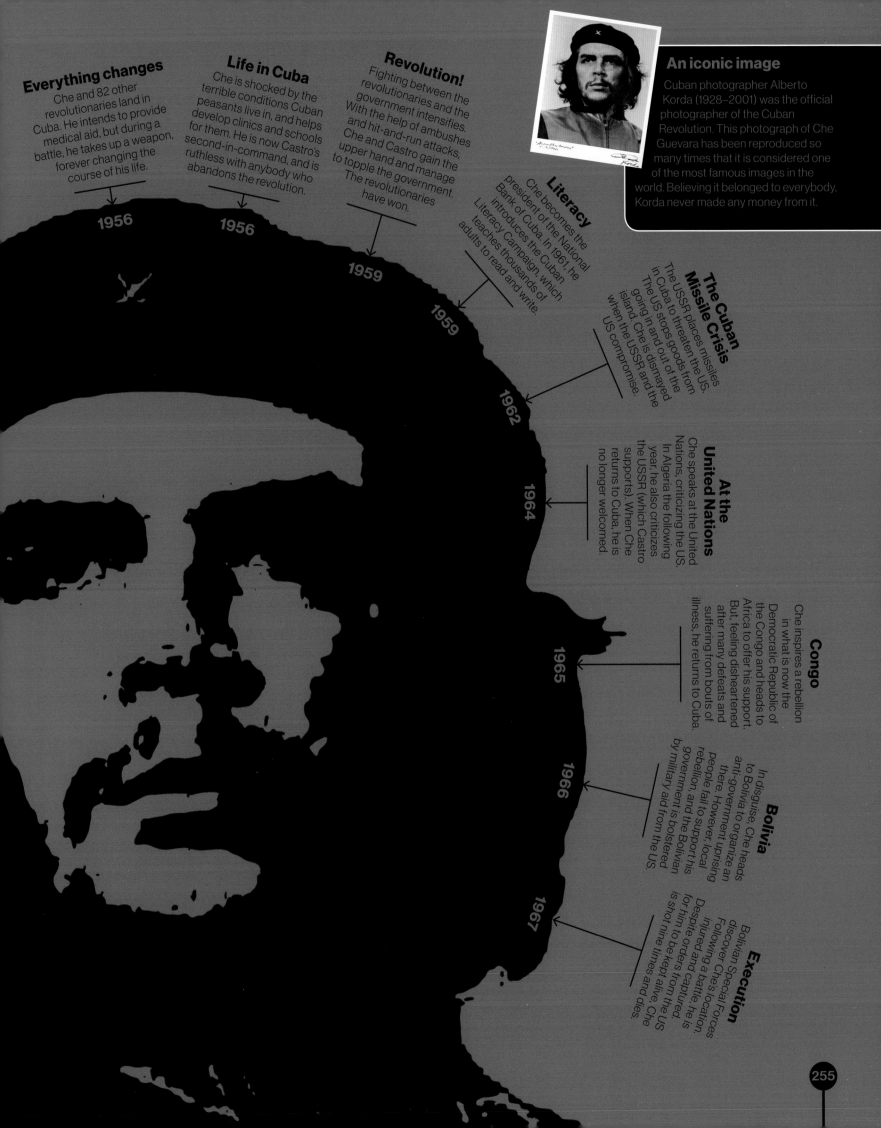

Everything changes
Che and 82 other revolutionaries land in Cuba. He intends to provide medical aid, but during a battle, he takes up a weapon, forever changing the course of his life.

1956

Life in Cuba
Che is shocked by the terrible conditions Cuban peasants live in, and helps develop clinics and schools for them. He is now Castro's second-in-command, and is ruthless with anybody who abandons the revolution.

1956

Revolution!
Fighting between the revolutionaries and the government intensifies. With the help of ambushes and hit-and-run attacks, Che and Castro gain the upper hand and manage to topple the government. The revolutionaries have won.

1959

Literacy
Che becomes the president of the National Bank of Cuba. In 1961, he introduces the Cuban Literacy Campaign, which teaches thousands of adults to read and write.

1959

An iconic image
Cuban photographer Alberto Korda (1928–2001) was the official photographer of the Cuban Revolution. This photograph of Che Guevara has been reproduced so many times that it is considered one of the most famous images in the world. Believing it belonged to everybody, Korda never made any money from it.

The Cuban Missile Crisis
The USSR places missiles in Cuba to threaten the US. The US to stops goods from going in and out of the island. Che is dismayed when the USSR and the US compromise.

1962

At the United Nations
Che speaks at the United Nations, criticizing the US. In Algeria the following year, he also criticizes the USSR (which Castro supports). When Che returns to Cuba, he is no longer welcomed.

1964

Congo
Che inspires a rebellion in what is now the Democratic Republic of the Congo and heads to Africa to offer his support. But, feeling disheartened after many defeats and suffering from bouts of illness, he returns to Cuba.

1965

Bolivia
In disguise, Che heads to Bolivia to organize an anti-government rebellion. However, local people fail to support his rebellion, and the Bolivian government is bolstered by military aid from the US.

1966

Execution
Bolivian Special Forces discover Che's location. Following a battle, he is injured and captured. Despite orders for him to be kept alive, Che is shot nine times and dies.

1967

255

Maya Angelou

Acclaimed novelist and poet Maya Angelou (1928–2014) was one of the greatest writers of the 20th century. She is best known for *I Know Why The Caged Bird Sings,* her vivid account of her childhood in the southern US. She was also a poet, dramatist, actress, and an activist for civil rights for African Americans.

1928
"I was born in St. Louis but lived there just for a few minutes in my life."
Interview with CNN (2011)
Maya is born Marguerite Annie Johnson in St. Louis, Missouri. Her parents separate when she is three. Maya and her brother Bailey are sent to live with their grandmother in Arkansas. Bailey nicknames Marguerite "Maya."

1931
"It was awful to be Negro and have no control over my life."
***I Know Why the Caged Bird Sings* (1970)**
In Arkansas, Maya faces racial discrimination and prejudice for the first time. She finds this extremely difficult to deal with.

1935
"In times of strife and extreme stress, I was likely to retreat to mutism."
Interview with *Smithsonian Magazine* (2003)
Maya returns briefly to her mother in St. Louis. While there, she is assaulted by her mother's boyfriend. Maya tells people what he did. When her mother's boyfriend is later killed, Maya believes her words have caused his death, and she stops speaking (becomes mute). She is mute for the next five years.

1941
"Her voice slid in and curved down through and over the words. She was nearly singing."
Describing her teacher reading from Charles Dickens in *I Know Why the Caged Bird Sings* (1970)
Maya lives with her grandmother. A teacher, Mrs. Flowers, helps her talk again and inspires a love of literature. Aged 14, she moves to California, living once more with her mother. She studies dance and drama.

1961
"If the heart of Africa remained elusive, my search for it had brought me closer to understanding myself and other human beings."
***All God's Children Need Traveling Shoes* (1986)**
Maya and her son travel to Egypt with South African civil rights activist Vusumzi Make. The following year, Maya and her son move to Ghana, where she lives for three years. She involves herself fully in African culture and politics.

Late 1950s
"A black person grows up in this country ... knowing that racism will be as familiar as salt to the tongue."
Interview for the American Academy of Achievement (1997)
Maya travels to New York. She meets African American authors and joins The Harlem Writers Guild (who help African American writers develop their skills). She hears civil rights leader Martin Luther King, Jr., speak. Maya begins to campaign for justice for African American people.

1945
"All my work, my life, everything is about survival ... one must not be defeated."
***Conversations with Maya Angelou* (1989)**
At 17, Maya gives birth to her son Clyde "Guy" Johnson. She is a single parent. Maya and Guy move to San Diego, where she works as a waitress and dancer. She marries a man called Tosh Angelos in 1951, and she changes her surname to Angelou. Their relationship ends after three years.

1944
"He asked me, 'Why do you want the job?' I said 'I like the uniforms ... and I like people.' And so I got the job."
Interview with Oprah Winfrey (May 2013)
Maya becomes the first female African American cable car conductor in San Francisco. Her mother tells her that, because she is black, she will have to work much harder than her colleagues in order to keep her job.

1969

"I've **always written**. There's a journal which I kept from about nine years old."

Interview with _Smithsonian Magazine_ (2003)
Urged on by friends, Maya turns her memories into a book, _I Know Why the Caged Bird Sings_. It is a vivid account of an African American childhood. The novel is wildly successful.

1978

"You may trod me in the very dirt, But still, like dust, **I'll rise**."

And Still I Rise (1978)
Maya's third volume of poetry, _And Still I Rise_, is published. It contains some of her best-loved lines and most famous poems.

1993

"Give birth again, to the **dream**."

From _"On the Pulse of Morning"_ (1993)
She becomes a global icon when she delivers her poem "On the Pulse of Morning" at the inauguration of President Bill Clinton. It speaks about America, and Maya's feelings on the good and bad aspects of American life.

2014

"I'll **probably be writing** when the Lord says, 'Maya, Maya Angelou, it's time.'"

Interview with _Time_ magazine (2013)
Maya dies at the age of 86. She had been writing right up until her death. Tributes pour in from a wide array of people—from media stars, such as Oprah Winfrey, to US presidents, including Bill Clinton and Barack Obama.

Maya Angelou
I Know
Why the
Caged Bird
Sings

1929
Special name
At birth, Martin is named Michael King, in honor of his father, a church pastor in Atlanta, Georgia. When Michael, Jr., is five, his father changes both his own and his son's name to "Martin Luther," after the 16th-century German religious reformer.

1944
BRIGHT STUDENT
From an early age, Martin displays a talent for public speaking and debating. He enrolls at Morehouse College as an early admission student at the age of 15. He receives a bachelor of arts degree and goes on to study theology (the study of God and religious belief). During his youth, he often feels humiliated by the discrimination that he and his family and friends experience on a daily basis.

1946
Moore's Ford Lynchings
Four young African Americans are murdered by a white mob in Martin's home state, an event known as the Moore's Ford Lynchings. Martin writes a letter to Atlanta's most popular newspaper. In his letter, Martin emphasizes that African Americans "are entitled to the basic rights of American citizens" — something repeatedly denied them.

1948
Following his father
Martin decides he wants to become a Christian minister and delivers his first sermon from the pulpit of his father's church, aged 18. The congregation vote to make him a minister and he is ordained, becoming an associate minister.

1953
MARRIAGE
Early in 1952, Martin is introduced to Coretta Scott. Two weeks later, he writes to his mother that he has "met his wife." A year later, Coretta and Martin marry, with his father conducting the service.

1955
Rosa Parks
An African American woman, Rosa Parks, is arrested in Montgomery, Alabama, for breaking the law by refusing to give up her seat on a bus for a white man. In response, Martin organizes a year-long boycott of the city's buses. It ends when the US Supreme Court rules that segregation laws are illegal.

Civil rights
The ideas behind the US civil rights movement were around for a while, but the movement really took hold in the mid-1950s. Many people fought for African American rights, and to bring about equality.

Septima Poinsette Clark (1898–1987)
A civil rights activist, Septima Poinsette Clark was instrumental in founding nearly 1,000 citizenship schools, which contributed to helping African Americans register to vote.

Lyndon B. Johnson (1908–1973)
The 36th president of the US, Lyndon B. Johnson signed laws that made racial discrimination and segregation illegal.

Malcolm X (1925–1965)
Like Martin Luther King, Jr., African American activist Malcolm X supported black Americans' efforts to empower themselves, but didn't believe in the racial integration that King wanted.

1957
Peaceful protest

Following the success of the bus boycott, Martin travels around the US, fighting for civil rights through peaceful protest. He is now the nation's foremost speaker for African American rights. He helps establish the Southern Christian Leadership Conference, an organization working to achieve equality for African Americans in all areas of US life.

1960
Prison

Martin takes part in a nonviolent anti-segregation protest in which he and other protestors occupy a segregated Atlanta department store and refuse to leave. As a result, Martin is arrested. He is sentenced to four months of hard labor in prison.

1963
"I HAVE A DREAM"

While in prison, Martin writes his "Letter From Birmingham Jail," in which he defends nonviolent resistance against racism. When released, he delivers his "I Have a Dream" speech to 250,000 people at the Lincoln Memorial in Washington, D.C., where he imagines a society where people are not judged "by the color of their skin, but by the content of their character."

July 1964
Civil Rights Act

The civil rights movement enjoys a huge victory when the Civil Rights Act is signed into law by President Lyndon B. Johnson. It makes any kind of discrimination or segregation on the basis of race illegal.

Oct 1964
Nobel Peace Prize

Time magazine names Martin as "Man of the Year." He is also awarded the Nobel Peace Prize for his resistance against racial prejudice in the US. At 35, Martin is the youngest person at the time to have received the award.

1967
Economic justice

Martin reveals his plans for a mass protest. Named the Poor People's Campaign, the movement is intended to bring about economic justice: the idea that everybody should have access to the basic things they need to live. This protest will include people of all walks of life from across the US.

1968
ASSASSINATION

Martin does not live to see the protest. He delivers a speech called "I've Been to the Mountaintop." Toward the end, he talks of the possibility of his untimely death as a result of speaking out about racial issues. The next day, Martin is fatally shot by an enemy of his work, James Earl Ray.

Martin Luther King, Jr.

An activist and a Christian minister, Martin Luther King, Jr. (1929–1968) was one of the leaders of the civil rights movement of the 1950s and 1960s, which campaigned for the rights of African Americans. A believer in nonviolent protest, his work helped tear down racial segregation (separation), then a part of the law, and inspire generations of activists looking for a fairer and more equal society.

> **"Now is the time to make real the promises of democracy."**
> **Martin Luther King, Jr.**
> **"I Have a Dream" speech (1963)**

Anne Frank

The Franks were a Jewish family living in Amsterdam, in the Netherlands, during World War II. The youngest child, Anne (1929–1945), kept a diary of her experiences hiding from Nazi officials, who were persecuting Jewish people. Her diary has been translated into 70 languages and is one of the world's best-known books.

> **"I don't think of all the misery, but of the beauty that still remains."**
>
> **Anne Frank,**
> *The Diary of a Young Girl (1947)*

Young people and World War II

World War II (1939–1945) turned the lives of people all over the planet upside down. Like Anne Frank, many young people's lives were cut short by the conflict.

Sophie Scholl (1921–1943)

German student Sophie Scholl was part of a nonviolent group that were against the Nazis. Found handing out anti-Nazi leaflets at her university, Sophie was convicted of high treason (betraying her country) and was murdered by the Nazis in 1943, aged 21.

Sadako Sasaki (1943–1955)

Japanese schoolgirl Sadako Sasaki survived the atomic bomb attack on the Japanese city of Hiroshima that brought about the end of the war in 1945. In 1954, she fell ill with leukaemia caused by the bomb. She died the following year.

June 1942

The diary

Anne receives a diary for her 13th birthday. She immediately begins to document her daily life—including the increasingly frightening restrictions placed on her and her Jewish friends and family.

1929

Born in Germany

Anne is born into a Jewish family in Frankfurt, Germany. She has a sister, Margot, who is three years older. Their parents, Otto and Edith, encourage them to read and write from a young age.

1933

LEAVING GERMANY

Adolf Hitler's anti-Jewish Nazi party wins an election in Germany. They attack Jewish people and their businesses. Fearing for their safety, more than 300,000 Jews leave Germany over the next six years. The Franks move to Amsterdam, in the Netherlands.

ADOLF HITLER

1942

Yellow star

All Jewish people in the Netherlands, including Anne, now have a black "J" marked on their identity cards (which everyone carries to prove who they are). They are ordered to wear a yellow star on their clothes so that officials can separate them from other citizens, making it easier for them to be discriminated against.

A yellow star marked with "Jude," the German word for "Jew." The Nazis forced Jewish people to wear this.

1939

War begins

Nazi Germany invades Poland, leading to the outbreak of World War II. The Netherlands is invaded in 1940, and the Nazis begin to persecute Jewish people there. The Nazis force Jewish people to live separately from others. The following year, Anne and Margot—both excellent students—are removed from their regular school and sent to a Jewish school.

July 6, 1942
Secret annex

When the family discover that Margot is to be sent to a Nazi work camp, they decide to go into hiding. They move into a secret annex (a hidden apartment) in Otto's work office. The entrance is hidden behind a bookcase. Life is hard (they have few comforts and must stay quiet), but Otto's work colleagues bring them food.

July 1942
More hide in the annex

Later in July, Anne's family are joined in the small annex by the Van Pels family—another Jewish family hiding from the Nazis. In November, dentist Fritz Pfeffer joins them. Anne finds the cramped living conditions very uncomfortable, but knows they will all be killed if found.

October 1942
HIDDEN AWAY

The group listen to the news on their little radio, and hear about the outside world from their helpers. They are terrified when they learn that Jewish people are being rounded up and sent to places called "concentration camps." The Nazis imprison Jewish people in terrible conditions in camps, before killing them.

August 4, 1944
DISASTER STRIKES

German police raid the annex and find the group hiding there. They are captured and taken to an overcrowded prison before being transported to the Westerbork Transit Camp in the northeastern Netherlands.

1943
Annex education

The Frank sisters hope to return to education as soon as the war is over. They keep up their studies in the annex. Anne wants to be a journalist, and she uses her entries in her diary to develop her writing skills.

1943
Annex relationships

Anne and 16-year-old Peter Van Pels become close, and they share a kiss. Anne begins to grow apart from her mother, Edith, but she soon feels bad about how she treats her, and resolves to be better.

PETER VAN PELS

September 1944
Auschwitz

They are sent to the Auschwitz concentration camp in Poland. Their heads are shaved, and they are each tattooed with a prisoner number. Men and women are separated. Anne's father will never see her again.

October 1944
BERGEN-BELSEN

Anne and Margot are moved to the Bergen-Belsen concentration camp in northern Germany. Their mother Edith is left behind. She soon dies of starvation. Anne is devastated to be separated from both of her parents.

1945
Legacy

Margot and Anne die within a few days of each other after disease spreads through the camp. Otto survives the war. He gathers Anne's writings, which are published in 1947. Anne's diary is translated into many languages, allowing children around the world to learn about World War II and understand what it is like to be persecuted.

Nina Simone

African American musician, songwriter, and activist Nina Simone (1933–2003) enchanted generations with her talent. She also raised awareness about, and campaigned for, civil rights for African Americans, often using her music to explore the realities of life for African Americans of her era.

> **"How can you be an artist and not reflect the times?"**
> **Nina Simone, *from an interview* (1960s)**

A musical talent
Eunice Kathleen Waymon is born in North Carolina, US. She learns to play the piano at an early age, and it soon becomes clear that she has a talent for the instrument. She begins to play the piano regularly during church services.

Classical music
Word of Eunice's talent spreads. She meets a pianist called Muriel Mazzanovich. Mazzanovich begins teaching Eunice, introducing her to the music of classical pianists such as Johann Sebastian Bach and Ludwig van Beethoven.

Early protest
After years of practice, Eunice is due to perform her first classical recital, but her parents are forced to give up their seats to white audience members. Displaying an early sign of her stance against racial segregation and inequality, Eunice refuses to perform until her parents are allowed to sit at the front.

Heartbreak
Eunice auditions for another scholarship to continue her musical education. Despite a great audition, her application to the Curtis Institute of Music, Philadelphia, is rejected. Eunice feels certain that she is rejected because she is black. While some argue that this is not the case, she is never given a clear reason why she is not accepted.

Musical dream
Realizing her talent, Eunice's local community in North Carolina contribute to a fund to pay for her education. After high school, Eunice receives a one-year scholarship to study music at the famous Juilliard School of Music in New York. She is one of the first black female artists to attend Juilliard.

1933

c.1939

1945

1950

1951

Musical pioneers

In their own unique way, each of these artists changed the sound of music and influenced the development of new types of music.

Billie Holiday (1915–1959)

African American Billie Holiday's songs were crucial in the growth of jazz music. Perhaps the most famous song she performed was "Strange Fruit", which told a story about a lynching (a type of racially motivated attack).

Ella Fitzgerald (1917–1996)

An African American singer, Fitzgerald was famous for using her voice to imitate instruments, known as scat singing. She was known as the "Queen of Jazz", an African American music style.

Aretha Franklin (1942–2018)

A gifted pianist, African American Franklin recorded her first album aged 14. She blended genres of music and was known as the "Queen of Soul", another African American music style.

NINA PERFORMING IN ALABAMA IN AUGUST 1963

Rally

Nina regularly speaks and performs at civil rights meetings and rallies. Some of the largest are the Selma to Montgomery marches in Alabama, when about 25,000 people walk 80 km (50 miles) to highlight unjust obstructions to African American voting rights. Nina is one of the many performers to inspire protestors to continue marching.

Emotional distress

Nina's career takes a huge toll on her mental health. She is diagnosed with bipolar disorder – which causes big mood swings in sufferers, something Nina struggles with in both her personal life and while performing. At times, Nina uses drugs to cope with her emotions. This only makes things worse.

Musical change

Many of her early records are about love, but when four black schoolgirls are killed in a racially motivated bombing in Alabama, Nina is furious. The tragedy leads to a change in Nina's music as she begins exploring her experiences as an African American.

An icon

In the later years of her life, close friends help Nina get her life and career back on track. Nina tours the world, giving some amazing performances. She dies from cancer at home in France.

Leaving America

After the assassination of many of the US civil rights movement leaders, the momentum and energy of the movement changes. Nina decides to leave the US, and spends several years living in countries such as Liberia, Switzerland, and France.

Political awareness

Nina channels her anger over the assassination of the civil rights activist Medgar Evers into some of her most political songs. Her music is banned in some southern states, but Nina continues to use her music to raise awareness of the civil rights movement.

A rising star

Determined to pursue a music career, Eunice gets a job singing and playing piano at a bar in New Jersey. She believes her family will not approve of this, so she adopts the name "Nina Simone" to keep it a secret. Her audience grows, which leads to a record deal in 1957. One of her first recordings is her version of the song "I Loves You, Porgy" (1958). It becomes a hit.

1954

1963

1964

1965

1970

c.1980s

2003

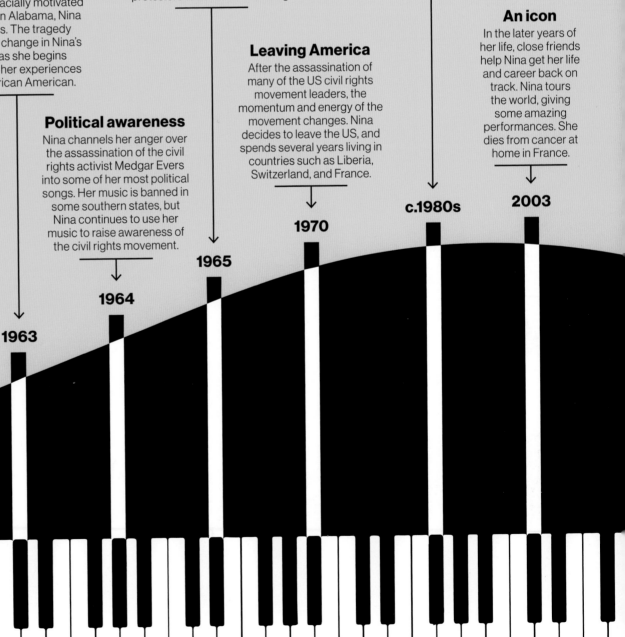

YURI GAGARIN

The first human in space

> **"I saw how beautiful our planet is. People, let us preserve and increase this beauty, not destroy it!"**
>
> **Yuri Gagarin, after his mission (translated in 1973)**

Yuri Gagarin (1934–1968), a Russian cosmonaut, made history in 1961 when he became the first human to travel into space. His 108-minute orbit of the Earth was a huge leap forward in the highly competitive Space Race between the world's two great superpowers, the Soviet Union (USSR) and the United States (US). Gagarin's achievement was presented to the world as a trouble-free triumph of Soviet technology—but the flight almost ended in catastrophe.

Vostok gets underway

In **1955**, both the USSR and the US announced their plans to launch the first artificial satellite into space. The USSR got there first, successfully sending Sputnik 1 out into orbit in **October 1957**. Meanwhile, Sergei Korolev, head of the USSR's space program, secretly gathered together a group of talented young engineers to design a crewed spacecraft. The model they came up with consisted of two sections—called the service module and reentry module—that separate when the spacecraft, called the Vostok, reenters the atmosphere. The sole cosmonaut on board is to be ejected from the reentry module, and land using a parachute. Production began in **1959**, with a launch planned for late **1960**.

Training and selection

In **September 1959**, an expert panel begins interviewing and testing candidates to become the first human in space. They undergo a series of tough physical, mental, and psychological tests, and in **March 1960**, the final 20 start preparing. Training involves classes; a daily fitness regimen; and exercises such as parachute jumps, weightlessness tests, and enduring long periods in an isolation chamber. By **May 30**, only six candidates remain. From the outset, Yuri Gagarin, a 26-year-old from a tiny village, impresses with his excellent memory, fast reactions, and good humor. He becomes the clear favorite.

Test flights

By **April 1960**, the first Vostok space capsule is ready for testing. Since no one knows whether a human will be able to operate the controls while weightless, the engineers decide to control the spacecraft by remote control from the ground. The first two launches end in failure, but on **August 19**, a test capsule carries two dogs—named Belka and Strelka—out into space and returns them safely 26 hours later. After two more successful tests in **March 1961**, Vostok 1 is declared ready to take a human into space.

Choosing Yuri

On **April 7**, the cosmonaut training committee finally makes its choice. Yuri Gagarin is selected, partly because they feel his humble background will please the Soviet leader, Nikita Khrushchev. Gherman Titov is chosen as a backup in case anything happens to Yuri before the mission. The two men are told on **April 9**, and Yuri gives a speech when the meeting is reenacted in front of TV cameras the following day. At **5 a.m.** on **April 11**, the rocket launcher and Vostok space capsule are towed out to the Baikonur Cosmodrome (in modern-day Kazakhstan) and are exhaustively tested throughout the day, while Yuri and Titov review the flight plans. They spend the evening chatting and playing pool.

"Let's go!"

At **5:30 a.m.** on **April 12, 1961**, Korolev wakes Yuri and Titov, neither of whom have had much sleep. The two cosmonauts are given breakfast and helped into their orange cosmonaut suits. Before they board the bus for the cosmodrome, Yuri pees on its back tires (this would become a tradition for later cosmonauts!). At **7 a.m.**, he steps into the cockpit of Vostok 1. Engineers plug Yuri into the spacecraft's monitors and perform a series of tests and checks, but there is a last-minute glitch when Yuri realizes that the hatch is not sealed properly. It takes technicians more than an hour to fix the seal. At **9:06 a.m.**, the rocket's engines fire, and Korolev radios "Preliminary stage … intermediate … main … LIFT OFF!" Yuri cries "*Poyekhali!*" ("Let's go!"), and, at **9:07 a.m.**, the spacecraft launches. Two minutes later, the booster rockets fall away.

In orbit

At **9:17 a.m.**, Vostok 1 reaches orbit above Earth. Ten seconds later, the space

capsule separates from the rocket. Traveling northeast across the planet, Yuri passes over Siberia and on to the northern Pacific Ocean. He radios that he is in good spirits. At **9:25 a.m.**, he starts traveling southeast across the Pacific Ocean toward South America, and 12 minutes later crosses to the northwest of Hawaii. At **10 a.m.**, news of the flight's success is broadcast on Radio Moscow. Everything proceeds as planned as the spacecraft passes over the Straits of Magellan and, at **10:10 a.m.**, it flies over the southern Atlantic Ocean.

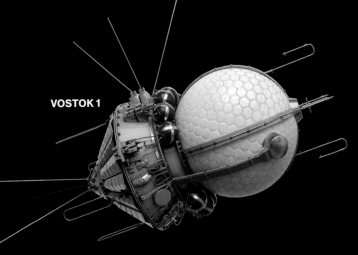

VOSTOK 1

Reentry and landing

At **10:25 a.m.**, the spacecraft turns around and fires its rockets forward to slow down, and mission control sends a command for the reentry and service modules to separate. Unexpectedly, however, the two modules remain attached by a bundle of wires. At **10:35 a.m.**, the spacecraft plunges back into the atmosphere above northeast Africa, but with the two modules still connected, it begins to spin. Yuri is violently shaken and a burning smell fills the cabin. He remains alert, and eventually the cables snap. As the tumbling begins to decline, Yuri—recognizing that the malfunction does not endanger the mission—calmly radios that everything is fine. At **10:55 a.m.**, 4 miles (7 km) from the ground, the hatch of the reentry module blows off and two seconds later, Yuri is launched into the air in his ejector seat. His parachute opens almost immediately, and at **11:05 a.m.**, he lands gently in a field in southern Russia's Saratov province.

A global hero

The mission achieves an important first for the USSR in the Space Race with the US. Yuri becomes a Soviet hero and a global celebrity, touring more than 30 countries as a Soviet goodwill ambassador, but dies in **1968** in an aviation accident, at the age of 34. Though he died young, he will forever be remembered as a space pioneer.

1938

Early years

Ellen is born in Monrovia, Liberia. Her father is the first member of the Gola tribal people to win a seat in the country's parliament.

1948

Moving around

Ellen and James move to the US. She earns a degree in accounting. They return to Liberia two years later, and Ellen pursues a career with the Treasury Department of Liberia. She divorces her husband after suffering abuse from him.

1961

Finance

She begins studying at the College of West Africa, in Monrovia. Ellen marries James Sirleaf in 1955. They will have four sons together.

1969

Further education

Ellen returns to the US to complete her education. She earns a degree in economics from the University of Colorado. In 1971, she obtains a Master's degree in public administration—the study of how governments make their policies work—from Harvard University.

Timeline

1972

Minister of Finance
Ellen moves back to Liberia. She becomes assistant Minister of Finance under President William Tolbert. In 1979, she rises to the position of Minister of Finance.

1980

Military coup
President Tolbert is overthrown and killed in a violent military coup (seizure of power) led by Samuel Doe. Ellen is put under house arrest. She is one of just four ministers of Tolbert's government to not be murdered. She flees to the US after her release.

1985

Arrest, prison, and exile
Ellen returns to Liberia and runs for the senate. She openly criticizes the government, which leads to her arrest and a term of nine months in prison. After her release, she leaves the country again. During her 12-year exile, she works for the World Bank and other financial institutions. A bloody civil war breaks out in Liberia in 1989.

1997

Presidential campaign
The civil war in Liberia ends in 1996. Ellen returns and runs for president against Charles Taylor. Taylor wins and his government charges Ellen for treason (betraying the country), which forces her back into exile.

2005

Becoming president
Ellen runs in the 2005 election against famous soccer player George Weah. She wins the election. Early on in her term she begins to work on sorting out the country's debt problems.

2011

Nobel Peace Prize
Ellen is awarded the Nobel Peace Prize. She is praised for her work to bring the period of war in Liberia to an end, and for her campaign to promote the safety of women throughout Africa.

2018

Stepping down
Ellen steps down after winning two more terms as president. She continues to provide support to women who want to have a career in politics.

Ellen Johnson Sirleaf

The first woman to become a head of state in Africa, Ellen Johnson Sirleaf (b. 1938) was the president of Liberia from 2006 to 2018. As president, she worked to improve the lives of all Liberians. She jointly won the Nobel Peace Prize in 2011 for promoting peace, and improving women's rights in Liberia.

National icons
Just like Ellen Johnson Sirleaf, these politicians overcame difficult circumstances in leading their nations. As a result, they have all become national icons.

Joseph Jenkins Roberts (1809–1876)
The first president of Liberia, US-born Roberts was also the first person of African descent to rule his country. After campaigning for Liberian independence, he sought foreign recognition for the country.

Vigdís Finnbogadóttir (b. 1930)
The world's first elected female president, Finnbogadóttir was president of Iceland for 16 years. She is the longest-serving elected female head of state in the world.

Angela Merkel (b. 1954)
Germany's first female leader, Angela Merkel is one of the most powerful women in the world. She carefully managed her country's response to an economic crisis in 2008, and is a firm supporter of green energy policies.

Fela Kuti

Nigerian musician and political activist Fela Kuti (1938–1997) used his great musical talent to take on the Nigerian military government in the 1970s and 1980s. He was a pioneer of a new musical genre called Afrobeat, and both his music and activism brought him critical acclaim and international fame.

Activist mother
Fela is born Olufela Olusegun Oludotun Ransome-Kuti in Abeokuta, Nigeria. His father is an Anglican clergyman and his mother is a feminist, activist, and musician.

1938

A musical child
From a young age, Fela shows an interest in music. He spends much of his childhood learning how to play the piano and drums. He later goes on to lead his school choir.

c. 1950

Leaving Nigeria
At the age of 20, Fela leaves Nigeria for London, England. His parents hope he will study medicine or law, but Fela wants to follow his passion for music. He enrolls to study classical music at Trinity College London.

1958

Koola Lobitos
During his time in London, Fela becomes interested in music from around the world. He forms a band, called Koola Lobitos. They combine American jazz with the lively rhythms of West African highlife music.

1959

Back to Nigeria
Fela graduates and returns to Nigeria, where he trains as a radio producer at the Nigerian Broadcasting Corporation. With highlife music growing in popularity, he re-forms his band with new members and records four tracks.

1963

Growing popularity
Koola Lobitos becomes increasingly popular, and they tour widely. Fela's band provides support to major international stars—including African American rock 'n' roll singer Chubby Checker—when they tour Nigeria.

1966

Afrobeat
Fela travels to Ghana in search of new musical inspiration. It is here that he coins the term Afrobeat to describe a new, progressive sound that blends Nigerian music with funk, jazz, and salsa.

1967

268

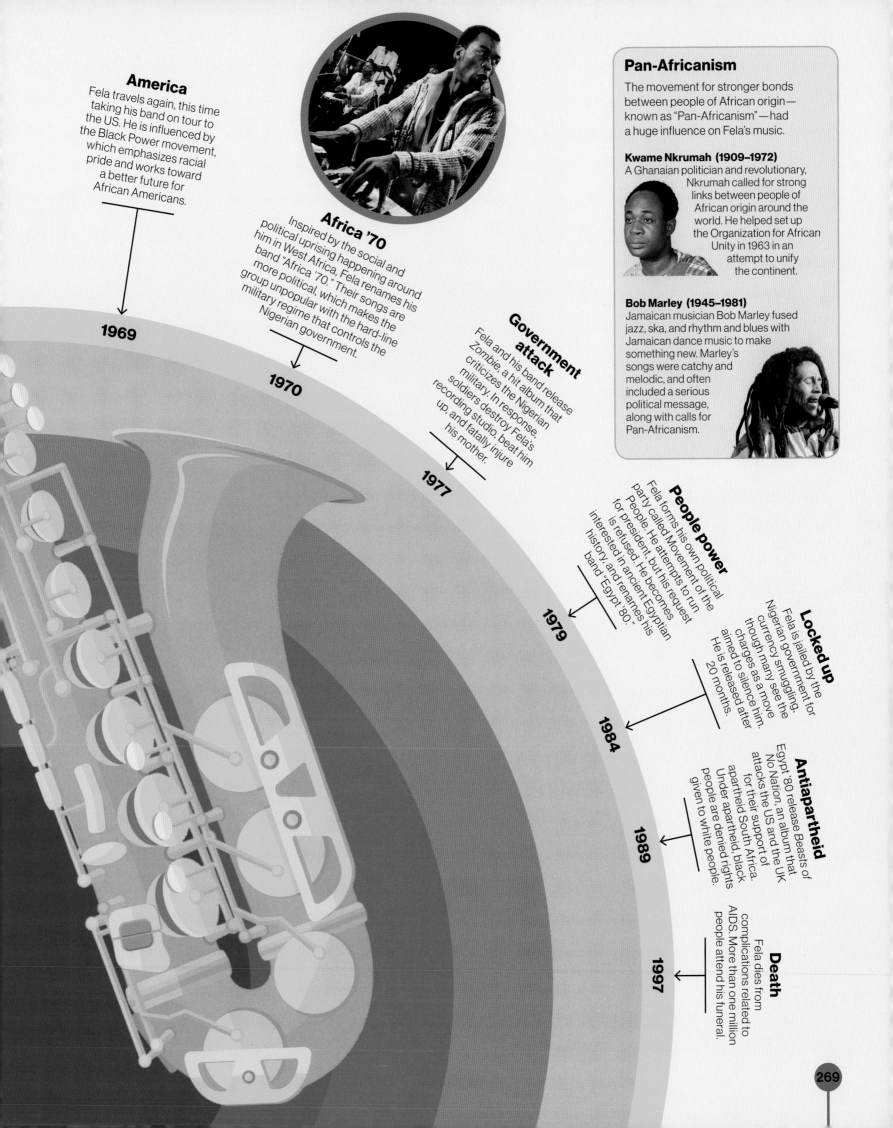

America

Fela travels again, this time taking his band on tour to the US. He is influenced by the Black Power movement, which emphasizes racial pride and works toward a better future for African Americans.

1969

Africa '70

Inspired by the social and political uprising happening around him in West Africa, Fela renames his band "Africa '70." Their songs are more political, which makes the group unpopular with the hard-line military regime that controls the Nigerian government.

1970

Government attack

Fela and his band release Zombie, a hit album that criticizes the Nigerian military. In response, soldiers destroy Fela's recording studio, beat him up, and fatally injure his mother.

1977

People power

Fela forms his own political party called Movement of the People. He attempts to run for president, but his request is refused. He becomes interested in ancient Egyptian history, and renames his band "Egypt '80."

1979

Locked up

Fela is jailed by the Nigerian government for currency smuggling, though many see the charges as a move aimed to silence him. He is released after 20 months.

1984

Antiapartheid

Egypt '80 release Beasts of No Nation, an album that attacks the US and the UK for their support of apartheid South Africa. Under apartheid, black people are denied rights given to white people.

1989

Death

Fela dies from complications related to AIDS. More than one million people attend his funeral.

1997

Pan-Africanism

The movement for stronger bonds between people of African origin—known as "Pan-Africanism"—had a huge influence on Fela's music.

Kwame Nkrumah (1909–1972)
A Ghanaian politician and revolutionary, Nkrumah called for strong links between people of African origin around the world. He helped set up the Organization for African Unity in 1963 in an attempt to unify the continent.

Bob Marley (1945–1981)
Jamaican musician Bob Marley fused jazz, ska, and rhythm and blues with Jamaican dance music to make something new. Marley's songs were catchy and melodic, and often included a serious political message, along with calls for Pan-Africanism.

Benito Mussolini (1883–1945)

Mussolini, an Italian politician, set up the Fascist Party of Italy. Fascists used violence and intimidation against their political opponents to seize power in the country.

1883
Born in Predappio, Italy, Mussolini is a bright but rebellious child, and is expelled from several schools.

1902
Mussolini becomes a socialist—believing that the citizens of a country should share in the wealth that the country produces.

1914
Mussolini is thrown out of the Italian Socialist Party for arguing that Italy should join World War I (WWI), which the party does not agree with.

1919

Mussolini forms the Fascist Party. They believe in strong leadership, military power, and the superiority of the Italian people.

1922
After a series of strikes, Italy's weak government is unable to control the country. Mussolini and his supporters march on the capital city, Rome, where he declares that he is the only one able to restore order. Mussolini is allowed to form his own government. He starts to gradually tear democracy down in the country.

1925
Mussolini declares himself the dictator of Italy. This means he rules the country alone, with unlimited power.

1939
Mussolini's Italy forms an alliance with Germany. When World War II (WWII) breaks out, Italy joins the war in support of Germany. Japan allies with Italy and Germany in 1940. Together, these three are called the Axis countries.

1945
The war turns against the Axis countries. Mussolini is captured by Italians and executed.

Adolf Hitler (1889–1945)

Adolf Hitler's racist and aggressive actions as German dictator started WWII. Under his rule, millions of Jews and others were mass-murdered, an event known as "the Holocaust."

1889
Raised in Linz, Austria, Hitler leaves school at 16 years old.

1914
Hitler fights for Germany in WWI. He is outraged when the country surrenders in 1918. He is angry at Germany's leaders, who he feels have betrayed the country.

1919
Inspired by Mussolini, Hitler joins a German fascist party. It is soon renamed the National Socialist German Workers' party, and is known as the Nazi Party. The Nazis seek to make Germany a strong country through rejecting the peace deal signed after WWI and expanding Germany's territory. They also want to get rid of people they see as enemies of Germany, such as Jewish people and political opponents. Hitler becomes the party's leader in 1921.

1923
Hitler attempts to seize power in Germany, but fails. As he serves time in prison, he writes *Mein Kampf* ("*My Struggle*"). It lays out his plans to change Germany by conquering land in eastern Europe, and by genocide (deliberately killing large communities of people). He is released after nine months of imprisonment.

1933
A series of financial crashes wrecks Germany's economy. With the country in crisis, Hitler seizes power. He passes laws that grant him the right to rule as a dictator. He begins to put his plans to change Germany into action.

1939

WWII begins when Germany invades Poland. The German army conquers large parts of Europe.

1942
The German invasion of the USSR is not successful, and the war begins to turn against the Axis countries. Their rivals, the Allies (USSR, UK, US, and China), start to win key battles.

1945
Germany's defeat is certain as the Allies close in on the country. Hitler kills himself rather than allowing himself to be captured.

Winston Churchill (1874–1965)

Prime minister of Britain for most of the war, Winston Churchill inspired his nation to stand up to Germany's aggression during the war.

1874
Churchill is born in Blenheim Palace in the UK, to an American mother and an English father.

1900
He joins the Conservative Party and enters politics.

1910
He becomes Home Secretary—one of the most important jobs in government. He resigns during WWI when the invasion of Gallipoli (in modern-day Turkey) that he had organized fails.

1933
No longer in politics, Churchill speaks out about the threat posed by fascism, and the Nazi Party in particular. His warnings are ignored at first.

1940
With the war underway, Churchill becomes prime minister of the UK.

July 1940

Germany begins an aerial bombing campaign of Britain known as the Blitz. During The Battle of Britain, Churchill gives rousing speeches to lift British morale. Britain holds firm, and Germany calls off the attack.

1941
Churchill works closely with American President Roosevelt and the USSR's Premier Stalin to coordinate their countries to defeat the Axis powers. They become known as "the Big Three."

1945
Just before the end of the war, Churchill's party loses an election, and he is no longer leader of the UK.

1965
Aged 90, Churchill dies at home from a stroke.

World War II (1939–1945) was the most devastating conflict the world has ever seen. During the war, millions of soldiers and regular people around the world lost their lives. Here are the most important leaders of the main countries that were involved.

Franklin Delano Roosevelt (1882–1945)

The 32nd US president, Roosevelt led America through some of the most difficult times in the country's history.

1882
Roosevelt is born in New York state.

1910
He enters politics as a Democratic Party politician.

1921
Roosevelt is diagnosed with poliomyelitis, a condition that paralyzes his legs.

1933
Roosevelt is elected president at a time when a financial crisis is devastating large parts of the US. He introduces laws that lead to economic stability.

1939
When WWII begins, the US is a neutral (not militarily involved) country. However, the country supports the Allied side with supplies and financial help.

1941

Germany's ally Japan attacks Pearl Harbor, a US naval base on the Pacific island of Hawaii. The US enters the war on the Allied side. It will mostly fight in the Pacific Ocean against Japan.

1942
At the Battle of Midway, the US manages to weaken the Japanese navy for the rest of the war. After this, the US begins to win the war in the Pacific.

1945
Roosevelt suffers a stroke, and dies a few months before the end of the war.

Joseph Stalin (1878–1953)

Joseph Stalin led the Soviet Union (USSR), the country that experienced the most devastation and loss of life during WWII.

1878
Iosif (Joseph) Vissarionovich Dzhugashvili is born into poverty in Gori, Georgia (then part of the Russian Empire).

1895
While studying to become a priest, Dzhugashvili becomes interested in socialism. He joins the Bolsheviks (a militant socialist political party) in 1901.

1912
Dzhugashvili adopts the surname "Stalin," meaning "man of steel" in Russian.

1917
The Bolshevik Party seizes power in Russia. The country joins with other states to become the Soviet Union (USSR) and is ruled by the Communist Party, whose policies are a more extreme form of socialism. Stalin plays a minor role in the revolution.

1922
Stalin becomes leader of the USSR after rising through the Communist Party's ranks.

1939
Stalin and Hitler sign an agreement not to engage in war with each other.

1941
Hitler breaks the agreement, and German troops invade the USSR. The Soviet Union allies with Britain and the US. Hitler's invasion of the USSR fails the following year.

1945

The Soviet armies capture the German capital city Berlin, which ends the war in Europe.

1953
Stalin is still leading the country when he dies at the age of 74 from a stroke.

Michinomiya Hirohito (1901–1989)

Emperor Hirohito was Japan's longest-living emperor. His country joined the war on the Axis side.

1901
Hirohito is born into the Japanese imperial family.

1926
When his father dies, Hirohito inherits the imperial throne and becomes the ruler of Japan.

1931
Japan invades China. Emperor Hirohito agrees to the use of chemical weapons and toxic gas against the Chinese—something that was banned by international law.

1940
Seeing an opportunity to use WWII to gain more territory, Hirohito allies with Germany and Italy and plans to attack targets in Asia.

1941
The US stops the export of vital raw materials to Japan. Hirohito orders the attack on the US naval base at Pearl Harbor. This attack causes the US to enter the war.

1945

The US drops powerful atomic bombs on the Japanese cities of Hiroshima and Nagasaki. Hundreds of thousands of civilians are killed, and tens of thousands are injured. WWII ends when Japan surrenders soon afterward.

1989
Hirohito dies from cancer. He had remained emperor until his death.

Wangari Maathai

Kenyan environmentalist Wangari Maathai (1940–2011) was the founder of the Green Belt Movement, an organization that has arranged the planting of more than 51 million trees worldwide. She spoke out against Kenya's corrupt government of the 1980s and 1990s, and suffered intimidation and arrest as a result. She won the Nobel Peace Prize in 2004.

> "Until you dig a hole, you plant a tree, you water it and make it survive, you haven't done a thing. You are just talking."
>
> **Wangari Maathai, Speech at Goldman Environmental Prize awards (2006)**

Return to Kenya

Wangari returns to Kenya to continue her studies at the University of Nairobi. Two years later, she receives her doctorate in veterinary anatomy, becoming the first Kenyan woman to earn a PhD. She becomes associate professor at the university, and campaigns for equal treatment for all staff.

Studying in the US

Wangari wins a scholarship to study in the US. She goes on to earn a Master's degree in Biology from the University of Pittsburgh. In the US, she witnesses Americans demonstrating against their government, and is inspired to speak up for her beliefs.

Nature lover

Growing up on a farm in rural Kenya, Wangari inherits a love of nature from her parents. She excels at school.

1940

1960

1969

Nobel Peace Prize

Wangari is awarded the Nobel Peace Prize for her work in the Green Belt Movement, and for speaking out about corruption in Kenya. She is the first African woman, and first environmentalist, to receive the award.

A billion trees

Wangari's autobiography, Unbowed, is published. She leads the United Nations' Billion Tree Campaign, designed to help combat climate change. This later becomes the Trillion Tree Campaign.

Death and legacy

Wangari dies of cancer. Ban Ki-moon, Secretary-General of the United Nations, pays tribute to her as a globally recognized champion for human rights and women's empowerment". The Wangari Maathai Foundation is set up in 2015 to support projects that continue her work.

2011

2006

2004

Political career

Wangari works with pro-democracy groups to unite opposition against President Moi's corrupt government. In 2002, Moi is forced into holding fair elections. Wangari runs as a parliamentary candidate. She is elected to parliament with 98 per cent of the vote.

1990s

Green Belt Movement

Wangari comes up with a simple solution: to plant more trees. She sets up the Green Belt Movement as part of the NCWK. The movement organizes women to start planting trees, and trains them in forestry, bee-keeping, and other trades that can earn income.

Protest

Wangari protests against the construction of a huge skyscraper on public park land in Nairobi. Her campaign forces the project's cancellation. She is later arrested and imprisoned, but is released and imprisoned, put pressure on the Kenyan government.

1989

Nobel Peace Prize winners

The Nobel Peace Prize has been awarded annually since 1901 to individuals or organizations who have done work to promote friendship between nations.

Kofi Annan (1938–2018)

A Ghanian diplomat, Kofi Annan served as Secretary-General of the United Nations from 1997 to 2006. In 2001, both Annan and the UN were jointly awarded the Nobel Peace Prize for their work to try to secure a more peaceful world.

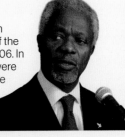

Leymah Gbowee (b.1972)

Leymah Gbowee is a Liberian peace and women's rights activist. She was a joint award winner of the Nobel Peace Prize in 2011. She brought together Christian and Muslim women to help bring an end to 14 years of devastating civil war in Liberia.

Tawakkol Karman (b.1979)

A women's rights activist from Yemen, Tawakkol Karman was also a recipient of the 2011 Nobel Peace Prize. She co-founded Women Journalists Without Chains in 2005 to support democracy and free speech in Yemen.

1987

1986

1977

1976

Opposition

Wangari's support for women's rights and environmental reform brings her into conflict with the Kenyan government run by President Daniel arap Moi. The dictatorship run by President government forces her to step down from her role at the NCWK.

International campaign

As the organization becomes increasingly successful, it establishes the Pan-African Green Belt Movement. About 40 delegates from other African countries travel to Kenya to learn how to set up similar programmes.

Activism

Wangari joins the National Council of Women of Kenya (NCWK), an organization of women from rural communities. She discovers that the government is encouraging farmers to cut down forests to grow crops for export instead of food for Kenyans. Cutting down trees is harming the nutrients in the soil, causing food shortages and damaging the environment.

Muhammad Ali

Boxing champion Muhammad Ali (1942–2016) was one of the greatest sportspeople the world has ever seen. Charismatic, witty, and courageous, he was an outspoken advocate for justice and equality, and an important icon for African Americans.

1942

"[My mother] taught us to love people and treat everybody with kindness. She taught us it was wrong to be prejudiced or hate."

Quoted in *Muhammad Ali, His Life and Times* by Thomas Hauser (1992)

Muhammad is born Cassius Marcellus Clay in Louisville, Kentucky. The eldest son of Cassius and Odessa Clay, he is the descendant of enslaved people and grows up in a segregated neighborhood.

1954

"My bike got stolen and I started boxing, and it was like God telling me that boxing was my responsibility."

Quoted in *Muhammad Ali, His Life and Times* by Thomas Hauser (1992)

When Cassius has his bike stolen, he tells the policeman, Joe E. Martin, he's going to "whup" the thief. Martin, the organizer of a boxing club, persuades him to learn to box instead.

1964

"Float like a butterfly, sting like a bee. Rumble, young man, rumble."

Speaking before fighting Sonny Liston (1964)

By February 1964, Cassius has won 19 fights without defeat. He is tall; physically imposing; quick; and full of charm, wit, and charisma. At 22, he defeats reigning champ Sonny Liston and is crowned world heavyweight champion for the first time.

1960

"When I won at the Olympics, that sealed it: I was the champ."

Interview with Oprah Winfrey (2001)

Cassius is chosen for the US Olympic boxing team. After winning three bouts in the qualifying round, he wins the gold medal in the final. The world takes notice. He turns professional two months later.

1954

"I never said I was the smartest. I said I was the greatest."

After taking an Army intelligence test (1964)

Young Cassius is no scholar, and can scarcely read or write when he leaves high school. During his six-year career as an amateur boxer, he wins title after title, including the Kentucky Golden Gloves annual competition six times.

1964

"Cassius Clay is a slave name ... I am Muhammad Ali, a free name— it means 'beloved of God.'"

Statement to the US media (1964)

In March, Cassius announces his conversion to Islam, and changes his name to Muhammad Ali. The US is simmering with racial tension, and his decision turns some white Americans against him.

1967

"If I thought the war was going to bring freedom and equality to 22 million of my people they wouldn't have to draft me, I'd join tomorrow."

Quoted in *Redemption Song* by Mike Marquseet (1999)

For religious reasons, Muhammad refuses to join the US Army to fight in the Vietnam War. He is arrested, stripped of his world title, and his boxing license is suspended. He is banned for three years. To millions of African Americans and other oppressed peoples, however, he becomes an unofficial spokesperson.

1971

"We all have to take defeats in life."

Interview on NBC News after losing to Joe Frazier (1971)

In his first big fight after returning to boxing, Muhammad and Joe Frazier compete in "The Fight of the Century" in New York. In the final round, Frazier's left hook knocks Muhammad down but he lifts himself from the canvas to continue fighting. Frazier emerges the victor on points, inflicting Muhammad's first defeat.

1974

"That all you got, George?"

Whispering in the ear of George Foreman during Round 7 of the "Rumble in the Jungle" (1974)

After losing his heavyweight title the year before, Muhammad—now 32—goes into a clash in Zaire (modern-day Democratic Republic of the Congo) against the undefeated champion, George Foreman, as the underdog. A billion people worldwide watch on TV as he downs Foreman in the eighth round and wins with a knockout. It is one of the greatest sporting contests of the 20th century.

2016

"Your soul and your spirit never dies."

TV interview in the UK (1977)

In 1996, Muhammad lights the Olympic cauldron during the opening ceremony of the Olympic Games in Atlanta. Fans are shocked at his frail appearance. He spends much of the following two decades out of the public eye. He dies, aged 74, in Phoenix, Arizona, and is mourned throughout the world.

1984

"Service to others is the rent you pay for your room here on earth."

Interview with *Time* magazine (1978)

Muhammad retires from boxing in 1981. Three years later, he is diagnosed with Parkinson's disease, a degenerative disease of the brain. He dedicates the rest of his life to helping others.

1975

"He could have whupped any fighter in the world, except me."

After fighting Frazier in Manila (1978)

In Manila, the capital of the Philippines, Muhammad again meets Frazier in a fight of unrelenting aggression. Fearing for their fighter's safety, Frazier's trainers end the fight between rounds 14 and 15. Muhammad wins, but he is also exhausted and is just about to retire from the fight.

Shirin Ebadi

A lawyer, writer, and university professor, Shirin Ebadi (b.1947) has fought tirelessly for human rights and has campaigned to stop discrimination against women and children. She was the first woman to become a judge in Iran, and went on to win the Nobel Peace Prize in 2003 for her work.

Ayatollah Ruhollah Khomeini (1902–1989)

An Islamic scholar and teacher who became the Supreme Leader of the Islamic Republic of Iran, Ayatollah Khomeini was imprisoned for opposing the rule of the Shah (the Iranian king) and later sent into exile, where he campaigned for a religious government in Iran. In 1979, the Shah fled Iran, fearing a revolution, and Khomeini returned home. The religious state he helped set up continues to rule Iran today.

Forced to step down

The country's new leaders force Shirin and the other female judges to step down from their roles. She is made a clerk, a very junior role, in the court that she once ran.

1979   1980s

Writing

Shirin and her colleagues protest about losing their jobs, but are ignored. She takes early retirement and uses her free time to write books and articles.

Revolution in Iran

A religious leader, Ayatollah Khomeini, takes control of Iran after the Iranian king is overthrown. The Quran becomes the basis of Iranian law. Women's roles are restricted and they lose many of their rights.

1979

Breaking barriers

She officially begins working as a judge, which makes her the first woman to become a judge in Iran. Shirin continues her studies, and gains her law doctorate two years later.

1969

Tehran University

Shirin wins a place at the Faculty of Law at Tehran University and three years later, graduates with a law degree. She immediately applies for a six-month placement at the Department of Justice.

1965

Childhood

Shirin Ebadi is born to a middle-class family in Hamadan, Iran. A year later, they move to the capital, Tehran. Her father works at Tehran University while her mother looks after Shirin and her brother and sisters.

1947

Scales of justice

Scales have been a symbol of justice since ancient times. They represent how evidence should be weighed, and how both sides of a legal case must be considered, and treated equally. This illustration is based on a set of scales that Shirin Ebadi owns.

A lawyer's license

After several attempts, she finally obtains a license to practice law. As a lawyer, she takes on many important cases. She defends women who have been treated unfairly by the Iranian government.

Jailed

Shirin shares evidence in court that connects government officials to the murders of students at the University of Tehran. She is jailed for three weeks and barred from practicing law for five years.

Supporting children's rights

She sets up the Association for Support of Children's Rights, which has thousands of members and runs a hotline for people to report abuse. She is the organization's president for five years.

1992   1995   1999

2001

Human Rights Defense Center

She helps set up a center to defend the human rights of people discriminated against in Iran. The government raids her office in 2008.

2002

A new law

Iranian mothers are not allowed to look after their children if they get divorced. After a young girl is killed by her father and stepmother, Shirin helps write a new law that forbids all forms of violence against children. It is passed by the Iranian parliament.

The Nobel Peace Prize

Shirin wins the Nobel Peace Prize for democracy and human rights," especially the "struggle for the rights of women and children."

2003

One of the most powerful women

Shirin is listed among the "Top 100 Most Powerful Women" in US business magazine *Forbes*. In 2006, the government of France awards her the *Légion d'honneur*, the country's highest award.

2004

Exile

Life becomes increasingly difficult for Shirin. She receives death threats, and pro-government demonstrators attack her home. She goes into exile in the United Kingdom, but continues to fight for change in Iran.

2009

> "An interpretation of Islam that is in harmony with equality and democracy is an authentic expression of faith."
>
> **Shirin Ebadi,**
> *Iran Awakening* (2006)

1-000100

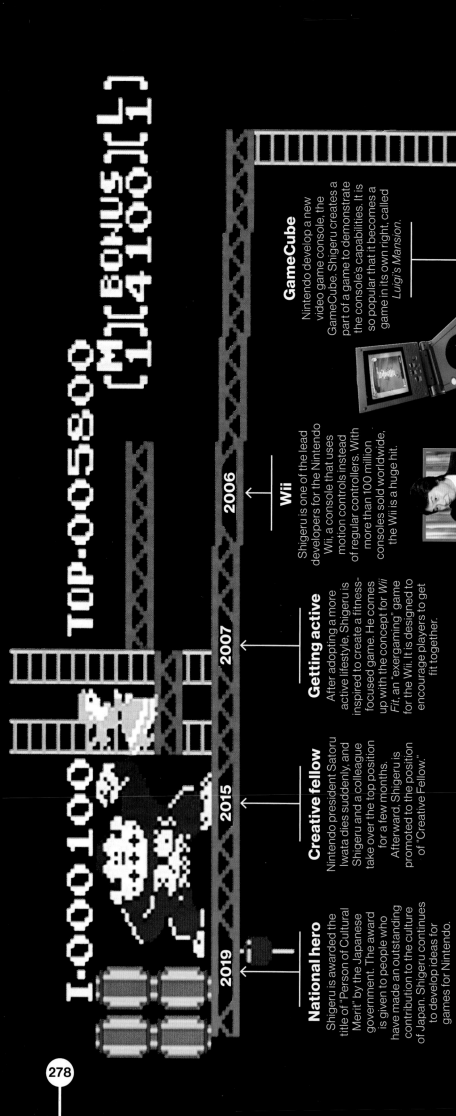

Donkey Kong

Shigeru is commissioned to design his first arcade game. Inspired by the film *King Kong*, he develops the game *Donkey Kong*. It is a platform game—a game in which players control a character that jumps over obstacles and climbs ladders to get to the next level.

1981

Mario Bros.

Shigeru creates the character of Mario, an action-seeking Italian plumber based on the jumping character from *Donkey Kong*. Mario becomes the star of Shigeru's next game, *Mario Bros.* Mario will appear in more than 200 video games.

1983

The Legend of Zelda

Nintendo make their own home video game console, and ask Shigeru to make a game for it. He creates *The Legend of Zelda*, an action-adventure game that goes on to sell more than 9 million copies.

1986

Nintendo 64

Nintendo release the Nintendo 64, their first video game console with 3-D graphics. Shigeru creates *Super Mario 64*, an open world–style game where Mario can move in any direction.

1996

GameCube

Nintendo develop a new video game console, the GameCube. Shigeru creates a part of a game to demonstrate the consoles capabilities. It is so popular that it becomes a game in its own right, called *Luigi's Mansion.*

2001

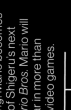

Wii

Shigeru is one of the lead developers for the Nintendo Wii, a console that uses motion controls instead of regular controllers. With more than 100 million consoles sold worldwide, the Wii is a huge hit.

2006

Getting active

After adopting a more active lifestyle, Shigeru is inspired to create a fitness-focused game. He comes up with the concept for *Wii Fit*, an "exergaming" game for the Wii. It is designed to encourage players to get fit together.

2007

Creative fellow

Nintendo president Satoru Iwata dies suddenly, and Shigeru and a colleague take over the top position for a few months. Afterward, Shigeru is promoted to the position of "Creative Fellow."

2015

National hero

Shigeru is awarded the title of "Person of Cultural Merit" by the Japanese government. The award is given to people who have made an outstanding contribution to the culture of Japan. Shigeru continues to develop ideas for games for Nintendo.

2019

Shigeru Miyamoto

One of the great pioneers of the video game industry, Japan's Shigeru Miyamoto (b. 1952) introduced imagination and adventure into the world of gaming. He has created some of the most popular video game series, such as *Donkey Kong*, *Mario Bros.*, and *The Legend of Zelda*.

A rural childhood

Shigeru is born in Sonobe, a rural town near Kyoto, in Japan. His parents do not have much money, but Shigeru keeps himself entertained by drawing and making puppets. He likes to explore the forests and caves in the countryside.

1952

Crossroads

He studies at Kanazawa College of Art, but finds it hard to find a job after finishing. Shigeru is interested in *manga* (Japanese comic books), and he considers becoming a *manga* artist.

1975

Nintendo

Shigeru's father manages to get him an interview with Hiroshi Yamauchi, president of the video game and toy company Nintendo. After presenting some ideas he has for toys, Shigeru is hired as an apprentice.

1977

Moving on up

Shigeru becomes Nintendo's first artist. He creates art for *Sheriff,* Nintendo's first arcade game. In 1980, he designs artworks for another arcade game, *Radar Scope.*

1978

Gaming pioneers

Video games have been incredibly popular since the invention of the first one, a simple tennis-based game, in 1958. As computer technology improves, games have become more creative, fun, diverse, and interesting.

Ralph H. Baer (1922–2014)

A German-American engineer, inventor and game developer, Ralph H. Baer created the first home video game console, the Magnavox Odyssey, in 1972. He helped inspire *Pong,* one of the first hit arcade games.

Sid Meier (b. 1954)

Canadian-American video game developer, designer, and producer, Sid Meier is the cofounder of MicroProse. His company produced strategy games that require players to solve problems, such as *Civilization* and *X-COM.*

Satoshi Tajiri (b. 1965)

Japanese video game designer Satoshi Tajiri is best known as the creator of the *Pokémon* series for Nintendo. Tajiri's childhood love of collecting insects inspired him to create a series of games based on the idea of collecting different characters.

Early life

Benazir is born and grows up in Karachi, Pakistan, the eldest daughter of Zulfikar Bhutto, a politician. At 16, she studies politics, philosophy, and economics at Radcliffe College in the US. In 1973, Benazir attends Oxford University in the UK, to study international law and diplomacy.

House arrest

Benazir and her mother Nusrat are placed under house arrest to prevent them from rallying support for Zulfikar. He is accused of conspiracy to commit murder, and after a trial, he is sentenced to death and executed in 1979.

Democratic hope

From London, Benazir criticizes General Zia's military regime and its defiance of civil and human rights in Pakistan. Advising her supporters against violence, she advocates for change through democracy.

1953   1977   1977   1979   1984

Military coup

After graduating from university, Benazir returns to Pakistan. A few days later her father, now prime minister of Pakistan, is removed by General Muhammad Zia-ul-Haq in a military coup (a seizure of power by the army). Martial law (military rule) is imposed, bringing democracy in the country to a standstill.

In exile

Benazir and Nusrat experience various forms of harassment from the government, from house arrest to long periods in prison. They both develop serious health issues that require medical attention. In 1984, in order to get treatment, they agree to exile themselves (leave Pakistan and not return), and move to London, England.

Benazir Bhutto

Overcoming several personal tragedies to become the first female leader of an Islamic country, Benazir Bhutto (1953–2007) was a divisive figure in Pakistan. To her enemies, her liberal and modernizing political ideas were dangerous, but her supporters saw her as a beacon of hope—a promoter of both democracy and women's rights in a politically male-dominated country.

Return
Martial law is lifted in December 1985. Benazir returns to Pakistan to campaign in the general election. Her reappearance on the Pakistani political scene shocks many when she calls for President Zia's resignation.

Covert campaigns
Benazir works to reduce the president's powers, but her rivals work with Pakistan's intelligence agency to set up an operation to remove her from power. A few months later the president dismisses her from office.

Conspiracy theory
Murtaza, Benazir's brother, is killed by the police. The siblings had fallen out as Murtaza felt he should lead the PPP. Many people suggest Benazir was behind the assassination. The allegations spur the president to dismiss her from office on corruption charges.

Political alliance
Benazir returns to Pakistan and joins the Alliance for the Restoration of Democracy, an alliance between the PPP and Pakistan Muslim League (PML-N), the two main political parties in Pakistan. She begins negotiations with President Musharraf to restore Pakistan to a civilian-led democracy.

1985   1986   1988   1990   1993   1996   1997   2006   2007

Party leader
Benazir's youngest brother, Shahnawaz, dies in mysterious circumstances. Many believe he was poisoned. During this period she becomes the leader of the Pakistan People's Party (PPP)—the political party her father set up in 1967.

All change
President Zia dies suddenly. Benazir's party win the most seats in the election, and she becomes the new prime minister. Though the president blocks many of her ideas, she is able to pass laws that improve human rights and women's rights.

Second term in office
Initiating an anticorruption campaign, Benazir is reelected for a second time as prime minister. A key priority is to modernize Pakistan by improving housing and health care, and reducing hunger.

Second exile
Benazir flees Pakistan before her corruption case goes to trial. During her exile, she continues to lead the PPP and to campaign for the restoration of democracy in Pakistan.

Assassination
Benazir plans to run in the 2008 elections. However, she is killed when her car is attacked while she is campaigning. An investigation is launched, but the identities of the people behind the attack remain a mystery.

Political obstacles
Conservative President Ghulam Khan often stopped Benazir's attempts to pass laws.

> **"I put my life in danger and came here because I feel this country is in danger."**
> **Benazir Bhutto,**
> **speaking on the day she was assassinated (2007)**

Oprah Winfrey

Rising from unrelenting poverty to become the "queen of all media," Oprah Winfrey (b. 1954) is one of the world's most influential people. She was the first African American multi-billionaire and is considered the greatest black philanthropist (charity-giver) in US history.

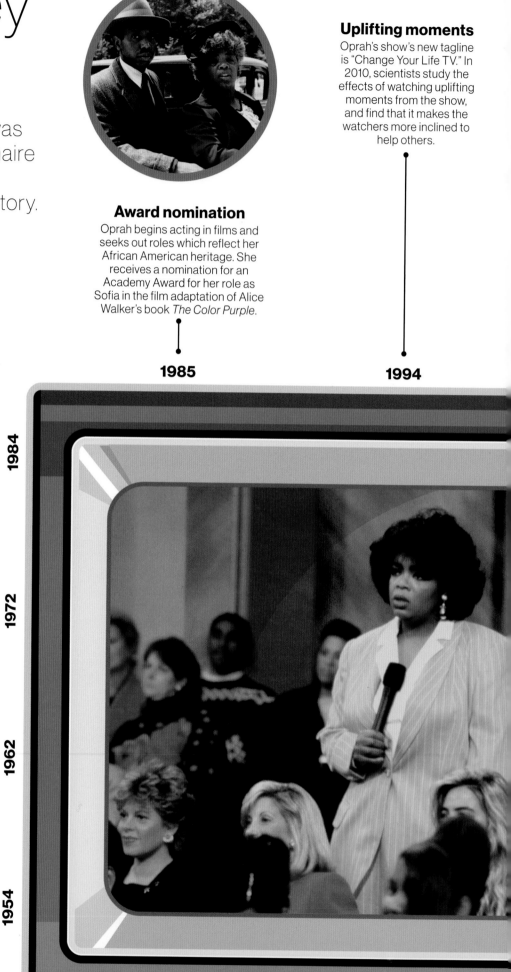

Award nomination

Oprah begins acting in films and seeks out roles which reflect her African American heritage. She receives a nomination for an Academy Award for her role as Sofia in the film adaptation of Alice Walker's book *The Color Purple*.

1985

Uplifting moments

Oprah's show's new tagline is "Change Your Life TV." In 2010, scientists study the effects of watching uplifting moments from the show, and find that it makes the watchers more inclined to help others.

1994

The Oprah Winfrey Show

On the show, Oprah discusses health, politics, and spirituality. Millions of viewers tune in each week to watch regular people and celebrities being interviewed by Oprah. The show is renamed *The Oprah Winfrey Show* in 1986, and runs for 25 seasons. Oprah sets up her own media company, Harpo, also in 1986.

1984

Radio and TV

Oprah begins announcing the news at the radio station, making her one of the first black female news anchors in the US. She works her way through local radio and TV stations. Eventually, she begins working on the morning show of a Chicago TV station.

1972

A new start

Oprah is abused by relatives in Mississippi. She leaves to live with her father in Tennessee, where she excels in her school studies. She begins to work in a local radio station during her final years in high school, and sticks with it into her early years at college.

1962

Potato-sack dresses

Born in Mississippi, Oprah is named "Orpah" at birth, but people found "Oprah" easier to pronounce. She is raised by her grandmother in rural poverty. They are so poor that Oprah wears dresses made from potato sack fabric. A bright and inquisitive child, she can recite verses from the Bible by heart at three years old.

1954

Book club

Oprah starts a book segment on her show called "Oprah's Book Club" to motivate her audience to read more often. Books that appear on her reading list top best-seller charts and sell millions of extra copies.

1996

LGBTQ+ support

Another effect of Oprah's show is that it brings stories about LGBTQ+ (lesbian, gay, bisexual, transgender, and queer) communities to the general public. Oprah invites comedian Ellen DeGeneres onto her show to give her a platform to discuss the reaction to Ellen coming out as a lesbian.

1997

Pioneering change

Oprah has paved the way for black Americans and other minority groups in television, film, and literature.

Alice Walker (b.1944)

An African American novelist, activist, and Pulitzer Prize winner. Alice Walker coined the term "womanist" for black feminists or feminists of color. Her most famous book is *The Color Purple*, which tells the story of poor black women in the American south in the 1930s.

Ellen DeGeneres (b.1958)

An American comedian, actor, and talk show host, Ellen was the first ever openly gay person to star in their own sitcom. She now hosts her own talk show where she interviews celebrities and regular people with special stories and talents.

1998

2007

2008

2018

Oprah's Angels

Oprah sets up Oprah's Angel Network, which provides grants and funding to nonprofit organizations. The network raises more than $80 million for charity programs from initial donations. After Hurricane Katrina (which hit the southern coast of the US, and caused 1,200 deaths) in 2005, the organization raised more than $11 million toward relief efforts.

Empowering change

Highlighting the HIV/AIDS crisis among South African children, Oprah travels around the country raising money and giving gifts. Understanding that education is the key to changing lives and enabling positive change in society, she establishes the Oprah Winfrey Leadership Academy for Girls near Johannesburg. It provides educational opportunities for girls from disadvantaged backgrounds.

Endorsing Obama

Oprah publicly endorses Barack Obama in his run to become US president in 2008. Election experts later credit the move with securing Obama up to 1.6 million extra votes from Oprah's viewers. In 2013, Oprah is awarded the Presidential Medal of Freedom as a result of her significant cultural contributions to society.

Museum exhibit

The National Museum of African American History and Culture opens a year-long special exhibit called "Watching Oprah" that centers around the profound cultural influence Oprah continues to have on the American public through television.

Rigoberta Menchú

Rigoberta Menchú (b. 1959) was a witness to the violence of the Guatemalan Civil War, and her political beliefs were formed by the turbulent times in her country. She became a vocal spokesperson against the atrocities committed against indigenous Guatemalans, and has dedicated her life to the pursuit of equality for her culture and people.

Flight to Mexico
The army murders Rigoberta's mother and brother. She flees to Mexico as it is too dangerous to stay in Guatemala. Rigoberta joins the United Nations Working Group on Indigenous Populations, who create a draft declaration of the rights of indigenous people. The declaration will be adopted by most nations in 2007.

Unrest
Born into the K'iche' Maya culture in Guatemala, Rigoberta grows up in a time of civil unrest between the government's ruling military regime and rebel groups supported by the country's indigenous people. A civil war breaks out in 1960, which leads to government-committed crimes against indigenous people.

Domestic work
Rigoberta spends a few months working as a domestic servant for a wealthy family. This period shows her the deep divide between indigenous and nonindigenous people in Guatemala.

Joining the union
She joins the Committee of the Peasant Union, a national group trying to secure basic labor rights for indigenous people. But efforts to improve their lives are seen as plots against the government, and are dealt with harshly by the military.

Peaceful protests
Rigoberta participates in nonviolent protests, and helps teach indigenous people to resist military oppression. During one protest, her father is killed in a fire started by the army at the Spanish embassy in Guatemala City.

Campaigning in exile
The Guatemalan authorities try to stop Rigoberta's protests by accusing her of being a guerrilla (rebel fighter). When that doesn't work, they make several attempts on her life, all of which fail.

1959   **1972**   **1979**   **1980**   **1981**   **1982**

Mayan fabrics
Traditional handmade fabrics play an important role in Mayan culture. Menchú always wears richly embroidered, multicolored garments to show the strength of indigenous traditions.

> **"I dream of the day when the relationship between the indigenous peoples and other peoples is strengthened."**
> **Rigoberta Menchú, Nobel lecture (1992)**

Nobel Peace Prize
Rigoberta receives the Nobel Peace Prize for her efforts to achieve justice for indigenous Guatemalans, and for her work toward cultural reconciliation (bringing cultures together) between indigenous and nonindigenous people of Guatemala.

Pursuing justice
Rigoberta files charges in a Spanish court against several of Guatemala's military officials. She accuses them of genocide (the mass murder of a cultural group), torture, and state terrorism against the nearly 200,000 people who were killed during the civil war.

Promoting peace
Guatemala's president, Óscar Berger, invites Rigoberta to join his government to help carry out Guatemala's peace agreement. She helps implement the parts of the agreement that relate to justice and reconciliation.

International focus
While in Paris, France, Rigoberta tells her life story to Venezuelan anthropologist Elisabeth Burgos-Debray in a series of interviews that become the basis of her autobiography. Her book *I, Rigoberta Menchú* focuses international attention on the atrocities committed during the civil war in Guatemala.

Foundation
Rigoberta returns to Guatemala to set up the Rigoberta Menchú Tum Foundation, which fights for justice for indigenous Guatemalans. After raging for 36 years, the Guatemalan Civil War ends in 1996 with a peace deal between the government and the guerrilla groups.

Continuing the fight
Rigoberta continues to be a voice for those who lack representation across the world. In recent years, she has turned her attention toward medical issues by fighting to make lifesaving cures cheaper and easier to obtain.

1983 **1992** **1993** **1999** **2004** **2019**

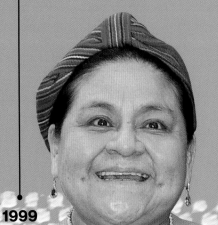

Marriage

He marries Michelle Robinson, a lawyer he meets while working for a Chicago law firm. They settle in Chicago's South Side and later have two daughters, Malia and Sasha.

Writer

Barack writes *Dreams from My Father*, a memoir of his childhood in which he explores issues such as race and identity. It is highly praised. In 2006, he publishes a second book, *The Audacity of Hope*.

Entering politics

Barack runs as a Democratic candidate for the Illinois State Senate. He is elected and serves eight years as a senator, debating and voting on laws for the state of Illinois.

Obamamania!

Barack runs for election to the US Senate in Washington, D.C. Young, charming, and eloquent, he appeals to a new generation of voters, and his speeches draw huge crowds. He is elected with 70 percent of the vote.

Law school

After deciding to become a lawyer, Barack enrolls at the prestigious Harvard Law School. He becomes the first African American president of the *Harvard Law Review*, an important law journal.

Kenya

Barack travels to Kenya for the first time to meet his father's family. He visits the grave of his father, who died in a car crash in 1982.

New York and Chicago

After graduating from Columbia University in New York City, Barack moves to Chicago, Illinois. He takes up a post as a community organizer, helping people who live on low incomes.

Barry

Barack is born in Hawaii to an American mother, Ann Dunham, and a Kenyan father, Barack Obama, Sr. As a kid, he is known as Barry. From the age of 10, he lives with his grandparents in Honolulu, Hawaii.

1961   **1983**   **1987**   **1988**   **1992**   **1995**   **1996**   **2004**

E PLURIBUS UNUM

Presidential seal

The Seal of the President of the United States is used as a symbol of the presidency. The seal shows a bald eagle—the national bird of the US—holding arrows and an olive branch to symbolize war and peace. When translated, the text in Latin reads "out of many, one"—an official motto of the country.

Barack Obama

Barack Obama (b.1961) was the first African American to be elected president of the US. A charismatic and articulate president, he introduced affordable health care, worked to improve the US' reputation abroad, and committed to tackling global warming.

Michelle Obama (b.1964)
Chicago-born lawyer and campaigner Michelle Obama pursued a successful career in law and city administration before becoming First Lady. She has campaigned on issues such as poverty, healthy living, and education, and published a best-selling memoir, *Becoming*, in 2018.

44th US President
Barack runs for the US presidency and campaigns with a message of hope and change. He wins the election and becomes the first African American to become US president. He must hit the ground running as the US is suffering from an economic crisis, with many people losing their jobs, savings, and even homes.

Nobel Prize winner
The new president is awarded the Nobel Peace Prize for his efforts to strengthen cooperation between nations. Much of his early presidency is spent trying to limit the damage of the economic crisis, and dealing with the wars in Afghanistan and Iraq that started before he became president.

Obamacare
Despite opposition, Barack pushes through the Affordable Care Act, popularly known as "Obamacare." Its aim is to make health care available to the poorest US citizens.

Second term
Barack is elected to a second term as president. He makes combating global warming a priority. He signs a major international agreement to reduce carbon emissions, the main contributor to global warming.

Leaving office
After his second term ends, Barack returns to private life. Both Michelle and Barack agree to write autobiographies. Barack occasionally gives speeches on issues that he worked on during his presidency, such as global warming.

2008
2009
2010
2012
2017

The first civilization

The Sumerians of southern Mesopotamia (modern-day Iraq) build the world's first cities. Sumer (the land of the Sumerians) is considered to be the first civilization (advanced society), as the people develop writing, a monarchy, and organized religion.

Taxation

Ancient Egyptians are the first people to pay taxes. The vizier (prime minister) appoints tax collectors to count how much grain and livestock each person owns. The Egyptians have no money system—instead people pay their tax in labor or grain.

Caste system

The caste (class) system develops in India. It divides people of the Hindu faith into four main castes: priests, warriors, merchants, and laborers. As the system develops, every aspect of an individual's life is increasingly decided by which caste they belong to, from the jobs they are allowed to do, to the person they are allowed to marry.

c.3300 BCE

c.3000 BCE

c.1000 BCE

Citizens through time

Most people automatically become a citizen of a country the moment they are born. This gives them the right to be protected by their government and, when they are old enough, the right to vote. In return, they have to obey the laws of the country in which they live. The automatic right of citizens to these freedoms is a modern idea, however. In the past, people have had to fight for rights that many today take for granted.

Declaration of Independence

After successfully ending British rule, American colonists create the Declaration of Independence. It states that "all men are created equal" and promises the right to "Life, Liberty, and the pursuit of Happiness." At this time, these statements do not apply to women and enslaved people.

1776

Revolution

Fed up with rising food prices, French people revolt against the king and his total power over France. The new French parliament publishes the Declaration of the Rights of Man, which guarantees citizens protection under law.

Votes for women

After a campaign by thousands of women lasting many years, New Zealand becomes the first country to grant women the right to vote. The US, Germany, and the UK will follow New Zealand's lead after World War I.

Communism

Ordinary Russians violently overthrow the Russian emperor, and communist revolutionaries seize power. Communists believe that all property and wealth should be shared by everybody. Russia becomes the first communist state, and later joins with other states to become the Soviet Union.

1789

1893

1917

Greek democracy

The ancient Greek city-state of Athens develops the world's first democracy, where citizens participate in politics. Several times a year, more than 6,000 men meet to vote on important matters. Women, enslaved people, foreign people, and children are excluded from taking part.

c.508 BCE

Law code

The first emperor of China, Qin Shi Huang, creates one of the first law codes (systems). Believing that humans are motivated only by their own interests, he establishes a harsh legal code in order to create and maintain order in society.

c.221 BCE

Roman togas

Male citizens in ancient Rome wear different types of clothing depending on their social class. Regular citizens dress in a plain white toga (loose garment), while purple togas are worn only by emperors. Enslaved people are only allowed to wear simple tunics.

c.100 CE

Feudal system

Medieval European society is organized according to the feudal system. The king gives lands to his noble lords, who in return vow to provide armies to protect him. A class of knights (mounted soldiers) fight on their lords' behalf. At the bottom of the pile are serfs, unpaid laborers who work the land to produce food in exchange for protection from those above them.

c.1000

The rise of nations

The Peace of Westphalia brings the Thirty Years War, a religious conflict in Europe, to a close. The agreement establishes, for the first time, fixed geographical boundaries for many of the countries involved. This leads to the idea of the nation state—the way we think about countries today.

1648

Bushidō

Armored warriors called samurai have high status in Edo-period Japan. They live by a code of honor called *bushidō*, which combines refined behavior with violence. Ideally, the perfect warrior should be as capable of writing a poem as they are of fighting an opponent.

c.1603

Matriarchy

For the Minangkabau people of Indonesia, women have a more prominent role in society than men. A woman is the head of the household, and passes her property to her daughter.

c.1350

Magna Carta

English nobles force the unpopular King John to sign the *Magna Carta* ("Great Charter"). It takes away some of the king's powers, and promises the nobles some rights. It is the first step toward making the monarchy answerable to law, and leads to the end of the feudal system.

1215

Human rights

The United Nations (UN) creates the Universal Declaration of Human Rights. This aims to secure basic rights—such as the right to life, freedom, and security—for every citizen in the world. Neglect and abuse of human rights, however, still continues.

1948

Civil rights

In the US, African Americans face segregation—meaning they are not allowed to have the same rights as white people or use many of the same facilities. Years of nonviolent protest and campaigning eventually leads to positive changes in the law, as segregation is banned.

1954

Citizens of nowhere

War and persecution has led to around two million people across the world becoming stateless. Stateless people are not protected by any country. Many are refugees, who often face difficult journeys in order to reach safety.

2015

Digital citizens

People are now able to use the internet to interact with others they may never meet in real life. Being a good digital citizen is all about being polite, truthful, and respectful of others' privacy.

2020

J.K. Rowling

Probably the most popular writer of her era, J.K. Rowling (b. 1965) has sold more than 500 million books, making her one of the top-selling authors of all time. Her books have introduced the wonderful world of reading to millions of children, and inspired a series of blockbuster movies.

Early years

Joanne Rowling (known as Jo) is born and raised in Gloucestershire in southwest England, and in South Wales. As a child, she loves to write fantasy tales.

1965

Movie adaptation

A major film company decides to adapt the books into a film series. The films star Daniel Radcliffe as Harry Potter, Emma Watson as Hermione Granger, and Rupert Grint as Ron Weasley.

2001

Harry Potter takes off

Harry returns to battle the heir of Slytherin in the second book in the series, *Harry Potter and the Chamber of Secrets*. As the success of the series grows, it seems as if every child is talking about the boy wizard with the lightning bolt scar, a snowy owl called Hedwig, and a "sorting hat."

1998

Fastest-selling book

The final book in the series, *Harry Potter and the Deathly Hallows*, sees Harry defeat Lord Voldemort once and for all. The book breaks all records by selling more than 10 million copies within 24 hours of its release.

2007

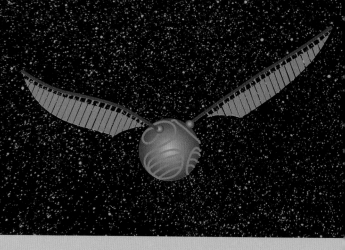

Companion of Honour

By now one of the wealthiest people in the UK, Joanne has donated millions of pounds to children's charities and medical research. Queen Elizabeth II appoints Joanne a Companion of Honour (CH) for her services to literature and philanthropy (charity).

2017

Fantastic beasts

Fantastic Beasts and Where to Find Them, a film written and produced by Joanne, premieres in New York. It features magizoologist Newt Scamander and his suitcase of fantastic beasts.

November 2016

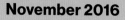

PLATFORM 9¾

A hero is born

While stuck on a train to Kings Cross Station in London, she comes up with the idea of a boy wizard called Harry Potter. In the book she goes on to write, Harry leaves Kings Cross on the *Hogwarts Express* to get to Hogwarts School of Witchcraft and Wizardry.

1990

Published author

Harry Potter and the Sorcerer's Stone—which tells the story of Harry's first year at Hogwarts— eventually finds a publisher. The publisher does not print many copies because it does not expect much interest. The book is an immediate hit. As its success grows, it wins several prizes.

1997

Getting started

Joanne begins writing the first *Harry Potter* book in Edinburgh, Scotland. Lacking childcare, she often writes in cafés with her baby daughter asleep beside her in a stroller.

1993

Crime writer

Joanne publishes the first book of a series for adults featuring a private detective who investigates crime. Instead of publishing them under the same name she used for the *Harry Potter* series, she decides to publish the series under the name Robert Galbraith, so people will not compare them to her Harry Potter books.

2013

Final film

The blockbusting series of *Harry Potter* movies concludes. Working their magic on the big screen, the *Harry Potter* movies break records as the largest-grossing film franchise in history.

CINEMA 10¢ GOOD ONLY ON DATE SOLD ADMIT ONE TK 037183 TK 037183

2011

HARRY POTTER AND THE CURSED CHILD

Harry's story continues

A theater play, *Harry Potter and the Cursed Child*, telling the story of a grown-up Harry Potter and his youngest son Albus Severus Potter, opens in London.

July 2016

Young dancer

Madhuri is born in Bombay (now Mumbai), India. She first takes an interest in dance at the age of 3, and at 9 wins a scholarship to train in Kathak, a form of Indian classical dance.

Movie debut

Madhuri plans to study microbiology, but this changes when she lands a part in a Bollywood film, "*Abodh*" ("*Innocent*"). The movie is a flop, but her performance is praised by critics.

1967

1984

Madhuri Dixit

Madhuri Dixit (b.1967) is one of the most popular and successful actors to emerge from India's Bollywood film industry. Praised both for her acting talent and her dancing skills, she has been nominated in India's annual Filmfare Awards—the Bollywood "Oscars"—a record number of times. She is also a campaigner for the rights of women and children.

1988

1990

Big breakthrough

Madhuri performs a dance to the song "*Ek Do Teen*" ("One Two Three") in the film "*Tezaab*" ("*Acid*"). The film is a huge success, and it catapults her to stardom.

First award

Madhuri wins her first Filmfare Best Actress Award for her starring role in the romantic drama "*Dil*" ("*Heart*").

Top Indian stars

The Indian film industry is the largest in the world, with Bollywood just one of many centers of film production. Films in India attract billions of people every year, and the industry has created huge stars.

Nargis (1929–1981)

One of the greatest stars of Bollywood, Nargis started out as a child actor. Her career took off with her first leading role in "*Taqdeer*" ("*Fate*") in 1943. She reached the peak of her career playing a brave, poverty-stricken woman in the epic drama *Mother India* (1957).

Meena Kumari (1933–1972)

Meena Kumari is often regarded as the greatest Indian film actor. She starred in 92 films over a 33-year career, and made history in 1963 by receiving all the Filmfare Award nominations for Best Actress for three different films. She was most famous for her tragic roles.

Sridevi (1963–2018)

Sridevi made her Bollywood debut in 1986, and went on to star in every genre of movie—from slapstick comedy to epic drama, often portraying women in difficult situations. She won three Filmfare Awards for her work.

Padma Shri Award

Madhuri is given the Padma Shri Award in recognition of her huge contribution to cinema. It is one of India's highest awards, given every year by the government on Republic Day, a national holiday.

Dance academy

Madhuri launches an online dance academy called "Dance with Madhuri." Users can learn how to dance like Madhuri by taking online classes.

Total Dhamaal

Madhuri returns to the big screen in *Total "Dhamaal"* ("*Total Blast*"), an action-adventure comedy. It is a huge success. Madhuri continues to act and dance in major films.

1992	2002	2007	2008	2011	2013	2014	2019

Dhak Dhak Girl

She gains the nickname "*Dhak Dhak Girl*" for her performance of the song "*Dhak Dhak Karne Laga*" ("*My Heart is Beating Fast*") in the movie "*Beta*" ("*Son*"). The film is the biggest hit of the year.

Devdas

Madhuri's acting and dancing in the film "*Devdas*" is well received by audiences and critics. The film is the most expensive Bollywood film ever made. It is a big success in India, and even gets noticed abroad, too.

Screen comeback

After taking a break from movies to start a family, Madhuri returns to the screen to star in "*Aaja Nachle*" ("*Come, Let's Dance*"). She plays a choreographer living in New York who returns to her hometown to save her old dance theater.

Dance judge

Madhuri's reputation as a great dancer leads to her becoming a judge for four seasons on the popular Indian TV show, "*Jhalak Dikhhla Jaa*", the Indian version of "*Strictly Come Dancing*" and "*Dancing with the Stars*".

UNICEF ambassador

She is appointed as an official supporter of the United Nations Children's Fund (UNICEF), promoting awareness of children's rights in India, especially the need for children to be protected from harm.

Dwayne Johnson

American Dwayne Johnson (b. 1972), first won fame as a professional wrestler, known as "The Rock"—a brash and entertaining character armed with many catchphrases. He later became a movie actor and a producer, and is now one of the highest-earning stars in US film history.

Acting career

After a few TV roles, Dwayne begins transitioning into a career as an actor. In his first acting role he plays his own father in an episode of the comedy That '70s Show. The following year he plays an alien gladiator who fights a crew member in an episode of Star Trek: Voyager.

"The Rock" emerges

He joins the Nation of Domination wrestling team and adopts the name "The Rock." His popularity rises as he provokes his rivals and their fans with his boastful fighting talk. In 1998, he wins the WWF championship, putting himself at the pinnacle of the professional wrestling world.

Professional debut

He begins his professional wrestling career with the World Wrestling Federation (WWF). He uses the name "Rocky Maivia," to honor both his father and his grandfather. He quickly impresses with his early contests in the organization.

Football player

While studying at the University of Miami, Dwayne joins the college's football team. A back injury later robs him of his dream of becoming a professional National Football League (NFL) player, and in 1995 he begins training as a professional wrestler.

Wrestling genes

Dwayne is born in Hayward, California. His Canadian father, Rocky Johnson, is a former professional wrestler, and his mother Ata is the daughter of Samoan-American wrestler Peter Maivia.

1972 1991 1996 1997 1999

Movie star
Dwayne makes his movie debut as the Scorpion King in the action film *The Mummy Returns*. In 2002, he returns to the role in *The Scorpion King*. The success of these films launches his acting career. He quickly becomes a top Hollywood actor, starring in hit films every year.

Samoan tattoo
A Polynesian tattooist in Hawaii completes a large tattoo covering most of Dwayne's chest and left arm. Based on a peʻa, the traditional tattoo for Samoan men, it represents his ancestors and his family history.

Luke Hobbs
Dwayne plays the role of federal agent Luke Hobbs in *Fast Five*, part of the *Fast and Furious* action movie franchise. His performance is a success, and he appears in a string of sequels and spin-off movies.

Seven Bucks Productions
He sets up Seven Bucks Productions, an entertainment production company. The name refers to seven bucks (dollars), which was all the money he had in his pocket when he gave up his football dreams.

Box-office draw
After the success of *Fast and Furious 6*, Dwayne's films for the year earn $1.3 billion at the box office. This leads to him being listed as the highest-grossing Hollywood actor for the year in *Forbes* (a business magazine), for the first time.

Moana
He is cast to voice Maui, the Polynesian trickster god, in the Disney animated movie *Moana*. He wins praise for his singing voice, and reveals that his inspiration for his performance was his Samoan grandfather, Peter Maivia.

Busy year
Dwayne appears in two huge movie remakes. He stars in *Jumanji: Welcome to the Jungle*, a fantasy adventure story that is a remake of a 1995 film, and *Baywatch*, based on the popular 1990s TV series about California lifeguards.

Mr. President
Dwayne dismisses rumors that he will run for election as US president in 2020, saying it is a job that requires years and years of experience. But the door is not shut on him running for office in the future.

2001
2003
2011
2012
2013
2016
2017
2018

> "In 1995, I had seven bucks in my pocket. I knew two things: I'm broke as hell and one day I won't be."
> **Dwayne Johnson, Twitter™ post (December 17, 2011)**

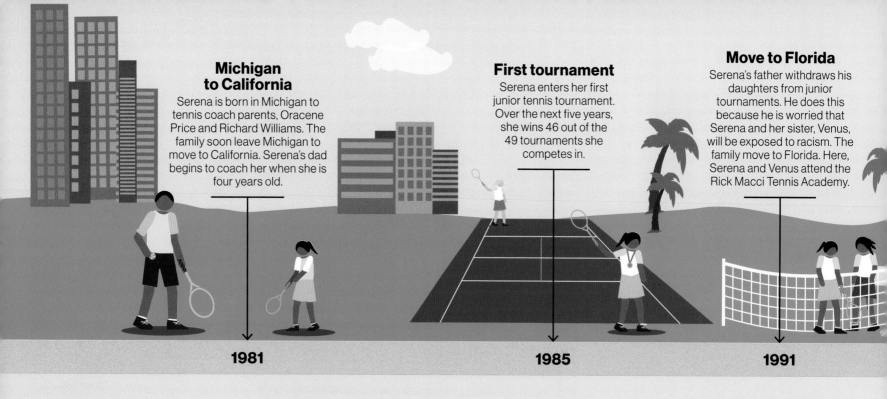

Michigan to California

Serena is born in Michigan to tennis coach parents, Oracene Price and Richard Williams. The family soon leave Michigan to move to California. Serena's dad begins to coach her when she is four years old.

1981

First tournament

Serena enters her first junior tennis tournament. Over the next five years, she wins 46 out of the 49 tournaments she competes in.

1985

Move to Florida

Serena's father withdraws his daughters from junior tournaments. He does this because he is worried that Serena and her sister, Venus, will be exposed to racism. The family move to Florida. Here, Serena and Venus attend the Rick Macci Tennis Academy.

1991

Serena Williams

One of the greatest tennis players of all time, Serena Williams (b. 1981) has won 73 singles titles, 23 doubles titles, and four gold medals at the Olympic Games. Williams' success is built on her power, agility, and mental toughness.

Tragedy strikes

After suffering from an injured knee for some time, Serena is forced to undergo surgery and takes time off to recover. A month later, her half-sister Yetunde is murdered. Serena does not return to tennis for eight months.

2003

2004

In top form

Serena returns to tennis, and wins the Australian Open in 2005. She goes on to win the US Open three years later, and by 2009, she has earned back her spot as the world's number one.

Illness

Doctors discover a blood clot in Serena's lungs. She is forced to take time away from tennis, and it is rumored that she might retire. Following surgery, her health improves, and she returns to training.

2011

Olympic winner

Serena's return means she does not miss the 2012 Olympic Games in London, UK. She takes home the gold medal for women's singles tennis by beating Maria Sharapova in the final. Her winning streak continues at the US Open, where she wins the title.

2012

Going pro

At the age of 14, Serena decides to dedicate her life to playing tennis professionally. After losing her debut professional match, she takes a break from competing and dedicates herself to training for the next two years.

Making an impact

Serena returns to competitive tennis. Aged 16, she beats professional tennis players Mary Pierce and Monica Seles at the Ameritech Cup, before losing to Lindsay Davenport in the semi-finals. At the end of a great year, she breaks into the top 100 players in the world.

1995

1997

Tennis greats

Over the past century, women's tennis has become one of the world's most popular sports. Its greatest players have become an inspiration to sports fans around the world.

Althea Gibson (1927–2003)
Described as a "forgotten pioneer," Althea Gibson was the first African American tennis player to win a tennis Grand Slam, in 1956. She won 11 Grand Slam tournaments over the course of her career.

Steffi Graf (b.1969)
Steffi Graf is the only tennis player to achieve a Golden Slam (winning four Grand Slam singles titles and an Olympic gold medal in one year). Over the course of her career, she was world number one for a record 377 weeks.

Venus Williams (b.1980)
Serena's older sister Venus is also a professional tennis player. She has won seven Grand Slam singles titles, and been ranked the world's best player three times.

1998

The "Serena Slam"

Serena wins the four Grand Slam tennis titles—the US Open, the French Open, the Australian Open, and Wimbledon. Her triumph is called the "Serena Slam" in the press. After an unbelievable year, Serena is now the number one player in the world.

Graduation

Serena signs a $12 million business deal with Puma, a sportswear company. A year later, she graduates from high school. Her tennis career goes from strength to strength, and she wins the US Open, her first major title.

2002

Engagement

Serena gets engaged to American tech business owner Alexis Ohanian. A year later, they marry and Serena gives birth to a girl, Alexis Olympia Ohanian, Jr.

Entrepreneur

Serena launches her own women's clothing company, Serena— perhaps a sign of what she wants to do when her tennis career is over.

Number one

After losing against Sabine Lisicki at Wimbledon, Serena returns to form at the US Open. She wins the title for the fifth time, and becomes the world's number one player for the sixth time in her career.

2013

2016

2018

LeBron James

Considered by many to be the greatest basketball player of all time, LeBron James (b. 1984) made his name playing for the Cleveland Cavaliers and the Miami Heat before moving on to the Los Angeles Lakers. He has been successful wherever he has played, and shows no signs of slowing down.

LeBron's Foundation

Affected by his experience of growing up in a single-parent home, he sets up the LeBron James Family Foundation. It aims to assist and empower single-parent families and children to succeed in education and daily life. He debuts with the US men's basketball team at the 2004 Olympic Games. They take home bronze medals.

First NBA final

Now captaining the team, LeBron makes his NBA finals debut with the Cleveland Cavaliers. He plays well, averaging 22 points per game across four games, but the team lose to the San Antonio Spurs.

LeBron goes big

After graduating from high school, LeBron decides to become a professional basketball player. He enlists with the National Basketball Association (NBA), and is drafted (chosen) by the Cleveland Cavaliers. He wins the NBA's "Rookie of the Year" award, given to the best new player in the league.

High school success

LeBron continues playing basketball under Walker and youth basketball coach Dru Joyce II. He joins his high school basketball team and leads them to success with three state championship wins.

Frank Walker

LeBron's life becomes more unstable. He and his mother often move homes, and he misses many days of school. LeBron's mother struggles to find work, and sends him to live with Frank Walker, one of his football coaches. Walker teaches him how to play basketball, and he joins a youth league basketball team.

American football

LeBron is playing with friends when a youth football coach, Bruce Kelker, passes by. LeBron tells Kelker that football is his favorite sport. To test LeBron's athleticism, he makes the children race. LeBron wins, and Kelker selects him to play for his youth football team.

Early life

LeBron Raymone James is born to Gloria Marie James and Anthony McClelland in Akron, Ohio. His father is absent for much of his childhood. As a young single mother, Gloria struggles to support their small family and they move often during LeBron's childhood.

2007

2004

2003

1999

1994

1992

1984

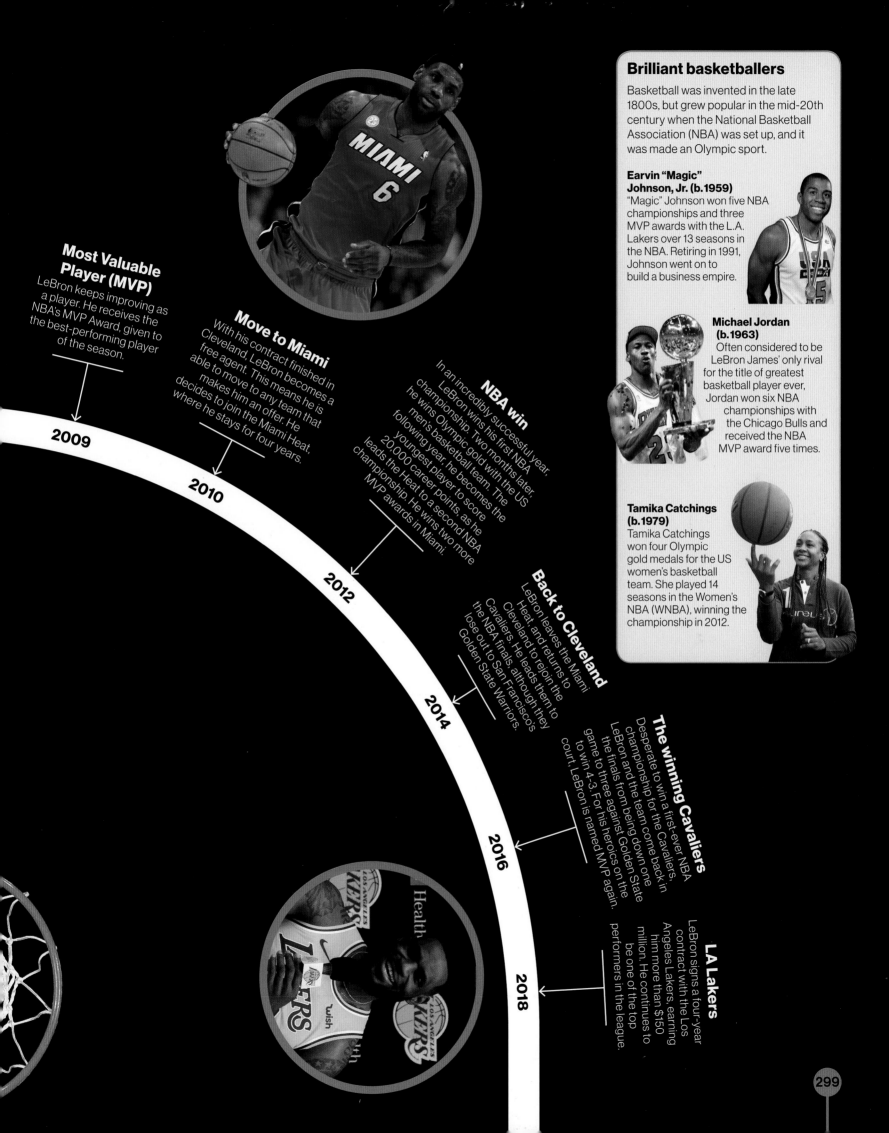

Brilliant basketballers

Basketball was invented in the late 1800s, but grew popular in the mid-20th century when the National Basketball Association (NBA) was set up, and it was made an Olympic sport.

Earvin "Magic" Johnson, Jr. (b.1959)
"Magic" Johnson won five NBA championships and three MVP awards with the L.A. Lakers over 13 seasons in the NBA. Retiring in 1991, Johnson went on to build a business empire.

Michael Jordan (b.1963)
Often considered to be LeBron James' only rival for the title of greatest basketball player ever, Jordan won six NBA championships with the Chicago Bulls and received the NBA MVP award five times.

Tamika Catchings (b.1979)
Tamika Catchings won four Olympic gold medals for the US women's basketball team. She played 14 seasons in the Women's NBA (WNBA), winning the championship in 2012.

Most Valuable Player (MVP)
LeBron keeps improving as a player. He receives the NBA's MVP Award, given to the best-performing player of the season.

Move to Miami
With his contract finished in Cleveland, LeBron becomes a free agent. This means he is able to move to any team that makes him an offer. He decides to join the Miami Heat, where he stays for four years.

NBA win
In an incredibly successful year, LeBron wins his first NBA championship. Two months later, he wins Olympic gold with the US men's basketball team. The following year, he becomes the youngest player to score 20,000 career points, as he leads the Heat to a second NBA championship. He wins two more MVP awards in Miami.

Back to Cleveland
LeBron leaves the Miami Heat, and returns to Cleveland to rejoin the Cavaliers. He leads them to the NBA finals, although they lose out to San Francisco's Golden State Warriors.

The winning Cavaliers
Desperate to win a first-ever NBA championship for the Cavaliers, LeBron and the team come back in the finals from being down one game to three against Golden State to win 4–3. For his heroics on the court, LeBron is named MVP again.

LA Lakers
LeBron signs a four-year contract with the Los Angeles Lakers, earning him more than $150 million. He continues to be one of the top performers in the league.

2009

2010

2012

2014

2016

2018

Lionel Messi

Star striker for Barcelona and the Argentinian national team, Lionel ("Leo") Messi (b. 1987) is often praised as being the best soccer player of all time. He has gathered a staggering number of records for both club and country, becoming Argentina's leading goal scorer and the only person to have scored more than 400 goals in the Spanish league.

Newell's Old Boys

Leo is born in the city of Rosario, Argentina, into a soccer-loving family. Aged six, he starts playing for his local youth team, Newell's Old Boys. He scores more than 500 goals in six years for them, and even entertains the crowds with ball tricks at halftime.

1987

Move to Spain

FC Barcelona in Spain give Leo a tryout, and are so impressed by his talent that they offer to pay for his medical treatment if he joins their youth academy. The club is in such a hurry to sign him that they hastily scribble down his first contract on a paper napkin!

2000

2003

1998

Growing pains

At the age of 10, Leo is diagnosed with a hormone deficiency which slows his growth. He needs expensive treatment, which his parents struggle to afford.

Barcelona debut

At the age of 16, Leo plays his first game for Barcelona's senior team in a friendly (noncompetition) game. He makes his competitive debut the following year, becoming the youngest player to represent Barcelona in La Liga (the top Spanish league).

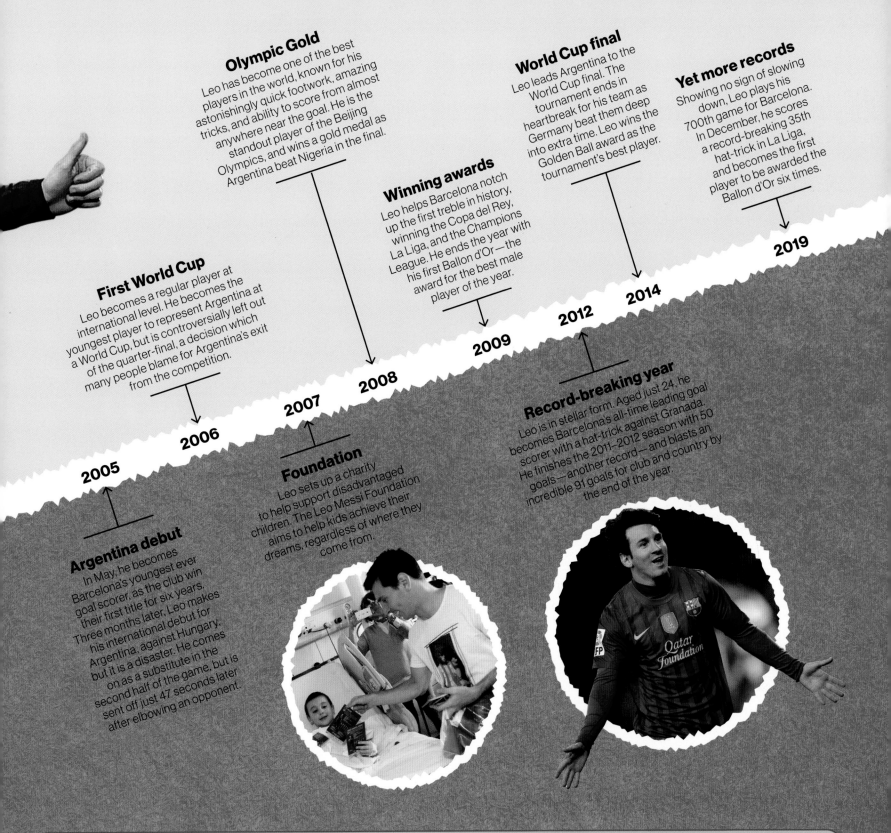

Olympic Gold

Leo has become one of the best players in the world, known for his astonishingly quick footwork, amazing tricks, and ability to score from almost anywhere near the goal. He is the standout player of the Beijing Olympics, and wins a gold medal as Argentina beat Nigeria in the final.

World Cup final

Leo leads Argentina to the World Cup final. The tournament ends in heartbreak for his team as Germany beat them deep into extra time. Leo wins the Golden Ball award as the tournament's best player.

Yet more records

Showing no sign of slowing down, Leo plays his 700th game for Barcelona. In December, he scores a record-breaking 35th hat-trick in La Liga, and becomes the first player to be awarded the Ballon d'Or six times.

Winning awards

Leo helps Barcelona notch up the first treble in history, winning the Copa del Rey, La Liga, and the Champions League. He ends the year with his first Ballon d'Or—the award for the best male player of the year.

First World Cup

Leo becomes a regular player at international level. He becomes the youngest player to represent Argentina at a World Cup, but is controversially left out of the quarter-final, a decision which many people blame for Argentina's exit from the competition.

2019

2014

2012

2009

2008

2007

2006

2005

Record-breaking year

Leo is in stellar form. Aged just 24, he becomes Barcelona's all-time leading goal scorer with a hat-trick against Granada. He finishes the 2011–2012 season with 50 goals—another record—and blasts an incredible 91 goals for club and country by the end of the year.

Foundation

Leo sets up a charity to help support disadvantaged children. The Leo Messi Foundation aims to help kids achieve their dreams, regardless of where they come from.

Argentina debut

In May, he becomes Barcelona's youngest ever goal scorer, as the club win their first title for six years. Three months later, Leo makes his international debut for Argentina, against Hungary, but it is a disaster. He comes on as a substitute in the second half of the game, but is sent off just 47 seconds later after elbowing an opponent.

Other greats

Soccer is a team game, but a few players have been so gifted that they have changed the course of a game with a moment of individual brilliance.

Johan Cruyff (1947–2016)
In the 1970s, the Dutch national team's philosophy of "Total Football"—where every outfield player was skilled at every position—produced some of the most exciting moments in soccer history. Many involved Johan Cruyff—for many the greatest player of all time.

Cristiano Ronaldo (b. 1985)
For over a decade, Portugal's star player has rivaled Messi as the greatest in the world. For most of the 2010s, the two dominated Spain's La Liga, as Ronaldo notched up five Ballons d'Or for Barcelona's great rivals, Real Madrid.

Marta (b. 1986)
A Brazilian midfielder, Marta became the first person of any gender to score goals at five World Cups. She has played club soccer in Sweden and the US.

> **"One child, one teacher, one book, and one pen can change the world. Education is the only solution."**
> **Malala Yousafzai, speaking to the UN (2013)**

Exposed

When the Taliban attack a number of schools, Malala speaks out. On the radio, she talks about the Taliban preventing women from accessing education. The New York Times makes a documentary film about her experiences, which exposes her identity.

Who is Malala?

Malala begins receiving death threats on social media. Returning from school, a Taliban assassin boards her bus and asks "Who is Malala?," before finding and shooting her in the face. Her life hangs by a thread, but she survives. Malala is initially treated in Pakistan before being flown to England for further medical help.

National Peace Award

At the age of just 14, Malala wins Pakistan's National Youth Peace Prize for her work. The award would later be renamed after her. Increased fears for her and her family's safety lead Malala to flee to the countryside to live with relatives.

Speaking out

Malala is encouraged to pursue education by her father, a teacher who runs a school for girls. She gives a speech called "How dare the Taliban take away my basic right to education?" after the Taliban ban girls' education in the Swat Valley.

Taliban rule

Hearing about her speech, a reporter with the British Broadcasting Corporation (BBC) approaches Malala's family to ask if she would write an anonymous blog. Under the fake name Gul Makai, Malala begins writing about life under the Taliban, who by this point are fighting a war against the Pakistani army—causing many in the Swat Valley, including Malala, to become refugees.

Heroic name

Malala is born in Mingora, a town in the Swat Valley (above) in Pakistan. Her name, meaning "grief-stricken," comes from the Afghani folk heroine Malalai of Maiwand. When she is 10, the Taliban seize power in the area.

1997

2008

2009

2009

2009

2011

2012

Malala Yousafzai

An activist for girls' and women's rights, Malala Yousafzai (b. 1997) is the youngest person ever to win the Nobel Peace Prize. At the age of 15, she was shot by a member of the Taliban—an Islamic extremist group—but she survived the attack. Her story brought international attention to the plight of girls and women in her country of Pakistan. She has gone on to speak up for women all over the world.

United Nations

Expressions of sympathy for and solidarity with Malala's story pour in from around the world. Following a long recovery, Malala is discharged and begins to adapt to a new life in England with her family. On her 16th birthday, Malala attends the United Nations General Assembly in New York and gives a speech on the importance of free education. She receives a standing ovation.

Nobel Peace Prize

Malala is awarded the Nobel Peace Prize in recognition of her work on the right of all children to education, and also for highlighting the suppression of children everywhere. Aged just 17, Malala is the youngest winner of a Nobel Prize in any field in history.

The Malala Fund

Malala opens a school for girls fleeing the Syrian Civil War. It is made possible by the Malala Fund—an international nonprofit organization set up by Malala and her father. The school serves over 200 young girls, aiming to help Syria's refugee crisis. He Named Me Malala, a documentary about Malala, is released.

Oxford

Having graduated from high school, Malala decides to continue her education by attending college. She is accepted to study Philosophy, Politics, and Economics at the prestigious University of Oxford in Oxford, UK.

Return to Pakistan

For the first time since the attack on her, Malala returns to Pakistan. She meets Prime Minister Shahid Khaqan Abbasi and gives a powerful speech, before visiting her home town. She describes this event as "the happiest day of my life."

We Are Displaced

Following Malala's experiences as a refugee, she writes We Are Displaced, featuring the stories of refugee girls from around the world. Malala continues to speak out for the voiceless millions experiencing oppression across the world.

2013

2014

2015

2017

2018

2019

Muhammad Ali Jinnah (1876–1948)

The countries we now know as India and Pakistan were colonies of Britain for hundreds of years. After leading the campaign for Pakistan's independence from Britain, Muhammad Ali Jinnah became the country's first leader when the country won its freedom in 1947. His struggle for justice and freedom is a huge inspiration to Malala.

The Information Age

Bill Gates
(b.1955)

A cofounder of Microsoft—the world's largest software company—Bill Gates has helped shape the Information Age.

1955
Bill is born in Seattle. He is small for his age, and suffers bullying in school. His mother is a teacher and businessperson, and his father is a lawyer.

1969
Bill's school is one of the few in his community to have a computer. He writes his first computer program aged 13—a version of the game tic-tac-toe.

1973
Bill goes to Harvard University to study mathematics and computer science.

1975
Bill and his friend Paul Allen create a highly successful programming language called BASIC for the Altair 8800 computer. He leaves Harvard University to develop more software (computer programs) and sets up Microsoft.

1980
Microsoft develops MS-DOS, a computer operating system. Bill makes a deal with the technology company IBM for MS-DOS to be used in their personal computers (PCs). As more and more people begin using PCs, Microsoft becomes the biggest computer software company.

1985
Microsoft releases the Windows operating system. Soon Windows is installed on 90 percent of the world's PCs.

2000
Bill steps down from leading Microsoft. He sets up a charitable organization with his wife Melinda. By 2019, they have donated more than $45 billion to causes, such as curing infectious diseases, across the world.

Steve Jobs
(1955–2011)

Before entrepreneur Steve Jobs formed Apple, PCs were difficult for regular people to use. Apple changed all this, and went on to produce some of the world's best-loved electronic products.

1955
Steve is born in San Francisco. He is introduced to Steve Wozniak (known as "Woz") by a mutual friend at the age of 16. The two become friends.

1976
Woz designs a new low-cost, easy-to-use computer. Steve thinks it can make money, and sells his van to help raise funds to build more of them. They sell fewer than 200 of the Apple I computer, but its follow-up, Apple II, is a great success. Steve builds a brilliant team of engineers, and takes charge of Apple's marketing. The company grows rapidly.

1984
Apple releases the groundbreaking Apple Macintosh. It is the first computer that allows users to interact with icons on screen, making it easier to use than the PC.

1985
Steve leaves Apple after the company's sales are lower than expected.

1997
Steve returns to lead Apple, which has struggled without him.

2001
Steve announces the release of iTunes music software and the iPod, a portable music player. Both are hugely popular.

2007
Apple releases the iPhone. It will go on to be the best-selling smartphone of all time.

2010
Apple release the iPad, a tablet computer. It quickly becomes Apple's fastest-selling product ever.

2011
Steve dies of cancer, after battling the disease for several years. By the time of his death, Apple is one of the world's biggest brands.

Larry Page and Sergey Brin
(both b.1973)

American computer science graduates Larry Page and Sergey Brin set up the internet search engine site Google. It is now the most-visited website in the world.

1973
Larry is born in Lansing, MI. Five months later, Sergey is born in Moscow in the Soviet Union (modern-day Russia). Sergey immigrates with his family to the US at the age of six.

1995
When Larry first meets Sergey at Stanford University, where they are both studying, they disagree on almost everything. But at college they soon end up working together on a new search engine called BackRub, and become close friends.

1996
Larry and Sergey figure out a way of ranking web pages that makes internet searches much more helpful. They rename their search engine "Google."

2000
Google becomes the world's largest search engine.

2004
Google launches Google mail—a free email service.

2005
Google releases the mapping service Google Maps. Larry and Sergey buy more than 200 technology companies, including the smartphone operating system Android, and the video-sharing site YouTube.

2009
Larry and Sergey spend more and more time exploring projects outside of Google, from driverless cars to renewable energy.

2015
Larry and Sergey found a new company, Alphabet, which collects their many technology companies. Google is the largest of them.

Computers, the internet, and mobile phones have brought about the Information Age—an era of huge change in how people communicate, work, and share information. Here are just some of the people who have developed, and used, these technologies to make that change happen.

Mark Zuckerberg (b.1984)

Mark Zuckerberg set up Facebook. The social media site has about 2.5 billion people using it every month, and has revolutionized communication.

1984
Mark is born in New York. At school, he develops a passion for computing. At the age of 12, he creates a messaging service called "ZuckNet" that enables his family to communicate within their home.

2003
At Harvard University, Mark designs a website that angers some of his fellow students and gets him into trouble with the university's authorities. Harvard shuts the site down within days and threatens Mark with expulsion.

2004

Mark and three friends launch "The Facebook"—a site where users create a profile and interact with each other. A million people join the site in under a year. Mark drops out of college and moves to Silicon Valley, California, to develop the site.

2006
Facebook opens to anyone over the age of 13. The site becomes incredibly popular, and gains 100 million users in under two years.

2012
Facebook buys Instagram, a popular photo-sharing app. Instagram's popularity helps fuel Facebook's success.

2018
A scandal hits Facebook when it is revealed that its users' data has been used in unlawful ways. Mark apologizes and vows to improve security.

Sheryl Sandberg (b.1969)

Sheryl Sandberg worked at Google before becoming one of the top leaders at Facebook. Her work and ideas have helped Facebook reach new users around the world.

1969
Sheryl is born in Washington, D.C. Her mother teaches French, and her father is an eye doctor.

1991
Sheryl graduates from Harvard University. She receives a prize as the top economics graduate of the year.

2001
After working for the World Bank and the US government, Sheryl joins Google. She helps make the company profitable and gains a reputation as one of the most successful managers in the US.

2007
Mark Zuckerberg meets Sheryl, and soon afterward hires her to be in charge of the day-to-day running of Facebook.

2008

Sheryl realizes that for Facebook to make money, it must be better at advertising. Within two years, she turns it into a profitable company (one that makes more money than it spends). She becomes the first woman on Facebook's board of directors (which controls what the company does).

2013
She publishes a best-selling book, *Lean In*. It encourages women to pursue their ambitions in the workplace, and reach for the highest roles in companies. Many people see her as a role model.

2018
Sheryl is in control of Facebook's response to the scandal about its users' data being misused. She helps come up with a set of new rules to ensure this problem does not happen in future.

Susan Wojcicki (b.1968)

Susan Wojcicki leads YouTube, the world's largest video-sharing website, and the second most popular site, behind Google.

1968
Born in California, Susan grows up at Stanford University, where her father is a physics professor. As a child, she thinks computers are boring, and prefers to make things.

1990
Susan graduates with degrees in literature and history from Harvard University. She takes her first computer science class while at college, and realizes how she can use her creative skills working in technology. She goes on to earn two more degrees, in economics and business.

1998
Susan buys a house in Menlo Park, California. To help her pay for it, she rents out her garage to Sergey Brin and Larry Page as they work on Google.

1999
She joins Google as marketing manager. One of her first jobs is to work on Doodles—interactive animations that appear on Google's home page to celebrate holidays and festivals.

2003
Susan comes up with the idea for AdSense, an incredibly successful advertising program. Advertising—companies paying Google to be advertised on their search engine—becomes Google's main source of income.

2005
Google launches a video-sharing site. Susan uploads the first video, "A purple Muppet singing a nonsense song" to it. She realizes the power of video when her kids love it.

2006
Google's video-sharing site is losing out to YouTube. Susan persuades her bosses to buy YouTube.

2014

Susan takes over as YouTube's leader. She increases its percentage of female employees, and helps the company reach a larger audience. YouTube users now watch more than a billion hours of video each day.

Greta Thunberg

Swedish activist Greta Thunberg (b. 2003) has inspired millions of people to take action against global warming. Her "skolstrejk för klimatet" ("school strike for the climate") started as a lone protest, but quickly spread via social media to become a global movement. Her message is that we all need to reduce our carbon emissions—the main cause of the climate emergency.

January 25, 2019
"Our **house is on fire** ... I want you to panic."
Speech to World Economic Forum, Davos, Switzerland (January 25, 2019)
Greta stresses to world leaders how urgently action is needed. She travels from Stockholm to Davos by train, which takes 32 hours, and calls out the hypocrisy of leaders who arrive to discuss global warming by airplane—a huge source of carbon emissions.

December 14, 2018
"You are **never too small** to make a difference."
Speech to UN Climate Change Conference, Katowice, Poland (December 14, 2018)
As Greta's protests gain momentum, she starts joining other demonstrations across Europe. She gives a string of speeches at high-profile conferences, delivering her message with clarity and power. By the end of the year, 20,000 students have held school strikes for the climate in more than 270 cities worldwide.

2003
"You would think the media and every one of our leaders would be talking about nothing else, but **they never even mention it.**"
TEDxStockholm talk (November 24, 2018)
Greta is born and grows up in Stockholm, Sweden. She is 8 years old when she first hears about global warming, and cannot understand why adults do not seem to care, or why the subject is not given more attention.

September 7, 2018
#FridaysforFuture
Campaign slogan
Initially protesting alone, she is soon joined by fellow students, parents, and teachers. She continues to protest every Friday under the slogan "Fridays for Future," and uses social media to encourage other students to stage similar weekly walkouts.

2014
"I'm sometimes a bit different from the norm ... Given the right circumstances being different is a **superpower.**"
Instagram™ post (August 31, 2019)
Aged 11, Greta's fears about global warming cause her to fall into a depression and she loses a lot of weight. She is diagnosed with Asperger's Syndrome, a condition that can make communicating with other people more difficult. She comes to see her condition as a strength that allows her to view the seriousness of the environment crisis with more clarity than others.

August 20, 2018
"Why should I be studying for a **future** that soon will be no more?"
***Declaration of Rebellion**, London, UK (October 31, 2018)*
After a series of unusual weather events hit Sweden, Greta protests by skipping school to stand outside the Swedish parliament every day until the Swedish elections in September. She demands that Sweden reduces carbon emissions to the levels agreed to in international law.

2016
"We can't save the world by playing by the rules. Because the **rules have to be changed.**"
TEDxStockholm talk (November 24, 2018)
In order to reduce her impact on the environment, Greta gives up eating meat and dairy products and refuses to fly. She persuades her parents to do the same.

February 21, 2019

"We have started to clean up your mess, and we will not stop until we are done."

Speech at European Economic and Social Committee, Brussels, Belgium (February 21, 2019)

Greta shares a stage with Jean-Claude Juncker, President of the European Commission. After her impassioned speech, Juncker announces that a quarter of the EU budget between 2021 and 2027 will go toward tackling global warming.

August 2019

"Unite behind the science."

Slogan on the *Malizia II*

Greta sets sail in *Malizia II*, a racing yacht, on a 14-day, zero-carbon trip from Plymouth, UK, to New York City. The trip gains global media attention. She meets former US president Barack Obama, and speaks to Congress to demand that lawmakers take note of scientific evidence about global warming.

August 31, 2019

"When haters go after your looks and differences, it means they have nowhere left to go. And then you know you're winning!"

Instagram™ post (August 31, 2019)

Greta's unapologetic approach to protesting causes some people to criticize her. Many of these comments refer to her appearance and make fun of her Asperger's, but Greta is not diverted by this rudeness.

September 20, 2019

"We are in the beginning of a mass extinction, and all you can talk about is money and fairy tales of eternal economic growth. How dare you!"

Speech to UN Climate Change Summit, New York City (September 20, 2019)

On September 20, 4 million protestors march worldwide—the biggest global warming protest in history. The next day, Greta delivers her most infuriated speech yet, warning world leaders that future generations will never forgive them. Her protest continues.

OLSTREJK FÖR IMATET

British and Irish people

Henry VIII (1491–1547)

Henry VIII ruled England, Wales, and Ireland. His wish to end his first marriage led to England's separation from the Catholic Church.

1491
Henry is born in Greenwich, London, to King Henry VII and Elizabeth of York. Henry becomes the heir to the throne in 1502 when his older brother Arthur dies.

1509
Following the death of his father, Henry becomes the King of England and Lord of Ireland at the age of 17. That same year, he marries his brother's widow, Catherine of Aragon.

1516
Henry and Catherine's only surviving child, Mary, is born. The king is disappointed, as he wants a male heir to succeed him.

1527
Believing that Catherine will never give birth to a male heir, Henry tries to have his marriage to her annulled (declared finished), but the pope refuses to allow it. Henry breaks away from the Catholic Church, ends his marriage to Catherine, and marries Anne Boleyn in 1533.

1534
Henry becomes the head of the Church of England.

1536
Henry and Anne fail to have a surviving son. Henry orders Anne's execution, and he marries Jane Seymour. Henry orders the seizure and sale of all Catholic religious buildings.

1537
Jane dies as she gives birth to a son, Edward VI. Henry marries Anne of Cleves, but he has the marriage annulled just six months later. Soon after, he marries Catherine Howard.

1542
Henry has Catherine Howard executed. The Crown of Ireland act makes him King of Ireland. He marries his sixth wife, Catherine Parr, the following year.

1547
Henry dies in the Palace of Whitehall, London. Edward VI becomes king, but dies at the age of 15 in 1553. Mary I (Henry's daughter with Catherine of Aragon) and then Elizabeth I (Henry's daughter with Anne Boleyn) are the next two rulers.

John Logie Baird (1888–1946)

Scottish engineer John Logie Baird developed one of the most world-changing inventions ever—the television.

1888
John is born in Dunbartonshire, Scotland. As a child, he shows an interest in engineering and inventing.

1914
John starts studying electrical engineering at the Royal Technical College in Glasgow. The outbreak of World War I this his studies short.

1915
John tries to join the British Army, but poor physical health prevents him from serving. Instead, he works as an engineer helping make weapons and ammunition for the war effort.

1924
After the war, John begins working on televising images over short distances.

1926
At the Royal Institution, London, John becomes the first person to demonstrate televised pictures of objects in motion.

1928
John unveils the world's first color television. That same year, his company, the Baird Television Development Company Ltd, makes the first successful transatlantic television transmission, from London to New York.

1930
The British Broadcasting Corporation broadcasts the first piece of televised drama made in Britain by using John's system.

1941
John continues to improve his techniques, developing a way of televising three-dimensional (3-D) images.

1946
John suffers a stroke and dies in Bexhill-on-Sea in East Sussex, England.

Jocelyn Bell Burnell (b. 1943)

Jocelyn Bell Burnell is a Northern Irish astrophysicist. She discovered rapidly rotating stars called pulsars—one of the most important breakthroughs of 20th-century astrophysics.

1943
Jocelyn is born in Belfast, Northern Ireland.

1965
Jocelyn graduates from college with a degree in physics. She begins studying for a PhD. She builds a huge radio telescope to study quasars, huge objects in space that give off radio waves.

1967
With her telescope, Jocelyn discovers some unusual radio signals that she cannot explain. She figures out that these are coming from a new type of star that pulses out jets of radiation as it rapidly spins. They come to be known as "pulsars."

1974
Jocelyn's groundbreaking discovery earns a Nobel Prize, but it is awarded to her research supervisor, Antony Hewish, and fellow astronomer Martin Ryle, who works in the same lab. Jocelyn is given no credit.

1999
Jocelyn is awarded a CBE (Commander of the British Empire) for her services to astronomy.

2003
Jocelyn becomes a fellow of the oldest scientific society in the world, the Royal Society in London, a high honor for scientists.

2018
Jocelyn is awarded the Breakthrough Prize in Fundamental Physics for her discovery of pulsars. She donates the prize money she receives to groups that encourage women and people from other under-represented groups to pursue careers in physics.

People from all over the United Kingdom and Republic of Ireland have gained world acclaim for their fascinating lives and groundbreaking achievements. Here are just a few more of these countries' most notable people.

Mary Robinson (b. 1944)

Mary Robinson is an Irish lawyer and politician who became the first female president of Ireland. Throughout her legal and political career, she has worked to improve lives for women and under-represented groups, and has campaigned to improve human rights around the world.

1944
Mary is born in Ballina, Ireland.

1967
Mary graduates from college with a degree in law. She goes on to study at Harvard Law School, one of the most prestigious law schools in the world.

1969
Aged just 25, Mary becomes a professor of law at Trinity College, Dublin. She is elected as a senator to the Seanad, Ireland's upper parliamentary house, a position which she will hold for the next 20 years. As a senator, she campaigns for equal rights for women and other important causes.

1990
Mary is elected as president of Ireland, the first woman to hold the position. She takes an active role in Irish and world politics.

1997
Mary steps down as president to serve as the United Nations High Commissioner for Human Rights. This is a high-profile and important role which highlights human rights issues throughout the world.

2009
US president Barack Obama presents Mary with the Presidential Medal of Freedom for her human rights work both in Ireland and internationally.

Tanni Grey-Thompson (b. 1969)

Tanni Grey-Thompson is a Welsh athlete and politician. She is the UK's most successful Paralympic athlete ever.

1969
Tanni is born in Cardiff, Wales. Her parents name her Carys, but her sister calls her Tanni, a nickname that sticks. She is born with spina bifida—a condition that causes her spine to not develop correctly. She uses crutches to help her walk and, eventually, a wheelchair.

1980
Tanni ignores her local government's wish to send her to a school for children with special needs. She attends a regular school in Penarth, Wales. It is there that she discovers her love for sports.

1988
Tanni wins a bronze medal for the 400m wheelchair race at her first Paralympic Games in Seoul, South Korea.

1992
Tanni wins the London Wheelchair Marathon, a race she will win five more times over the next 10 years. Later in the year, she wins four gold medals and one silver medal at the Barcelona Paralympics in Spain.

1996
Tanni wins another four medals—one gold and three silver—at the Atlanta Paralympics.

2000
Tanni wins four gold medals at the Sydney Paralympics in Australia. She is awarded an OBE (Order of the British Empire) for her services to sports.

2004
In her last Paralympic Games, Tanni wins two gold medals.

2010
Tanni is appointed as a Peer in the House of Lords, the UK's upper parliamentary house. She uses this position to advise on subjects such as disability rights, welfare reform, and sports.

Zadie Smith (b. 1975)

Zadie Smith is an award-winning English writer and college professor.

1975
Zadie is born in London to an English father and a Jamaican mother.

1997
While in college, Zadie begins sending her short stories to student publications. Her writing gets noticed, and she signs a publishing deal. Zadie graduates with a degree in English.

2000
Zadie's first novel, *White Teeth*, is published. It is about the UK's colonial past and the way it treats people from its former colonies. It wins numerous awards and becomes a best-seller.

2002
Zadie is elected as a fellow of the Royal Society of Literature. Her second novel, *The Autograph Man*, is published. It is about a man who is obsessed with celebrities.

2005
Zadie's third novel, *On Beauty*, is published. It is short-listed for the Man Booker Prize and wins the Orange Prize for Fiction, two of the most prestigious awards for literature.

2010
Zadie is appointed as a professor of fiction at New York University.

2012
Zadie's fourth novel, *NW*, is published. It is set in northwest London.

2016
Swing Time, Zadie's fifth novel, is about two girls who tap dance. It earns her another nomination for the Man Booker Prize.

North American people

Mistahi-maskwa (c. 1825–1888)

First Nations Canadian Mistahi-maskwa (also known as Big Bear), was a Cree chief. As European settlers expanded west over what is now Canada, he tried to unite and protect his people who had lived on the land for centuries.

c. 1825
Mistahi-maskwa is born near Fort Carlton (in modern-day Saskatchewan, Canada).

1865
Mistahi-maskwa becomes the chief of a small group of Cree people. He is known for being a good hunter and a strong warrior, important skills for a Cree chief.

1876
The Cree people are suffering because of a terrible famine. The Canadian government offers the Cree, Ojibwa, and Assiniboine peoples food supplies in exchange for their land. Most chiefs agree, but Mistahi-maskwa strongly opposes, arguing that it is unfair to First Nations peoples, and that this will end their way of life.

1882
Mistahi-maskwa holds out for a better deal, but none comes. As the famine takes hold, his people's trust in him begins to diminish. He signs the government's deal, and agrees for his people to be moved to a reservation (an area set aside for First Nations people to live on).

1885
Cree people previously under Mistahi-maskwa's control murder nine white settlers at Frog Lake, Alberta. Despite Mistahi-maskwa's attempts to stop the violence, the government holds him responsible and finds him guilty of treason (betraying the country). He is put in prison.

1887
Mistahi-maskwa is released halfway through his three-year prison sentence because of poor health.

1888
Mistahi-maskwa settles on the Little Pine reservation, where he later dies.

Theodore Roosevelt (1858–1919)

Theodore Roosevelt was a soldier, politician, and naturalist who became the 26th president of the United States.

1858
Theodore is born in New York City. He suffers from poor health as a child. He takes up regular exercise to improve his health and well-being.

1884
Theodore's wife and mother die of illnesses within hours of each other. He writes "the light has gone out of my life" in his diary.

1898
Theodore joins the US Army. He fights in the Spanish–American War. Afterward, he is recognized as a war hero for his service.

1901
Theodore becomes US vice president to President William McKinley. Later that same year, McKinley is assassinated. Theodore becomes the 26th US president at the age of 42—the youngest-ever president.

1904
Theodore is reelected as president. During his time in office, he expands the power of the presidency and increases the US' involvement in world politics.

1909
After serving his second term, Theodore steps down as president. He travels through Africa and Europe before returning to the US.

1919
Theodore considers running for president again, but he dies before the election takes place.

Katherine Johnson (1918–2020)

Katherine Johnson overcame racism and sexism to become key to the success of the US Space Program. She helped put the first US astronaut into space, and the first-ever humans on the moon.

1918
Katherine is born in West Virginia.

1928
Many African American children suffer from poor access to proper schooling. Katherine enrolls in a neighboring county's high school at the age of 10.

1937
At just 18, Katherine proves herself to be an academic star, and graduates from West Virginia State College with degrees in mathematics and French.

1953
Katherine starts working as a "human computer" for the US space agency, NASA. Before electronic computers, these "human computers" worked complex mathematical calculations by hand.

1961
She is selected to calculate the flight path for the Freedom 7 mission, which takes the first US astronaut into space.

1969
Katherine is part of the team that calculates the trajectory (the path of a flying object) of the Apollo 11 mission, which puts the first humans on the moon.

1986
Katherine leaves NASA. She often visits schools to talk about the importance of mathematics education.

2015
President Barack Obama presents her with the Presidential Medal of Freedom, the highest civilian honor in the US, for her work with NASA.

2020
Katherine dies on February 24, 2020, at the age of 101.

People from across North America have gained world renown for their fascinating lives and groundbreaking achievements. Here are just a few more of this incredibly diverse continent's most notable people.

Neil Armstrong (1930–2012)

Neil Armstrong was the first person to walk on the moon. His historic triumph represents one of humankind's most incredible achievements.

1930
Neil Armstrong is born near Wapakoneta, Ohio. He discovers a passion for aviation at a young age.

1946
Neil earns his pilot's license on his 16th birthday.

1949
Neil serves in the US Navy as a pilot during the Korean War.

1955
He graduates with a degree in aeronautical engineering, the study of how aircraft work. He begins working as a pilot testing aircraft for the US Air Force.

1962
Neil becomes an astronaut for NASA.

1966
Neil goes to space for the first time as part of the Gemini 8 mission—testing spacecraft for a future trip to the moon.

1969
Neil is named commander of the Apollo 11 moon mission. On July 20, he becomes the first human being to set foot on the moon. He instantly becomes an American hero, and the achievements of Apollo 11 are celebrated around the world.

1971
After leaving NASA, Neil becomes a professor of aerospace engineering. He teaches classes to pilots, and leads a life mostly out of the public eye.

2012
Neil dies at the age of 82.

Ruth Bader Ginsburg (b. 1933)

Ruth Bader Ginsburg is a US Supreme Court Justice (judge). She has become a popular public figure, known for her trailblazing career, incredible intelligence, and sharp wit.

1933
Ruth Bader is born in Brooklyn, New York, to a Jewish family.

1954
Ruth graduates from Cornell University with a bachelor of arts degree. A few days later, she marries Martin D. Ginsburg, and adds his surname to her own.

1956
Ruth goes on to study law at Harvard Law School. She later transfers to Columbia Law School, where she graduates first in her class in 1959.

1960
Ruth initially struggles to find work, as not many lawyers are women at this time. She secures a position as a legal clerk. Her career goes from strength to strength as she takes on numerous high-profile cases. She successfully argues before the Supreme Court on several occasions to protect women's rights and promote gender equality.

1972
Ruth becomes Columbia Law School's first-ever permanent female law professor.

1980
President Jimmy Carter nominates Ruth to the US Court of Appeals for the District of Columbia Circuit, an important and highly regarded role.

1993
President Bill Clinton nominates Ruth to the Supreme Court of the United States (SCOTUS). She is one of only nine justices on the SCOTUS at any time. She becomes the second woman, and first Jewish woman, to sit on the court.

2016
A collection of Ruth's speeches and writings, *My Own Words*, is released. The earliest material in the book is from when Ruth was an eighth-grade student.

Selena (1971–1995)

Selena Quintanilla-Pérez was a Mexican-American singer and musician from Texas. One of the most popular Latin artists of all time, Selena helped bring Mexican-American Tejano music to bigger audiences.

1971
Selena is born in Lake Jackson, Texas.

c.1980
Selena shows a talent for music from a young age. She starts singing in her family's band Selena y Los Dinos ("Selena and the Guys"). They play Tejano music at her parents' restaurant and at local events.

1981
Selena y Los Dinos start to record their music. At this time, Tejano music is mostly dominated by male singers, so success is slow at first.

1987
Selena wins two major awards at the Tejano Music Awards. The band's popularity explodes.

1989
Selena records her first solo album, *Selena*.

1992
After two successful solo albums, her breakthrough record, *Entre a Mi Mundo* ("*Enter My World*") is released. The album is number one on the US Billboard Regional Mexican Albums chart for 19 weeks.

1994
Selena becomes the first female Tejano artist to win a Grammy, for her album *Live*.

1995
Selena is shot by Yolanda Saldivar, the former president of her fan club. Selena is just 23. Her final album, *Dreaming of You*, is released after her death. It is her biggest success, and brings the "Queen of Tejano music" to more people than ever before.

Glossary

Terms defined elsewhere in the glossary are in italics.

abolition
The act of doing away with something completely.

activist
Someone who campaigns to bring about social or political change.

allies/Allied powers
People or countries working together. In World War I and World War II, the Allies or Allied powers were the countries fighting against Axis powers.

anti-Semitism
Prejudice and hostility toward Jewish people.

apartheid
In South Africa, a government policy of racial *segregation* that lasted from 1948 to 1994.

armistice
An agreement that is reached to end a conflict.

assassination
The murder of a key figure by surprise attack, usually carried out for political or religious reasons.

astronomy
The study of the universe.

atom
The smallest part of an *element* that has the same chemical makeup as that element.

Axis powers
Nations on Germany's side in World War II, including Italy and Japan.

bacteria
Microscopic, single-celled (see *cell*) organisms (see *organism*), some of which are responsible for serious diseases.

bankrupt
A legal declaration that a person or company cannot pay their debts.

BCE
Before common era. The years before 1 CE (Common Era). This abbreviation has largely replaced BC (Before Christ).

bipolar disorder
A mental health condition that causes extreme mood swings.

blockade
The isolation of an area so as to prevent supplies from entering or leaving.

boycott
A form of protest that involves not buying, using, or interacting with something.

caliph
The title of the religious and political leader of Islam (in the *Islamic world*).

capitalism
An economic system based on the private ownership of property and free competitive conditions for business.

CE
Common Era. The years from 1 CE to the present day. This abbreviation has largely replaced AD (Anno Domini, which is Latin for "in the year of the Lord").

cell
The basic unit from which all living organisms are made.

Christian
A follower of Christianity.

citizen
A person who belongs to a city or a bigger community such as a state or country.

city-state
A self-governing, independent state consisting of a city and its surrounding area.

civilization
The *culture* and way of life of people living together in an organized and developed society.

civil disobedience
A peaceful form of protesting where citizens refuse to obey laws that they consider unjust.

civil rights
The rights of citizens (see *citizen*) to be socially and politically equal.

civil war
A war among opposing groups of people of the same country.

classical
Refers to the ancient Greek or ancient Roman world.

colonization
The act of sending settlers to establish a *colony* in another country, sometimes involving taking political control over the people already living there.

colony
An area under the political control of another state; or the group of people who have settled there.

communism
The political belief in a society in which wealth and ownership of property are shared.

concubine
An unofficial or lesser wife.

Congress
The law-making branch of the US government.

constitution
A set of laws or rules that determine the political principles of a government.

court
The household, advisors, and favorites of a *sovereign*. Also a place where legal cases are decided.

coup
The sudden violent or illegal seizure of power by a group.

Crusades, the
Military expeditions of the 11th to 13th centuries in which *Christian* knights tried to seize the city of Jerusalem from *Muslim* control.

Cubism
An artistic style that represents objects using simple shapes.

culture
The customs, beliefs, and behavior shared by a society.

daimyo
A Japanese lord.

democracy
A form of government based on rule by the people, usually through elected representatives.

depression
In history, a period of drastic decline in economic activity, marked by widespread unemployment and hardship.

diaspora
The dispersion of people from their original homeland.

dictator
A leader who rules a country alone, with no restrictions on the extent of their power.

DNA
Deoxyribonucleic acid, the chemical that stores genetic information inside living cells (see *cell*).

dynasty
A royal family ruling a country for successive generations.

element
A substance in which all the atoms (see *atom*) are the same, and which cannot be broken down by another substance.

emancipation
The process of being set free from political or social restrictions.

emperor/empress
The ruler of an *empire*.

empire
A group of lands or peoples brought under the rule of one government or person (the *emperor/empress*).

Enlightenment, the
The period of European history, in the 1700s, when radical thinkers tried to reach a new understanding of society, government, and humanity, and then reform them.

enslaved person
A person who is held against their will as the property of another.

evolution
The gradual change of species over generations as they adapt to the changing environment.

exile
Forced absence from a person's home or country.

fascism
An ideology stressing nationalism, which places the strength of the state above individual citizens' welfare.

feminism
The belief that women should have the same rights and opportunities as men.

feudalism
A political system under which lords granted land to people of lower rank in return for loyalty, military assistance, and services.

fossil
The remains or impression of a prehistoric plant or animal, often preserved in rock.

frequency hopping
A method of transmitting radio signals securely by changing the transmitter frequency.

genocide
The deliberate murder of an entire people.

Great Depression
A worldwide economic catastrophe that began in 1929 in the US.

guerrilla warfare
A type of warfare in which small groups of fighters make surprise attacks against a larger force.

guild
An organization in 11th–14th-century Europe formed by skilled workers or merchants of the same craft or trade to protect its members and control business.

habitat
The area where an animal naturally makes its home.

heresy
Beliefs, held by a member or members of a larger religious group, that are considered to be in conflict with that group's established beliefs.

Holocaust, the
The *genocide* of the Jews, and other minorities, by Nazi Germany between 1933 and 1945.

humanitarian
Someone who works to help improve human welfare.

Islamic world
A term for the countries where Islam is the main religion. It includes parts of North Africa, the Middle East, and Asia.

martyr
A person who is killed for refusing to renounce his or her religious beliefs.

mausoleum
A large tomb, or an impressive building for housing several tombs.

medieval period
Also known as the Middle Ages, the period in European history that lasted from about the 5th to the late 15th century CE.

Mesopotamia
The region of modern-day Iraq lying between the Tigris and Euphrates rivers, where many of the earliest *civilizations* began.

monarchy
A type of government in which a king or queen is recognized as head of state, even though he or she may have no real political power.

Mughal
A member of the *Muslim dynasty* that ruled much of India between the 16th and 19th centuries.

Muslim
A follower of Islam.

nation
An independent country, or one or more countries whose people share historical, linguistic, or cultural (see *culture*) ties.

naturalist
A scientist who studies living creatures and their *habitats*.

natural selection
The process whereby organisms better adapted to their environment tend to survive and produce more offspring.

nobility, the
A name for the people who belong to the highest social class in a society, usually just below the *sovereign*.

nomad
A person who moves from one place to another to find fresh pastures and water for livestock.

nucleus
The center of an *atom*.

oracle
An ancient priestess or priest who provided advice or prophecies for believers.

organism
Any living thing, including an animal, a plant, or a microscopic life-form such as a bacterium (see *bacteria*).

paganism
A term used for the religious beliefs of the ancient Greeks and Romans and other early European peoples before the coming of Christianity. Now used more widely for any non-major religion.

patent
The exclusive rights held by an inventor or company to make use of a specific process or invention.

peace treaty
An agreement that ends a conflict between countries.

pharaoh
The title of the ruler of ancient Egypt, who was traditionally seen as both a ruler and a god.

philosophy
A set of ideas or beliefs.

pilgrimage
A religious journey a person makes to a holy place.

pioneer
A person who is the first or among the first to do something important.

pogrom
An organized massacre of a particular group, usually used to mean attacks on Jewish people.

pope
The title of the religious leader of the Catholic Church.

prehistory
The time before the development of *civilizations*, and before the invention of writing.

propaganda
Information spread publicly to put forward political views; propaganda is sometimes used to cause deliberate harm to a person or group.

Reformation, the
A 16th-century reform movement of the Catholic Church in Europe. During the Reformation, many churches broke away from the Catholic Church to become Protestant churches.

Renaissance, the
A period of European history, beginning in the 14th century, when far-reaching changes occurred in the arts and intellectual life.

republic
A country without a hereditary monarch (see *monarchy*) or *emperor*. Modern republics are usually headed by presidents.

revolt
An organized uprising intended to overthrow whoever is in authority.

revolution
A sudden and fundamental change in society brought about by an organized group of protestors.

samurai
A Japanese warrior who owes allegiance to a *daimyo* and follows a strict code of honor.

script
The written characters that make up a writing system, such as an alphabet.

segregation
Separation, particularly of one race from another within a racist social system.

shogun
One of the military leaders who ruled Japan in the name of the *emperor*.

siege
To surround and *blockade* a city or fortress with the intention of capturing it.

socialism
The belief that the government should have some control over the economy and be able to spread wealth more evenly among the people.

Solar System, the
The sun, together with its orbiting planets, including Earth, and smaller bodies such as asteroids.

sovereign
A ruler or head of state exerting supreme power.

suffrage
The right to vote.

suffragette
In the early 20th century, a person who fought for women to have the right to vote.

sultan
In some Islamic countries, the traditional title given to the ruler.

Surrealism
A 20th-century movement in art and literature that used ideas from dreams to spur creativity.

terrorism
The unlawful use of violence and intimidation, usually against *citizens*, in the pursuit of political aims.

theology
The study of the nature of God and religious beliefs.

treason
The crime of betraying one's country.

United Nations
An international organization of countries set up in 1945 that aims to promote peace, security, and cooperation between its members.

vaccination
Precautionary medical treatment, usually given by injection, that stops people contracting a disease.

Viking
Scandinavian seafaring raiders, traders, and explorers who were active in Europe in the 8th to the 11th centuries.

Zionism
The movement to create and maintain a homeland for the Jewish people in Israel.

Index

Page numbers in **bold** indicate main entries.

318

Acknowledgments

The publisher would like to thank the following for their assistance in the preparation of this book: Additional writing: Edward Aves and Tayabah Khan. Fact-checking and editorial assistance: Bharti Bedi. Editorial assistance: Sarah MacLeod. Special consultant: Toby Buckley. Design assistance: Anna Pond, Samantha Richiardi, and Mary Sandberg. Project Picture Researcher: Aditya Katyal. Assistant Picture Researcher: Geetika Bhandari. Jacket DTP Designer: Rakesh Kumar. Jackets Editorial Coordinator: Priyanka Sharma. Managing Jackets Editor: Saloni Singh. Production Manager: Pankaj Sharma. Senior DTP Designer: Neeraj Bhatia. DTP Designer: Vijay Kandwal. Retouching: Steve Crozier. Database assistance: Jamie MacNeill. Proofreading: Debra Wolter. Index: Helen Peters.

The publisher would like to thank the following for their permission to reproduce their photographs:

(Key: a-above; b-below/bottom; c-center; f-far; l-left; r-right; t-top)

2 Alamy Stock Photo: Daniel Bockwoldt / dpa picture alliance (br); dpa picture alliance (ftl); Dinodia Photos RM (ftr); Granger Historical Picture Archive (fcra); GL Archive (cra). **Bridgeman Images**: Pictures from History (crb). **Getty Images**: Daniel Berehulak (cb); Bettmann (tl); Leemage (tr); Walter Dhladhla / AFP (ca); Gérard Géry / Paris Match Archive (fclb); Roger Viollet Collection (clb); John Lamparski (b). **Rex by Shutterstock**: AP (fcla). **12-13 Dreamstime.com**: Sergii Kolesnyk. **12 Alamy Stock Photo**: Adam Eastland (clb); Peter Horree (crb). **Bridgeman Images**: Charles Edwin Wilbour Fund (cl). **Dreamstime.com**: Jaroslav Moravcik (bl). **Getty Images**: Phillip Hayson / Photolibrary (ca). **13 Alamy Stock Photo**: Granger Historical Picture Archive (cra); Peter Horree (tc). **Getty Images**: Lansbricae (Luis Leclere) / Moment (c). **14 Alamy Stock Photo**: Peter Horree (tl). **15 Alamy Stock Photo**: www.BibleLandPictures.com / Zev Radovan (tc). **16 Getty Images**: De Agostini Picture Library (cla). **17 Alamy Stock Photo**: colaimages (crb); Granger Historical Picture Archive (c). **Getty Images**: De Agostini / A. Dagli Orti (ca). **18-19 Alamy Stock Photo**: Photo 12 / Archives Snark (c). **20-21 Alamy Stock Photo**: Artexplorer (t). **20 Alamy Stock Photo**: GL Archive (crb); World History Archive (br). **21 Alamy Stock Photo**: Classic Image (br). **22-23 123RF.com**: Laurent Davoust. **24 Alamy Stock Photo**: Art Collection 2 (tl); Prisma Archivo (bl). **24-25 Getty Images**: Hulton Fine Art Collection / Heritage Images / Fine Art Images (b). **25 Alamy Stock Photo**: GL Archive (cla). **Bridgeman Images**: Pictures from History (c). **27 Alamy Stock Photo**: Abbus Archive Images (tr); Dinodia Photos RM (tc); Dinodia Photos / Indian Pictures RF (br). **Dreamstime.com**: Aapthamithra (cr). **28 Alamy Stock Photo**: CPA Media Pte Ltd / Pictures From History (cla). **Dreamstime.com**: Silvershot55 (tr). **SuperStock**: The Art Archive / Art Archive, The aa335637 (fcla). **28-29 Alamy Stock Photo**: The Picture Art Collection (b). **29 Alamy Stock Photo**: David Davis Photoproductions RF (cr); Granger Historical Picture Archive (tl). **30 Getty Images**: Hulton Archive (tr). **30-31 123RF.com**: Laurent Davoust. **Getty Images**: De Agostini / G. Dagli Orti (b). **32 Alamy Stock Photo**: Granger Historical Picture Archive (bl); The Print Collector / CM Dixon / Heritage Images (cl); WBC ART (clb). **32-33 Alamy Stock Photo**: Photo12 / Archives Snark (c). **Dreamstime.com**: Ovydyborets. **33 Alamy Stock Photo**: Charles Phelps Cushing / Classicstock (tr); Lanmas (cra). **Bridgeman Images**: The Stapleton Collection (br). **34 Alamy Stock Photo**: Atlaspix (tr); incamerastock / ICP (clb). **bpk**: Ägyptisches Museum und Papyrussammlung, SMB / Else Grantz (cl). **Dorling Kindersley**: Bolton Library and Museum Services (bl). **34-35 123RF.com**: Josef Prchal (c). **Dreamstime.com**: Marek Uliasz. **35 Bridgeman Images**: Alinari (tr). **Dreamstime.com**: Matthijs Kuijpers (br). **37 Alamy Stock Photo**: (br); The Picture Art Collection (bc); John Reveley (tr); Realy Easy Star (cra). **40 Bridgeman Images**: (tl); De Agostini Picture Library / © A. Dagli Orti (cla); Pictures from History (cl). **Getty Images**: Leemage / Photo Josse / Corbis Historical (crb). **Mary Evans Picture Library**: Iberfoto (cb). **40-41 Bridgeman Images**: Pictures from History. **41 Rex by Shutterstock**: Gianni Dagli Orti (cr). **42-43 Alamy Stock Photo**: Images & Stories. **44-45 Alamy Stock Photo**: The Granger Collection. **45 Alamy Stock Photo**: Robert Chiasson / All Canada Photos (bl); Christopher Vernon-Parry (br). **46-47 Alamy Stock Photo**: Alfio Scisetti. **Getty Images**: Hulton Archive (Spine sketch). **46 Alamy Stock Photo**: FLHC 61 (bc); Historic Images (clb). **47 Alamy Stock Photo**: Archivah (br); Historisches Auge Ralf Feltz (tl); Ivan Vdovin (fcla); Prisma Archivo (cla); Robert Preston (c). **50 Alamy Stock Photo**: Guenter Fischer / Imagebroker (tl); Godong (br). **50-51 Dreamstime.com**: Rodrigolab (c). **51 Alamy Stock Photo**: Stephen Coyne (tr); CPA Media Pte Ltd / Pictures From History (tc); Peter Horree (fr); J Marshall - Tribaleye Images (br); Colin Marshall (bc). **52 Alamy Stock Photo**: Interfoto (bl); Quagga Media (tc). **52-53 123RF.com**: wlad74 (c). **53 Alamy Stock Photo**: FineArt (ftr); Granger Historical Picture Archive (tr); Pictorial Press Ltd (cra). **Dreamstime.com**: Alexstar (cr); Horst Lieber (crb). **Getty Images**: De Agostini / Biblioteca Ambrosiana (tc). **54-55 Dreamstime.com**: Ovydyborets; Shirophoto (texture). **56 Alamy Stock Photo**: The Picture Art Collection (cb). **Bridgeman Images**: (crb); © British Library Board. All Rights Reserved (cb); Pictures from History (r). **57 Bridgeman Images**: © Photo Josse (tl). **iStockphoto.com**: MatiasEnElMundo (br). **58-59 Getty Images**: Massimo Rumi / Barcroft Media. **60-61 123RF.com**: Yuliia Pushkar. **Getty Images**: De Agostini / M. Seemuller (t). **60 Alamy Stock Photo**: Heritage Image Partnership Ltd / © Fine Art Images (cb). **Bridgeman Images**: (ca, br). **61 Alamy Stock Photo**: Heritage Image Partnership Ltd / © Fine Art Images (br). **62-63 Alamy Stock Photo**: Robertharding / Peter Barritt. 64 Alamy Stock Photo: Heritage Image Partnership Ltd / The Print Collector (ca); The Picture Art Collection (bl). **64-65 Dreamstime.com**: Björn Wylezich (b). **65 Alamy Stock Photo**: Jenny Pate / Robertharding (tr). **68 Alamy Stock Photo**: SIRIOH Co., LTD / PortForLio (tr). **Dreamstime.com**: Elwynn. **69 Alamy Stock Photo**: Art Collection 3 (tc); Niday Picture Library (ftr). **Bridgeman Images**: Pictures from History (tr, br). **70-71 Dreamstime.com**: Snowboy234. **Getty Images**: UniversalImagesGroup / Universal History Archive (b). **70 Alamy Stock Photo**: Axis Images (tr). **71 akg-images**: Bible Land Pictures / www.BibleLandPictures.com (tr). **72-73 Dreamstime.com**: Tupungato. **73 akg-images**: Album / Oronoz (crb). **Alamy Stock Photo**: Chronicle of World History (tr); UtCon Collection (cra). **74 Alamy Stock Photo**: Gustavo Tomsich / Marka (tc). **75 Getty Images**: Jean-Luc Manaud / Gamma-Rapho (tr). **76-77 Bridgeman Images**: © Look and Learn. **76 Alamy Stock Photo**: Heritage Image Partnership Ltd / Fine Art Images (br); The Picture Art Collection (tc); Prisma Archivo (cl); HeritagePics (clb); Ian Dagnall Commercial Collection (c). **78-79 123RF.com**: Laurent Davoust. **Dreamstime.com**: Ke77kz (background). **V&A Images / Victoria and Albert Museum, London**: (t). **78 Alamy Stock Photo**: Digital Image Library (bl); Heritage Image Partnership Ltd / The Print Collector (br). **79 Alamy Stock Photo**: Heritage Image Partnership Ltd / © Fine Art Images (bc); Karl Kost (bc); IanDagnall Computing (crb). **80 Alamy Stock Photo**: bilwissedition Ltd. & Co. KG (bl). **80-81 Alamy Stock Photo**: Science History Images / Photo Researchers (b). **Dreamstime.com**: Ovydyborets. **81 Alamy Stock Photo**: GL Archive (cra); Heritage Image Partnership Ltd / © Fine Art Images (ca). **Dreamstime.com**: Dariusz Leszczynski (tl). **82 Alamy Stock Photo**: Falkensteinfoto (cl). **Getty Images**: United Archives (cla). **82-83 123RF.com**: Andrei Zaripov (background). **83 Alamy Stock Photo**: The Artchives (ca); Interfoto (tl); bilwissedition Ltd. & Co. KG (tr); North Wind Picture Archives (br); Alfio Scisetti (b/manuscripts). **Bridgeman Images**: (tc). **86-87 Alamy Stock Photo**: Granger Historical Picture Archive. **86 Getty Images**: adoc-photos / Corbis Historical (bl); De Agostini Picture Library (tl). **87 Alamy Stock Photo**: Balfore Archive Images (cra); Niday Picture Library (bl); The Picture Art Collection (ca). **Bridgeman Images**: Sonia Halliday Photographs (tr). **88 Alamy Stock Photo**: IanDagnall Computing (bc). **Bridgeman Images**: (cr). **89 Alamy Stock Photo**: GL Archive. **90 Alamy Stock Photo**: Chronicle (cla); Gerry McNally (clb). **Bridgeman Images**: (tr). **91 Alamy Stock Photo**: GL Archive (cra); Prisma Archivo (tr); Ivan Vdovin (tc). **Bridgeman Images**: Look and Learn (bc). **92 Dreamstime.com**: Aleksey Baskakov (tr). **93 Alamy Stock Photo**: Agefotostock / Historical Views (tl); The History Collection (tr); Marka / Jarach (ca); Chronicle of World History (cra); The Picture Art Collection (br). **94-95 123RF.com**: andreykuzmin (background). **Alamy Stock Photo**: Universal Art Archive. **95 Alamy Stock Photo**: The History Collection (bl); The Picture Art Collection (bc). **Getty Images**: Hulton Archive / Imagno (br). **98-99 Alamy Stock Photo**: Dinodia Photos RM (b); Manjik photography (bc). **98 Alamy Stock Photo**: Interfoto (tr). **Bridgeman Images**: Dinodia (tc). **99 123RF.com**: Ann Dudko (cla). **102-103 Alamy Stock Photo**: Artokoloro Quint Lox Limited (cb); Tatjana Urosevic / Zoonar GmbH (bc/frame). **103 Alamy Stock Photo**: ART Collection (br, cra); Artepics (ca); GL Archive (cr). **104 Alamy Stock Photo**: National Geographic Image Collection / W. Langdon Kihn (tr). **105 Alamy Stock Photo**: North Wind Picture Archives. **106 Alamy Stock Photo**: Pictorial Press Ltd (tc); The Picture Art Collection (tl). **107 Alamy Stock Photo**: Archivah (cb); Falkensteinfoto (tl); Artokoloro (br). **108 Bridgeman Images**: PVDE (tr). **Dorling Kindersley**: Science Museum, London (cb). **Getty Images**: De Agostini / G. Nimatallah (bl); Foodcollection RF (crb). **108-109 Science Photo Library**: David Parker. **109 Alamy Stock Photo**: Ricardo Rafael Alvarez (br); The History Collection (tc); Archivart (tr). **Bridgeman Images**: Pictures from History (bl). **Science Photo Library**: Paul D Stewart (tl). **110-111 Alamy Stock Photo**: Granger Historical Picture Archive. **110 Bridgeman Images**: © James Reeve (crb). **112-113 123RF.com**: Pissanu Prempree (b). **112 Alamy Stock Photo**: incamerastock (tl); The Picture Art Collection (tc); World History Archive (tr). **Bridgeman Images**: (cla, cr). **Getty Images**: Fine Art Images / Heritage Images / Hulton Archive (cra). **113 Alamy Stock Photo**: Eduardo Fuster Salamero (cla). **Getty Images**: Leemage (br). **114 Alamy Stock Photo**: Hi-Story (bl); Peter Horree (tl); Niday Picture Library (tr); World History Archive (clb); IanDagnall Computing (clb/Thomas Jefferson). **114-115 Alamy Stock Photo**: Luciano Leon (b). **115 Alamy Stock Photo**: IanDagnall Computing (tr); Lebrecht Music & Arts (cra). **118 Alamy Stock Photo**: ART Collection (bc). **118-119 Alamy Stock Photo**: Giuglio Gil / Hemis.fr. **120-121 Alamy Stock Photo**: Tim Macpherson / Cultura RM. **Dorling Kindersley**: Wilberforce House, Hull City Museums / Bridgeman Images (b). **120 Alamy Stock Photo**: The Picture Art Collection (br). **121 akg-images**: NTB scanpix / Scanpix (tr). **Alamy Stock Photo**: World History Archive (bc). **122 Alamy Stock Photo**: FineArt (tr); Science History Images / Photo Researchers (bl, cb); IanDagnall Computing (ca); The Picture Art Collection (cra). **123 Bridgeman Images**: Granger (tc). **124 Alamy Stock Photo**: IanDagnall Computing (bl). **124-125 Dreamstime.com**: Jakkapan Jabjainai. **125 Alamy Stock Photo**: Heritage Image Partnership Ltd / © Fine Art Images (cra); The Picture Art Collection (cla); Pictorial Press Ltd (tr). **Getty Images**: Bettmann (cr). **128 Alamy Stock Photo**: Pictorial Press Ltd (c). **Getty Images**: Archive Photos / Stock Montage (bl). **129 Alamy Stock Photo**: Chronicle (tl); Pictorial Press Ltd (tc, tr); Historical Images Archive (cra); World History Archive (c). **132 Alamy Stock Photo**: Pictorial Press Ltd (bl). **132-133 Getty Images**: Universal Images Group / Universal History Archive. **133 Alamy Stock Photo**: 19th era (cr); IanDagnall Computing (tl); Science History Images / Photo Researchers (tc); ZUMA Press, Inc. / Globe Photos (tr). **134 Getty Images**: M. Seemuller / DEA (br). **135 Alamy Stock Photo**: GL Archive (bc); The Picture Art Collection (bl). **Getty Images**: De Agostini Picture Library (br). **138 Alamy Stock Photo**: The Artchives (tl); Heritage Image Partnership Ltd / © Fine Art Images (tr); Artepics (tc). **138-139 Dreamstime.com**: Marcin Wos. **139 Alamy Stock Photo**: ART Collection (tc); Artepics (tl); incamerastock / ICP (tr). **140 Alamy Stock Photo**: Granger Historical Picture Archive (br). **140-141 Science & Society Picture Library**: Science Museum. **141 Alamy Stock Photo**: NASA Image Collection (cr); PJF Military Collection (cra). **142 Alamy Stock Photo**: Art Collection 2 (bl); PvE (bc); Artokoloro (br). **143 Alamy Stock Photo**: Historic Collection (bc). **Bridgeman Images**: © Archives Charmet (tr). **144-145 Alamy Stock Photo**: GL Archive. **145 Alamy Stock Photo**: The Natural History Museum, London (tr). **Dorling Kindersley**: Oxford Museum of Natural History (clb). **150 Alamy Stock Photo**: FLHC 90 (bl); Pictorial Press Ltd (cb). **150-151 Alamy Stock Photo**: PjrStatues. **151 Alamy Stock Photo**: Glasshouse Images / Circa Images (tc); Karen Humpage / The Print Collector / Heritage Images (crb). **Bridgeman Images**: © British Library Board. All Rights Reserved (cra). **153 Alamy Stock Photo**: The Print Collector / Heritage Images. **154 Alamy Stock Photo**: Charles Phelps Cushing / Classicstock (tr); Stocktrek Images, Inc. (bl). **154-155 Alamy Stock Photo**: Chronicle (cb). **Dreamstime.com**: Leelloo. **155 Alamy Stock Photo**: Everett Collection Historical (bl); Glasshouse Images / JT Vintage (bc/John Wilkes Booth). **Getty Images**: Bettmann (bc). **158 Alamy Stock Photo**: Granger Historical Picture Archive (cra); IanDagnall Computing (bl). **159 Alamy Stock Photo**: The Granger Collection (bc); Universal Art Archive (tc); Photo 12 / Ann Ronan Picture Library (tr). **Dreamstime.com**: Jgroup / James Steidl (br). **160 Alamy Stock Photo**: incamerastock (bl); WorldPhotos (fclb); Pictorial Press Ltd (clb); Sputnik (cr, cla). **160-161 Dreamstime.com**: Fiftyfootelvis (hammer & sickle). **161 Alamy Stock Photo**: The Granger Collection (br). **Getty Images**: Patrik Stollarz / AFP (tr). **162-163 Alamy Stock Photo**: PictureLux / The Hollywood Archive. **164-165 Dreamstime.com**: Elen33. **164 Alamy Stock Photo**: Alpha Historica (bl); Granger Historical Picture Archive (clb). **166 Alamy Stock Photo**: Granger Historical Picture Archive (bl); Xinhua (bc/Tu Youyou); World History Archive (bc). **166-167 Dreamstime.com**: Donfiore. **Science Photo Library**: Moredun Animal Health Ltd (bacteria). **167 Alamy Stock Photo**: Horizon International Images Limited (cb); Peter Horree (cla); North Wind Picture Archives (tc). **Getty Images**: Roger Viollet Collection (br). **168-169 123RF.com**: Laurent Davoust. **168 Alamy Stock Photo**: Art Collection 2 (b); The Picture Art Collection (br). **171 Alamy Stock Photo**: IanDagnall Computing (l). **174 Alamy Stock Photo**: Frank A. Rinehart / Hi-Story (bl). **Bridgeman Images**: Peter Newark American Pictures (bc). **174-175 Alamy Stock Photo**: World History Archive (b). **175 Getty Images**: Bettmann (br). **176 Alamy Stock Photo**: CPA Media Pte Ltd / Pictures From History (tr). **Getty Images**: Quinn Rooney (cla). **177 Alamy Stock Photo**: World History Archive (tc/Qianlong). **Bridgeman Images**: Pictures from History (cr). **Getty Images**: Archive Photos / Pictorial Parade (tc); Hulton Royals Collection / Hulton Archive (tr). **178-179 Dreamstime.com**: Mmphotos2017. **178 Alamy Stock Photo**: GL Archive (tr). **Dreamstime.com**: Hupeng (bl). **180 Alamy Stock Photo**: GL Archive (tc); History and Art Collection (tl); Historic Images (tr). **180-181 123RF.com**: Laurent Davoust. **181 Alamy Stock Photo**: Granger Historical Picture Archive / Nadar (tl); Lebrecht Music & Arts (tc); Hirarchivum Press (tr). **182 Alamy Stock Photo**: Hi-Story (tl). **Getty Images**: Universal Images Group / Leemage (tr). **183 Alamy Stock Photo**: PvE. **184 Alamy Stock Photo**: (cr). **185 Alamy Stock Photo**: Chris Hellier (br); (c). **186-187 123RF.com**: Laurent Davoust. **186 Alamy Stock Photo**: Pictorial Press Ltd (tr). **Bridgeman Images**: Peter Newark Pictures (bl). **187 Bridgeman Images**: Peter Newark Pictures. **188-189 Science Photo Library**: Nikola Tesla Museum. **188 Getty Images**: Stefano Bianchetti / Corbis Historical (bc). **189 Alamy Stock Photo. 190 Alamy Stock Photo**: GL Archive (bl). **Getty Images**: Bettmann (crb). **190-191 Alamy Stock Photo**: Archive Pics (b/background 2 X3). **Getty Images**: Hulton Deutsch / Corbis Historical (b/background 1 X3). **191 Alamy Stock Photo**: Chronicle (tc); Shawshots (cb); Trinity Mirror / Mirrorpix (cl); The Picture Art Collection (tc/Laura Cereta); FLHC 30 (tr). **192 Alamy Stock Photo**: Alpha Historica (bc); Granger Historical Picture Archive (cb); GL Archive (bl); Everett Collection Inc (br). **Dreamstime.com**: Ovydyborets (X4). **193 Alamy Stock Photo**: Glasshouse Images / Circa Images (cb); Granger Historical Picture Archive (ca); The History Collection (br). **Dreamstime.com**: Ovydyborets (X3). **Getty Images**: Archive Photos / Gado / Levy / Sheridan Libraries (tl). **196 Alamy Stock Photo**: IanDagnall Computing (tr); SuperStock / RGB Ventures / Library of Congress (bl). **197 Alamy Stock Photo**: Granger Historical Picture Archive (bc/Ernest Rutherford). **Getty Images**: Maurice Jarnoux / Paris Match Archive (br). **McCord Museum, Montreal**: Miss Harriet Brooks, nuclear physicist, Montreal, QC / 1898, 19th century / II-123880 (bc). **Wellcome Collection**: Thomas S G Farnetti (cr). **198 Alamy Stock Photo**: GL Archive (tl). **Madam C. J. Walker Collection, Indiana Historical Society: (tr). 199 Alamy Stock Photo**: State Archives of Florida / Florida Memory (crb); WDC Photos (cr). **Black History Photograph Collection (S0336). The State Historical Society of Missouri, Photograph Collection**: (br). **202-203 Alamy Stock Photo**: Dinodia Photos RM (b). **202 Alamy Stock Photo**: Dinodia Photos RM (bl); World History Archive (tl). **203 Alamy Stock Photo**: Dinodia Photos RM (tr, cr); Trinity Mirror / Mirrorpix (cra); Ninja Flags (br). **Getty Images**: Universal Images Group / Universal History Archive (ca). **204 Alamy Stock Photo**: Everett Collection Historical (cla/Sun Yat-senEverett Collection Historical); Pictorial Press Ltd; Lebrecht Music & Arts (bl). **205 Dreamstime.com**: StrippedPixel (crb). **207 Getty Images**: Popperfoto (tl). **208 Alamy Stock Photo**: Granger Historical Picture Archive (cra); Pictorial Press Ltd (ca). **Getty Images**: Bettmann (tl). **208-209 Dreamstime.com**: Nouwens (b). **209 Alamy Stock Photo**: dpa picture alliance / Uwe Zucchi (tl); Everett Collection Historical (tr). **210 Alamy Stock Photo**: Heritage Image Partnership Ltd / © Fine Art Images (tc). **Wellcome Collection**: (cra). **210-211 123RF.com**: pichai pipatkuldilok. **211 Alamy Stock Photo**: Heritage Image Partnership Ltd / © Fine Art Images (bl). **Getty Images**: ullstein bild (tr). **212-213 123RF.com**: Laurent Davoust. **212 Alamy Stock Photo**: Everett Collection Historical (b). **213 Alamy Stock Photo**: Everett Collection Historical (tl). **Getty Images**: Bettmann (cr). **214 Carl Van Vechten photograph © VanVechtenTrust**: Beinecke Rare Book and Manuscript Library, Yale University (l). **215 Alamy Stock Photo**: Everett Collection Historical (ca); The Protected Art Archive (ca/Dust Tracks). **Bridgeman Images**: (tr). **Getty Images**: Archive Photos / PhotoQuest (bc, tc); Archive Photos / Underwood Archives (tc/Langston Hughes). **216-217 123RF.com**: Laurent Davoust. **216 Getty Images**: Bettmann (clb/Background). **217 Alamy Stock Photo**: World History Archive (ca). **Getty Images**: Bettmann. **218-219 Courtesy of Smithsonian. ©2020 Smithsonian.**: (b). **218 Bridgeman Images**: Underwood Archives / UIG (tr). **219 Alamy Stock Photo**: Archive Pics (ftl); GL Archive (tl); Pictorial Press Ltd (br). **Bridgeman Images**: Granger (cra). **Getty Images**: George Rinhart / Corbis Historical (tc). **Science Photo Library**: Sputnik (tr). **220 Alamy Stock Photo**: David Cole (bc/Margaret Thatcher); World History Archive (tc); Granger Historical Picture Archive (tr); Sputnik (bc); Barry Iverson (br). **Bridgeman Images**: (tl). **221 Getty Images**: George Stroud / Hulton Archive (tc); Universal History Archive (tr). **Rex by Shutterstock**: AP (br). **222 Alamy Stock Photo**: BNA Photographic (c). **Rex by Shutterstock**: Traverso (bl). **223 Alamy Stock Photo**: Allstar Picture Library (tr). **Getty Images**: Hulton Archive (cl); Daniel Simon / Gamma-Rapho (cr). **224 Alamy Stock Photo**: Marka / EPS (tc). **Getty Images**: Stefania D'Alessandro (ca). **Rex by Shutterstock**: ITV (cla). **225 Getty Images**: Alfred Eisenstaedt / The LIFE Picture Collection (bl). **226 Alamy Stock Photo**: Peter Horree (cla). **Getty Images**: Jack Mitchell (tl). **226-227 Dreamstime.com**: Bluedarkat (main image). **227 Alamy Stock Photo**: FAY 2018 (crb); Archivart / © Banco de México Diego Rivera Frida Kahlo Museums Trust, Mexico, D.F. / DACS 2020 (cr). **Bridgeman Images**: Fine Art Images / © Banco de México Diego Rivera Frida Kahlo Museums Trust, Mexico, D.F. / DACS 2020 (tc). **Dreamstime.com**: Dwi Cahya Wahyuni (crb/image frame). **Getty Images**: Jeff Greenberg (bc). **228 Alamy Stock Photo**: GL Archive (tl). **Library of Congress, Washington, D.C.**: LC-USZ62-73770 (tc). **228-229 Dreamstime.com**: Daniil Peshkov. **229 Alamy Stock Photo**: Historic Collection (tc); IanDagnall Computing (tl). **Getty Images**: Bettmann (tr). **230 Alamy Stock Photo**: ART Collection (tr); Hilary Morgan (bl). **Getty Images**: Bob Thomas / Popperfoto (crb). **230-231 Alamy Stock Photo**: Ian Trower (b/background). **231 Alamy Stock Photo**: Bill Greenblatt / UPI (bc/St Louis); Lordprice Collection (c); WENN Rights Ltd (br). **Dreamstime.com**: Stephen Noakes (cra). **Getty Images**: Patrick Eagar / Popperfoto (cb); Tony Triolo (bl). **232 Alamy Stock Photo**: Archive PL (cr); UtCon Collection (cla); Photo12 / Ann Ronan Picture Library (bl); Oote Boe (cr/identity document). **232-233 Alamy Stock Photo**: PjrStudio (background). **Dreamstime.com**: Cienpies Design & Communication (Paperclip x2). **233 Alamy Stock Photo**: US National Archives (cr). **234-235 Dreamstime.com**: Alexey Kuzin (c). **234 Alamy Stock Photo**: Pictorial Press Ltd (tr). **Getty Images**: Francois G. Durand (cla). **235 Alamy Stock Photo**: Alpha Historica (br). **236 Getty Images**: Bettmann. **237 Alamy Stock Photo**: Alpha Historica (cr). **238 Rex by Shutterstock**: United Artists / Kobal (bc). **238-239 Getty Images**: Clarence Sinclair Bull / Moviepix. **239 Alamy Stock Photo**: Interfoto (tr). **Getty Images**: Bettmann (tl, tc); Corbis Historical / Sunset Boulevard (cla). **Science Photo Library**: US National Archives and Records Administration (bl). **240-241 Getty Images**: Bettmann. **240 Alamy Stock Photo**: @Painet Inc. (bc/Corazon Aquino); ZUMA Press, Inc. (cb); Sputnik (bc, br). **Dreamstime.com**: Ovydyborets (X5). **241 Dreamstime.com**: Ovydyborets (X3). **Getty Images**: Bettmann (clb); Laurent Maous / Gamma-Rapho (c); Gérard Géry / Paris Match Archive (br). **242-243 Getty Images**: Jurgen Schadeberg (t). **242 Bridgeman Images**: Spaarnestad Photo (br). **Getty Images**: Deborah Feingold / Corbis Historical (cl). **243 Getty Images**: Walter Dhladhla / AFP (bl). **244-245 Getty Images**: Alfred Gregory / Royal Geographical Society. **245 Alamy Stock Photo**: Keystone Press / Keystone Pictures USA (cr). **Dreamstime.com**: Daniel Prudek (tl). **246 Alamy Stock Photo**: Sergei Fadeichev / TASS (cl); World History Archive (crb). **247 Getty Images**: Hulton Archive (bl); Keystone-France / Gamma-Keystone. **248-249 Dreamstime.com**: Konstantin Nechaev. **248 Getty Images**: Universal Images Group / Universal History Archive. **249 Alamy Stock Photo**: Heritage Image Partnership Ltd / From the Jewish Chronicle Archive (tr); Science History Images / Photo Researchers (cr). 250 **Alamy Stock Photo**: Atomic (bl). **Getty Images**: Jackie Ghossein / The Sydney Morning Herald / Fairfax Media (br); Ronald Leslie Stewart / Fairfax Media (tr). **251 Dorling Kindersley**: Mark Winwood / RHS Wisley (tc). **Getty Images**: Trevor James Robert Dallen / Fairfax Media (br). **254 Alamy Stock Photo**: Mariano Garcia (tr); ZUMA Press, Inc. / Keystone Pictures USA (bc). **Getty Images**: Lois Herman / Corbis Premium Historical (clb). **254-255 Alamy Stock Photo**: Witold Krasowski (c). **255 Alamy Stock Photo**: Historic Collection (tc). **257 Rex by Shutterstock**: AP (br). **258-259 Getty Images**: Robert W. Kelley / The LIFE Picture Collection. **258 Alamy Stock Photo**: GL Archive (bc). **Bob Fitch Photography Archive, Department of Special Collections, Stanford University Libraries**: (bl). **Getty Images**: Robert Parent / The LIFE Images Collection (br). **260 Alamy Stock Photo**: United Archives GmbH / IFA Film (bl). **Dorling Kindersley**: Imperial War Museum, London / By kind permission of The Trustees of the Imperial War Museum, London (crb). **Getty Images**: Anne Frank Fonds, Basel (tr); Archive Photos / Authenticated News (ca); Hulton Archive / Stringer (cb). **260-261 Alamy Stock Photo**: Granger Historical Picture Archive (Tape x20). **261 Alamy Stock Photo**: History and Art Collection (bc); Keystone Pictures USA (ca); Pictorial Press Ltd (cr). **Anne Frank House:** (cla). **Getty Images**: Anne Frank Fonds Basel (cb). **262 Getty Images**: Jack Robinson / Archive Photos (cl). **263 Getty Images**: Bettmann (tc, tr); Grey Villet / The LIFE Picture Collection (cl); Michael Ochs Archives (tc/Ella). **264 Alamy Stock Photo**: Granger Historical Picture Archive (tl). **Getty Images**: Popperfoto (b). **265 Alamy Stock Photo**: Science History Images / Photo Researchers (bc). **266-267 A UMNS photo by Mike DuBose. Photo #GC0380. April 29, 2008. 267 Alamy Stock Photo**: Peter Cavanagh (br); The History Collection (bl); Keystone Press / Keystone Pictures USA (bc). **268 Alamy Stock Photo**: Eden Breitz (cl). **Bridgeman Images**: Hannah Assouline / Opale (b). **268-269 Dreamstime.com**: Al4k14 (saxophone). **269 Getty Images**: Hulton Archive / Keystone (cra/Kwame); ullstein bild (tc); Pete Still / Redferns (cra). **270 Alamy Stock Photo**: AF archive (tc); Chronicle (tl); Universal Images Group North America LLC / DeAgostini / DEA PICTURE LIBRARY (tr). **270-271 Alamy Stock Photo**: Granger Historical Picture Archive. **271 Alamy Stock Photo**: AF archive (tc); ZUMA Press, Inc. / © Supplied By Globe Photos, Inc / Globe Photos (tl). **Getty Images**: Neil Leifer / Sports Illustrated (tr). **272 Getty Images**: Micheline Pelletier / Corbis Historical (bl). **272-273 Dreamstime.com**: Leremy (Background (silhouette)). **273 Alamy Stock Photo**: dpa picture alliance (br); ZUMA Press, Inc. (cr). **Getty Images**: William Campbell / Sygma (bc); Eric Feferberg / AFP (tl); Ernesto Ruscio (cb). **274-275 Getty Images**: Don Morley / Allsport. **276 Alamy Stock Photo**: dpa picture alliance (bl). **Getty Images**: Hulton Archive / Keystone (ca); Joel Robine / AFP (cl). **277 Rex by Shutterstock**: Sipa (cra). **278 Alamy Stock Photo**: Lynne Sutherland (tr); Hugh Threlfall (ca). **Getty Images**: Edge Magazine (br); Yoshikazu Tsuno / AFP (c). **278-279 Alamy Stock Photo**: Jamaway. **279 Alamy Stock Photo**: dpa picture alliance (crb); BJ Warnick / Newscom (tr). **Getty Images**: John Lamparski (tc); The Washington Post (cr). **280-281 Alamy Stock Photo**: Xinhua (t). **280 Getty Images**: Daniel Berehulak (br); Gamma-Rapho / Patrick Siccoli (bc). **281 Getty Images**: Saeed Khan / AFP (bc). **282 Alamy Stock Photo**: The Hollywood Archive / PictureLux (tc). **282-283 123RF.com**: Aloysius Noble Patrimonio (b/vector tv). **Alamy Stock Photo**: Everett Collection Inc / © King World Productions (bc). **283 Alamy Stock Photo**: Everett Collection Inc (cra); UPI / Brian Kersey (crb). **Dreamstime.com**: Tauha2001 (tl). **Rex by Shutterstock**: Noah Berger / AP (ca). **284-285 iStockphoto.com**: ByronOrtizA (b). **285 Alamy Stock Photo**: History and Art Collection (tc); WENN Rights Ltd (bc). **Getty Images**: Rolando Gonzalez / AFP (ca); Johan Ordonez / AFP (cra). **286 Alamy Stock Photo**: Stock Experiment (tc). **Dreamstime.com**: Joe Sohm (br). **Getty Images**: Hulton Archive / Apic (cla). **287 Alamy Stock Photo**: Akademie (cra); GL Archive (br); BJ Warnick / Newscom (cb); Andrea Spinelli (tc). **290 Press Association Images**: PA Archive / Andrew Matthews (bl). **290-291 Getty Images**: Xuanyu Han / Moment. **292 Alamy Stock Photo**: agefotostock / Historical Views (tl). **292-293 Alamy Stock Photo**: The Hollywood Archive / PictureLux (tr). **293 Alamy Stock Photo**: Dinodia Photos RM (ca/Nargis, ca); ZUMA Press, Inc. (cra); WENN Rights Ltd (c). **294 Alamy Stock Photo**: Everett Collection Inc (cla). **294-295 Getty Images**: Kevin Mazur (c); Universal Images Group / View Pictures / James Newton. **295 Alamy Stock Photo**: AF archive (tr, cra); PictureLux / The Hollywood Archive (tc). **Getty Images**: Robert Beck / Sports Illustrated (cr). **297 Getty Images**: AFP / Intercontinentale (ca); Bob Martin / Hulton Archive (cra); Clive Brunskill (cra/Venus Williams). **298 Getty Images**: Jeff Haynes / AFP (tr); Michael J. LeBrecht II / Sports Illustrated Classic (cla). **298-299 Getty Images**: Al Bello (bc). **299 Getty Images**: Yiorgos Doukanaris (cb); Doug Pensinger (tc); Harry How (bc); National Basketball Association / Andrew D. Bernstein (cra); Jeff Haynes / AFP (cra/trophy). **300-301 Dreamstime.com**: Maxwell De Araujo Rodrigues. **301 Getty Images**: Quique Garcia / AFP (clb); Lluis Gene / AFP (c); Popperfoto (bc/Johan Cruyff); Dean Mouhtaropoulos (bc); David Ramos (br). **302-303 Daniel Bussiere | DAN23**: (b). **302 Alamy Stock Photo**: Edward North (c). **Getty Images**: Mohammad Rehman / AFP (tc). **303 Getty Images**: Gamma-Keystone / Keystone-France (br). **Rex by Shutterstock**: Matt Dunham / AP (tc). **304 Alamy Stock Photo**: ES Imagery (tl); Chuck Nacke (tc). **Getty Images**: James Leynse / Corbis Historical (tr). **304-305 Dreamstime.com**: Sergey Khakimullin. **305 Alamy Stock Photo**: Aflo Co. Ltd. / Nippon News (tc); dpa picture alliance / Kay Nietfeld (tl). **Getty Images**: Kimberly White (tr). **307 Alamy Stock Photo**: Daniel Bockwoldt / dpa picture alliance (l). **308 Alamy Stock Photo**: Ian G Dagnall (tl); Geraint Lewis (tr). **Mary Evans Picture Library**: Imagno (tc). **309 Alamy Stock Photo**: Tomek Surdel (tl); WENN Rights Ltd (tc, tr). **310 Alamy Stock Photo**: Pictorial Press Ltd (tc). **Getty Images**: Michael Ochs Archives / NASA / Donaldson Collection (tr). **Library and Archives Canada**: O.B. Buell / C-001873 (tl). **311 Alamy Stock Photo**: Granger Historical Picture Archive (tc); RGB Ventures / SuperStock / NASA (tl). **Getty Images**: Cesare Bonazza / Contour (tr). **500 Getty Images**: Anne Frank Fonds, Basel (bl/remove); WPA Pool (t/remove).

All other images © Dorling Kindersley
For further information see: **www.dkimages.com**